《符号与传媒》2020 年春季号，总第 20 辑

中国知网（CNKI）来源集刊　中文科技期刊数据库来源集刊
超星数字图书馆来源集刊　万方数据库来源集刊

符号与传媒
Signs & Media

主编　曹顺庆　赵毅衡
四川大学符号学-传媒学研究所　主办

总第20辑

20

四川大学出版社

项目策划：黄蕴婷
责任编辑：黄蕴婷
责任校对：欧风偃
封面设计：墨创文化
责任印制：王　炜

图书在版编目（CIP）数据

符号与传媒．20 / 曹顺庆，赵毅衡主编．— 成都：四川大学出版社，2020.4
ISBN 978-7-5690-3728-9

Ⅰ．①符… Ⅱ．①曹… ②赵… Ⅲ．①符号学－文集 Ⅳ．①H0-53

中国版本图书馆 CIP 数据核字（2020）第 063355 号

书名　符号与传媒（20）
Fuhao Yu Chuanmei（20）

著　　者	曹顺庆　赵毅衡
出　　版	四川大学出版社
地　　址	成都市一环路南一段 24 号（610065）
发　　行	四川大学出版社
书　　号	ISBN 978-7-5690-3728-9
印前制作	四川胜翔数码印务设计有限公司
印　　刷	郫县犀浦印刷厂
成品尺寸	170mm×240mm
插　　页	2
印　　张	17.5
字　　数	321 千字
版　　次	2020 年 4 月第 1 版
印　　次	2020 年 4 月第 1 次印刷
定　　价	70.00 元

扫码加入读者圈

◆ 读者邮购本书，请与本社发行科联系。
电话：(028)85408408/(028)85401670/
(028)86408023　邮政编码：610065
◆ 本社图书如有印装质量问题，请寄回出版社调换。
◆ 网址：http://press.scu.edu.cn

四川大学出版社
微信公众号

编者的话

《符号与传媒》（第 20 辑）终于跟读者见面了。我们见证了中国符号学这十余年的发展历程，加上对数字的情节，总在催促着我们进行一番总结回顾。但思来想去，还是准备将意向性让给文本，用叙述叙述叙述，以无情寄托深情。

本辑“哲学符号学”研究专辑中，赵毅衡提出“文本意向性”，明确了文本发出者与解释者中间的意义规则，让困扰文学与艺术的艺术性问题有了新解；张碧从马克思主义符号学视角切入，梳理象征、符号与信号三种符号类型的演变及其背后的社会文化批判；颜小芳以存在符号学视域审视福柯的晚期主体思想，讨论他对“说真话”的诠释。在关注“有”的同时，学者们也思考“无”，“‘无意味’的符号学研究”中，马西莫·莱昂内探讨符号随机性及其意义体系，打开了意义探索的新视角；谭光辉论无情之情，“佛系”人格背后的社会意义让人深思。

意义之辩在“中国俗文化的符号学研究”“传播符号学”与“广义叙述学”中继续展开。黄维樑从对《文心雕龙》的诠释着眼思考应对“瑕疵文本”的态度；谢清果、陈瑞分析了礼乐文化在黔中屯堡中的演化传播；林升栋等学者从表情包的设计发掘东西方的文化差异；唐小林用演示和记录区分了社会形态，对人类社会的宏大文本进行叙述学的观照；王安以美杜莎的语象叙事分析性别的政治博弈，见微知著。此外，学者们在本辑中对符号噪音、新闻价值、交流叙述，电影造梦等话题展开的讨论同样精彩。

按照惯例，我们提交了 2019 年符号学年度发展报告，整理汇集了一年来中国符号学领域的重要论著与学术活动，供读者参考。

Editor's Note

This is the twentieth issue and also the tenth anniversary of *Signs & Media*, which has had the honour to witness a boom in Chinese semiotic studies over the past decade. It seems that a "fetish" for numbers should prompt us to review this significant decade. However, we decided to yield the "intentionality" to the text, to let the "narrative" narrate and to express affections by "insignificance".

In this issue's section on "Philosophical Semiotics", Zhao Yiheng advances the term "textual intentionality" to clarify the signifying mechanism between the sender and receiver of the text, providing a new way to define "artifacthood" in literature and art. Zhang Bi elaborates the evolution of symbol, sign and signal and the sociocultural critiques of them that have been presented by Marxist semiotics. Yan Xiaofang adopts existential semiotics to reflect on Foucault's late thoughts on the subject and his discussion of "truth-telling". Semiotics is not only about "significance" but also about "insignificance". In our new section entitled "Semiotics of Insignificance", Massimo Leone examines "randomness" and its categories in terms of semiotics, indicating a novel approach to meaning studies, and Tan Guanghui discusses the term "emotionlessness", focusing on the social meaning of the Buddha-like personality.

Discussions of meaning are also found in other sections of this issue: "Semiotics of Non-Orthodox Chinese Culture", "Semiotics of Communication" and "General Narratology". For instance, Huang Weiliang ponders "flawed text" in *The Literary Mind and the Carving of Dragons*; Xie Qinguo and Chen Rui analyse the communication of the traditional rites and music culture of the Tunpu of Guizhou province; Lin Shengdong et al. discuss the cultural differences in Eastern and Western emoji; and Tang Xiaolin considers human society as a macro-narrative text and attempts to distinguish social formations into two basic narrative types as demonstrating and recording. Finally, Wang An explores the sexual politics of literary works in terms of Medusa *ekphrasis*. Our contributors also extend their discussion into many other topics, such as noise, news value, communicative narratives, and the dream making of films.

In addition, following the spring issue tradition, we provide the 2019 edition of the annual report on the development of Chinese semiotic studies, recording for your reference the important works and activities over the past year.

目　录

哲学符号学

“无意味”的符号学研究

中国俗文化的符号学研究

传播符号学

广义叙述学

报告与书评

Contents

Philosophical Semiotics

Semiotics of Insignificance

Semiotics of Non-Onthodox Chinese Culture

Semiotics of Communication

General Narratology

Report and Book Review

哲学符号学

符号学“瑕疵文本”说：从《文心雕龙》的诠释讲起

黄维樑

摘　要：赵毅衡指出，“符号学即意义学”；如何寻求符号文本的确切意义，赵毅衡提出“伴随文本”理论。李卫华论文《从伴随文本释“文之为德也大矣”》据赵氏理论寻求一个文本的意义，但发现对此文本（出自《文心雕龙》的一个句子）的解释众说纷纭，未能确解。笔者认为“文之为德也大矣”和《文心雕龙》的《风骨》篇一样，都可称为瑕疵文本，即文本本身含义不清或互相矛盾。古今中西的“瑕疵文本”所在多有，本文略举数例说明之。本文以《文心雕龙》的《论说》篇和《指瑕》篇，作为瑕疵文本之所以存在的背景说明；换言之，此二篇可作为解释“瑕疵文本”说的伴随文本。

关键词：符号学，伴随文本，瑕疵文本，《文心雕龙》

On “Flawed Text” in *The Literary Mind and the Carving of Dragons*

Huang Weiliang

Abstract: “Semiotics is the study of meaning ”, according to Zhao Yiheng, who coined the term “co-text” for studies of the exact meaning of a semiotic text. In his paper “A Study of ‘ *Wen*, or Pattern, is a Great Power

Indeed' from the Perspective of Co-text", Li Weihua, sought out the meaning of the crucial first sentence of *The Literary Mind and the Carving of Dragons* on the basis of Zhao's theory, but found a great number of different interpretations. The present author argues that this sentence, along with the same book's famous chapter "Feng Gu" ("The Wind and the Bone"), themselves constitute "flawed texts": texts with unclear or contradictory meanings. There are many "flawed texts" in ancient and modern works from both China and the West. This paper uses two chapters—"Lun Shuo" ("The Treatise and Discussion") and "Zhi Xia" ("Literary Flaws")—from *The Literary Mind and the Carving of Dragons* to explain the existence of "flawed text". These two chapters can be deemed co-texts in expounding the concept of "flawed text".

Keywords: semiotics, co-text, flawed text, *The Literary Mind and the Carving of Dragons*

DOI: 10.13760/b.cnki.sam.202001007

符号学论著丰硕，在这一门学问领导群伦的赵毅衡，对符号学做了言简意赅的解释："符号是用来承载意义的，不用符号无法表达、传送、理解意义，符号学即意义学。"（赵毅衡，2018）文字是人类的一种符号，甚至可说是最重要的符号；由文字构成的文本（text），尤其是文本中的经典（classic）文本，其一词一句一段以至全篇的意义为何，这样的讨论，当然属于符号学的范畴。这样的讨论，涉及中国传统的训诂学、来自西方的诠释学（hermeneutics），也与中西的文学批评理论如中国的笺注和评点、西方的精细分析（explication de text）和文本细读（close reading）等密切相关。如何理解以至确定（如果可能的话）某文本（或称"符号文本"；本文中"文本"和"符号文本"二词交互使用）的意义，符号学有其理论和方法。赵毅衡提出了"伴随文本"这个概念。他指出：伴随文本是"伴随着符号文本一道发送给接收者的附加因素"（2012，p. 143）；他在一个讲座中曾再解释，以下是该讲座的报道的一个片段：

他（赵毅衡——笔者注）认为，伴随文本是文本"边上"携带的大量符号元素，包括副文本、型文本、前文本、同时文本、链文本、先文本和后文本几种类型。"我们的思想意识本来就是一部合起

> 的伴随文本词典，等着文本来翻开，来激发而已”，他强调，“没有伴随文本，就无法理解任何文本”。（数字文化与传媒研究中心，2018）

笔者对符号学认识有限，曾读过一篇符号学论文用“伴随文本”的理论来解释经典文本，即李卫华的《从伴随文本释“文之为德也大矣”》一文（2019）。笔者打算从李氏此文对《文心雕龙》全书首句“文之为德也大矣”的解释说起，提出“瑕疵文本”的概念，看看是否可作为符号学理论的一个小小补充。如果同样或类似的“瑕疵文本”概念已有人提出过，笔者自然要请知识者赐教。先引李文的提要如下：

> 《文心雕龙》开宗明义即为《原道》，而《原道》开篇之句“文之为德也大矣”，是极为重要也极富争议的一句话，是一个浸透了社会文化因素的复杂构造。要正确理解这一句话的含义，必须从它的伴随文本入手。将“文之为德也大矣”视为一个文本，其最重要的伴随文本就是《原道》篇中的其他文字。对“文之为德也大矣”的解释，必须放在《原道》篇的具体语境中，做到上下顺畅，文脉相承。而《原道》篇之外、《文心雕龙》之外的其他所有文化文本，则作为文外伴随文本，影响着读者对“文之为德也大矣”的理解和解释。

李卫华征引历来多位《文心雕龙》学者对“文之为德也大矣”的解说，而这些学者解说时，基本上是根据种种可有的伴随文本——“文之为德也大矣”这句话、《原道》全篇、《文心雕龙》全书、《文心雕龙》的时代及以前甚至以后的多种文献，特别是与“德”这个词语，以及“文之德”“文之为德”不同构词式引起的不同的可能解说——来解释“文之为德也大矣”这句话的意义。换言之，包括李卫华在内的历来《文心雕龙》学者根据的伴随文本，就是上面赵毅衡讲座所说的“副文本、型文本、前文本、同时文本、链文本、先文本和后文本”。可以补充说明的是：历来对“文之为德也大矣”（以至对其他很多经典文本语句）的诠释，都在不同程度、不同层面上利用过伴随文本，而赵毅衡的伴随文本理论，乃对这个诠释现象涉及的种种文献以及上述种种诠释理论和方法，在学理上做了厘清，做了系统化论述，使伴随文本成为符号学的一个术语。

李卫华论文的结论是：

> 《原道》全篇均可视为“文之为德也大矣”的文内伴随文本，以

全文意义的通畅为标准，“文之为德也大矣”之“德”，无论释为德教、性情、功用、规律或道的体现，都有不足或牵强之处。而将“X之德”、“X之为物”作为“X之为德”的文外伴随文本，通过对三者表意的比较则不难发现，“X之为德”重在“X”而不重在“德”，“之为德”通常只起复指作用。中国古代文论重感悟而轻概念，将字义落得太实往往反而破坏了文意的表达。因此，不如就将“之为德”视为对“文”的复指，将“文之为德也大矣”直接译为“文真是很伟大呀!”反而更为贴切。①

把“德”解释为“德教、性情、功用、规律或道的体现”，李卫华是将龙学者范文澜、冯春田、罗宗强、王元化、杨明照、张光年、赵仲邑、周振甫的诸种说法，加以整理综合。笔者这里另外随机抽样地列举几位龙学者对“德”的解释——张少康：“刘勰此处（即‘文之为德也大矣’——笔者注）之‘德’，指的是‘文’和天地并生的特点”（1987，p. 24）；王运熙、周锋：“德：性质、意义”（1998，p. 3）；王志彬：“德：有多种解释，此处按‘事物的属性’和‘道的形式表现’作解”（2012，p. 3）。

加以比照，就可发现张少康、王运熙、周锋、王志彬四位的说法，和上述李卫华所整理综合的诸说，不尽相同或大为不同。可能还有多种不同的解释。2005年出版的戚良德《文心雕龙分类索引》告诉我们，解说《原道》篇的论著共有173篇（章），涉及的作者不止这里所列的范文澜等和张少康、王运熙、周锋、王志彬四位。索引所列的篇章，解说《原道》篇时，不免会对首句“文之为德也大矣”加以诠释；而对“德”字怎样诠释，可能和上面所引各种说法有所不同。换言之，“德”的意义，可能更是众说纷纭。“德”是个非常复杂的符号。

《文心雕龙》另一个复杂的符号，比“德”的解说更为众说纷纭的，是以“风骨”为论述焦点的《风骨》篇。先引述《风骨》篇的一些句子：“是以怊怅述情，必始乎风；沈吟铺辞，莫先于骨。故辞之待骨，如体之树骸；情之含风，犹形之包气。”引文分别解释了“风”和“骨”的意义；类似的分别解释“风”和“骨”的句子还有不少。本篇中另外又有“风骨”合起来成为一

① 这里所引李卫华的意见中，有“中国古代文论重感悟而轻概念”之语。这个说法可斟酌。中国古代文论里，诸如《毛诗序》的风雅颂、赋比兴等，都是概念；《典论·论文》的奏议、书论、铭诔、诗赋等“四科”，也都是概念；《文心雕龙》里面的丽辞、比兴、事义等，也都是概念……中国古代文论对相关概念的解说，也许不够详明细致，但我们不应该说中国古代文论“轻概念”。

词的解释，如："若风骨乏采，则鸷集翰林；采乏风骨，则雉窜文囿。"

1987年陈耀南撰《文心风骨群说辨疑》一文，分析数十篇有关《风骨》篇的论著，其作者包括黄侃、范文澜、周振甫、王运熙、祖保泉、张长青、张文勋、石家宜、牟世金、王更生、蔡钟翔、张少康、曹顺庆、目加田诚等人。诸家对《风骨》的解释，差别甚大，陈氏把诸种不同的解释分为十余类。1995年出版的《文心雕龙学综览》中，汪涌豪综述"风骨"研究成果，指出对此词的解释，主要有12种说法，其中第1种："风即文意，骨即文辞"；第6种："风即文辞，骨即文意"。请注意，两个说法对"风"和"骨"意义的解释，正好相反。其余较有影响力的解释："9. 风骨是风格形成的基本条件。10. 风骨即风格。11. 风骨即格调。12. 风骨是力。"

由于"风骨"众说纷纭，对其意义为何，学者没有共识，陈耀南认为《风骨》篇的内容与文字，有点"扑朔迷离，闪烁不定"。汪涌豪只综述各家的说法，其本人没有加以评论。另一位龙学者周振甫在其主编的《文心雕龙辞典》中的《释风骨》一文里说："从《风骨》篇看，刘勰讲的风骨有矛盾。"(1996, p. 187)

笔者读《文心雕龙》，钦佩其体大虑周、高明而中庸之际，极言其价值之际，希望让"雕龙"成为"飞龙"广播四方之际，并没有把此书神圣化，认为它一字一句都是文学理论的真理，都是无懈可击的。笔者在台北出版的*Tamkang Review* 1994年春夏号发表"Fenggu"一文，指出《风骨》语意有含糊处、矛盾处，篇章本身有问题，此篇可说是《文心雕龙》的一个瑕疵。"风骨"一词意义难明，《文心雕龙》英译者施友忠（Vincent Y. C. Shih）干脆把此词翻译为"the Wind and the Bone"；笔者没有良策，只好音译为"fenggu"。研究我认为有瑕疵的这个篇章，困惑叹息之余，倒是收获了"唯藻耀而高翔，固文笔之鸣凤也"这意象鲜明的句子——我尝试这样解读：有"风骨"的文学作品，就是"藻耀而高翔"的"鸣凤"；虽然"风骨"和"鸣凤"两者，在想象里既不形似也不神似。

有才有识的老中青龙学者，不论怎样集思广益，不论怎样经历"头脑风暴"（brainstorming），不论怎样祭出各式各样的"伴随文本"以助解说，都未能对"文之为德也大矣"和"风骨"的解释达成基本的共识（不敢祈求"定于一尊"的"定义"）。这表示这一句、这一篇用词有不精准处，或内容有含糊、矛盾处，其文本诚然有问题。笔者称这样有问题的文本为"瑕疵文本"（flawed text）。《文心雕龙》还有别的瑕疵文本，本文未及举例并论述。

瑕疵文本古今中西并不少见。莎翁名剧《哈姆雷特》的名段首句的"To

be or not to be”究竟是什么意思，向来众说纷纭，各种汉语翻译也就差别甚大。例如，朱生豪翻译为“生存还是毁灭”，卞之琳翻译为“活下去还是不活”，梁实秋翻译为“死后还是存在，还是不存在”，真是各译其释（根据译者的解释而翻译）。之所以如此，是因为“To be or not to be”这个符号文本本身有问题，有瑕疵。莎翁戏剧的其他名段，如《麦克白》中的“To-morrow，and to-morrow，and to-morrow”词组，意思清晰，不是瑕疵文本。

刘季春指出，乔志高所翻译的美国作家菲茨杰拉德（Scott Fitzgerald）的《了不起的盖茨比》（*The Great Gatsby*，亦译《大亨小传》），译文有句子费解；他对照原文，发觉原文就是费解的。这里说的费解译文“对人不乱下断语是表示一种无穷的希望”来自费解的原文“Reserving judgments is a matter of infinite hope”。（刘志高，2018）蔡思果翻译狄更斯的《大卫·科波菲尔》（*David Copperfield*），曾一边翻译一边告诉文友：大小说家的文句多有差池以至错误的地方。卡夫卡的小说手稿，根据整理者和出版者的讲述，也有诸多不善不妥的字句。韦勒克（Rene Wellek）在其现代文学批评史中指出，艾略特（T. S. Eliot）的批评文章里，每有用词意义含糊以及内容前后龃龉的地方。凡此种种有问题的语句和篇章，都可称为“瑕疵文本”。

文学研究者细读小说文本，古人张竹坡发现《金瓶梅》的人物年岁前后对应不妥；今人潘铭燊发现《红楼梦》叙事时间有先后错乱，人物年龄时大时小（1988，pp. iii—viii）。虽说是经典名著的“大醇小疵”，到底是瑕疵，也因此，《金瓶梅》和《红楼梦》是另一类型的瑕疵文本——可说是大的瑕疵文本，因为其瑕疵是读了整个《金瓶梅》或《红楼梦》文本才被发现的。葛浩文（Howard Goldblatt）翻译了莫言的好几部长篇小说，夫子自道，说他翻译时，往往对原著内容加以删削，甚至把情节结构加以调整改动。莫言的小说，在葛浩文眼中，在某种意义上，也是一种瑕疵文本——也是大的那一种。[①]

追求完美的人，容不得瑕疵的存在。然而，任何杰出以至伟大的写作人，谁的书写能自夸为白璧无瑕呢？无论如何精心写作、刻意经营，作品篇幅一多，作品数量一多，能白璧微瑕就已经难得了。《文心雕龙》非常重视文字的妥善运用，《练字》篇指陈“缀字属篇”的毛病，要操翰者避免。《指瑕》篇

---

① 葛浩文的文章大概两三年前发表于上海出版的《东方翻译》。顺便说明一下，本文所举例论述的“瑕疵文本”，其文本本身几乎没有形象性可言。形象性强的文本，如李商隐的《锦瑟》，其主题有多种解释，难定于一尊。我们应该用“象征”（symbol）理论来理解，即一个象征性意象可有多种含义，也因此不应把《锦瑟》这样的文本视作“瑕疵文本”。

指陈写作的种种毛病，包括用词含义模糊不清；它指出："晋末篇章，依稀其旨，始有'赏际奇至'之言。""依稀其旨"即含义模糊不清的意思。"文之为德也大矣""风骨""To be or not to be""Reserving judgments is a matter of infinite hope"等都是含义模糊不清的词句。

《文心雕龙》有《论说》篇，刘勰解释"论"这种文体，意谓议论性文章，有一个"锋颖精密"的要求。"锋颖精密"的"锋颖"指笔锋要锐利，"精密"指立论要严谨。对于"精密"的要求，《论说》篇有下面的补充："必使心与理合，弥缝莫见其隙；辞共心密，敌人不知所乘。"牟世金这样译为白话："必须做到思想和道理统一，把论点组织严密，没有漏洞；文辞和思想密切结合，使论敌无懈可击。"（1995，p.271）《论说》篇还有"义贵圆通"和"要约明畅"的说法，意思是论文的立论要能够自圆其说，不会前后矛盾，用词要简约明白，而非含糊不清。

然而，知易行难，古今中外如一，白璧微瑕甚至白璧多瑕是种种人为劳作的常态，刘勰岂有不知？也因此《指瑕》篇曰："古来文才，异世争驱。或逸才以爽迅，或精思以纤密，而虑动难圆，鲜无瑕病。"好一句"鲜无瑕病"！我们要认识"文之为德也大矣"等瑕疵文本之为瑕疵文本，要了解其整个符号学背景，《指瑕》篇和《论说》篇可作为这个议题的伴随文本来加以说明。

对种种符号文本，包括经典文本、名著文本的解释，赵毅衡的"伴随文本"说告诉我们，可以动用的各种相关资料（即伴随文本）从近到远有哪些类别，帮助我们有层次、有次序地寻找答案。然而，我们所面对的文本，可能是有缺陷、有瑕疵的。"瑕疵文本"这个认识，有助于我们避免过分执着，去求取文本意义的终极答案。陶渊明"好读书不求甚解"，这位隐逸诗人的宗师，是个"普通读者"；我们这些学者、学人，则是"专业读者"[①]，是应该求甚解的。然而，"求之不得，寤寐思服，……辗转反侧"，实在辛苦，更可能徒劳。有时应该豁达一点，大而化之一点。"风骨"的确切意义我"求之不得"，我摘《风骨》篇的"藻耀而高翔，固文笔之鸣凤也"，以之为文学作品的一种极佳风格的形容，以之为我研究这个瑕疵文本的一大收获。李卫华应用"伴随文本"说求取"文之为德也大矣"的确切意义，未能成功。她大而化之把这文本解读、"翻译"为"文真是很伟大啊"。这样的解读深得我心，在《"情采通变"：以〈文心雕龙〉为基础建构中西合璧的文学理论体系》

---

① 余光中有"普通读者""专业读者"二分的说法，见余光中《凭一张地图》中《专业读者》一文（2014，pp.20—24）。

（2016）一文中，我对这一句正有“文学伟大”的理解。而《文心雕龙》，虽然有瑕疵，仍然是一本伟大的文论著作。

引用文献：

陈耀南（1988）．《文心》“风骨”群说辨疑．求索，3，89－97，58．

黄维樑（2016）．文心雕龙：体系与应用．香港：文思出版社．

陆侃如，牟世金（1995）．文心雕龙译注．济南：齐鲁书社．

刘季春（2018）．我读乔志高译〈大亨小传〉——兼谈文学和翻译批评．上海翻译，6，77－83，94．

刘勰（2012）．文心雕龙（王志彬，译注）．北京：中华书局．

李卫华（2019）．从伴随文本释“文之为德也大矣”．载于赵毅衡（主编），符号与传媒，18，185－198．成都：四川大学出版社．

潘铭燊（1988）．石头记年日考．香港：中国学社．

数字文化与传媒研究中心（2018 年 10 月 24 日）．符号与意义——赵毅衡：“论伴随文本”．

王运熙，周锋（1998）．文心雕龙译注．上海：上海古籍出版社．

汪涌豪（1995）．风骨．载于杨明照（主编），文心雕龙学综览．上海：上海书店出版社．

余光中（2014）．凭一张地图．北京：国际文化出版公司．

张少康（1987）．文心雕龙新探．济南：齐鲁书社．

周振甫（编）（1996）．文心雕龙辞典．北京：中华书局．

赵毅衡（2018）．符号学作为一种形式文化理论：四十年发展回顾．文学评论，6，146－155．

赵毅衡（2012）．符号学．南京：南京大学出版社．

作者简介：

黄维梁，博士，香港中文大学中文系教授。

Author:

Huang Weiliang, Ph. D., professor of Department of Chinese Language and Literature, The Chinese University of Hong Kong.

Email: szwlwong@163.com

Textual Intentionality in Art and Literature

Zhao Yiheng

Abstract: Intentionality, the speculation projected by consciousness toward an object, is the starting point of any activity directed at meaning. It includes the intentionality of the sender of a text and that of the receiver, as well as the seemingly subject-less "textual intentionality" between the two. The sender's intentionality comprises the intentions of both the artist and, more importantly, the demonstrator. Demonstration involves placing the text into a cultural category, which exercises a decisive influence on the interpretation of the receiver. In the reception of an artistic or literary text, the textual intention is a crucial link in determining the "artifacthood" and intrinsic quality of the text. In every artistic and literary text are left a large number of intentional traces that call for interpretive intentionality. The more "meaning indeterminants" are present in the text, the greater is the demand on the interpretation and thus the higher is the interpretative tension.

Keywords: intentionality, demonstration, text, textual intentionality

论文本意向性

赵毅衡

摘　要：意向是意义活动的出发点，它是意识面向对象发出的获义观照。意向不仅是文本发出者的意向性、文本解释者的意向性，还有处于这二者之间的文本具有的特殊的“文本意向性”。文本所体现的意向，既是艺术家的意向留下的注重痕迹，更包括展示确立的文本的文化范畴，这对于意义解释有决定性影响。在符号文本的接受和解释中，文本体现的诸种意向性，是关键环节。文本需要靠它才能面对接收者确立艺术性。尤其当文本中有大量的意义不定点时，文本意向性对解释施加压力，形成文本的解释张力，此时的解释行为对文本的意义就有决定性作用。

关键词：意向性，展示，文本，文本意向性

DOI: 10.13760/b.cnki.sam.202001001

Ⅰ. Intentionality in Art and Literature

Meaning lies where consciousness meets the material world. This correlation is maintained by the intentionality projected by consciousness, which is the starting point and initiator of meaning-directed activity. No discussion of meaning can ever draw a veil over the compound nature of intentionality, which includes the intentions of both the sender and receiver. Furthermore, we have to focus on a third, and more complicated, intentionality that lies between them: the so-called textual intentionality. The text itself has neither consciousness nor intention, yet has within itself scores of intentional traces left by its sender that become objects of the receiver's intention. The conflict between the intentionality of the sender and the receiver toward those traces plays a vital role in generating the meaning of art and literature.

In terms of consciousness, the world can be divided into at least two parts: things (including substances, events and others' intentions) and their texts, represented by any medium. Of the aforementioned three types of intentionality, only the sender can deal with things directly. The receiver merely faces the texts of art and literature, which by no means present things directly but rather in an inevitably mediatised form and made up of symbols. This paper does not circumvent the discussion of the intentionality in artistic and literary texts; on the contrary, in studying this field, it deals with the daunting question of "textual intentionality".

However, before proceeding with that discussion, this paper re-evaluates the role of the demonstrator's intention, which constitutes a great deal of the sender's intentionality and yet is somehow easily neglected. How does a receiver come to know that what he or she is facing belongs to a artistic or literary text? The receiver can only be well prepared for the corresponding interpretive intentionality when the demonstration of the text displays its distinctive intentionality. Compared with that of the demonstrator, the creator's intentionality takes the inferior place.

For nearly half a century, the heated debate on how to define art and literature has focused on the status of intentionality, as one point of contention. "The dispute over Kafka's intentions" is one example that has revealed the difficulties of solving this puzzle. As Levinson, the renowned arts scholar, pointed out, "artifacthood", aside from being embodied in texts of artistic symbols, is even more to be found in the link between texts and cultural histories. Such a link places intentionality within the works, making them into art. This is what Levinson meant by his proposal for "defining art historically": some texts are considered artworks for they are the outcome of "the making of something which is intended for regard or treatment as previous art works have been regarded or treated" (Oppy, 1992, p. 154). Here the word intended refers precisely to the textual intentionality, while which follows "as" places the text into a category. The genre of artistic and literary texts requires a receiver to establish itself as art.

Another scholar, Kolak, gave a seemingly straightforward counterexample in "Art and Intentionality": in his will, Kafka asked his friend Brod to burn his manuscripts of the novels *Der Prozeb* and *Das Schloss*, thus exhibiting both a denial of artistic intentionality for these texts and an attempt to avoid the link between these works and "previous artworks". In spite of this, these works still turned out to be monuments in the history of literature. Levinson, seemingly, had good reason to refute this. What he meant was that regardless of what he thought before dying, the artistic intentionality was *in* Kafka's works—before, during, and even after writing them—and could never be erased even by his own final will. Levinson, who objected to intentionality, further contested that while Kafka undoubtedly had contradictory intentions for his novels, which intention weighed the most was still to be decided; what was certain was that his novels were truly artistic texts, and this was unaffected by anyone's intention. Consequently, the "actifacthood" accords with the quality of the text, with no regard paid to the sender's intentions.

It seems that the intentionality of art and literature is much more complicated than generally thought. The author's own intention is not equal to that of their texts. Initially, Kolak and Levinson disputed the intentions of Kafka himself, but in time their discussion switched to whether demonstrators or publishers can offset the author's intention with their own. If, instead of Kafka's novels, what is discussed here is the "piggy Picasso" in South Africa that recently gained widespread attention, then it would be much better understood. The "art circle" seemed to treat the works of that pig as artworks for they were sold at a 100 000 yuan each, in a case similar to that of the famous deceased orangutan artist "Congo", whose paintings were reportedly sold for 10 000 yuan (Sina, 2016).

Biologists have not yet decided whether animals have intentions to create art, but the intention of demonstrators, such as galleries and auction houses, could not be more explicit; demonstration injects the artistic intention into texts, forcing us to interpret the pig's works as if guided by the intention of "fine arts". Therefore, when facing a symbolic text, the interpreter, to a great extent, is confronting the competition and coordination of the intentions of more than one subject. In the case of Kafka, apparently, the intention of his executor Brod mattered a lot more than his own.

The concept of "art" relates somehow to artificiality in Chinese and Western languages. In Western languages, the word "art" is defined as "human skill or workmanship as opposed to nature". The Chinese character "藝" initially meant "to plant", with the "木" in the top left standing for plants, and the right part meaning to cultivate by hand: the character "術" is explained in *Shuowen Jiezi*, a Chinese wordbook analysing the form and origin of Chinese characters, as "the path in a city", or perhaps the "way" or "approach". Evidently, this concept has derived from manual skills in both Chinese and Western languages, which brings to notice the question of intentionality. In Western languages, the word "art" has retained the clear connotation of "artificial" by sharing the same word root; in Chinese, by contrast, the artificiality of art needs to be highlighted.

Artworks, as artifacts, are supposed to possess artistic intentions. The scribbles of apes or elephants, even those that are very similar to works created by true artists, are disclaimed by many on the grounds that animals could never have the intention to create an artwork. Nonetheless, these symbolic texts are equipped with artistic intentions by being put to be displayed as artworks. Once demonstrated (such as in an auction house), they immediately gain enough cultural co-textual pressure; the force to consider them as artworks incorporates them into the artistic category. According to the already quoted definition of Levinson, they are "intended for regard or treatment as previous art works have been regarded or treated", leaving interpreters no choice but to interpret them with the expectations for real works of art.

An unavoidable question is whether artworks can be made by nature. It is true that natural things or events have often been seen as arts, but despite the longstanding practice of describing these objects as "miraculous masterworks of nature", there can be no artistic intention assigned to geological processes or biological evolution without a firm belief in deities. The only way that completely natural things can really be turned into artworks is through the artistic demonstration; tree roots, strange-looking stones, or human bodies are not art, but they can become art if they are injected intentionality by demonstrators. This is not to mention mountains or rivers, which can be placed within a demonstrative frame, or displayed in a "sight-viewing way". Demonstration, the pivotal link in generating intentionality, may sometimes be hidden or ignored, but must always exist. Demonstrated things are no longer purely natural things, for the artistic intention has been added.

A mediatised text should undoubtedly become an artwork if the boundaries between intentional meaning, textual meaning, and interpretive meaning are clear enough. In human societies, it is the artistic demonstration (rather than the work's creation) that renders the text with its final intentionality, because it somehow activates the cultural mechanism and places the text within the relational network of art.

The artistic demonstration is an intention with a strong tendency for sociability: caves of primitive murals, medieval churches, editors' compilations, and contemporary galleries and art festivals are all significant mechanisms to construct literary and artistic intentionality. Music performers and singers, for instance, realise the essence of music by adding a "hyper-intentionality" to the intentions of lyricists and musicians. This all shows that the demonstration intention, as a "second-order intentionality", outweighs the original intention, which is very likely to not exist at all (such as the case of animal "painters"), be no longer discoverable (such as the *Homeric Hymns*), or be shadowed by demonstration such that its importance has faded (such as Kafka's final will).

Readers often do not recognise that the text they are facing is subject to a social and cultural intentionality that forces them to examine the text as an artwork. A poem, for example, will not be read as a poem if not written in separate lines or rhymes, or with no title or subtitle establishing it as a poem. Neither will readers seriously interpret the images in such a "non-poem". Some, perhaps those who are sentimental enough, might consider that a text somehow has some "deeper meaning". However, if they read the text as a poem, they may find deep meaning even where there is in fact nothing. Hence, the artistic intentionality of artists cannot ensure the generation of artworks. Only demonstration can precisely determine a symbolic text as being a literary or art work. Facing such a demonstration, supported by the whole mechanism, receivers have no opportunity to conduct a pure speculation free of cultural convention. In Althusser's terms, the viewers are "interpolated" by the cultural mechanism into the place of artistic interpreters. Such an "interpolating" force works because our interpretation has been "formatted" by culture.

Artistic demonstration, by forcing interpretation to accord with artistic intentionality, combines texts with the art mechanism in the culture to "locate" them. As the Chinese aesthetician Zhu Qingsheng's (2000) daring title has it, "No one is an artist, and no one is not an artist". Perhaps it would be better phrased from the perspective of demonstration intentionality as, "No text is definitely an artistic text, and no text is definitely not an artistic text". Alternatively, perhaps we are to see artworks as waiting to be set free from their rigid physicality, in which form vases or sculptures are just sealed up and keeping interpreters away; after all, only in the arts can the irreconcilable antagonism between subjectivity and objectivity be set aside. In sum, the sender's intention will by no means determine whether a symbolic text belongs to art or literature; what plays the decisive role is rather the intention to demonstrate that text as artistic or literary.

Ⅱ. Textual Intentionality

The academic history of intentionality has seen the vital concept gradually evolve, from its beginning as some kind of psychological activity, to becoming a presentation of pure consciousness, to a mode in which the world of meaning is formed, and eventually to an interpretive way of constructing cultural communities.

The concept of intentionality was first proposed by the German philosopher Brentano in the 19th century as an object-oriented psychological activity (Bretano, 1974, p. 88). His student Husserl, who saw intentionality as the cornerstone of phenomenology, accepted Brentano's opinion that an intention is directive, but refuted its psychological structure. Once clarified by Husserl, intentionality can be simply put as a *meaning* intentionality, shown by an abstract connotation structure of consciousness.

As for the aforementioned "textual intentionality", how can a text—a non-subject—have intentions? One easily concluded explanation is that from the text the creative subject's intention can be recognised. As a matter of fact, however, textual intentionality is beyond the control of any individual subject, meaning that it not only belongs to an artist—a single writer or painter, perhaps—but, more importantly, is inherent in the social category added to the text by the demonstrator, therefore being a product of social and historical subjectivity. The combination of assorted elements serves to verify that texts become the intentionality of cultural history.

Except for performances where some of the creators directly face the receivers, in the interpretation process for most literary or artistic texts these two groups will not meet. Instead, receivers or interpreters directly face the texts and are influenced by textual intentionality. The concept of "textual intentionality" has not yet been approached in any straightforward way, though many scholars, particularly those in analytic philosophy, have engaged in discussions based on similar concepts. While intentionality, as many have believed, is a core issue for phenomenologists, it is, in fact, semiotic theorists, who have been most concerned with the intentionality presented in texts, who underpinning the arguments in this paper.

The semiotician Eco, for example, put forward the idea of the "text's intention", believing that an intention must be presented in texts to be interpreted. Kaye Mitchell called this the "intention of the form": some intentionality carried in the textual form (Mitchell, 2008, p. x). Important in this context is the 1943 paper of Mukarovsky from the Prague School, "Intentionality and Unintentionality in Art", and Searles' classic 1983 work in the philosophy of language, simply titled *Intentionality*.

Mukarovsky classifies various elements of a text into "Intentionality Elements" and "Unintentionality Elements". The former refers to the elements comprising a text that were generated by the "writer's intentionality". Meanwhile, however, the signs created for literature and art differ from those aiming at usage (i. e. "signs for communication"), being not for the purpose of effectively conveying a certain meaning. What matters most in artworks, therefore, is the unified significance composed by both the intentional and unintentional elements. Mukarovsky further explained that the so-called "unintentionality" really is not intended by the author, representing those parts of a text that cannot be incorporated into the creator's intentions. These elements altogether form interpretive obstacles that need to be supplemented by perceivers. In this way, Mukarovsky echoes Ingarden's "indeterminacy" from the perspective of semiotics. The splendid explanation of the term "intentionality" given by Searle, meanwhile, is quite close to the textual demonstrator's intentionality discussed in this paper. To make a text literary or artistic means representing it in the form of literature and art. For this reason, textual intentionality, namely the creative and demonstrative intention embodied in symbolic texts, is more of a cultural characteristic rather than the outcome of individual intentions highlighted in Phenomenology (McIntyre & Woodruff, 1982, p. 78).

Though seemingly abstract, textual intentionality has a concrete form in the genre classification of texts, so it is a vital part in the "textual metalanguage" in addition to being a kind of text-imposed cultural pressure on interpretation. Textual intentionality, when it comes to the meaning of artistic texts, dwarfs the "artistic quality" of the textual form, for the classification of textual genre—a matter of cultural form—decides the textual meaning. Similarly, in terms of the expression of textual intentionality, the form category matters more than the content.

In the history of modern thought, there is abundant material regarding intentionality, and the role of textual intentionality in art has gained particular attention from the movements of Phenomenology and analytic philosophy. However, this paper still faces the difficulty that each side in the discussion of intentionality uses exclusive terms in presenting their statements, and there still lacks of any straightforward illustration of the textual demonstrator's intentionality. To find support for the arguments in this paper, the statements of different schools of thought must be scrutinised.

Ⅲ. Demonstration and "Indeterminacy"

The question now arises of how textual intentionality guides the interpreted artistic meaning. One consideration of this is Husserl's analysis of Dürer's copper etching *Knight, Death and the Devil*. First, the viewer takes the etching as an "image carrier"; second, the viewer recognises some images presented by the lines, "the knight on the horse", "Death", "the Devil", and so on; thirdly, an artistic reflection occurs, through which the viewer sees the substantiality displayed by these images consisting of black lines: a knight of flesh and blood. These three processes (image vehicle—image object—image subject) cannot proceed without imagination. Husserl thus offered a vivid description of the process of the viewer from perception to recognition, from the perspective that the generation of meaning requires the blending of the viewer's intentionality.

Ingarden, a literary theorist in the phenomenological tradition, provided a further explanation: the artwork that an interpreter faces is neither a physical object nor a conceptual one, but a pure intentional object combining the two (Ingarden, 1973, p. 56). Further developing Husserl, Ingarden (1973, p. 10) suggests four levels of literary work: first, sounds and phonetic composition; second, sense-groups and sentences; third, schematic outer appearance though which appear various images described in the work; and fourth, objects described by the events of intentionality.

The contribution made by Ingarden lies in his emphasis on the "filling-in" from interpreters to artistic texts. The third level in the consciousness of interpreters, the schematic level, cannot represent every aspect of the real object. There are, in this layer, a series of "indeterminants", where meaning is incomplete or unclear. He called the process by which interpreters supplement these "the concretization of the intended objects" (Ingarden, 1973, p. 145).

This "intention tension caused by indeterminants" is precisely where interpretation is activated. The truth is that literary and artistic texts retain the maximum amount of "indeterminancy" to form a tension in the interpreting process. Therefore, those texts are able to activate the meaning intentionality of interpreters, and provoke their pursuit for the completion of meaning. For example, untitled music, abstract art, and avant-garde drama are all equipped with numerous "indeterminants", thus forcing the interpreters to strive for the meaning. Writers and artists may not know about this theory, even while they compete on it instinctively, resulting in their creative works possessing an increasing amount of indeterminancy to the point that it can nearly dominate those works. Such literary and artistic texts require a near reconstruction from their interpreters, thus becoming works of "open meaning".

Though varying in terms and approaches, many other scholars have observed the same process. Culler (1975, p. 129), for example, raised the concept of "naturalisation". In 1996, the German narratologist Monica Frudnick further proposed, in her book *Establishing A "Natural" Narratology*, that the standard for achieving "naturalness" is set by oral expression. Once a narrative text can be expressed by its readers as "natural" in oral presentation, then the turbulences in this text have been straightened out and intelligibility has been achieved. Frudnick's remark once again made "secondary narrative" controversial, whereby a group of scholars, including Richardson, strongly opposed it by putting forward "unnatural narratology" (Alber, Nelson, Iverson, & Richardson, 2010). They believed that a great deal of narratives cannot be expressed as "natural" in oral presentation, which means they are "unable to be clear and coherent". The author of this paper, therefore, proposed four approaches to the "secondary narrative": correspondence, collation, compromise, and creation (Yiheng, 2014). These approaches cannot be achieved without the intentionality of interpreters, and all belong to the readers' intentional responses to the "indeterminants" in artistic texts. Only by reconstructing intentionality can literature and art derive their meaning.

The ancient Chinese may have shown a more profound understanding of "indeterminants". In the poetics of Zen Buddhism they are called the "barriers of a text", with the understanding that words in a text both facilitate and hinder understanding; they can advance the interpretation or, more likely, obscure the meaning. Tang Xianzu, a writer in the Ming Dynasty, made an excellent remark:

> When Dharma came from India, from heart to heart he imparted Buddhist spirit to his disciples. With the five scriptures of Zen Buddhism emerging and prevailing, the usage of words was again popular among monks. This was probably because after Buddhism spread to China, the majority of Buddhists acquired its spirit by listening to doctrine explanation. The other reason may be that the heart-to-heart way had fallen into a rut; for example, instead of directly explaining doctrines, the Buddha just picked a flower while another saint beckoned a smile. Moreover, in the Zen tradition, a branch from orthodox Buddhism, *kasaya*, a vestment worn by monks, is used as a token of imparting doctrines. However, due to the tradition to use words to express ideas, Chinese people tried to remove barriers in understanding words by the means of words, so as to achieve the sudden enlightenment hoped for in Zen Buddhism. (Xianzu, 1982, p. 1072—73)

Another scholar at the end of the Ming Dynasty elaborated more clearly on the function of "indeterminants": "If meaning is made clear, it is good; if not, better: where there is ambiguity, there is space for interpretation." (Fuzi, 2008, p. 76)

It can be said that indeterminancies in literary and artistic texts are the evidences left by the sender's intentionality that has already departed, so as to summon the interpreter's intentionality to come. The combination of the two intentionalities makes the works of literature and art purely intentional objects. For example, the reading method differs for prose or poems, for to read poems is to perceive a deeper symbolic meaning, which leaves more meaning gaps needing to be filled. A short text is prose when put in an anthology, but a poem among other poems; when it is read as a prose or a poem, even the same words can have totally different meanings. Once produced, a text must be interpreted according to the methods determined by its genre, that is the "expectation" caused by textual intentionality.

This is even more the case in other forms of art. What makes Duchamp's *Fountain* and Warhol's *Brillo Boxes* "artworks" is their being demonstrated at art exhibitions; likewise with performance art, which is firstly performed as some sort of art rather than someone running wild; likewise with animals' paintings being considered fine art because, instead of being discarded like rags, they are exhibited as fine arts; likewise with installation art, on which jokes are made about "ignorant" housekeepers who clear out collections worth millions of dollars like garbage. Art is something created by humans, and consists of mediatised texts of symbols. Upon seeing a demonstrated text, an interpreter will immediately understand the genre intentionality in the text; then, from his or her experience, will evoke the "prior understanding" toward the genre. An agreement between the interpreter and a cultural tradition has been reached before the interpretation takes place; the agreement is to interpret the work in accordance with some existing formula of the genre category. The interpreter, nonetheless, might be completely unaware of the process, for the interpreting model is almost all his or her intuition, and may scarcely require much effort at all.

References:

Alber, J., Nelson, H., Iverson, S., & Richardson, B. (2010). Unnatural narratives, unnatural narratology: Beyond mimetic models. *Narrative*, 18(2), 113–136.

Bretano, F. (1974). *Psychology from the empirical standpoint*. London, UK: Routledge & Kegan Paul.

Culler, J. (1975). *Structuralist poetics: Structuralism, linguistics and the study of literature*. Ithaca, NY: Cornell University Press.

Fuzi, W. (2008). *Comments on selected Ming poetry*. Baoding, CHN: Hebei University Press.

Ingarden, R. (1973). *Cognition of the literary work of art*. Evanston, IL: Northwestern

University Press
McIntyre, R. & Woodruff, S. D. (1982). *Husserl and intentionality: A study of mind, meaning and language.* Dordrecht, NL and Boston, MA: D. Reidel Publishing Company.
Mitchell, K. (2008). *Intention and text: Towards an intentionality of literary form.* London, UK: Continuum.
Oppy, G. (1992). On defining art historically. *The British journal of aesthetics*, 32.
Qingsheng, Z. (2000). *No one is an artist, and no one is not an artist.* Beijing, CHN: Commercial Press.
Sina. Retrieved from: http://collection. sina. com. cn/dfz/henan/yj/2016－11－29/doc－ifxyawmp0524453. shtml
Xianzu, T. (1982). Preface to meeting of five lanterns. In *Complete Works by Tang Xianzu*. Shanghai, CHN: Shanghai Guji Press.
Yiheng, Z. (2014). On the secondary narrativization. *Fujian forum*, 1, 121－127.

Author:

Zhao Yiheng, professor of Semiotics & Narratology of Sichuan University, director of ISMS research team.

作者简介：

赵毅衡，四川大学文学与新闻学院符号学与叙述学教授，符号学—传媒学研究所所长。

Email: zhaoyiheng2011@163. com

马克思主义关于社会符号学类型的文化考察及批判

张　碧

摘　要：关于象征、符号与信号三种符号学类型的基本属性，马克思主义批评曾进行科学性界定，并以此为逻辑依据，根据对三种符号学类型间嬗递关系的社会考察，就现代社会文化体系及交往过程中意义的单义化趋势进行了深入辨析和批判，从而彰显出马克思主义的社会文化批判立场及精神救赎理念。

关键词：马克思主义，符号学类型，考察，批判

Marxist Cultural Theory and Social Critique of Semiotic Types

Zhang Bi

Abstract: This paper takes up the scientific definitions given by Marxists to the essential attributes of three semantic types: symbol, sign and signal. From this logical basis, Marxists conducted a social investigation of the transmutation of the relationships between these three semantic types, advocating for their clear distinction and critiquing the trend to simplify notions of meaning in cultural systems and in the process of communication in modern society. The Marxist critique of semiotic types further highlights the socio-cultural critical standpoint taken by Marxist thinkers and relates to the idea of spiritual salvation.

Keywords: Marxism, semiotic types, cultural theory, critique

DOI: 10.13760/b.cnki.sam.202001002

20世纪的欧洲马克思主义批评呈现出极为多元的发展态势。其中，以波兰、匈牙利、南斯拉夫等东欧社会主义国家马克思主义者为代表的东欧马克思主义，以及主要以西欧、南欧等某些资本主义国家马克思主义者为代表的西方马克思主义，共同构成当代欧洲马克思主义发展格局的重要板块。

拥有不同学术谱系的欧洲马克思主义学者，从马克思主义基本原理出发，对人类社会中“象征”“符号”和“信号”三种符号学类型的基本特征，进行了科学性讨论[①]；同时，他们在此基础上，通过对三种符号学类型之间嬗变或替换关系的描述，深入探讨了现代社会中意义的单义化倾向，以此作为其现代社会文化批判及现代性精神救赎的重要视域。

一、三种符号学类型的表意过程特征及意义张力差异

长期以来，“象征”（symbol）、“符号”（sign）与“信号”（signal）三种符号学类型，受到西方人文社会科学界的广泛关注和运用。尽管学界对三者间关系的界定较为庞杂[②]，但一般而言，可做以下梳分和界定：

在当代学界，“符号”通常指在索绪尔（Ferdinande de Saussure）结构主义传统的意义上，其表意过程（signification）建立在系统内的差异性基础上，并在特定社群内体现出“任意性”（arbitrariness）与“约定性”（conventionality）的符号学类型，换言之，符号根据能指和所指任意结合的表意原则，在特定群体内逐渐获得约定俗成、相对稳定的意义。

“象征”的表意过程，体现出其能指形式对某种对象内涵的直接再现，且这种再现过程本身具有包容性和表意的张力。象征往往与某种抽象观念直接结合，从而呈现出某种价值属性或倾向。因此，一般而言，象征的主要特质或功能，便体现为通过一定能指形式，对特定群体的某种精神价值进行储蓄、积淀，并以此维持、激发这一群体的伦理秩序、文化生活乃至生产机制等。原始时期的原始神话及相应的祭仪、图腾等，由于寄寓着某一历史阶段中特定社会群体充沛的情感因素和精神价值，故而是人类社会中最初的象征形态。

此外，“信号”往往被与上述两种符号学类型相提并论。关于信号，学界

---

① 本文所述的“符号学”（semiotics 或 semiology），采取学界对这一概念的广义式理解，指以不同符号学类型为研究对象的学科，并非仅仅关注文中所涉的“符号”（sign）这一种符号学类型的学问。后同。

② 一个具有代表性的例子：意大利马克思主义语言学家费鲁奇奥·罗西-兰迪（Ferrucio Rossi-Landi）即持有独到的观点，认为象征只是符号的类型之一。（1977，p.9）

通常将其界定为一种仅存在于信息发出者和接受者之间的单义性符号学类型，接受者只能被动接受其单独的信息意义，并据此做出相应的单一反应。相对于前两种符号学类型而言，信号的接收形式迥然相异，对此，不同学者均曾提出过相关见解：翁贝托·艾柯（Umberto Eco）指出，信号与符号的差异，在于它无法具有符号那样“指代他物的约定俗成性”（1979，p. 19）；查尔斯·莫里斯（Charles Morris）则认为，信号与象征的最大区别在于信号不需要接受者的阐释行为。（1955，p. 25）这些阐释，均描述出信号存在于发出者和接受者之间且不受接受者阐释行为和语境的影响而产生其他意义的单义性属性。

三种符号学类型在表意过程方面的不同，造成其各自意义张力，或曰意义丰富程度的差异。一般而言，象征由于直接关涉作为情感或精神观念的对象，具有较强的意义延伸性，故其意义张力最为明显，也便最具有情感性及诗性品质①；对于符号而言，其意义由特定社群经过较长时间“约定俗成”的表意过程而确定，因此其意义更为稳固，意义张力亦相对较弱；信号是一种单义性符号学形式，因此意义张力显然是最弱的。

马克思与恩格斯指出，当人类通过生产劳动工具进行劳动时，其精神、思想便不得不与世界发生联系，于是人类的意识以及语言便在劳动的作用下产生；同时，人类的劳动是一种集体性、社会性活动，在社会性劳动的分工、合作过程中，人类便自发地产生交往诉求。（马克思，恩格斯，1960，p. 34）这样，人类精神世界的社会性特征也在各种符号学类型的中介作用下得以呈现，而人际交往过程中的意义形态也是特定社会心理结构，乃至相应的社会结构的表征。在人类社会不同历史阶段，人类交往活动往往体现出象征、符号及信号三种符号学类型并存、嬗变或替换的复杂关系。对于秉持历史唯物主义立场的马克思主义者而言，考察不同符号学类型及以其为媒介的现代交往范式及其文化体系，便成为对人类社会活动进行科学性探讨的重要途径。

二、马克思主义批评对社会符号学类型的科学考察

如上所述，各种符号学类型无不是人类进行社会性协作、交往的产物，

---

① 关于意义的张力及与情感性及诗性的关系问题，英美新批评业已做出诸多经典论述。值得注意的是，在西方马克思主义内部，德拉·沃尔佩（Galvano della Volpe）以其“有机语境论”（contexuales-organicos），同样对该问题进行了详尽阐述。详见其 *Critica del gusto*（Milán：Feltrinelli，1963，pp. 107—118）。

体现出人类的类属性。在这一认识基础上，西方学界的马克思主义者关于不同社会符号学类型的基本质态及其彼此间的关系，进行了不同维度的科学考察。

在其《马克思主义与语言哲学》（*Marxism and the Philosophy of Language*）中，巴赫金（Mikhail Bakhtin）曾体现出鲜明的马克思主义方法倾向。[①] 与学界关于符号的一般性结构主义认识不同，巴赫金在该作中提出，符号是特定群体或阶级意识形态的产物，并能够根据意识形态之间的冲突与融合而产生相应的全新意义，因此符号意义具备不断生成并更新的动态机制。同时，巴赫金关于“信号”的论述虽着墨不多，但其学术意义却十分深远。（Petrilli & Ponzio，2005，p. 157）巴赫金提出，“在任何情况下，信号都与意识形态范畴（domain of ideological）毫无关系；与它有关系的，是技术装置世界（world of technical devices）及广义的生产性设施”。（Volosinov，1973，p. 68）信号更多地出现于现代社会生产技术之中，是存在于信息发出者和接受者间的恒定的信息承载者，且具有不受意识形态语境影响的基本属性。由此可见，由于符号具有动态的意义生成机制，而信号更多地体现为发出者和接受者间的单义化作用/反应机制，因此两者的差异主要体现为意义生成机制的动态性和恒定性，这便是符号与信号在意义张力方面存在差别的主要原因。

由于历史语境及人类社会经验的变动不居，亦即社会历史自身的多样性，尤其是当不同社会阶层的意识形态之间产生冲突、对抗及交融时，社会群体便根据其特有的社会实践目的，对符号的表意机制加以变动，从而使其在形式及内容层面发生相应的变化，并产生出一系列全新的意义。

英国马克思主义者雷蒙·威廉斯（Raymond Williams）借助巴赫金的“复调”概念，同样对促使新符号不断生成并使符号具有意义张力或意义多样化的机制属性予以了一定论述。同时，威廉斯也认识到，在具体社会活动中，信号所具有的信息单一性指向，使得社会成员在接受其传达的信息后，仅仅机械而被动地做出程序化的反应，无法对信息做出源自主体视域的其他理解和阐释。符号的复调性正是使其与信号产生本质差异的原因。由此，威廉斯

---

① 当代学界大多认为，该作虽署名为瓦伦丁·沃洛辛诺夫（Valentin Volosinov），但实为巴赫金所作。另，关于巴赫金的马克思主义者身份，学界亦有争议，但包括伊格尔顿（Terry Eagleton）在内的不少国内外学者坚定不移地将其视为马克思主义者。本文根据学界多数意见，认为其《马克思主义与语言哲学》一作体现出明显的马克思主义方法。相关论题，参见张冰《〈马克思主义与语言哲学〉是马克思主义的吗?》（载于《中国人民大学学报》2013年第6期）。

同样从意识形态语境中信息接收者对符号的阐释作用方面，对符号与信号做出了本质区分："符号——正如其社会性经验一样，这些社会性经验是符号得以形成的基准……符号的特征不像信号仅仅具有固定、稳定而永不变更的涵义。……它往往被用于各种各样的社会范畴之中，并在这些不可胜数的新语境中相应产生出新的涵义。"（Williams，1977，p. 39）威廉斯对符号与信号关系的阐释，显然是对巴赫金观点的进一步发展。两位学者从不同群体或阶级间意识形态的交流及冲突角度阐释了符号的多元表意机制，并由此将其与信号做出区分。尽管与索绪尔对符号的经典界定不同，但他们却通过对符号与信号在表意过程中意义张力维度的比较，对其差异性进行了历史唯物主义的科学分析，从而隐含地表达出社会意义张力的重要性。当然，关于这种社会意义多样性的精神内涵及价值，两位学者未做进一步论述。

较之巴赫金与威廉斯，波兰马克思主义者亚当·沙夫（Adam Schaff）则从语用学角度，强调了符号或语言及现实间的关系（佩特丽莉，庞奇奥，2013，p. 183），尤其是信号在人类社会中的交往实践功能。他从索绪尔对符号的界定方式出发，认为"符号最突出的功能在于它是交往途径，以及某种交流意图"（Schaff，1962，p. 175），同时，"信号的意图往往旨在激发（或变更、阻止）一项行为（action）；信号之所以能够突显——在与意向性行为（action）间的联系方面，往往具有偶发性"。（p. 184）在现代社会生产活动和日常交往活动中，两种符号学类型都能够发挥交往功能，尤其是信号，由于其反应机制建立在人际交往行为的刺激与反应的基础上，因而能够在社会群体的特定场合内发挥实践性指令功能。这种认识对信号在现代人类社会中的交往功能进行了基本界定，也为马克思主义对现代社会信号化状况的批判埋下了伏笔。

值得注意的是，在沙夫看来，具有强烈意义张力及情感特征的象征在交往活动中发挥交往功能的效率虽不及信号，但在某些特定场合，例如祭祀、仪式中，象征通过对集体思想及情感的展现，体现出某种张力性较强的意义向度，并以此调动和激发民众产生不同的情感及思想价值，从而能够为人类社会精神生活增添某种诗性品质。同时，通过对象征和符号与信号的表意机制的比较，沙夫暗示了这样一种观点：象征的情感性意义张力特质，具有某种特殊的精神价值向度，这也使其与符号，尤其是信号的工具性特征的差异被突显出来。（p. 193）然而，沙夫同样主要从科学维度来认识几种符号学类型的基本社会属性及功能，并未就其精神价值进行充分论述。

上述学者，基本以马克思关于社会性是人类的类属性这一经典判断为基础，并从科学认知的角度考察和界定了几种符号学类型各自的基本特征和社会生成机制，尤其对其各自的意义张力特征进行了基本性界定及隐而不彰的价值判断。事实上，在人类的交往体系及文化体系中，几种具有不同意义张力程度的符号学类型间的嬗递，以及在意义张力方面渐次降低的趋势，也反映出人类社会在特定生产条件下社会心理结构的递变，并相应体现出人类交往模式及文化景观的蜕变，而这正应当是马克思主义的社会文化批评的重要考察维度及对象。因此，上述马克思主义者关于符号学类型的科学界定，为马克思主义批评从几种符号学类型间的意义差异方面，充分深入对现代社会中人类的交往方式及文化体系以及深藏其中的生产关系的价值考察和批判之中，提供了逻辑论证的基础。

三、列斐伏尔对现代社会交往范式单义化的批判

在马克思主义批评传统中，现代性问题始终受到审慎而辩证的价值判断。对于 20 世纪的西方马克思主义而言，文化与哲学往往是其主要研究对象，体现出浓郁的人本主义倾向，而对现代性问题的审视、反思及批判，也一度成为其评价现代社会的主要维度与方式。其中，法兰克福学派的诸多成员描述并论证了现代社会中工具理性对价值理性的压制与撕裂、话语制度对人类心理结构的强制性规约等异化现象，彰显出鲜明的现代社会批判立场，并由此延伸出精神救赎观念。鉴于此，作为西方马克思主义的代表之一，法国马克思主义者列斐伏尔（Henri Lefebvre）及其弟子鲍德里亚（Jean Baudrillard）等人通过对现代社会中符号学类型间嬗变关系及过程的考察，对隐藏于其中的现代性缺陷及政治逻辑进行了深入批判，由此拓展了马克思主义的社会批判视域及路径。

列斐伏尔持有与法兰克福学派相类似的现代社会文化批判立场，并将批判视野延伸至资本主义社会日常生活的现代性问题。关于现代性，包括西方马克思主义传统在内的西方近代学界有着极为多样而复杂的界定途径与阐述立场，而列斐伏尔亦形成了独到的马克思主义式的理解方式："马克思在频繁运用'现代'一词时，将其界定为资产阶级、经济增长的兴起，以及资本主义的确立、资本主义政治的呈现"（Lefebvre，1995，p. 169）；同时，他援引波德莱尔（Charles Baudelaire）关于现代性的经典论述，指出现代性是现代人所特有的"短暂性及流动性"的心理结构。（p. 170）综合而言，列斐伏尔对现代性的理解可表述为：与社会物质生产领域以及上层建筑的现代化过程

相应的人类心理及意识结构。

社会意义活动直接产生、作用于人类心理结构，其本质体现为人类对蕴含、承载着某种意义信息的各种意义形式的生产、理解与接收。同时，社会的现代化活动，往往以某种意义形式作用和表征于人类心理结构。列斐伏尔提出，现代化社会的经济、政治及文化等诸多领域业已呈现出人际交往及文化体系的形式化、去意义化的“恐怖主义”（terrorism）特征[①]，并且该特征也在人类心理结构中普遍呈现，形成现代性缺陷。形式化，成为现代社会诸多领域最为主要的意义样态，而在这种现代社会语境中，人类生活领域中所应当蕴藏的丰富内涵被剥夺，进而体现出现代人心理结构的僵化以及对生命本真体验的缺失。对现代社会中“恐怖”形式的反思，成为列斐伏尔现代社会批判的重要维度，而其基于符号学维度的现代性省思，正源于这一基本思想框架。

关于几种符号学类型各自的本质及特征，列斐伏尔与前述马克思主义者的认识差异主要体现在符号上。他基本采纳了索绪尔对符号的结构主义式界定，指出符号的任意性和约定性集中体现为人类特定群体对对象及概念的群体化规定过程，并由此不断形成涵盖这一群体的语言、话语（discourse）等表意体系：“语言专横而必要性地使用词汇来确认感觉和行动，并不断地消除模糊性和误解。”（Lefebvre，2008，p. 282）此处，列斐伏尔特别强调了符号整合特定群体内部关于对象的表意方式的逻辑性（logical）功能，亦即在符号体系内部，不同符号表意方式之间具有统一协调性（coherence）（p. 283）；也就是说，群体成员往往以统一性表意形式，亦即语言、话语等符号形式，来表征社会实践的诸多方面，使得混沌的世界通过诸多符号分节（articulation），逐渐形成庞大的符号体系，而这种符号体系与自然及社会实践间的关系具有稳固的逻辑统一性，亦即表意过程的相对恒定和单一性。

同时，信号作为一种指示性单义机制，其主要特点体现为“并不或极少提供信息，它仅仅具有提示‘阻止’或‘同意’、‘排除’或‘允许’的功能”（p. 279）。值得注意的是，对于除沙夫等人外的多数马克思主义者疏于阐述的“象征”，列斐伏尔同样有清晰的界定。在他看来，象征能够被寄予和表达特定群体一系列丰沛的情感及价值因素：“象征，往往意指一种情感的投入品，一种感情充沛的事物（如恐惧、魅力等），这些情感能够在某个特定的区域内

① 详见列斐伏尔 *Everyday Life in the Modern World* 一书中“Terrorism and Everyday Life”一章。

得到积淀，并因而在任何地方都能‘表达’每个人的利益。”（p.141）

由此，三种符号学类型的差异便体现在“信号完全呈现和消逝于其自身功能范畴中；符号（语词）只有在符号群及其相互影响中才有其合理性……而象征则代表它自己，充盈着丰富的意义”（p.284）。与符号和信号相比，象征的主要差异体现为往往能够在特定群体内彰显出丰富的意义及精神内涵。三种符号学类型无不以各自不同的表意实践，表征着人类社会在不同历史语境中各项生产、交往活动的具体内容，并呈现出相应的意义模式。

西方历史自上古时期直至近现代，其社会文化形态的转换过程，往往是由三种符号学类型形态间的递变而得以呈现的，“象征的显赫地位，曾经持续许多世纪之久，它们源自自然，却暗含着特定的社会内涵（implications）。但在我们西方文明的最近几个阶段，尤其是在印刷术被发明后，从象征到作为符号的、权威性日益增强的书写词汇间，存在明显的转换。如今，一种从符号到信号的进一步的转换即将产生”（Lefebvre，1984，p.62）。马克思指出，缩减社会必要劳动时间并不断提高生产效率，成为资本主义现代社会的基本特征。（马克思，2009，pp.52－54）因此，生产过程及生活中对交际效率的追求，便同样成为现代社会的基本特征。从象征到符号，再到信号的嬗变，由于逐渐向单义性、信息传达的快捷性和有效性方向发展，故而在现代社会生产、生活中的交际效率方面呈渐次上升趋势；但相应地，信息传达有效性的渐次升高，却也预示着意义张力，即意义丰富程度及其价值理性的相应衰弱。这种趋势，暴露出人类精神领域的萎缩与现代性的缺陷。

从古希腊这一西方思想源头时期直至现代社会产生前，思想、真理——或曰“逻各斯”（logos），往往以神话式象征形式得以呈现；在具体社会生活中，象征也常以神话样态出现，蕴含并彰显着人类群体的感性认识、深挚情感和忠贞信念等丰富的意义内涵，为群体成员提供阐释世界及生命存在意义的方式，也为维系社会生产与生活提供行为及伦理的规范依据。尤其在西方中世纪语境中，象征往往通过宗教神话发挥表达、凝聚特定群体的精神、情感、意志的功能（Lefevre，2009，p.231）。在现代社会，尽管象征在社会群体中依然能够发挥类似功能（Stevenson，2003，p.98），但当科学理性成为近现代人类思想方法的主流，尤其是马克斯·韦伯（Max Weber）宣告祛魅时代来临之际，符号逐渐以消解及伪装的方式取代着象征的社会作用，使人类思想观念的表达方式往往不再体现为充满着丰沛情感意义及神话意味的象征，而是以逻辑性的语言－文字（即符号）获得书写，以符号相对恒定而统一的意义形式表述着人类的思想与真理，并不断取消或替代着神话象征中的多义性及精神性言说："象征和神话传说转变成了话语主题"（Lefebvre，2008，p.302），"符号开始大量繁殖（书写、书面数字等），且无法与象征和平共处"（p.303）。对于这种现象，法国哲学家克里斯蒂娃（Julia Kristeva）同样予以描述："符号从更少的维度来指涉整体……较之象征，符号显得更加具体化。"（1986，p.70）这种状况的成因主要在于，符号相对固定的社会表意方式及迅捷的符码传达效率优势使其更符合现代社会对生产及生活中交往效率的要求，因此在现代印刷业语境中，印刷文字与其他现代媒介的符号一样，替代和限制着象征符码的超验性精神效应。对此，本雅明（Walter Benjamin）在论述机械复制艺术与充满灵氛（auro）的前现代艺术间的差异性时，业已进行了经典性阐释。这样，便出现上述符号取代象征的历史文化状况，社会文化体系也在一定程度上，初步呈现出符号所具有的意义统一性的形式特征。

必须指出的是，尽管象征同样能够通过语言文字而发挥功能（例如《圣经》等经典著作具有宗教象征功能），然而，以印刷文字等现代媒介为传播途径的象征品，在其符码传播的社会性、广泛性与效率性方面，均远低于作为符号系统的印刷文字，因此在现代传媒语境中，象征仍旧无法避免被符号取代的命运。

对于当代社会而言，最令人不安的是其交往及文化体系的信号化倾向。在一味追求高效率的当代生产及生活过程中，人际信息沟通的有效性被提升到人类历史上无以复加的程度，尤其是现代工业化、技术化生产方式的广泛兴起，促使信号以其高效的信息传递支配着现代人的感知及心理结构。以信号灯为例。在红、绿两色面前，司机机械地执行"停止"或"前行"指令，并由此形成"指示/应答"的机械心理反应模式。当然，信号不仅体现为诉诸感官的物理性信息指示，在列斐伏尔看来，所有源于现代科技理性、窄化人类思维与意识的单义系统，无一不是信号的体现。现代社会中的诸多信号，以向社会成员传达某种单向指示信息的方式，约束、指示和组织着社会成员的行动方式，并逐渐将其心理领域塑形为某种单向性意义结构。在现代社会，信号往往比符号更加全面地侵入现代社会的各个领域，影响着现代人的日常生产及生活方式，也更为严重地禁锢着现代人对诗性精神世界的感知与体验。

德国哲学家卡西尔（Ernst Cassirer）曾指出，信号代表动物的刺激性生存本能，而象征则体现人类的智慧及灵性；人类一旦失去象征对心灵世界的升华与引导，其意识及行为便可能退化至动物为维持基本生存而做出的生理性、信号性本能反应："一旦失去象征体系（symbolism）……人类生活将被拘囿于在其生理性需求和现实利益的狭小圈子里，也便无法寻求指向‘理想性世界’的途径，而这个世界恰以宗教、艺术……等不同维度，向人类敞开大门。”（Cassirer，1944，p. 62）与其相似，列斐伏尔同样意识到现代社会意义领域中象征被信号取代的恶果。尽管象征依然广泛存在于现代日常生活中，但建立于科技理性基础上的单义化意义系统却不断消解着充盈于象征之中的丰沛的情感意义，从而侵蚀着人类的思维、情感世界，其中，信号尤可能以其单义性功能，使人类在僵化的社会交往模式及文化体系中失去通过象征所进行的超验性和神圣性幻想与精神追求，也因此失去对人类存在意义的价值性思考。

自 18 世纪始，西方诸多文学家及艺术家都曾试图通过文学或艺术途径，借助神话象征所蕴含的浪漫主义诗性因素[①]，化解以科学理性为基础的现代性思维对人类精神生活的僵化。列斐伏尔亦感慨道：“瞧瞧那些试图取消戏剧性、象征性、去除意指效应的人们吧！……失去了象征，没有了虚构，在这生活与生命间，你与我如何进行这残酷的对话?”（Lefebvre，1995，p. 100）在现代社会中，生产与生活领域对效率的一味追求，促使社会文化活动日渐呈现出单义化趋势，致使人类逐渐失去关于事物意义建构的主体性思虑，从而亦失去对自身所处境遇的、生命本真意义的反思。这样，列斐伏尔同样主张以一种浪漫主义的诗性审美态度和生活方式，使现代人从工具理性的思维与生活方式中解放出来，并充分意识到：在诸多符号学类型中，诉诸丰沛的意义性、情感性及伦理性的象征，承载着某个群体、民族乃至整个人类对自身生存境遇的记忆，并体现出人类精神世界永久的诗性诉求，从而最具有使现代人恢复盎然诗意的价值理性特质，“通过强化‘人类’（beings）或‘事物’的直接、基本的在场的方式，象征体系复制了它们的存在（existence）”（Lefebvre，2008，p. 301）。

总之，在现代社会中，象征向符号，尤其是信号的转换，是人类丰富的情感及思维意义向无意识机械反应的蜕变，是建构诗性世界的努力逐渐衰落的过程，它标志着人性的倒退，亦体现出现代性的精神缺陷。因此，列斐伏尔站在西方马克思主义立场上，对现代社会交往方式及文化体系的单义化倾向进行了严厉的抨击，并提出以象征中的浪漫主义审美方式化解现代社会中

① 自 18 世纪以来，作为文化思潮的浪漫主义（Romanticism），因对以科学理性为精神内核的历史进步的不同理解，而在其内部呈现出不同的思想倾向及国别传统。本文所涉浪漫主义，主要指以反思现代文明、复兴人类诗性精神生活为旨归的德国浪漫主义思想传统，亦涉及英国、法国浪漫主义传统中与之相关的思想倾向。

深陷单义化泥淖的人类精神，也由此延续了西方马克思主义为克服现代性缺陷而引发的精神救赎思考。

四、鲍德里亚对现代社会单义化倾向的多重批判

早年的鲍德里亚曾体现出鲜明的马克思主义批评旨趣（Baudrillard，1993a，p. 20），业已成为学界公论。[①] 具有马克思主义批评倾向的鲍德里亚，大致采取了列斐伏尔对几种符号学类型的界定方式，进一步认识到现代社会符号学类型的嬗变及其历史内涵，并对其中的现代性缺陷进行了必要的社会批判。

延续列斐伏尔的批判思路，鲍德里亚十分强调对资本主义社会中现代媒介文化形态的单义化趋势的省察，“被媒介化的东西……是被形式/符号所重新掌控的东西，它被结合成模式，受符码的支配”（2013，p. 74）。在鲍德里亚看来，现代媒介中的符号，以其单义化的符号学形态，发挥着维护资本主义社会政治既定秩序的意识形态功能，“（媒介）所指涉的，不是真正的物，不是真正的世界或指称的（referential）维度，却是从一个符号指向下一个符号”（Baudrillard，1998，p. 125），媒介中符号[②]的意义不再由指称物（referent），亦即符号所指涉的社会现实语境决定[③]，而仅仅通过符号系统内部诸多组成要素间的互相指涉而生成、存在，符号也便相应丧失了获取多元意义的基本机制，由此在传播过程中仅能表达某种单一观念，并呈现出排斥其他意义价值的封闭性特征。这样，在资本主义现代社会语境中，作为社会制度维护者的编码者在符号信息的编码过程中，为其植入有利于维护资本主义现有政治、社会秩序合法性的意识形态，“电视‘信息’不是所播出的视像，是所强加的新型关联和知觉模式”（p. 123），符号在被诸多社会个体解码及消费的过程中，通过向其灌输技术官僚所指定的某种单一意识形态，迫使民众失去对政治、社会等领域中历史事件进行独立反思的意识及能力。显然，鲍德里亚对现代媒介符号化的批判对象由资本主义的一般现代性问题转向了

---

① 学界一般认为，鲍德里亚早期的《物体系》《消费社会》是体现其马克思主义思想倾向的代表作。其《符号政治经济学批判》虽同样关注符号学类型问题，但其立场与批评旨趣已与马克思主义产生分裂。

② *The Consumer Society* 一书的英译者此处使用了“symbol”一词，对应法文版的“symbole”，但从其所指涉的现代文化传媒语境来看，此处实指“sign”。

③ 关于“指称物”在马克思主义符号学批评中的方法意义，参见张碧《西方马克思主义批评理论对指称物的运用及意义》（载于《文艺理论研究》2014 年第 4 期）。

更具现实性的资本主义社会政治领域。

列斐伏尔对资本主义现代社会中信号化趋势的批判，同样影响到鲍德里亚。尽管较少使用“信号”这一表述，且往往将之与“符号”等术语混用，但鲍德里亚在阐述现代媒介传播文化的过程时，分明体现出对现代传媒技术信号化特征的批判。

麦克卢汉（Marshall McLuhan）曾提出，现代媒介形式是使人类形成新型心理感知结构的重要原因，而媒介内容本身则无足轻重。（McLuhan，1964，p. 94）在这一基础上，鲍德里亚提出，现代媒介往往通过迫使接收者消费其体系中的信号而形塑人类心理感知模式。现代媒介为文化制品进行单义性编码活动，使大众文化呈现出明显的信号化特征，“交往体系在整体上从复杂的语言语法结构，转型为二元性‘问/答’的信号体系”（Baudrillard，1993b，p. 62）。然而，信号对现代大众文化的普遍支配，使诗性话语的意义多样性特质丧失殆尽，无法体现人类思想、智慧等精神要素的延展与创新。

此处，鲍德里亚再次强调了象征在现代社会中的精神价值。鲍德里亚意识到，在西方前现代社群中，人类往往通过宗教祭仪的活动形式，以血肉、红酒和面包等象征道具作为具体交往媒介，传达特定场合中的精神文化韵味；而在现代社会中，现代人却往往通过网络、无线广播等现代媒介来进行交流，这些媒介活动“往往由刺激－反应、提问－回答这样的模式构成”（Baudrillard，1998，p. 105），它们并不以媒介自身内容感染参与者的精神世界，而是使其仅仅满足于在这种交往、互动活动中所获取的刺激，从而在无意识中削弱甚至忽略交往内容的精神意蕴。因此，具有浓郁情感象征意味的前现代交往方式，蜕变为建立于现代科技基础上的信号系统：“交往活动不会像以往那样，通过象征媒介来完成，而是通过技术手段”，“人们所共同浸渍其中的不再是‘文化’：鲜活的身体、灵动的群体（所有为仪式和盛宴带来象征和活力的事物）……而是由符号和参照物组成的怪异躯壳”。（p. 103）显然，较之列斐伏尔，鲍德里亚对现代社会交往方式中符号、信号取代象征的倾向，从西方马克思主义的文化批判立场上，予以了更为辩证而全面的考察，并将对资本主义现代社会的现代性的反思进一步延展到具体政治领域，从而体现出更为深入的批判思路。

鲍德里亚曾敏锐地觉察到现代社会中符号取代象征的趋势。在对现代家庭陈设的考察中，鲍德里亚认识到，在传统家庭中，代表着传统道德的家具，作为家庭父权秩序意义的承载者，发挥着明显的象征作用；在现代社会中，家具则平等地参与对家庭整体意义系统的建构过程，也便因发挥出结构主义式符号功能而相应地失去昔日的象征意义。对此，学界的论述较为完备，兹不赘述。

值得注意的是，鲍德里亚与列斐伏尔一样，体现出某种浪漫主义批判倾向。在他看来，古董和藏品尽管同样可以被纳入功能性的符号系统之内，却由于发挥着象征时间的功能，而使自身从符号系统中脱颖而出。通过古董，人类能够依稀品味到苍茫而神秘的历史况味及蕴含于其中的真实内韵(authenticity)。诚如本雅明所言，前现代时期的艺术品，往往以其巫术般的灵氛撩动现代人的心魄。尤其在充满工业秩序的现代社会中，古董更能使人类通过对久远世界的玄想，从工具理性中获得一丝浪漫主义的精神解脱。鲍德里亚同样认为，古董所蕴含的历史象征，能够使其在家庭陈设的符号系统中保持相对独立的状态，并以此洋溢出某种超越世俗的精神气质："古董象征着精神超越以及某种在现实中的冥想，滋养着人们的神话性观念与个体观念……它们弥散在人世间，重新安置着这个世界，与功能组织（functional orgnization）不断延伸着的属性分庭抗礼。"（Baudrillard，1996，pp. 79－80）即便被安置于符号系统性的家庭陈设中，古董也能够从由诸多陈设所共同构成的共时性结构中，体现出某种指向久远历史的象征价值。

由此，通过对象征与符号关系的描述，鲍德里亚在彰显出某种浪漫主义式现代社会批判立场时，亦体现出西方马克思主义关于现代社会的精神救赎诉求。

五、作为"自为的"类本质对象化的象征

由此可见，列斐伏尔与鲍德里亚都认识到，象征所具有的情感性、意义丰富性及超验性特征对现代人而言，具有使其从单义化乃至形式化导致的现代性精神危机中获得精神救赎的可能性，这正是列斐伏尔极力主张恢复象征在现代社会中价值地位的主要原因。然而，两人更多的是在一种抽象意义上谈及象征的现代救赎功能，但从马克思主义角度深入论证象征在人类社会交往及实践中的本质属性时，两人受到了限制，也未能充分阐释象征在马克思主义社会文化批评中的独到价值[①]，因而未能在根本上超越19世纪的浪漫

---

① 值得一提的是，本雅明（2013）也曾提及象征的精神超越性特质，但与列斐伏尔等一样，对象征本质的论证似不甚充分。

主义。

对此，匈牙利马克思主义者阿格妮丝·赫勒（Agnes Heller）对象征的本质进行了更为深入的探讨。在列斐伏尔理论的基础上[①]，赫勒提出，象征指代的往往不仅是某个单一概念或指令，而是一系列审美及伦理等精神价值的综合："象征不只牵涉意义，还往往同价值或一系列综合性价值相关——以语言或物质性形式再现这些综合性的价值"（Heller，1984，p. 142）；象征是人类在劳动实践中创造出来的特殊符号学类型，是表达特定人类群体诸多情感、审美及伦理价值的媒介，也是能够使人类普遍从中直观自身的重要精神形式。

同时，赫勒将人类对自然及社会中所有对象的占有及实践后的产物称为"自在性"类本质对象化（species-essential objectivations "in itself"）（pp. 117－119），亦即所有经过人类实践加工改造并体现出人类某种社会性意志的物质性或精神性产物。所有"自在性"类本质对象化产物，无不是作为社会性存在的人类集体实践的结果，这显然是对马克思的"人具有类属性或社会属性"这一经典命题的延伸。这样，赫勒便理所当然地将包括象征在内的诸多符号学类型一并归于"自在性"类本质对象化产物的范畴。此处，赫勒虽已意识到却未能明确指出这样一种观点：与其他一般性"自在性"类本质对象化产物不同，象征往往以其鲜明的意义丰富性、情感性等价值特征，彰显出人类对置身其中的物质世界的精神创造及超越性体验，换言之，象征具备了被赫勒命名为"自为性"类本质对象化（species-essential objectivations "for itself"）的基本品质——成为超越一般物质性"自在性"类本质对象化水平并达到"特定的时期内触及的人性的自由度"的精神性自由境界的类本质对象化产物。（p. 119）值得注意的是，列斐伏尔等人有时在不自觉中，将象征表述成了代表着诸多人类个体在深陷俗务泥淖中时聊以自我解脱的精神超越性，但至为重要的是，象征，体现出具有类本质的或曰社会性存在样态的人类，在历史活动，亦即现实性的生产、生活的实践过程中，普遍具有的对物质有限性的超越诉求，以及对人类共有的精神自由状态的追求这一恒久目标；同时，亦体现出作为社会性存在的人类，对具有精神自由性的理想社会状态的普遍性精神追求。质言之，象征应当被理解为承载着人类特定群体某种超越性精神意志的意识形态。

---

① 赫勒在对现代日常生活的批判路径等许多方面，均曾受列斐伏尔影响。她关于"符号"与"信号"的界定基本与列斐伏尔一致，本文不再引述。

总之，唯有从作为人类的类本质——社会属性——的对象化这一角度来理解象征，才能真正将对象征的精神价值的阐释还原至马克思主义的历史唯物主义方法视域，也才能使西方马克思主义传统所强调的精神救赎路径获得更为合理的延续与升华。

六、结语

关于人类社会中符号学类型的特征及其关系，马克思主义进行了细致的理论探讨，不同马克思主义者对符号学类型的观照，存在考察维度和价值立场等诸多方面的差异。巴赫金等人将不同符号学类型视为人类社会交往过程及文化体系的不同表征形式，并从意义的丰富性角度，对符号学类型间的关系所隐含着的社会逻辑进行了科学性探讨，从而体现出马克思主义对方法科学性的基本诉求。但更为重要的是，列斐伏尔、鲍德里亚等则在这种科学认知基础上，通过对现代社会中交往方式及文化体系中象征的衰退、符号及信号化普遍兴起现象的分析，对其深层的历史社会逻辑进行了深入批判，并提出以象征中类似于德国传统的浪漫主义精神来化解由社会文化单义化所导致的人性危机。同时，赫勒则为阐释象征的现代价值进一步提供了来自马克思主义理论传统的合理途径。由此，他们关于符号学类型各自特征及嬗变关系的探讨，进一步延续了马克思主义批评关于符号学的建构（秦佳阳，2014，p. 221)，以及人类现代社会发展状况的理论思考。

引用文献：

本雅明（2013）. 德意志悲苦剧的起源（李双志等，译）. 北京：北京师范大学出版社.

波德里亚，让（2013）. 游戏与警察（张新木等，译）. 南京：南京大学出版社.

马克思，恩格斯（1960）. 马克思恩格斯全集（第三卷）. 北京：人民出版社.

马克思（2009）. 资本论（第一卷）. 北京：人民出版社.

佩特里莉，苏珊；庞齐奥，奥古斯托（2013）. 亚当·沙夫马克思主义思想中的人文主义、语言哲学及社会批判. 载于曹顺庆，赵毅衡（主编），符号与传媒，2. 成都：四川大学出版社.

秦佳阳（2014）. 符号学转向：评张碧、唐小林主编《欧洲马克思主义符号学派》. 载于曹顺庆，赵毅衡（主编），符号与传媒，1. 成都：四川大学出版社.

Baudrillard, J. (1993a). *Baudrillard live: Selected interviews*. Mike Gane(Ed.). London, UK and New York, NY: Routledge.

Baudrillard, J. (1993b). *Symbolic exchange and Death*. (Iain H. Grant, Trans.). London,

UK: Sage Publications.

Baudrillard, J. (1996). *The system of objects*. (B. James, Trans.). London, UK and New York, NY: Verso.

Baudrillard, J. (1998). *The consumer society: Myths and structures*, Los Angeles, CA and London, UK: Sage.

Cassirer, E. (1944). *An essay on man: An introduction to a philosophy of human culture*. New York, NY: Yale University Press.

Eco, U. (1979). *A theory of semiotics*. Bloomington, IN: Indiana University Press.

Heller, A. (1984). *Everyday life*. (G. L. Campbell, Trans.). London, UK and Boston, MA: Routledge and Kegan Paul.

Kristeva, J. (1986). *The Kristeva reader*. Toril Moi (Ed.). New York, NY: Columbia University Press.

Lefebvre, H. (1984). *Everyday life in the modern world*. (Sacha Rabinovitch, Trans.). New Brunswick, CA and London, UK: Transaction Publishers.

Lefebvre, H. (1995). *Introduction to modernity*. John (Moore, Trans.). London, UK and New York, NY: Verso.

Lefebvre, H. (2008). *Critique of everyday life* (Volume 2). (John Moore, Trans.). London, UK and New York, NY: Verso.

Lefebvre, H. (2009). *State, space, world: Selected essays*. (Gerald Moore, Trans.). Minneapolis, MN and London, UK: University of Minnesota Press.

McLuhan, M. (1964). *Understanding media: The extensions of man*. New York, NY: McGraw-Hill Book Company.

Morris, C. (1955). *Signs, language and behavior*. New York, NY: George Braziller, INC.

Petrilli, S. & Ponzio, A. (2005). *Semiotics unbounded*. Toronto, CA and Buffalo, NY: University of Toronto Press.

Rossi-Landi, F. (1977). *Linguistics and economics*, Paris, FR: Mouton.

Schaff, A. (1962). *Introduction to semantics*. Oxford, UK: Pergamon Press.

Stevenson, D. (2003). *Cities and urban cultures*. Philadelphia, PA: The McGraw-Hill Companies, Inc..

Volosinov, V. (1973). *Marxism and the philosophy of language*. (Ladislav Matejka & I. Titunik, Trans.). New York, NY: Seminar Press.

Williams, R. (1977). *Marxism and literature*. Oxford, UK and New York, NY: Oxford University Press.

作者简介：

张碧，文学博士，西北大学文学院副教授，博士生导师，主要从事西方文艺学、符号学及西方文学研究。

Author:

Zhang Bi, Ph. D., associate professor and doctorial supervisor at the Faculty of Liberal Arts, Northwest University. His research interests are in Western theory of literature, semiotics and Western literature.

Email: china_zhangbi@163.com

“直言”与“理想自我”的建构：存在符号学视域下对福柯晚期主体思想的阐释

颜小芳

摘　要：与早期对主体的理性而冷峻的批判相比，福柯临终前的讲课因为笼罩着死亡阴影，反而流露对生命的深情眷念和赞颂。与权力相比，生命与自我才是福柯最关心的问题。福柯回顾一生，想要追根溯源。看看早期欧洲人如何生活，他回到了苏格拉底，打捞出几乎快在欧洲思想史中销声匿迹的犬儒主义，来给自己一生做总结。福柯从“直言”入手，提出了“说真话”的伦理向度，并以此为契机，挖掘欧洲被埋没的实践哲学传统，提出“生命美学”主张，为“理想自我”建构注入新的生命内涵，给世人留下除思想遗产之外，极其珍贵的生命信仰、生活希望。

关键词：直言，福柯，生命美学，理想自我

Parrêsia and the Construction of the Ideal Self—An Interpretation of Foucault's Late Thoughts on the Subject in the View of Existential Semiotics

Yan Xiaofang

Abstract: In the “shadow of death”, Foucault's final lectures showed a deep affection and admiration for life when compared with the coldly rational critique of the subject that characterised his earlier work. In these lectures, life and the self were the issues of greatest concern to Foucault, rather than power. Looking back upon his whole life, Foucault wanted to find out how early Europeans lived. Returning to Socrates, he recovered Cynicism, which had almost disappeared from the history of European thought, and found that it resonated with his own life. Starting with *Parrêsiazesthai*, he put forward the ethical dimension of "truth-telling". From there, Foucault dug into Europe's buried tradition of practical philosophy, and claimed that it revealed an aesthetics of life that contributed new meaning to the construction of an "ideal self" and left the world an extremely precious set of beliefs and hopes for life that go beyond the heritage of thought.

Keywords: *Parrêsiazesthai*, Foucault, aesthetics of life, ideal self

DOI: 10.13760/b.cnki.sam.202001003

1970 年 4 月 12 日，福柯在法兰西学院教授哲学思想史课程，直到 1984 年 6 月他因艾滋病去世，除去休假的 1977 年，福柯在 13 年间，一共讲授了 13 门新课；其中最后一门课的讲稿《说真话的勇气》法文版于 2009 年整理出版，2011 年英文版出版，2016 年中文版由钱翰、陈晓径首次翻译出版。正如格罗所说，"1984 年的冬天，福柯的生命似乎都打上了苦行禁欲的烙印，而彼时的他也正在描述犬儒者的苦行生活。"（福柯，2018，p. 284）这已非纯粹的学术活动，而是生命诉求。辞世前三个月，福柯在学院中公开说的最后的话是："太晚了。那么，谢谢。"（p. 280）连同他未完成的研究课题，这句"遗言"给后人留下了丰富的阐释空间。在最后这门课中，福柯依然延续了早期思考与研究问题的方法，但较明显的是，与早期对主体的理性而冷峻的批判相比，福柯临终前的讲课，因为笼罩着死亡阴影，反而流露对生命的深情眷念和赞颂。与权力相比，生命与自我才是福柯最关心的问题。福柯回顾自己的一生，想要追根溯源。看看早期欧洲人如何生活，他回到了苏格拉底，打捞出几乎快在欧洲思想史中销声匿迹的犬儒主义，来给自己一生做总结。福柯从"直言"入手，提出了"说真话"的伦理向度，以此为契机，挖掘欧洲被埋没的实践哲学传统，提出"生命美学"主张，为"理想自我"的建构注入新的生命内涵。

一、从被动形成到主动建构——主体建构的理论背景

福柯在最后一次课程中探讨的问题，其出发点是"一个位于整个西方哲学中心、古老而传统的问题"，"即主体和真相之间的关系问题"。（p. 5）福柯说，在《主体解释学》乃至之前，他就已开始了这样的研究。福柯早年一直

都在批判主体；这个批判使其理论鲜活、锐利，但却无法让人心安、慰藉，福柯老是提到忏悔者与神父，他可能需要一个理论，来安放被批判和解构之后，那个已疲惫不堪、破碎凋零的自我。

福柯早期思想的关键词主要是"主体"与"权力"——"我所研究的，毋宁说是探索我们文化中，有关我们人类的各种不同的主体化模式的历史。"（高宣扬，2005，pp.222－223）他通过知识考古的方式，提出历史上"主体形成的三种方式"（Peters，2004）。第一种主体形成方式可用于考察欧洲特有的理性文明特征，即把疯子排斥、隔离出去，导致疯子主体产生；在此基础上形成正常人的主体。与"疯子"类似的是在《规训与惩罚》里，犯人的主体也是通过隔离而成；正常人、理性社会修建了监狱，将犯人排斥出去，从而建构了犯人主体。符号学的"文化标出性"理论认为，社会总由二元结构形成；所谓主体与非主体，在同一个系统中，通过颉颃、对抗的方式，划分出正项、异项，来实现绝大多数人的身份认同，以维持系统的稳定。因而主体与非主体身份、地位不同，但并无本质区别。身份是能指划分所指的结果，其本质是符号对真实生存的替代。莫伟民说："人之序与符号之序是不相容的，活着的、劳动着的和讲着话的人只存在于话语消失的地方。"（2011，p.8）故而福柯写作《词与物》与《知识考古学》，目的就是要质疑西方的真理意志，恢复语言符号所具有的事件性和实在性，"最终消除能指的统治权"（莫伟民，2011，p.6），让存在回归人自身。第二种主体形成的方式，福柯认为是人文学科知识区分的结果。这点特别符合符号学对人的定义：人是符号的动物；主体是知识建构的产物。人是话语建构的主体。根据莫伟民的看法，"话语"这个词在福柯的《词与物》与《知识考古学》中含义是有变化的。在《词与物》中，"话语"指的是起表象作用的古典语言，它与人的存在是对立的；在《知识考古学》中，福柯对"话语"的内涵进行了纠正，认为"话语"具有实在性和事件性。莫伟民进一步指出："人的存在与话语的存在是不相容的"（2011，p.8），人从不存在到存在再到消失，都是西方认识型知识的基本顺序发生变化的结果。

很显然，福柯对权力和知识话语体系中主体的生存状况很不满意，他热切渴望一个理想自我的存在，但这必须在现代文明之外去寻找，于是他将目光投向了古希腊。福柯在生命的最后四年转向古代，探讨古希腊、古罗马、基督教的主体模式建构方式。他发现欧洲人在古代没有现代人文学科的知识机构，其建构主体的方式乃通过自身建构，即按照自己的理想模式、意愿、想法把自己变成主体。这就是主体形成的第三种方式。

前面两种方式中，主体都是被建构，即由外力推动而成的；福柯发现，古代欧洲人竟然能够自己建构自己，这种主动的自我建构方式，就是福柯说的“自我技术”（汪民安，2016，p. 1），即自己通过特定的技术和手段，来重新塑造自己。那么，主体自我建构的领域在哪里呢？福柯认为，它对应三个领域：性的领域（包括性的实践、行为，如何使用性、对待快感，培养自我，塑造自我）、自我教育（自我关心，希腊人、罗马人通过自我教育，能够让自我变成什么样子；自我培养跟导师的关系尤其重要；如何通过自我学习变成主体）和说话的领域，即通过“讲真话”的方式，关心自己，塑造自我。这三个领域，就是我们今天所说的生活/生命哲学。

福柯生命的最后时日关注的重点是话语领域与生活实践的结合，即通过“说真话”的方式，重新塑造自我与他人的关系，它超越了话语符号分析的立场，这种重估主体价值的研究，已经是塔拉斯蒂所说的“存在符号学”（Tarasti，2000）领域，即重拾被结构主义符号学忽略的价值和主体，并进行分析、重估。塔拉斯蒂认为“符号的功能性这些年来几乎变成了一个审美标签”（Tarasti，2015，p. 11），随之而来的就是“价值现实逃离了我们的掌控，一切事物成为纯粹技术性的功能性问题”（p. 11），这样就会导致“价值仍然完全是外在的、先验的，人们无需相信它们的实存：只有意见、语言、话语，但没有先验范畴”，其结果必然会如格雷马斯所说“没有真理，只有关于真理的陈述”（p. 11）。当然福柯早年也是这样看待主体及话语的产生的，但很显然，福柯也看到了主体解构而产生的一系列问题。余碧平说：“当代责任理论的缺点就在于把责任这个伦理概念法律化或科学化了，它成了人逃避成为道德责任人的手段。即使有人为发生的错位或灾难负责，那也只是法律或科学意义上的，而与道德良心无关。”（福柯，2010，p. 6）对此，塔拉斯蒂认为，存在符号学正是将主体和价值重新请回符号学领域，“任何情况下，此在的主体完全对其价值选择负责”（Tarasti，2015，p. 11），即便“如果他天生缺乏某些价值，例如他缺乏教育，他也应该承担其团体责任；例如，他缺少‘发送者’（学校、父母、老师），用叙述学术语表示；他仍然对其所选择的先验价值、他怎样将其模态化进他的价值行动、价值行动的种类与及其随之而来的模态性负有存在性责任”（p. 14）。福柯晚年对主体的思考正好向这一伦理学维度敞开。

二、生活哲学——被遗忘的哲学传统

福柯在疾病和死亡阴影之下，提出要阅读一批重要文本，它们主要包括：

《回忆苏格拉底》《裴多篇》《拉凯斯》《阿尔喀比亚德》等。福柯认为，《拉凯斯》和《阿尔喀比亚德》两篇文章都有“关心”原则，都提到应该关心年轻人的教育。只不过在《阿尔喀比亚德》里，它提到的是要照顾灵魂，而在《拉凯斯》里，它提到的是要照顾生活，而这正好形成西方哲学的两大主题：“一方面是一种置身于认识灵魂氛围中的哲学，把对灵魂的认识转变为关于自身的本体论。另一方面是一种考验生活的哲学，考验作为道德材料和自身艺术的生活（bios）。将《拉凯斯》和《阿尔喀比亚德》对话两相比较时，就能较为轻易地辨认出柏拉图哲学、古希腊哲学、西方哲学这两大主题。”（福柯，2018，p. 106）故而，在福柯看来，古希腊哲学的重要命题——“认识自我”，就具有了两个维度，一个走向灵魂，指明一种可能的形而上学话语空间，另一个指向作为生存或生命的生活（bios），要在整个生命的过程中，加以考验和检验，因为“认识自己的话语应当确定人类赋予其自身生命的可见外形”。如此，“说真话”的危险，并不是形而上学的危险，而是“这个说真话现在要遭遇的危险是要向人们说，他们需要从勇气获得什么，他们给予生活一个风格要付出什么代价”。因此，“要发现灵魂的时候，就需要说真话的勇气。要给予生活以形式和风格的时候，也需要说真话的勇气” （福柯，2018，p. 200）。故而，从“认识自己”这个原则，就延伸出两条路线，一条是“必须找到并说出灵魂的存在”，另一条则是福柯晚期最看重的，“给生活（bios）一种可见的形式，和谐的美的形式”（p. 322），这正是“生存美学”的任务。

生命，生活，对应的古希腊文是“bios”。它可以是一个美的作品；主体把生命生活构建为审美形式的对象；其生活、生命在其他人眼中表现出来的外观，以及他死后可能在别人的生命中留下的印迹，在古代，无论中西，这都曾经是美学考虑的对象。而生命本身，作为美的对象却较少被人们赋予美的风格，且在欧洲历史上，它遭到了双重压制：形而上学哲学的压制和美学本身的压制。生活的问题及对其的探讨，在西方哲学领域不断被弱化、边缘化、消散，乃至遗忘；正是这个遗忘，才让形而上学哲学（理论哲学）达到顶峰，但即便如此，它还是顽强地体现了出来。这种美学的开端，在福柯看来正是犬儒主义。

犬儒主义的创始人是安提司特涅斯，他是苏格拉底的学生。由于他经常在雅典郊外一个叫作库诺萨尔革斯的体育场同人交谈，而“库诺萨尔革斯”（拉尔修，2010，p. 274）这个词正好由“犬”和“白”两个词构成，因此，该地方的意思，就是“白犬”，由此一些人就认为这是“犬儒”一名的由来。而安提斯特涅斯本人也被起了一个绰号，叫“单纯的狗”。（p. 274）犬儒学派最著名的人物是第欧根尼·拉尔修，他称自己是一只受到人们赞扬的猎犬，但那些赞扬他的人却无一敢同他一起去狩猎。有人曾问他做了什么事被称为狗，他回答说："因为对那些给我施舍的人，我摇尾；对那些不给我施舍的人，我狂吠；对流氓无赖，我则大加撕咬。"（p. 280）在克尔希达斯的短长格诗中，他曾这样描写第欧根尼："他真正是宙斯的儿子，天狗第欧根尼。"（p. 287）第欧根尼死后，他所生活的城邦的长者们和当权者特意为他立了一根柱子，上面有一尊大理石雕成的狗。他的同胞还立了一个青铜像来纪念他，上面写着："时间甚至可以使青铜朽去，但第欧根尼，整个世代都无法抹去你的荣耀。因为只有你给予终有一死的人以自足生活的教导，向他们指出最容易的生存之路。"（p. 288）这墓志铭，算是总结了第欧根尼最伟大的功绩，那就是教导人们"关心自我"，认识自我的灵魂，从而过上独立、自足、有尊严的生活，而真的生活方式远比理论教义重要。

在福柯看来，犬儒者之美，就体现在生活方式与"直言"的一致，这就是真正意义上的"真实"。或者问，如何让生命印迹变成美的东西呢？根据福柯的观点，那就是说真话——直言："犬儒主义的稳定特征就是直言的人，说真话的人"（2018，p. 206）；"直言（parrêsia）在犬儒者和犬儒主义的标志中总是占据着最重要的地位"（p. 207）。生命可能具有的最美的形式如何与直言（parrêsia）实践直接联系在一起，这在犬儒身上得到了最好的体现。

三、"直言"与"理想自我"的建构

"直言"或曰"说真话"，从词源上看，指的是"某种说出一切的活动"，古希腊文是"pan rêma"。"Parrêsiazesthai"意思是"说出一切"，而"parrêsiastês"就是"说出一切的人"。根据钱翰的翻译，这个词的希腊文拉丁拼法是"parrêsia"（福柯，2018，p. 4）。这是福柯晚期著作中最核心的术语，余碧平翻译成"说真话"（福柯，2010，p. 400），钱翰翻译成"直言"，赵灿翻译成"诚言"（赵灿，2017，p. 32），各有特色，也都很妥当，但从用语习惯上看，"直言"既简洁，又接近口语，因此也就更容易被接受。

福柯通过对苏格拉底临终时嘱咐其门徒献祭一只大公鸡给阿斯克勒庇俄斯这个故事的正面阐释，维护了苏格拉底的尊严，肯定了苏格拉底能够坚持真理、保持独立的品格，认为这正是对"直言"这一哲学实践活动的践行。苏格拉底超越死亡，给人们留下了"关心自己"这条原则。福柯在1982年的讲座第一次课时提到，"关心自己"（古希腊语为"epimeleia heautou"）在古希腊文化中延续了很长时间，但福柯却大致在1981年才使用。“‘Epimeleia’和‘meletê’的相似性既意味着训练，也同时指沉思。”（福柯，2010，p.13）因此，这个词实质上就是训练自己将注意力向内转，从专注于外在世界到专注自身。这就是“关心自我”的基本意义。《论语》里也有类似的说法，叫作“求诸己”；佛教也有“佛不外求”。实际上，无论东西方文明，“关心自己”都是在“认识自我”基本原则之下自我觉醒和自身成长的必要操作。“就苏格拉底—柏拉图哲学而言，‘关心自己’是在《阿尔西比亚德》中提出并阐发的。”（福柯，2010，p.168）当然“关心自己”，不仅是要关心自己的身体，还包括真实看见自己的灵魂，并看到它如何与真理发生关系。故而在福柯的阐释中，直言生效的范围，也就从城邦过渡到个体自我内心。就这样，福柯的“直言”理论从其对政治权力进行批判的先前思路中开辟出提倡个人修身的伦理向度，亦即通过修身来塑造“理想自我”，从而达到重新改变他人和社会的目的。“修身”是中国和西方古代都很重视的一个命题。古希腊时的“修身”思想，其完美践行者是苏格拉底，他能够做到行为方式与灵魂保持完全一致，这种不分裂、纯粹的个体生命，正好是“真的生活”的体现。儒家也特别重视修身，但它往往与“外圣”联系起来；修身、齐家、治国、平天下，是君子的必修课，也是帝王之学。儒家的修身，并不导致对现实生活与社会秩序的否定，而福柯意义上的直言，具有改变现实，甚至革命的要求。其路线是，通过认识自我、照顾自我，而发现灵魂真正的需求；同时将其他人引向这一对自己的关心，又引向了照顾他人的可能性。照顾他人，本质上也是照顾自我，大家都改变了，就是在推动社会改革和进步。

犬儒主义在直言与其生活模式的一致性方面赢得了福柯的赞扬，犬儒主义由此将生存变成了真正的艺术。“犬儒者，就是拿着棍子、拿着褡裢的人，穿着斗篷、穿着拖鞋或赤脚的人，留着大胡子的人，肮脏的人。他也是到处游荡的人，他不属于任何社会，他们没有房子、家庭、家乡和祖国……他是乞丐。”（福柯，2018，p.211）这是犬儒主义者基本的生活形式。虽然犬儒主义的情况有些复杂，但总体而言，特别是早期的犬儒主义者，大都是“好的和可以接受的犬儒主义的犬儒者”（p.209）。生存形式与表达真理之间的对应关系，是犬儒主义者最根本的特征。如果用符号学的方式，分析犬儒主义者的话，那么，他们在符号的能指、所指、主体间形成了三位一体，符号不仅仅是一种形式，或意义建构的方式，更是真理的在场：“生活作为真理发出光芒的和原始野性的东西直接在场，这就是犬儒学派所表现出来的东西。”（福柯，2018，p.216）那么，福柯的主体理论，也就超越了结构主义符号学的局限，表达了对主体、真理、价值等本质性事物的期许和回归。

在犬儒者那里，可以找到很多有关行为方式的表述，其中最重要的一项是关于身体特征的描述，那就是裸体。这是真理敞开的方式，即不遮蔽、不隐藏、不撒谎："生命的选择成为真理的轰动性展示，一无所有的生命成为在肉体上建构真理的展示剧院"（福柯，2018，p. 2），所以裸体是犬儒者直言精神的实践形式，也是其哲学本身。"'犬儒者'指的是'真理的看门狗'，而真理则指'赤裸裸的东西'。"（p. 2）

犬儒者往往通过榜样、叙述、事迹和例子来展示其信仰，而不是用理论的、教条的教学。在犬儒主义这里，生活的目标不是重新激活原始思想的内容，而是重新记忆生活中的要素和情节；它唤起的不是源自理论学说的意义，而是让人们通过真实生活重建道德衰落之后做人的力量。与柏拉图主义或亚里士多德主义对理论传统的重视相比，犬儒者表现出一定的"反哲学"倾向。犬儒者反对的是书斋里的哲学，根据福柯的说法，当"哲学变成教授的职业的时候，哲学生活、哲学伦理、哲学的英雄主义、哲学传统就无法继续存在下去了"（福柯，2018，p. 263），这正是19世纪初哲学的境况。当哲学成为教授的职业时，哲学就开始消失了；与此同时，一部分人用另一种方式，重新开始哲学生活，这就是福柯说的"离开浮士德，进入革命"的"革命生活"（p. 264）。这种意欲建立实践规范的哲学态度，就是福柯所说的哲学英雄主义，而践行它的人，则被称为"哲学英雄"。哲学英雄的生活，是犬儒传统的一部分，且在后世流传下来。

通过研究犬儒主义在西方思想史中的演变历程，福柯找到了被传统理论哲学所湮灭、遗忘的一个主题，那就是："真的生活的主题"，"在生活的形式中表现真理、实践、生产真理"；而这一"真的生活的主题"，与普通人日常生活关系最密切的就是"什么是真爱"和"什么是真的生活"，这是哲学中最根本的问题。

福柯围绕这个主题，首先提出了"真"的四种形式："非隐藏、非混杂、正直、不变和无损耗"（福柯，2018，p. 272）。与之相对应的"真爱"的四个特点，分别如下：第一，真爱是没有隐藏的爱情；第二，真爱是没有混杂的爱情；第三，真爱与正直和公正相符合；第四，真爱绝不变化或生异，真爱永葆青春，天长地久。而真爱的定义又使得对"真的生活"的研究更进了一步。于是，真的生活也有四个特征。第一，真的生活是一种无所隐藏的生活，"这种生活可以赤裸裸地面对一切光亮，面对一切人的注视"，"不隐藏任何动机和目的"，"所说与所想，所说与所欲，所想做的与将做的，这之间没有任何隐瞒和曲折，没有任何东西遮挡其所想的事实，言必信，行必果”，“没有城府”，“简单和真实”。（福柯，2018，p.275）第二，真的生活指的是“没有混杂的生活”，“没有善恶的混杂，没有快乐与痛苦的混杂，没有罪恶与美德的混杂”，是“没有分裂的生活”。所有分裂的生活，都是人们通往真理的阻碍，因为分裂的人，是被各种欲望控制的人，这些人没有能力获得真理。总之，真的生活与混杂的生活对立，生命一旦混杂，就不再是真的生活。第三，真的生活是正直的生活，也是符合原则、规范的生活。也就是说，真的生活，不仅仅是个人的生活，同样也在社会生活、公共生活和政治生活中。可见，福柯并不反对规范和秩序，恰恰相反，福柯认为，一定的秩序和规范恰恰是个体能够过上真的生活的前提和保证。第四，真的生活是不变质的，摆脱了动摇、变化、变质和堕落，从而保证自身的自由和独立，不依赖、不屈服任何可能的统治，是一种自我管理、自我满足的幸福生活。在第四个方面，自我管理最重要。自我管理目的是让自我成为真正的主体，过上自主的生活，它不仅对自我有益，也可以帮助他人，最后可以对全人类有益。在福柯看来，尽管犬儒主义在西方历史中经历了复杂的演变历程，但总体上，犬儒者的生活是真的生活。自我应该通过实践真的生活，建立自由独立的主体，这就是福柯理想中的个体主体。

四、结语

纵观福柯一生的经历及其创作可以发现，福柯的学说与其生存状态紧密相关。生命的本质在于变化和成长，故而福柯的学说也并非一成不变，甚至还充满矛盾。自我不是先天的，它可以通过反思去构建，而最重要的是在实践中去形成。尤其在《说真话的勇气》中，“福柯通过苏格拉底这样的知行合一的典范，把话语和行为的主体重新汇聚起来，说真话具有了超越语言之外的意义，它不是以符号呈现的逻各斯，而是与具体生活密切相关，是指导寻常日用、生活抉择的逻各斯。这种与生活世界、与个人修身融为一体的逻各斯才是直言”（福柯，2018，p.9）。

人类永远都需要价值和真理。解构和批判的目的，只不过是为了建立更理想的社会，而这个落脚点就是每一个个体生命。自我与他人、自我与社会的矛盾、冲突是永恒的，但自我价值的实现永远都要以他人、社会乃至整个人类为旨归，故而主体不可能真正消失。

但福柯在表达对主体回归的渴望的同时，仍不忘警惕过分强调真的生活的一系列危害。福柯很感性，但也时刻清醒。他关心欧洲和美国的无政府主义以及恐怖主义的问题，它们是将真的生活推向极致的产物："为了真理而死（人肉炸弹、自杀式袭击），它转向了戏剧性的和疯狂的极限，这种为了真理的极限勇气……直至为此丧失生命或者杀死他人，在欧洲思想的漫长源流中，可以找到这种东西。"（福柯 2018，p. 230）且对生活风格的过分强调，忽略公共秩序和伦理，势必导向资产阶级的堕落或极左疯狂。所以，福柯也呼吁建立规范而理性的社会秩序。在宗教活动和政治实践之外，福柯也看到了犬儒主义正深刻影响当代艺术的发展与走向。艺术上的犬儒行为，最终会导致艺术的生活化，而不是生活的艺术化。前者降低艺术的水准和品位，而后者才是真正的生活美学。这是福柯晚年对主体问题的思考给予我们的启示。

主体问题一直是符号学研究的前沿、疑难问题。一切流动的事物都在寻求表达，而符号的表达之于流动的事物而言，有时无疑是抽刀断水。存在符号学即对这一棘手研究对象努力进行符号表达的尝试。谁能画出精神的地图？赫拉克利特说，人不能两次踏入同一条河流。因此，"存在符号学"本身就如同一个想象中的符号，无论是塔拉斯蒂早期在其师格雷马斯"符号矩阵"基础上利用经典存在哲学遗产而"创立"的"主体符号方阵"（塔拉斯蒂，2012，p. 84－85），还是近期转向的"Zemic"（Tarasti，2015，pp. 26－27）模式，都需要接受者/读者发挥各自的理解能力和悟性，去填充这份精神地图中的空白。塔拉斯蒂说，存在符号学的关键概念是"超越"（Tarasti，2015），即存在符号学研究一切超越中的事物。超越的事物是现实中缺乏但却存在于我们心灵或观念中的事物。除了经典符号学分析方法，研究者还必须综合运用直觉、领悟、情感等方式，才能更为完整地把握研究对象。（颜小芳，刘源，2018）在主体与真相的关系中，福柯找到的存在符号是"勇气"。勇气并非主体特属，却是理想主体的品质。因为没有压力和对抗，勇气不可能产生。直言是勇气的结果，也势必要承担勇气所需的代价。勇气的意义早已溢出能指的固定范围，蔓延至人的整个生存。故而福柯的主体研究，是对传统、静态、结构主义符号学的超越，并与存在符号学产生了交集。

引用文献：

福柯（2001）. 词与物（莫伟民，译）. 上海：上海三联书店.

福柯（2010）. 主体解释学（余碧平，译）. 上海：上海人民出版社.

福柯（2018）. 说真话的勇气：治理自我与治理他者Ⅱ（钱翰，陈晓径，译）. 上海：上海人民出版社.

高宣扬（2005）. 福柯的生存美学. 北京：中国人民大学出版社.

拉尔修（2010）. 名哲言行录. 桂林：广西师范大学出版社.

塔拉斯蒂（2012）. 存在符号学（魏全凤，颜小芳，译）. 成都：四川教育出版社.

汪民安（2015）. 自我技术：福柯文选Ⅲ. 北京：北京大学出版社.

颜小芳，刘源（2018）. 论存在符号学电影批评理论建构的可能性与现实性——以电影《一个乡村牧师的日记》为例. 广西科技师范学院学报，33（6），39－43

赵灿（2017）. 诚言与关心自己：福柯对古代哲学的解释. 上海：上海人民出版社.

Peters, M. A. (2004). "Educational research: 'Games of truth' and the ethics of subjectivity". *Journal of educational enquiry*, 5(2).

Tarasti, E. (2000). *Existential semiotics*. Bloomington, IN: Indiana University Press, 2000.

Tarasti, E. (2015). *Sein und Schein: Explorations in existential semiotics*. Berlin, GER: De Gruyter Mouton.

作者简介：

颜小芳，文学博士，南宁师范大学文学院副教授，研究方向为比较文学和符号学。

Author:

Yan Xiaofang, Ph. D. of Literature, associated professor in School of Literature, Nanning Normal University. Her research interest is comparative literature.

Email: 67514129@qq. com

“无意味”的符号学研究

Accepting Randomness*

Massimo Leone

Abstract: The article first defines three types of randomness: ontological, phenomenological, and epistemological randomness. It then introduces a fourth semiotic definition of randomness, as something that does not arise from intrinsic ontological characteristics, or from the imperfect perceptibility and, therefore, phenomenological unfathomability of a subjacent regularity, or from the unsuitability of the formula that is supposed to grasp and, possibly, control it, but from the way in which a metalanguage is created in order to describe and make sense of irregularity. In keeping with this definition, the article then reconceptualizes Charles S. Peirce's semiosis and introduces the distinction between interpretants and scales of interpretation, and elaborates on the notions of over-complexification, over-simplification, and significance. It concludes that the efforts of scholars of all fields in the future will have to be directed toward the task of understanding the correct scale at which understanding of reality must take place, and social coordination and action as a consequence of it.

* A first version of this paper was presented at the COST—COMPACT (Comparative Analysis of Conspiracy Theories) conference held at the University of Dubrovnik, 18—19 October 2018; I thank the EU program COST and the organizers for such a splendid opportunity.

Keywords: randomness, semiosis, scale of interpretation, oversimplification, overinterpretation

论随机性的接受

马西莫·莱昂内

摘 要：本文首先定义了随机性的三种类型：本体论随机性、现象学随机性以及认识论随机性，进而给出了第四种也即符号学式的定义。随机性不来自内在的本体论特征，也不是因为我们不具备完全的感知力，因此它是底层规则性在现象学意义上的不可测性。它的产生也不是因为它不与那些似乎可以被掌握甚至被控制的准则不相符。随机性是通过制造可以描述以及理解不规则性的元语言而形成的。为了说明上述定义，本文重构皮尔斯符号过程这一概念，区分解释项与解释范围之间的差异，并阐明过度复杂化、过度简化以及意义等概念。本文最后指出，不同领域的学者应当在将来致力于探索一个正确的范围，在这种范围中对实在的理解必然会发生，同时探索对实在的理解作为一种结果所需的社会协调和行动程度。

关键词：随机性，符号过程，理解范围，过度简化，过度解释

DOI: 10.13760/b.cnki.sam.202001004

ἀνθρώποισι γὰρ
τοῖς πᾶσι κοινόν ἐστι τοὐξαμαρτάνειν:
1025ἐπεὶ δ᾽ ἁμάρτῃ, κεῖνος οὐκέτ᾽ ἔστ᾽ ἀνὴρ
ἄβουλος οὐδ᾽ ἄνολβος, ὅστις ἐς κακὸν
πεσὼν ἀκῆται μηδ᾽ ἀκίνητος πέλῃ.

(Sophocles, *Antigone*, V, 1023-27)

Ⅰ. Semiosis on Thin Ice

In one of the episodes that compose *The Decalogue* (see Campan, 1993; Garbowski, 1996; Simonigh, 2000; Badowska & Parmeggiani, 2016; Vaillancourt, 2016; see also Wach, 2000; Haltof, Agusti, and Anton, 2004),

Polish director Kieslowski's[①] masterly cinematic reflection on the Ten Commandments, a scientist lives with his young son near a lake. The lake freezes in winter, allowing people, including children, to skate on it. The young son is impatient: the lake is freezing but it is not certain yet that the ice is thick enough so as to tolerate his weight. The father, therefore, elaborates a complex formula in order to determine the status of the ice. The result is mathematically evident: the son can go to the lake and skate on it with no fear, the ice will hold. The father, however, could not calculate, in his formula, that a random homeless person had camped overnight at the lake, near the place where the son would then go skating. The campfire lit by the homeless, indeed, makes the ice a little thinner. The ice breaks. The son dies. The father desperately stares at his formula.

This episode contains a narrative in which the manifestation of evil is evident. The suffering that a father feels for the death of his son is anthropologically universal. There is no doubt, then, that the movie tells a story of misfortune and the sorrow that it entails. But what is the origin of evil in the episode? Members of the human species, like all other living beings, are destined to perish. Although that is a biological certainty, it is culturally difficult to accept. Entire symbolical systems are created so as to cope with what is, nevertheless, a biological platitude. One of the main elements that make the inexorable chronology of death culturally unacceptable is its indeterminacy. It is not evident when the organism of a human being will perish, also because this datum depends not only on the biological information contained in the organism itself, such as its genetic predisposition to develop cancer, for instance, but also on the uncountable interactions that this biological structure will have with an environment that, in the case of human cultures, is exceedingly complex. It is difficult to accept that, in the environment in which we live our daily life, there is, mostly invisible, a pattern of elements that, in the short, medium, or long term, will interact with the genetic content of our body and ultimately kill us. Some of these elements are

---

① Krzysztof Kieslowski, Warsaw, Nazi-occupied Poland, 27 June 1941—Warsaw, Poland, 13 March 1996.

known because science has singled them out as direct causes for potential disease and even death. A popular Italian idiom says "bacco, tabacco, e venere riducon l'uomo in cenere"①, a not-too feminist proverb about how drinking alcohol, smoking tobacco, and womanizing are supposed to shorten a man's life. But what about other factors whose impact on the length and quality of our life is not clear yet, but will nevertheless play a decisive role in introducing suffering, sorrow, and eventually death in our lives.

In the episode narrated in the movie, for instance, what elements should be eliminated or at least curtailed so that evil does not manifest itself in the life of this family by dramatically and prematurely killing a young child, survived by his father? The story told by Kieslowski is a moral apologue about the hubris of science. It is, from a certain point of view, a highly originally and narrative rendering of the Commandment "thou shall not have other gods". The father believes that, through science, and precisely through physics and mathematics, he can control the environment and foresee the future, preventing risks. Risk, indeed, is the possibility that the environment changes in the future in such a way that it will worsen one's conditions of life in it, even to the point of terminating such life. Through calculus, the father turns this possibility into probability. His confidence in scientific knowledge is such that he dares entrusting his own son's life to it: given his weight, the temperature of the air, the weather forecasting, the temperature of the ice, and its current thickness, there will be no risk for the son to skate on it. There would not be any risk, indeed, and the formula with its consequent calculus would be correct, if a totally unexpected element did not intervene to slightly modify the scenario, but to modify it significantly enough as to kill the son.

From an anthropological perspective, it is interesting to analyze what people say when a relative, friend, or acquaintance dies. Besides the common expressions of sorrow, many people will spontaneously produce counterfactual scenarios. In some cases, concocting them will be relatively easy: if he had not developed a passion for skydiving, he would still be alive. In some other circumstances, though, counterfactual scenarios will be more difficult to come

① Literally, "Bacchus, tobacco, and Venus turn a man into ash."

up with. It will not be so straightforward to single out what elements in the environment, life choices, or behavioral patterns should have been eliminated so as to come up with a plausible hypothesis for a longer life.

The tragic aspect of Kieslowski's episode consists in the fact that, when the son died and the father realized that his formula was not correct, the homeless person whose campfire had thinned the ice had already gone. There is no trace of his presence and impact on the environment that the father may fathom. It is only the god-like observation point that the movie grants to its spectators that allows them to infer what has really happened, while the father is left in complete darkness. There is a rational cause for the death of the child. In his case, indeed, the counterfactual narrative could recite as follow: if the homeless person had not existed, or if he had set the campfire elsewhere, the child would still be alive. There is a reason, however, for which Kieslowski chose exactly this element, and not another, to tragically upset the environment whose measures the father's formula calculates. The homeless person is a clear symbolical evocation of what, in life, comes and goes, appears and disappears, manifests itself out of the blue, surprises. It is not simply a structural element of the environment that the formula has neglected to model. It is an evocation of randomness. It is the imponderable, that is, literally, what cannot be calculated.

In the context of Kieslowski's *Decalogue*, and in relation to his poetics, the episode has a religious undertone: science aims at a full grasp of the universe, and arrogantly turns into a technique for the complete mastery over the environment, yet a terrible punishment for this hubris comes from a transcendent dimension, which tragically underlines the condition of ignorance and fragility in which human beings must live and justifies their resort to religion and faith. Given the structural impossibility to control the environment, its risks, and its dangers to human life, the only possibility is to hope, to pray, or, at least, to remain fully aware of the structural limitations of human scientific knowledge.

Ⅱ. Three Kinds of Randomness

Outside this religiously inspired framework, though, the tragic apologue prompts a reflection on the definition of randomness. Philosophy has long meditated on the nature of what is evoked in various languages as chance, randomness, casualness, and so on. Without delving into this complex philosophical field, and without focusing, for the moment, on the semantic distinctions between different terms and concepts in this area, it is certainly fundamental to distinguish between ontological, phenomenological, and epistemological randomness. (see Svozil, 2018; Giberson, 2016; Church & Hartman, 2019)

Ontological randomness consists in the idea that reality, as it is, including the reality of the environment in which human beings live and die, is characterized by intrinsic irregularity. Apparent pockets of regularity might appear in reality, yet they are an exception and actually an illusion. They are the equivalent of that well-known phenomenon that consists in having the illusory impression of understanding some bits of discourse in a conversation that is uttered in a totally unknown language. Another example of this illusion is pareidolia, for instance, the impression of being able to recognize, in the shape of clouds, some distinctive figures. Belief in ontological randomness usually entails either nihilism or fideism. Given the randomness of reality, humans can either give up any hope of controlling it or developing the idea of a transcendent grasp over it.

In phenomenological randomness, reality is not thought of as irregular *per se*, but as manifesting itself in a way that does not allow one to infer its underpinning systematicness. According to this view, in the episode narrated by Kieslowski, for instance, the final accident is not simply the result of imponderable chaos, but the outcome of a pattern whose regularity and, therefore, controllability is not evident.

The hypothesis of phenomenological randomness is, therefore, strictly related to that of epistemological randomness: a supreme scientist might indeed come up with a formula that takes into considerations not only some physical variables such as the temperature of water in a lake and the weight of a child's body but also some apparently imponderable variables such as the propensity of homeless people to lit up a campfire in some areas of an urban settlement.

Without deepening the question that some variables in the environment might be intrinsically impossible to grasp, mostly because of the interaction between observation and determination, it is evident that, in the movie episode as well as in the history of epistemology, science is in the middle of a tension between ontological and phenomenological conceptions of randomness. The entire scientific endeavor might be described as the ongoing attempt to reduce more and more the domain of the former betting on the existence of the latter.

Ⅲ. Random Networks

This stark contraposition, however, is increasingly nuanced by the awareness that the existence of pockets of regularity within an ocean of randomness might not be casual in itself but depend on a complex dynamic of scales, levels, and emergence. The scientific domain in which this awareness is currently the most developed is probably that of the mathematical theory of networks. (see Battistoni, Caldarelli, and Garas, 2018; Zattoni, Perdon, and Conte, 2020) This theory, which is too complex to be summarized here, in a nutshell shows that, given the presence of two elements, such a sender and a receiver in a phone conversation, it is probable that certain patterns of exchange of information will arise. Applying these same patterns to conversations that happen among three people, however, or, even more macroscopically, applying them to conversations that simultaneously involve dozens of participants, like in Whatsapp chats, for instance, would be a mistake. There is a structural resemblance between the two kinds of conversations, yet the scale of the latter is such that, in comparison with the scale of the former, leads to the emergence of new patterns, which are probably not random *per se*, but which appear as such if one attempts at grasping their structure, and especially their probable future evolution, through models that are based on conversation experience gathered at lower levels of complexity scale.

This leads to a fourth and alternative definition of randomness, which is neither ontological nor phenomenological nor epistemological, but is, essentially, semiotic. Randomness does not arise from intrinsic ontological characteristics, or from the imperfect perceptibility and, therefore, phenomenological unfathomability of a subjacent regularity, or from the unsuitability of the formula that is supposed to grasp and, possibly, control it, but from the way in which a metalanguage is created in order to describe and make sense of irregularity. From this point of view, randomness emerges from the adoption of a metalanguage issued from lower levels of complexity of interaction for the description and interpretation of higher levels of it. In the theoretical framework of mathematical network analysis, for instance, the virality of a conspiracy theory that spreads throughout digital social networks appears as random or even as chaotic if it is described and analyzed with models of interaction that apply to exchanges at a different scale. What is totally unreasonable at this scale, however, for instance that the final result of the conversation might be such that is completely unintelligible in relation to the individual contributions of the interlocutors, might turn out completely reasonable at a superior scale, where the way in which individuals, through their communicative behaviors, affect the final setting of the network and the predominant cognitive and emotional representations circulating through it, substantially changes.

Ⅳ. Semiotic Randomness

Defining randomness in semiotic terms, that is, as an epistemological randomness that specifically emerges from the application of a framework of intelligibility to a phenomenological situation and, therefore, from the opaqueness that results in adopting frames whose diagrammatic complexity is inadequate to the scale of complexity of the range itself of phenomena under observation, requires a fuller consideration of the problem with respect to the kind of semiosis that it involves. The customary description of semiosis in the terms coined by Charles S. Peirce usually entails a certain amount of repetition, if not a manifestation of recursion. In Peirce, whose semiotic understanding in this as in other domains is essentially modeled after Kant's gnoseology, the ontological dimension *per se* cannot be grasped by the human mind, which, through the senses, can only receive the phenomenological stimuli that this ontology supposedly emanates, stimuli whose conformation ultimately depends on the interaction between the structure of reality and that of cognition, defined as the system of the bodily sensorium and the cognitive reception of it.

An object of potential knowledge, therefore, is only perceived under certain respects or capacities, in a way that can be effectively evoked in optical terms (an optical metaphor being already implied in the etymology and meaning of the concept itself of "respect", coming from the Latin "respicio", whose many acceptances all revolve around the idea of looking at something from a particular angle): ontology never appears in full light, but is lit by cognition in such a way that only a part of it becomes visible, whilst the rest of it remains in darkness or in nuanced shadows. What determines the particular nature (that is, the intensity and the angle) of the light projected onto the ontology of reality is a combination of nature and culture, of the neurophysiology of cognition interacting with the cultural patterns that, in a human society, determine the formation of cognitive habits.

The way in which a certain interplay of the cognitive physiology of the species and the symbolical patterns that it has deposited in cultural memory casts a given light onto the supposed ontology of reality is what the semiotics of Charles S. Peirce synthetically calls an "interpretant". An interpretant is the conjunction of natural and cultural schemes that predetermine the potentiality of the way in which reality might become significant to human cognition and understanding. It is just a potentiality, and not an actuality, for a myriad of codeterminations can actually inflect this particular angle and cause idiosyncratic variations of it. Such inflections too can be either natural or cultural, or a combination of both. Cognitive impairments of various kinds, including some temporary oscillations in the regularity of apperception, like in hallucinations or *déjà-vus*, can create actual interpretations, or interpretive tokens, diverging from the interpretive type of an interpretant; similarly, its cultural regularities are even more subject to fluctuations due to the unceasing modification of linguistic and cultural patterns in society.

Thus far, nothing is particularly novel in this account of semiosis in the terms of Charles S. Peirce. The questionable aspect of such account, indeed, emerges especially in relation to the fact that this model is not presented as static, but as dynamic. That is certainly necessary. Peirce contributes enormously to the understanding of the human cognition by suggesting that the ontological reality is not seen simply through the light of a single interpretant but through the cumulative effect of a chain of them. So as to continue with the same optical metaphor, one might compare this process to that of an object that is lit by a source of light, whilst another source of light simultaneously enlightens the first, and a third one affects the visibility of both the second and the third one, and so on and so forth in a superposition of cognitive angles whose final effect is a summation of all the lights intertwining over the object itself. What is known of the ontology of reality, therefore, is not simply the selection operated by an interpretant, but that brought about by a chain of them.

Ⅴ. Semiosis Unchained

The designation of such conjunction of cognitive angles is a particularly complex and delicate subject. Why should one call this conjunction "chain" and not "series" or "system"? What does the chosen designation reveal of the way in which Peircean semiotics imagines the cumulative effects of many interpretants on the final cognition of an object? The metaphor of the chain suggests that, first, all the interpretants are somehow linked with each other and, second, that they come with a certain sequence. The mental process of the association of thoughts or mental images is often used in order to explain the way in which a chain of interpretants might affect the final result of a semiosis. This metaphor is certainly effective, but only to the extent that it is understood not as a random wave of mental images or thoughts, but as a concatenation of them that, as random as it may appear at first sight, actually follows a certain pattern.

That entails that the metaphoric description of the chain of interpretants must be understood, like many cognitive models in Peirce, not chronologically but logically. It is true that, from the point of view of the phenomenology of interpretation and cognition, one has the impression that interpretant A is interpreted by interpretant B, which is in turn interpreted by interpretant C, and so on and so forth, A coming before B, B before C, and C before the following interpretant. That impression, however, is only an epiphenomenon of the most essential dynamic that links these interpretants not chronologically but logically, that is, according to a kind of causation. Interpretant C coming after interpretant B, which comes after interpretant A, is because something, either in nature or in culture, in the structure of the neurophysiology of cognition or in its cultural schematization, as well as in the interaction of both, determines this sequence. In other words, and in Peircean terms, an indexical logic seems to underpin the concatenation of interpretants that superpose their cumulative lights on the cognition of a certain object, although such indexicality, as always in Peirce, does not emanate from purely causal relations but from the way in which they are structured in individual and cultural cognition.

That is why an interpretant never strictly determines the following one, but is somehow determined by it. That is, in a nutshell, the difference between a causal understanding of indexicality, which is an improper interpretation of Peirce's thought on the subject, and a real understanding of indexicality: an interpretant A is in its turn interpreted by an interpretant B, which therefore inflects the effect of the first one cognition, but the emergence of B is not determined by A. If that were the case, interpretants would concatenate always in the same way, without any possibility of deviation. Hence, all interpretations would actually end up in the same result, which is not the common empirical experience of how a chain of interpretants works. On the contrary, the fact that indexicality in a chain of interpretants is never deterministic, accounts for the apparently chaotic nature of its concatenation.

To recapitulate: in Peirce, ontology supposedly exists but affects cognition through a natural and cultural filter, whose essence though Peirce characterizes not through a static diagram, like Kant, but through a dynamic diagram, semiosis, whose dynamicity is actually guaranteed by its triadic nature. The interposition of a third element into a relation opens up to the possibility of further interpositions, and so on and so forth potentially add infinitum. From the gnoseological point of view, however, as it was indicated earlier, it would be simplistic to understand this dynamic and triadic character of cognition in chronological and causal terms, meaning that each step in the chain of interpretants comes before the following one and actually causes it.

On the opposite, this dynamic and triadic character must be interpreted in logical and indexical terms, meaning by indexicality an approach that might take into account and explain the cumulative effect of the concatenation of interpretants as well as its apparently chaotic mushrooming. Why is it apparent? Because such concatenation, although it is not a chronological but a logical one, and although it is not a causal but an indexical one, actually follows some laws, or at least such as the assumption that the present paper would like to adopt. These laws are not those of physical causation but those of cognitive causation, which are essentially the laws of intentionality.

Understanding individual and cultural cognition as semiosis implies that, at each step of the chain of interpretants that leads from the supposed ontological source of it up to the final determination of meaning, there is freedom, not necessity. Neither individuals nor cultures are ever physically compelled to think about reality as they do. That means that intentionality rules at every step of cognition, for at every ring in the chain of interpretants there is the possibility of choice. Each choice, then, somehow retroacts on the previous ones, until a particular quality of light, given by the superposed lights of all the interpretants that have chained up in the semiosis, manifests itself in cognition. The triadic model of the sign, the diagram of semiosis, and the notion of the chain of interpretants are nothing but an elegant philosophical attempt at explaining the fact that the light of knowledge is infinitely changing, yet it is not unpatterned. Neither is intentionality. Affirming that it is involved at each step of semiosis, and for each ring of the chain of interpretants, does not mean that such intentionality is anarchic. It follows, on the contrary, patterns that are pre-configured by both the nature of cognition and the culture of it.

Ⅵ. Semiosis in Chains

What is the origin, then, of the impression of chaoticity and randomness attached to the idea of "unlimited semiosis"? It is to this regard that the conceptual metaphor of "the chain of thoughts" comes short of explaining the actual dynamic of "the chain of interpretants". In a typical session of mental associations, either individual or in couple or in group, the word (and idea) A will lead to the word (and idea) B, which will lead to the word (and idea) C, and so on and so forth, through a sequence that is free but not unpatterned, intentional but not unstructured. That is evident when this mental activity is turned into a group play: to the stimulus-word "water" one might answer with "fire", or with "lake", but not with "triangle", for the rhizomatic structure of the cultural encyclopedia deposited in common sense does not allow this association, at least not in the Western culture.

This game, however, only imperfectly renders the nature of the dialectics between indeterminacy and determination in unlimited semiosis; in the game, indeed, the equilibrium of this dialectics is always constant, or depends, at the most, on the structure of the semantic connections irradiating from each word. There is, that is true, a cumulative effect in such game, but its resonance is limited. When I say "water", and someone else says "lake", and I subsequently say "sea" to that, "sea" and "water" are connected, but the impact of the first word on the emergence of the third one is only chronological, not logical, it is causal, not indexical. I say "sea" because someone else said "lake", and this someone else said "lake" because I, in turn, had said "water" before, but the word "sea" is not connected anymore with the word "water" directly but through the chronological and causal mediation of the word "lake". The nature of the interplay between determinacy and indetermination, necessity and freedom, remains unchanged at every step of the game.

Such is not the case in that special game that is unlimited semiosis. When an interpretant casts its light on an object, and is in turn cast light upon by another interpretant, the final light depends on the interplay and superposition of the first two. Also, at each new light that superimposes its pattern of luminosity and darkness, brightness and shadows onto an object of cognition, thus patterning its reception in semiosis and understanding, the equilibrium between determinacy and indetermination, necessity and freedom, changes. As the chain of interpretants that lit up a certain object stretches forward, extending through cognition, the level of determination changes according to a logic of scale. As a consequence, it would be a mistake to believe that all the interpretants involved in a semiosis determine the final meaning of an object in the same way; on the contrary, they do so with a cogency whose scale decreases as subsequent interpretants are involved in the semiosis itself.

The metaphor of a stone thrown into a pond is perhaps particularly adequate to evoke the growing level of indeterminacy in the concatenation of interpretants. Interpretants that are close to the point in which the stone falls are sharper in definition and contour (the stone in the metaphor represents the object, an object that turns invisible at the same moment in which the water rings its, the stone's, fall produces start to appear, and is therefore only supposed to have existed both logically and chronologically); such first rings emerge starkly as perfect circles around the spot in which the stone has fallen and are, hence, also easy to be considered as its signs; as one moves away from the center, however, one comes across circles, although connected in shape with the nearest ones, and although appearing simultaneously with them (a chronological substratum persists in the metaphor but it should be disregarded so as to understand the logical nature of semiosis), whose appearance becomes less and less defined, until they seem to merge with the surrounding water and vanish into it.

Other aspects of this metaphor are worthy of consideration. The number of rings that are seen around the point in which the stone has fallen into the lake somehow depends on the attention of observers, but also on the adopted instruments of observations. The more one considers outer rings in water, the more the adopted instruments of observation must change, since they, the rings, will not be visible any longer, and at some stage will actually turn into vibration, until they will actually disappear into that same indistinction from which the throwing of the stone, that is, the mutual impact of the object with the plexus of cognition and culture, has had them emerge and give shape to their phenomenology.

Ⅶ. Semiosis and Semiosphere

The metaphor should suggest some conclusions about the nature of the semiotic definition of randomness and its consequences for the approach of social sciences to the notion of emerging phenomena. An intriguing morphological resemblance holds between the metaphor of the stone thrown into the pond and the rings it gives shape too (metaphor through which the present paper has sought to visualize the dynamic and logical functioning of unlimited semiosis especially as regards the quality of interpretants in their concatenation and the relations they have among themselves and with the center) and the diagrammatic metaphor of the semiosphere. In Lotman's semiosphere too, indeed, there is a center that defines the conditions according to which meaning irradiates all around, yet these conditions are respected in an increasingly loose way as one moves from the center toward the periphery, until the semiosphere appears as so poorly structured that it actually yields to neighboring centers of gravity and structuration, that is, to other semiospheres. Interestingly, the analogy between the metaphor that explains the nature of the concatenations of interpretants in unlimited semiosis and the schematic metaphor of the semiosphere also concerns the way in which the periphery of the structure is imagined, that is, as a liminal area where meaning inexorably sinks into chaos and indistinction, in the case of semiosis, into chaos and barbaric behaviors, in the case of the semiosphere.

Such analogy, whose articulation could expand even more, should suggest that, in treating the semiotic randomness of meaning, one should adopt the same constructivist perspective that predominates in the current understanding of the relation between a semiosphere and its outer world. When a sign emerges, that occurs because an individual mind, that is, an interpreter, has turned the reception of physical stimuli from the environment, through the filters of both the physiology of perception and the influence of culture, into an occasion for meaning. The inner nature of this operation is such, though, that such emergence cannot be simply reduced to a coupling, to the dyadic attribution of a meaning to a stimulus. On the contrary, the semiosis provoked by the stimulus comes about through that concatenation of interpretants whose dynamic the metaphor of the stone in the pond has tried to describe. On the one hand, the fact that this dynamic, instead of simple coupling, characterizes semiosis is probably adaptive: the former allows individuals to respond to the environment in much more a creative and flexible way than the latter would do.

On the other hand, if interpretants were mushrooming around a given object in a totally random, chaotic, unpatterned, and unstructured way, then the adaptive character of this cognitive mechanism would probably turn into a social impairment: no pragmatic coordination among members of a group would be possible if their interpretations of a simultaneously received stimulus or series of stimuli could not somehow give rise to a certain degree of isomorphism and, therefore, coincidence and understanding. Incidentally, that is also the reason for why human mutual understanding is so different from merely machine coordination: human beings successfully understand each other, and therefore efficaciously act together, not because they coordinate their actions, but because they coordinate their thoughts, including those particularly complex thoughts that we call emotions.

Ⅷ. Interpretive Scales and Meta-habits

Such coordination is possible because individuals in a group are somehow compelled by shared common sense not much to adopt the same interpretants (that is a usual but wrong simplification of what happens in social interactions according to Peirce's semiotics) but rather to adopt the same scale of interpretants. They spontaneously yield to a meta-habit that consists in urging them to curtail concatenations of interpretants to the extent that is required in relation to the scale of semiosis that is predominant in a certain exchange. When the philosopher meets another philosopher in a roundtable at a congress, for example, they would both betray their role and disobey the rule of their communicative exchange were they to engage in a stereotypical conversation about a given philosophical topic. Avoiding the stereotype of the habit is difficult in philosophy too, and even more difficult is the trap of the stereotypical effect of meta-habits, yet if the two philosophers embrace their mission to the utmost extent, they should actually engage in an unceasing activity of deconstruction and reconstruction of semiotic habits. Were they to meet at lunchtime, though, and exchange platitudes with other eaters, the scale determining the formation of habits in such case would be completely different; of course one is free to philosophize at lunch table as well, but with the risk of upsetting or simply annoying or at least puzzling those who, instead, abide by the non-written norms of conversation among strangers and simply exchange small talk.

According to this modeling of semiosis, when a stone hits the surface of water of the pond, and sinks into it, simultaneously creating the visible traces of this impact, that is, the rings that irradiate from the center of it (out of metaphor: when the ontology of reality hits the senses through cognition and cultural habits of interpreting), a halo is created around the object, another optical metaphor to render the complex superposition of lights that the interpretants superimpose on each other in unlimited semiosis. This halo of meaning becomes increasingly fuzzy and ethereal moving away from the center of the impact, until it actually merges with the surrounding luminosity, or is overshadowed by the light created by other centers of semiosis. If the structure of the sign itself requires already a non-dyadic and, therefore, complex modeling, since it systematically emerges from a triadic interaction, the modeling of this halo of unlimited semiosis requires even more complex diagrams, which should take into account not only the sequence of interpretants in the concatenation of them that emanates from the center of semiosis, but also the multilayer and complexly stratified patterns that these interpretants cumulatively create around a semiotic event.

At each superposition, indeed, the extent of freedom of intentionality increases, to the point that, as the chain of interpretants moves away from its center, the constraints that common sense imposes on them become virtually absent, so that the periphery of the halo surrounding the semiotic event tends to vanish into unpatterned light. In the proximity of a semiotic event (that is, the impact of the ontology of reality with the senses through cognition), not only sociocultural meta-habits but also and perhaps primarily cognitive mechanisms favor the formation of habits. What is a habit, indeed, if not the socially shared attribution of a certain measure to the ring of light that surrounds an object through an interpretant? Habits, though, can always be challenged, exactly because of their stemming from a triadic and non-dyadic relation. That means that, on the one hand, common sense tends to crystallize unlimited semiosis into conventional understanding; in normal everyday conversation, for instance, the meaning of most objects is not constantly challenged but received through the regular structuring pattern of common sense. On the other hand, though, individuals as well as groups are at least potentially always able to deconstruct these habits.

Ⅸ. Inhabited and Uninhabited Semiosis

Another improper vulgate of Peirce's semiotics interprets this potentiality of deconstruction always unidirectionally, that is, in the sense of the possibility of dismantling existing social habits of interpretation by increasing the scale of patterning required in a certain semiotic event and, therefore, producing a reading that sees more rings around the stone, stretches the observation of the sign's halo farther, and detects patterns in more remote stretches of the concatenation of interpretants through semiosis. That is what poets and artists do spontaneously and what semioticians themselves do systematically, seeking to pattern the social circulation of meaning through articulations that are thicker than those provided by common sense.

The opposite possibility, though, is commonly neglected: whereas the arts and semiotics usually work for the a wider intelligibility of the field of semiosis of an object, pushing its habits forward through the creation of more sophisticated scales and, therefore, meta-habits of interpreting, a symmetric force is also active in all semiospheres, exerting an opposite impulse towards the narrowing down of semiotic habits. All instances of oversimplification work exactly through this dynamic: they encourage interpreters to actually stop their semiotic efforts short of the range of possibilities that are provided by common sense itself.

These two trends, the one that operates so that interpreters rearticulate their habits through the adoption of meta-habits that respond to a more sophisticate scale of interpretation than that provided by common sense, and the other one, on the contrary, that exerts its agency in the opposite sense of not only disfavoring such complexification but urging, also, toward the simplification of the existing habits through the adoption of meta-habits stemming from a narrower semiotic scale, deserve a better characterization. Surprisingly, indeed, they might be found responding to the same necessity, which is the one of making sense of emerging phenomena in the ontology of reality, as it is perceived and received by the senses and cognition.

In other words, re-articulations of interpreting habits through either over-complexification or oversimplification might just be two alternative but analogous ways to respond to a mismatch between existing patterns of interpretation and the complexity of reality. That is quite evident in historical circumstances in which individuals and groups must deal with the existence and social effects of emerging phenomena, that is, with the fact that increasing of quantity and speed of relations and interactions in a system leads the system itself to produce phenomena that cannot be explained anymore by the scale of understanding that has proven to guarantee successful interactions in that same system. For instance, application of digital and telematic technology to the financial field has increased the quantity and speed of interactions in it to the extent that it has given rise to emerging phenomena, that is, outcomes that could not be explained with the logic of understanding that was commonly adopted as a standard scale of interpretation in such domain of interactions.

Reactions to this mismatch can be twofold: on the one hand, a dismantling of existing meta-habits so that semiosis can be reactivated and possibly lead to taking into account interpretants which were previously excluded from the range of crystallized habits of meaning. For example, some scholars might relinquish their most deep-seated interpretive meta-habits and start considering not only human beings but also machines and even disembodied financial algorithms as independent economic agents, or start to describe and interpret interactions in the economic and financial domain as if they were interactions at another level and scale of complexity, for instance, organisms in biological systems of interaction.

On the other hand, inadequacy of the common interpretive habits can also lead to the opposite trend of reducing the scale of interpretation, dismantling the current meta-habits in the sense of an increased simplification of understanding and curtailing, as a consequence, the levels of interpretants considered in making sense of reality. In extreme cases, the oversimplification may be so drastic as turning a semiotic event into a physical event, a triadic relation into a dyadic one. That is, for instance, the cognitive logic beyond many conspiracy theories, which socio-culturally operate in a direction that is opposite to what is taken by paradigm-changing social scientists: instead of rearticulating the meta-habits of interpreting so that they take into account interpretants that were not modeled by the previous habits, they discard even presently modeled interpretants as insignificant, thus producing simpler explanations of reality. On the one hand, then, increasingly sophisticated macro-economic theories end up detecting agencies also where they would remain unseen and undetected by the previous interpreting patterns: algorithms start to be part of a larger picture. On the other hand, the picture shrinks to such an extent that only a very reduced number of elements remains part of it: Jews move it all. The first interpretive trend starts to see an agency that was hitherto unseen; the second interpretive trend starts to disregard agencies that were hitherto part of the system, neglecting the fact, for instance, that so many important operators in the global financial systems have no relation with Judaism.

Along the metaphoric lines proposed earlier, in the first case scholars adopt theoretical and sometimes even empirical instruments so as to see rings where they would previously see only water; in the second case, conspiracy theorists get rid of existing theoretical and even empirical instruments so as not to see some of the further rings irradiating from the stone, concentrating only on those that are starkly visible to everyone. The optical metaphor is valuable too: on the one hand, another beam of light is projecting onto the existing ones, superimposing its halo on them; on the other hand, existing lights are switched off so that only one stark luminous focus is projected onto reality.

Ⅹ. Over-complexification, Over-simplification, and Significance

Clearly, operations of over-complexification extend the range of the significant: what was considered as random, chaotic, unpatterned, and unintelligible becomes structured, patterned, and decipherable. Analogously, operations of oversimplification evidently shrink the domain of the significant, turning into insignificance all that lies outside of the visible rings turned into meaning by the narrow-scale, weedy meta-habits selected by curtailing the level of articulation of common sense. These two tendencies, which manifest themselves at the levels of both individual and social cognition, also have an equivalent in the development of the semiosphere, which can either include more and more external and hitherto considered as chaotic and insignificant elements within the circle of patterned and understandable meaning (through complex operations of transduction and translation across the frontiers of the semiosphere, operations that work exactly in the direction of altering and increasing the scale of meta-habits adopted to make sense of reality), or, conversely, shrinking the circle of the semiosphere, expelling as insignificant many phenomena that were hitherto included in the domain of the meaningful; such dynamic manifests itself, for instance, when metaphors of "naturality" or "authenticity" are adopted so as to exclude from the range of the significant, from that of the morally acceptable, and even from that of the legally permissible, practices of meaning that were previously part of common sense, albeit only at the margins of it: societies may, for instance, adopt meta-habits whose scale is narrow enough to reinterpret admissible systems of kinships, excluding from the range of the significant same-sex marriages, interreligious marriages, or even interethnic marriages (as it tragically occurred with anti-Semitic racist laws in Nazi Germany).

Over-simplification leads to narrowing down the span of understanding but is, nevertheless, a successful socio-cultural trend in some contingencies, and especially, as it was indicated earlier, in cases of increasing quantity and speed of relations and interactions within a system. The reasons for such success can be explained in relation to the fictional anecdote, Kieslowski's movie, evoked at the onset of the present paper. The father in the movie is an interpreter whose interpretation of the ontology of reality tragically fails. Reality presents to it the severest of all final counter-interpretants, that is, death. The son's accident leads to the incontrovertible conclusion that the father's adopted habit of interpretation was wrong, at the semiotic, epistemic, and even ontological level. Indeed, most of the habits of interpretation followed to explain reality in conspiracy theories were also wrong, and would probably also prove mortally if they were left to lead to full courses of action. That is actually occurring to a certain extent in the case of some conspiracy theories, for instance those in accordance to parents' stopping vaccinating their children, thus giving rise to epidemics in their children's schools, fortunately with consequences that are, at least thus far, less serious than what was faced by the father in Kieslowski's movie.

The case of this father, though, is different. He does not adopt a conspiracy theory or a clearly non-scientific interpretation of the reality of the lake. For instance, he does not tell his son to skate unworried on the thin ice of the lake because he, the father, will actually pray for the ice not to break. He is actually adopting a system and scale of interpretation, that of present-day mathematics and physics, which is acclaimed and unchallenged in the domain of contemporary sciences. Physics is what allow airplanes to fly, after all. Indeed, the father's tragic mistake does not consist in adopting physics as matrix of meta-habits for interpreting reality, but in adopting it in relation to the wrong domain. The father, tragically, does not understand the difference between an ideal lake and the real like, between the ice of physics and the ice of nature, between a laboratory where only a number of variables are allowed to interact in the field of an experiment, and a level of complexity of reality outside the laboratory, where the number of these variables explodes.

As a consequence, although physics is clearly not a conspiracy theory, the father adopts it in the same way as conspiracy theories are usually embraced, that is, so as to drastically curtail the scale of complexity characterizing the formulation of interpretive meta-habits and semiotic interpretations. That happens because this kind of over-simplification is not without virtues (or rather, pseudo-virtues). In Kieslowski's movie, for example, oversimplification introduced by mathematics and physics allows the father to give his son a rapid and unambiguous answer, which happens to be the wrong one, unfortunately. A father with no mathematics and no physics would have probably more safely adhered to common sense, and told the son to wait, and advised him to see first whether other people were skating, and even probed the ice himself before letting his child skating on it.

Out of the example, drastic over-simplifications are successful for, by reducing the number and scale of potentially significant elements considered in the process of making sense of reality, they give rise to fast coordination and immediate action. Anti-Semitism tragically spreads for many reasons, but one of them is certainly related to the pragmatic efficacy to which its oversimplification gives rise: the extermination of all Jews will give rise to the elimination of the economic crisis. It is quite simple to federate a community of ideas, emotions, and actions around such a simple and straightforward plan. On the contrary, the subtleties of scholars, not to speak of those of philosophers and semioticians, do not as immediately lead to coordination and even less to action. They can actually bring about more ambiguities, indeterminacies, and inaction. They increase the range of freedom to which intentionality is entitled to, thus making the social coordination of intents more difficult. They intrinsically strive, in the long term, for the reduction of the domain of randomness, yet in the short term, and especially in the eyes of the over-simplificators and their audiences, appear as agents of chaos and indeterminacy.

Ⅺ. Conclusions: Hoping for Mistakes

That is the case with medical science too; in fostering and moving forward the frontier of understanding, medical researchers must actually challenge commonsensical ideas that are at the basis of most medical practices, including the simple practices of self-medication. That should warn one about the fact that attention to the "accidents of over-simplification" should be paralleled by an equally keen attention to the "accidents of over-complexification". Unsuccessful interaction with the ontology of reality takes place not only when the scale of meta-habits is overly reduced, but also when it is overly increased. The father that over-simplifies the lake through physics makes a mortal mistake; but the father who would over-complexify it, for instance, by telling his son not to skate, lest a nuclear plant explode in that moment, melting the ice on the spot, would certainly save the son's life, but would also unduly shrink his, the son's, interaction with the environment. In the frame of this over-complexification, the son would never skate.

The efforts of scholars of all fields in the future will therefore have to be directed toward the task of understanding the correct scale at which understanding of reality must take place, and social coordination and action as a consequence of it. Over-simplifications as well as over-complexifications of all sort should be progressively discarded toward an ideal of reasonable interpretive style, whose main virtue should be that of adopting suitable frames and meta-habits for guiding the interpretations of phenomena. The application of a poetical frame to the understanding of an airplane aerodynamics should be avoided as much as the application of a physical frame to the understanding of a sonnet; after all, everyone likely prefers to fly in airplanes engineered through physics and read sonnets written through poetry, whereas everyone would be terrified to fly in a airplane engineered by a poet, but perhaps also to read a poem penned by an engineer (unless he or she doubles as poet adopting an alternative interpretive style).

Extending the domain of significance over randomness is certainly an important human task in the long term, but in the short term should not give rise to the paralysis of common sense and action either. The only way to guarantee such balance between excesses of under-interpretation and excesses of over interpretation is to learn from mistakes; the clash between an interpretation and a recalcitrant reality provides, indeed, fundamental evidence in Peirce's semiotics, for it is exactly the resilience of reality that guarantees the evolution of habits and especially meta-habits towards more and more suitable frames of understanding. It is only to be hoped that the mistakes that will be necessary to change the scale of interpretation will not have to be too serious. Had the father in the movie a second son, he, the father, would not tell him to skate on the lake on the basis of a mere mathematical calculus, yet how tragic the mistake would be leading to such a better consideration of reality. Getting rid of pernicious ideologies and astute demagogues will be fundamental in order to let reality speak through the mistakes of the human interaction with it.

References:

Badowska, E. & Parmeggiani, F. (Eds.). (2016). *Of elephants and toothaches: Ethics, politics, and religion in Krzysztof Kieslowski's "Decalogue"*. New York, NY: Fordham University Press.

Battiston, S., Caldarelli, G. & Garas, A. (2018). *Multiplex and multilevel networks*. Oxford, UK: Oxford University Press.

Campan, V. (1993). *Dix brèves histoires d'image: Le Décalogue de Krzysztof Kieslowski*; foreword by Jean-Louis Leutrat. Paris, FRA: Presses de la Sorbonne

nouvelle.
Church, I. M. & Robert J. H. (Eds.). (2019). *The Routledge handbook of the philosophy and psychology of luck*. New York, NY: Routledge.
Garbowski, C. (1996). *Krzysztof Kieslowski's decalogue series: The problem of the protagonists and their self-transcendance* [East European Monographs, 452]. Boulder: East European Monographs; New York, NY: Columbia University Press.
Giberson, K. W. (2016). *Abraham's dice: Chance and providence in the monotheistic traditions*. Oxford, UK: Oxford University Press.
Haltof, M., Agusti, J. & Anton, M. (Eds.). (2004). *The cinema of Krzysztof Kieslowski: Variations on destiny and chance*. New York, NY: Columbia University Press.
Simonigh, C. (2000). *La danza dei miseri destini: Il Decalogo di Krzyzstof Kieślowski*. Turin ITA: Testo & Immagine.
Svozil, K. (2018). *Physical (A) causality: Determinism, randomness and uncaused events*. Cham, CHE: Springer.
Vaillancourt, Y. (2016). *Jeux interdits: du Décalogue à la trilogie de Kieślowski*. Québec, CAN: Presses de l'Université Laval.
Wach, M. (2000). *Krzysztof Kieslowski: Kino der moralischen Unruhe*. Köln: KIM, Katholisches Institut für Medieninformation; Marburg, GER: Schüren / (Arte Edition.) / (Edition Film-Dienst ; [Bd. 1].)
Zattoni, E., Perdon, A. M. & Conte, G. (Eds.). (2020). *Structural methods in the study of complex systems*. Cham, CHE: Springer.

Author:

Massimo Leone, professor of semiotics in University of Turin, Italy, chief editor of *Lexia*. His research field is cultural semiotics.

作者简介：

马西莫·莱昂内，意大利都灵大学符号学教授，国际期刊 *Lexia* 主编，研究领域为文化符号学。

Email: massimo.leone@unito.it

论“无情”：人类的情感规则如何面对“佛系”人格的挑战

谭光辉

摘　要：“无情”这个词有多种意思，第一个意思是没有情感；第二个意思是不要受情感牵制，不要为情所伤，要破除执念；第三个意思是指无情之物；第四个意思是没有某种特定的情感。中国古代的各种“无情说”都不是说人可以做到没有情感。西方古代哲学由于重视理性而将理性与情感分开，但后来又证明没有情感理性亦不可能。人之所以不可能没有情感，是因为人是追求意义的动物。情感是人追求意义的原因，情感决定意义的方向和本质，意义活动必然产生一个情感结果。人类社会以情感为基础建立了显在的和潜在的社会规则。“佛系”人格因具有不同于社会多数人的情感而显得更加“无情”，但“佛系”人格并非无情，而是用一种特殊的情感状态表达了对社会潜规则的某种不满，预示着需要建立新的社会价值观念。“佛系”人格让我们体会到情感的意义和价值，同时也让我们明白我们的情感世界到底出了什么问题。

关键词：无情，佛系，情感研究，情感符号学，情感现象学

On “Emotionlessness”: How the Human Rules of Emotion Face up to the Challenge of a Buddha-like Personality

Tan Guanghui

Abstract: In Chinese, the concept of “emotionlessness” has multiple meanings: the first is the absence of emotion; the second is to be unaffected by emotions, unhurt by emotions, and for emotions to be fleeting; the third is emotionless things; and the fourth is the absence of specific emotion. None of these kinds of emotionlessness in ancient Chinese thought meant that people could be emotionless. Ancient Western philosophy first separated reason from emotion to emphasise the former, but later found the separation impossible because emotion and reason go hand-in-hand. It is impossible for human beings to have no emotions, because human beings are animals pursuing meaning and emotion motivates that pursuit. Emotion underlies the direction and essence of meaning, while meaningful activities inevitably produce an emotional result. Human society establishes explicit and potential social rules based on emotion. A Buddha-like personality appears "emotionless", but in fact expresses a kind of dissatisfaction with the latent social rules through a particular emotional state, thus indicating that new social values need to be established. A Buddha-like personality enables us to appreciate the meaning and value of emotions while simultaneously helping us to understand what is wrong with our emotional world.

Keywords: Emotionlessness, Buddha-like personality, emotion research, semiotics of emotion, phenomenology of emotion

DOI: 10.13760/b.cnki.sam.202001005

一、"无情"的概念辨析

关于"无情"，庄子与惠施曾有一场著名的辩论，载于《德充符》篇，原文如下：

> 惠子谓庄子曰："人故无情乎?"庄子曰："然。"惠子曰："人而无情，何以谓之人?"庄子曰："道与之貌，天与之形，恶得不谓之人?"惠子曰："既谓之人，恶得无情?"庄子曰："是非吾所谓无情也。吾所谓无情者，言人之不以好恶内伤其身，常因自然而不益生也。"惠子曰："不益生，何以有其身?"庄子曰："道与之貌，天与之形。无以好恶内伤其身。今子外乎子之神，劳乎子之精，倚树而吟，据槁梧而瞑。天选子之形，子以坚白鸣!"（庄周，2016，pp. 28—29）

在这段辩论中，庄子替换了惠施"无情"的概念，从而使无情有了两个意思。惠施所说的"无情"是指没有情感；庄子所说的"无情"，是指要顺应情感规律，不要让情感损害身体健康，回归本真状态。按张辉的说法，庄子所言"无情"，就是"指抛弃附加于人本真之上、纷扰人天然德性的世俗虚妄之情，恢复自然真情，而不是没有任何情感"（2016）。庄子和惠施都承认，作为人，要真正做到没有情感是不可能的。只不过，庄子认为人可以通过内心修炼，达到超然情感之外的状态，不因为情感而伤害身体本性，要遵守自然规律，而不让情感超过自然生命的需要。无情不是不要情感，而是不受情感牵制，也不过多追求非必要情感。

与庄子的观点极为相似，佛教也力劝世人不要被情感控制，要"破执"。道教认为"无情即圣人"，佛教禅宗认为"无情即佛祖"。（张松辉，2015，p. 189）佛教教义中有很大部分都在谈情感控制，"'反情'二字几乎就是佛教哲学的基本立场"（洪涛，2007）。朱松苗认为："如果说道家的'无情'指的是人们不要被情感所伤，那么禅宗则是要求人们要看透这种情感，而不是不要情感，情感还是可以有的，只是不要执著于这种情感。"（2016，p. 217）破除执著，乃能获得自由，达到"空"的境界。禅宗所说的"无情"，还有一个意思是"无情感之物"，指的是山河大地、树木花草、瓦砾砖石，与"人"相对。禅宗中有一派认为无情有性，无情说法。无情也有佛性，也能成佛，甚至也在说法。无情说法只有无情才能听得到，人无法听到。（方立天，2015，pp. 435－436）禅宗意见并不统一，"无情有性"是湛然最有特色的表现，但华严宗认为湛然的立论没有依据。（文海，2014，pp. 85－86）无论哪派，实际上已经默认了一个前提，即只有人才有情感，而且只要是人，就一定有情感。

"无情"还有一个意思，指没有特别的爱意或没有某种特定的情感，与"多情"相对。苏轼《蝶恋花》中名句"多情却被无情恼"，用的就是这个意思。这里的"无情"，指的是没有如"墙外行人"那种特别的情感，并非指"墙内佳人"没有感情，不然何以"墙内佳人笑"呢？苏轼还在《竹枝词》中用谐音写到过"无情"："东边日出西边雨，道是无晴却有晴。"这里谐音的"无情"仍然是此意。而梁遇春的散文《无情的多情和多情的无情》中所谈的"情"，专指爱情，意思是有众多爱情的人实际上是不懂爱情的，所以叫"多情的无情"；而像乔治·桑那样每一次都认真地爱一个人，却因此爱了无数人，这就是"无情的多情"。（梁遇春，2016，pp. 86－90）这里所说的"无情"，指的是"无爱情"。现代汉语中所说的"无情"，也主要使用"没有某种特定情感"之义，比如"冷酷无情"的人，并非说这个人没有情感，而是说这个人对他人没有爱或同情之类的情感。“水火无情”“翻脸无情”中的“无情”，则指不给面子或不留情面。

以此观之，中国历史上虽多有“无情”之说，但从未承认人可以做到没有情感。没有情感，甚至没有某种情感，都不符合“人”的标准。孟子说：“人皆有不忍之心。”“无恻隐之心，非人也；无羞恶之心，非人也。”这是因为，“恻隐之心，仁之端也；羞恶之心，义之端也。”（1997b，pp. 2690－2691）孟子为了强调仁、义的重要性而指出了两种情感的重要性，对情感类型未进行穷举。如果一一罗列，这个情感清单可以拉得很长。作为一个人，没有任何一种情感，可能都是不完整的，也就不会符合人类的行为规范。悲、喜、欲、惧、爱、恶、恩、怨，缺了任何一种，谁还敢相信他是一个完整的人？“有情”是人的本质规定性，是所有终有一死的凡人的必备品质。有此观念，才会有“天若有情天亦老”的名句，你要是不死的神仙、永恒的天，才有资格具备“无情”的品质。中国古代思想，无一例外，都把情视为人的天然伴生物。只有人才具有情感；没有情感的，不能称之为人。无情，是一种具有超越性的理想品质，或者指暂时缺乏某种具体情感的状态。

二、无情是否可能？

中国古代哲学多拿人的品性修为说事，所以在谈论无情的时候，多用来指一种情感超越性，即一种不受日常情感控制的心性品质。只有在诗人的口中，“无情”才用来指没有某些具体的情感特征。西方哲学的讨论没有中国哲学这样复杂，无情感就是无情感，无情感的东西才有更强大的力量。怀特海（Alfred North Whitehead）认为，正是那些无情感的力量（senseless agencies），比如蒸汽和蛮族，驱动它们各自的文明脱离秩序模式，“这些无情感的力量便是希腊哲学家有时称之为‘强制力’、有时称之为‘暴力’的东西”（2014，p. 10）。“无情感的力量”，既不同于中国禅宗所说的“无情之物”，也不同于庄子所说的“不以好恶内伤其身”之精神修养，而是指一种人所不能控制的东西。

与中国哲学更关心人自身的情感不同，西方哲学向来都更注重理性的作用。在古希腊人的观念中，即使是众神，也不是无所不能的，在这些神灵的背后，“是更为严苛、没有人类情感的命运在操纵一切。所以古希腊的研究者注重的是什么样的生活才是最正当的，而不注重上帝与人世间的关系”（威尔斯，2016，pp. 193－194）。希腊神话、史诗、宗教中的诸神，都是有情感的存在，"诸神展示了人类具有的情感和对人类事务的关心"（梯利，2014，p. 5）。哲学不是宗教，更注重探索存在于诸神掌控之外的理性。从苏格拉底开始，哲学家们就开始相信，用理性和逻辑的方法可以获得真理。这一思想差异导致中国哲学与西方哲学的典型差别：中国哲学更关心情感，而西方哲学更关心理性。

西方大多数哲学家都认为，情感与理性是相异乃至矛盾的力量，处于人性的两端，一端是情感和非理性，一端是认知和理性。在这个哲学框架下，奉行理性主义的哲学家就可以明确地宣称无情感是可能的。至少，理性主义者在进行理性思考的时候，可以宣称没有情感的参与。但是，"情感神经科学的研究现在已经证明，长期以来把情感和理智作为对立并列的两极是错误的"，"人类的理性，更具体地讲，人类的决策依靠情感，没有情感，人们不能把握选择的效价或效用"。论据非常有力："当大脑皮层，特别是前额回，如果与情感的核心部位——皮下神经组织之间的联结中断时，个体的任何决策行为都有困难，而且几乎总是作出不理性的或者不是最优的决策。"（特纳，斯戴兹，2007，p. 18）情感都是在某种理性的指导下产生的，而理性总是有情感的参与，或者有某种情感目标。以此观之，要真正做到无情感，几乎是不可能的，因为缺少了情感中枢，人的生活将变得不可想象。"没有情感我们就会失败，没有情感我们就会失去据以作出判断的方向和尺度。"（阿尔茨特，比尔梅林，2004，p. 154）失去了判断的方向和尺度，人也就不可能依靠理性做出正确的判断，理性就会因为失去人性而变得毫无用处。王弼在《周易正义》中说道："天本无情，何情之有？而物之性命，各有情也。所禀生者谓之性，随时念虑谓之情，无识无情，今据有识而言，故称曰'情'也。"（邢昺 1997a，p. 14）只要是有意识有性命之物，就必然会"随时念虑"，就必然有情感。

宋明理学提出"性即理"，"性"相当于"理性"，"情"就是"情感"。性与情之关系，程朱之前就讨论颇深。中国古代关于性情关系的讨论，曾礼军将其概括为三个方面："性体情用"说、"性阳情阴"说和"性水情波"说。（曾礼军，2016，p. 76）比如，孔颖达认为"情者，性之欲也"（邢昺，1997a，p. 17），王安石认为"性生乎情"，（1996，p. 736）都是"性体情用"说的代表；董仲舒、王充等人是"性阳情阴"说的代表，认为性与情没有主辅之分，一阴一阳，都是人之内在品质；杨慎（杨升庵）则是"性水情波"说的代表："波兴则水垫，情炽则性乱。波生于水，而害水者波也；情生于性，而害性者情也。"（杨升庵，2002，168）这些学说为宋明理学奠定了理论基础，情与理被分割开来看，且褒理而贬情，恰如西方哲学将理性与情感分割开来对待一样。

情理关系经过千年探讨，虽无定论，却留下大量的真知灼见和共识。其中一个最大的共识是，有无情感是判断人之为人的一个本质规定。现代人工智能的发展进一步证明了这一论断。没有情感的人工智能不是真正的人工智能。机器只有有了情感，才能被称为智能机器，而且，机器只有拥有了情感，才可能进行自主判断，做出独立的选择。机器在实现智能时不能没有情感的参与。（李蕾，王小捷，2016，p. 236）只要是人，就不可能做到无情感；只有有了人类的情感，才可以称为真正的人。

现在的人工智能在理智的某些方面已经远超人脑，但在自主情感方面，仍遭到瓶颈，机器人仍然只能在人为其设定的目的和方向中工作，因而达不到人的标准。王峰认为："机器没有情感，这是一个基本的人类主义预设。"他认为情感计算是可能的，人的情感与人工智能情感可以是两种不同的情感系统，二者的情感反应可以一致，情感机制不必相同。（2019）情感机制问题，可以让它继续保持神秘性，而情感反应则可以通过计算模仿。问题随之而来：既然情感机制不可模仿或计算，那么仅仅是情感反应与人类相似的人工智能是否是真正的智能？为什么人类特有的情感对于人是不可或缺的？

三、情感之于人在何种意义上不可或缺？

情感之于人不可或缺，是因为情感参与了一切意义建构行为。人是符号的动物，更是意义的动物。没有情感，意义没有发生的可能，也没有发生的必要。

首先，情感是人追求意义的原因。如果被问及"人为什么要存在"，我们可以得到一大堆哲学解释、宗教解释或进化论解释。符号学家则会说，人为追求意义而存在。如果被问及"人为什么要追求意义"，那么从哪个角度都难以给出一个令人满意的解释，所以很少有人敢问，更少有人敢答，似乎追求意义是人天生的本能，无需回答为什么。其原因可能在于，回答问题的路径必须是理性的，而答案却不得不归结到情感上。简言之，人之所以要追求意义，只不过是为了获得某种情感上的满足。甚至人创造符号，比如创造语言，可能也是因为情感需要。卢梭说："激情逼出了第一句言语［voix］。""同情（feeling），而不是理性，创造了人。""语言起源于何处？精神的需要（moral needs），亦即激情（passion）。""逼迫着人类说出第一个词［voix］的不是饥渴，而是爱、憎、怜悯、愤怒。”（2003，pp. 14—15）卢梭大概非常准确地解释了人创造符号，亦即追求意义的动力源。人们常把人类探索知识的动力归结为求知欲，而求知欲的“欲”，就是一种情感。人之所以愿意运用理性思考去获得真知，其根源正是人有这种获得真知的欲望。机器人不会主动去获得知识，是因为它没有获取这种知识的欲望。安·兰德曾在耶鲁大学发表激情洋溢的演说：“人与其他生命物种的特殊区别就在于他在种种选择面前可以凭借着意志做出决定。”“欲望并不是本能，生存的欲望并没有告诉你生存所需要的知识，甚至连人的生存欲望都不是天生就具备的。”“人不得不成为人——这是他自己选择的；他不得不将自己的生命视为一种价值——这是他自己选择的；他必须选择学会去爱护它；它不得不去发现生命需要的种种价值，实践美德。”是什么促使人在生存之道上做出如此多的选择？兰德用盖尔特（Galt，《阿特拉耸耸肩》一书的主角）的话总结道：“你必须做出选择，让你的思想和生存之爱决定吧。”（兰德，2016，p. 93）归根结底，是“生存之爱”这种情感，决定了人的一切选择，包括选择理性、知识、生存、美德，等等。之所以某些选择有意义，并非真有一个意义在那里等着人去选择或认识，而是因为如此选择才符合人的情感需要。正是因为这个原因，凯文德（Nancy Cavender）等人认为，“每一个词语和表达既有认知意义，又有情感意义”（凯文德，卡亨，2016，p. 160）。几乎任何一个词语，对一些人而言可能是褒义的或中性的，而对另一些人而言可能是贬义的，反之亦然。选择一个词语，都已经暗含了一次情感选择；任何一个选择，已经显现出一个情感倾向。

其次，情感决定意义的方向，从而决定了意义的本质。任何意义的产生，必先有意向性。没有意向性，意义无从发生。海德格尔指出：“从字面看，意向（Intentio）的意思就是：自身一指向（Sich-richten-auf）。每一体验、每一心灵行为都指向着某物。表象是对某物的表象，回忆是对某物的回忆，判断是关于某物的判断，猜测、期待、爱、恨——都是对于某物的。”（2014，p. 38）从这个意义上看，意向性似乎与情感无关。但是，如果再进一步追问，问题就会显现出来：任何“某物”的呈现，细节是无限丰富的，是什么决定了意向的方向？谢文郁指出：“意向是一种人的意识的倾向性活动”，“所有的倾向都是一种情感”，所以，“意向性就是一种情感指向，或者说，意向性分析归根到底是一种情感分析”，“一旦意识指向某物，一定是具有了某种倾向性，即拥有了某种情感”。由此，他认为，意向性本身就是一种情感，是认识活动的动力，进而，“在不同的情感中，对象呈现出不同的意义。情感具有对对象本质的界定功能”。(2016）此论非常精彩，非常准确地指出了情感的赋义功能。“情感总是指向一个对象并对它进行赋义。”（谢文郁，2016，pp. 273－274)关于情感对意向性方向的影响，学界早已展开广泛的论述，比如汤普森就说过：“身体感受不是不向世界开放的自我闭合（self-enclosed)。相反，它们以某种情感的（affective）方式或氛围呈现出事物，因此深深地影响我们如何感知和回应事物。”（2013，p. 21）问题似乎没有完结。情感固然可能决定意向的方向，但相反的过程仍然可能发生，由意向性而得的认识也可能影响情感。海德格尔曾经提到过舍勒的一篇文章——《喜好和知识》，他认为舍勒是第一个弄清楚了问题的人：“意向行为是完全不同的，比如，甚至喜爱和憎恨也基于认识。”（海德格尔，2015，p. 169）对于情感与意向性的关系，哲学界意见不一。一部分人认为并非一切心理现象都是有意向性的，比如胡塞尔就认为情感并非都是有意向性的；另一部分人则认为一切心理现象都是有意向性的，比如布伦塔诺。一些人认为认知影响情感，比如海德格尔和舍勒；另一些人则认为情感影响认知，比如谢文郁；还有一些人认为认识和情感是相互影响的，比如唐孝威（2008，p. 304）。本文认为，认识活动和情感是相互影响的，可以找出大量证据。从意向性和意义生成的角度看，情感的作用不可忽略。至于情感本身是否受认知活动影响，则是另一个问题。

最后，任何意义活动必然产生一个情感结果。由于情感是符号－意义活动的原因，并且决定了其方向，所以符号－意义活动必然产生一个情感结果。这个观点可能很容易招致反对意见，因为人们已经假定认知活动与情感无关，而且习惯于将人类的符号活动分为认知活动与情感活动等不同的类型。进一步追问我们就会发现，任何认知活动必然伴随情感活动，因为任何认知活动都必然是在元认知结构中发生的，而元认知的基本成分之一就是元认知体验。“元认知体验是指伴随着认知活动而产生的情感体验。”（唐龙云，等，2015，p. 235）元认知体验既可能发生在认知活动之前，也可能发生在认知活动之后。比如说，在学习某个科学知识之前，我们可能产生好奇、焦虑等情感，在懂得这个知识之后，则可能产生满足、喜悦等情感。任何符号行为都伴随着元符号体验，元符号体验是所有符号－意义活动的必然结果，所以情感是符号－意义活动的必然结果。

综上所述，情感贯穿于符号－意义活动的整个过程。情感在人的意义活动过程中是不可或缺的。对作为动物性的人，情感或许不是必需的；对作为符号性和社会性的人，情感必然是必需的。要真正做一个无情之人，并非易事。

四、"佛系"人格之无情对社会潜规则的挑战

以上长篇累牍的论述，无非是想说明，对于具有社会性的人而言，情感是必需的。社会靠情感维系，各种社会规则以情感为基础建构，社会用情感管理人类。用情感管理人类有很多好处，其中最大的好处之一是人不必每次行动都在试错，而是可以有预见性地调节，从而提高人类整体的生存概率。由于这个原因，人类社会的诸多规则，无论是显在规则（比如法律体系等）还是潜在规则（比如道德观念等），都以情感为依据。休谟早就认为，道德是建立在情感之上的，而不是建立在理性之上的。（斯特德，1992，p.240）哈奇森也认为，唯有情感才能推动道德行为的发生，唯有情感才是道德的真正根源。（李家莲，2012，p.91）史次耕在给《孟子·公孙丑》中的"离则不祥"句做注的时候说："儒家伦理道德，建立在情感上，故家庭以情感为主。设若父子不和，则非家庭之福。"（1980，p.196）这些道理很好理解，例子就在身边。人类要结成群体，需要爱；要远离坏人，需要厌恶；要让对我们好的人继续对我们好，需要感恩；要阻止对我们不利的行为，需要抱怨。要让人乐于继续生存，就要让他喜悦；要让人不想再继续生存，就要让他悲哀；要鼓励人行动，就要利用欲望；要阻止人行动，就要利用恐惧。恰当地利用人的情感，可以有效地调节行为。社会规则的目的，就是调节人的行为，所以社会规则都以情感为基础。由于社会规则以情感为基础，所以人类就形成了一整套符合情感规律的道德规范和法律条款。

举例来说，2005 年 12 月，中央电视台联合央视国际和新浪网发起了"最缺乏公德的行为"调查活动，排在前列的几种行为依次是：向窗外扔污物；上公共汽车不排队，一拥而上；在旅游景点、名胜古迹上乱写乱刻；宠物随地大小便，主人不清理；行人翻栏杆，随意横穿马路；下雨天开车溅湿行人；公交车上，年轻人不主动给老弱病残孕让座；传播垃圾电子邮件、手机短信；看电影、演出时，大声说话、喧哗、到处走动；在街上乱吐口香糖。（朱力宇，张伟，2013，pp.36－37）之所以认为这些行为缺乏公德，原因主要是这些行为在一定程度上损害了其他人的利益，让其他人产生了不同程度的怨恨情感。公众对某行为怨恨的程度，决定了该行为违背社会公德的强弱程度。公众对其怨恨极强的行为，往往就是法律禁止的行为。

除了道德规范和法律条款，人类的其他行为准则大多也都有情感依据。比如，常人的行为准则，以积极进取、是非分明、追求幸福等为正面价值，

“人应该朝着和安止于光明和美丽之境”，“青年人的人生观应该是乐观向上、朝气蓬勃、积极有为，而不应该是悲观低落、灰暗气馁、碌碌无为的。”（徐小跃，2018）简言之，多数人都认为，青年人应该以上述有正面价值的追求为向往和热爱的对象，如果实现这样的目标就应该产生喜悦感。如果这些大家认为应该追求的东西不能给某些青年人带来喜悦感，大家就会感到无所适从，不知如何是好。

“佛系”青年正是这样一种人：大家认为应该感到喜悦的事，他们不喜悦；大家认为应该感到悲伤的事，他们不悲伤；大家认为应该感到愤怒的事，他们不愤怒；大家认为应该追求的欲望，他们不感兴趣。汪行福将“佛系”青年的特征概括为如下四点：“（1）一切都行，看淡一切、安静自然、随遇而安、一切随缘的人生观；（2）有也行，没有也行，不争不抢、不求输赢的得失观；（3）兴趣第一，做事有自己喜欢的方式和节奏；（4）做什么无所谓，把本职工作做好，不揽事、不贪功也不卸责的职业观。”（2018）王金林认为“佛系”青年的特征是“以低欲望、低需求、低消费的姿态‘拒绝’（不管是主动还是被动）加入这场消费盛宴”（2018）。总之，“佛系”青年的情感状态与社会大多数人不同。大家都认为应该有激情的时候，他们没有激情，持一种“不走心”淡然心态。“淡然”就是情感淡化，相对普通人而言，显得“无情”。

“佛系”青年的无情，是一种相对意义上的无情，与庄子、禅宗所讲的无情意思非常接近。不同之处在于，第一，“佛系”青年把庄子、禅宗曾经奉劝世人不要被情感控制、要破除执念的思想真真切切地变成了人生原则。庄子、禅宗是在谈理想和境界，而“佛系”青年则是在实践。第二，庄子、禅宗并不否认普通人的情感，他们主要谈的是对情感的控制和超越，而“佛系”青年的情感则不同于普通人的情感，在价值观层面已经发生了变化。从某种意义上说，“佛系”青年的无情，比庄子、禅宗所说的无情更彻底。

上文说过，人类的行为准则和社会规则，多以普通人的情感为依据和根源，这些规则面对不具有符合惯常规则的情感的人时就变得无效、无力。“佛系”青年的情感和心态，并不对法律、道德等规则形成任何挑战，而是对社会日常潜规则形成挑战，因为这些日常潜规则对他们而言无效。比如社会潜规则是以物质、金钱、荣誉、地位等吸引人更努力地工作，而“佛系”青年则以“有也行，没有也行，不争不抢”的态度对待之，一切都行，无所谓，所以这条潜规则就对他们无效。社会潜规则是，所做之事要服从多数人的需要，所以为多数人服务的人能够获得更大的利益，而“佛系”青年以自己的兴趣为第一，做事有自己的方式和节奏，不以他人好恶为转移，因此这条潜规则对他们也无效。社会潜规则是，工作做得出色、有更大功绩的人就有机会获得更多的奖赏和更高的地位，而“佛系”青年只把本职工作做好，不揽事、不贪功，因而这条潜规则对他们仍然无效。当社会潜规则对一大批人都无效时，社会感到恐慌，于是就有人指出是“佛系”青年的情感和心态出了问题，应当加以引导和纠正。

洪涛发现，明清主情思潮经历了从“本色论”到“童心说”“性灵论”“情至论”，再到“情教说”“情正论”，最终坠入“情幻论”的发展历程，比如《长生殿》中的唐明皇、《红楼梦》中的贾宝玉等人物，都在经历一番深刻的情感历程之后，最终归于情空情幻。洪涛认为，佛道有情无情的观念给予主情思潮深刻影响，他最后得出的结论是：“在某种普遍的虚无主义心绪中，佛禅最终彻底进入了中国人的情感世界，成为中国人处理世俗情感的最后方式，某种意义上也表明了明清以后中国人情感资源的枯萎状态。”（2007）如果佛教中的“无情”思想确实被当时中国人普遍接受，表明了明清以后中国人情感资源的枯萎状态，那么“佛系”青年的出现，也势必表明当下中国人情感资源的某种枯萎状态。

细思之后我们会发现，在任何社会和时代，情感资源都不会真正枯萎。影响人们情感的关键因素是世界观和人生观。世界观和人生观，影响人对世界和他人的叙述方式，从而生成不同的情感。“佛系”的无情并非没有情感，而是说情感世界与大众不一样，其无情本身就是一种特殊的情感，因为“佛系”心态，本就是一种有倾向性的选择。“佛系”人格，让人感觉到是在挑战社会的情感规则，“佛系”的出现使人们警觉：要不是社会出现了问题，就是“佛系”青年自身发生了某种病变。但通过以上反思我们会发现，“佛系”青年反映的是新一代青年人生观和世界观的一些微妙变化。一方面，他们以一种非对抗的方式对现存的社会潜规则表达了失望和不满；另一方面，他们希望以一种情感无作为的方式瓦解社会潜规则，从而使建立一种新的规则成为可能。“佛系”青年的出现，确实值得整个社会反思：我们习以为常的行事原则是否具有天然的合理性？我们毕生追求的价值是否真的有价值？当整个社会加速运转的时候，我们到底应该紧跟时代大潮，还是应该在某些时候停下来问问初心？

我们有理由相信，在物质条件和符号环境发生了极大变化之后成长起来的中国青年，其世界观和人生观必然与之前的人们有所不同。“佛系”人格的出现，对我们也是一个提醒：只有用无情做对比，我们才能真正体会到情感的意义和价值，也才能明白我们的情感世界到底出了什么问题。

引用文献：

阿尔茨特，福尔克；比尔梅林，伊曼努尔（2004）．动物有意识吗（马怀琪，陈琦，译）．北京：北京理工大学出版社．

方立天（2015）．中国佛教哲学要义（中）．北京：宗教文化出版社．

海德格尔（2014）．时间概念史导论（欧东明，译）．北京：商务印书馆．

海德格尔（2015）．从莱布尼茨出发的逻辑学的形而上学始基（赵卫国，译）．西安：西北大学出版社．

洪涛（2007）．有情无情：佛道渗透中的沉沦与超越．内蒙古社会科学（汉文版），1，pp. 130－134．

怀特海，A. N.（2014）．观念的冒险（修订版）（周邦宪，译）．南京：译林出版社．

凯文德，南希；卡亨，霍华德（2016）．生活中的逻辑学（杨红玉，译）．北京：中国轻工业出版社．

兰德，安（2016）．谁需要哲学（张旭东，译）．北京：华夏出版社．

李家莲（2012）．道德的情感之源：弗兰西斯·哈奇森道德情感思想研究．杭州：浙江大学出版社．

李蕾，王小捷（2016）．机器智能．北京：清华大学出版社．

梁遇春（2016）．无情的多情和多情的无情．载于相遇，只为住进你心里．天津：天津人民出版社．

卢梭（2003）．论语言的起源：兼论旋律与音乐的摹仿（洪涛，译）．上海：上海人民出版社．

史次耕（1980）．孟子今注今译．台北：台湾商务印书馆．

斯特德，巴里（1992）．休谟（周晓亮，刘建荣，译）．济南：山东人民出版社．

汤普森，埃文（2013）．生命中的心智：生物学、现象学和心智科学（李恒威等，译）．杭州：浙江大学出版社．

唐龙云等（2015）．心理学基础．杭州：浙江大学出版社．

唐孝威（2008）．脑与心智．杭州：浙江大学出版社．

特纳，乔纳森；斯戴兹，简（2007）．情感社会学（孙俊才，文军，译）．上海：上海人民出版社．

梯利，弗兰克（2014）．西方哲学史（贾辰阳，解本远，译）．北京：光明日报出版社．

汪行福（2018）．佛系是一种消极的善．探索与争鸣，4，29－33．

王安石（1996）．原性．王安石全集（宁波，刘丽华，张中良，校点）．长春：吉林人民出版社．

王峰（2019）．人工智能的情感计算如何可能．探索与争鸣，6，89－100，159，161．

王金林（2018）．佛系：反消费症候式的内置式出走．探索与争鸣，4，39－42．

威尔斯，H. J.（2016）. 世界史纲（孙丽娟，译）. 北京：北京理工大学出版社.
文海（2014）. 天台宗与法华经. 北京：宗教文化出版社.
谢文郁（2016）. 形而上学与西方思维. 南宁：广西人民出版社.
邢昺（1997a）. 十三经注疏（上）. 上海：上海古籍出版社.
邢昺（1997b）. 十三经注疏（下）. 上海：上海古籍出版社.
徐小跃（2018）. "佛系"是伪佛：中国传统文化如何消解佛系. 探索与争鸣，4，47－50.
杨升庵（2002）. 性情说. 王文才，万光治. 杨升庵丛书（三）. 成都：天地出版社.
曾礼军（2016）. 古代文学的文化批评与学术反思. 哈尔滨：黑龙江人民出版社.
张辉（2016）.《庄子》"无情"说发微. 长安大学学报（社会科学版），4，115－120.
张松辉（2015）. 道冠儒履释袈裟：中国古代文人的精神世界. 长沙：岳麓书社.
朱力宇，张伟（2013）. 职业道德与法律. 北京：高等教育出版社.
朱松苗（2016）. 论儒道禅之情：以《论语》《庄子》《坛经》为中心. 武汉：武汉大学出版社.
庄周（2016）. 庄子. 长沙：岳麓书社.

作者简介：

谭光辉，博士，四川师范大学文学院教授，博士生导师，研究方向为符号学、叙述学、中国现当代文学。

Author:

Tan Guanghui, Ph. D., professor of Chinese and Literature College, Sichuan Normal University, member of ISMS research team. His academic interests are semiotics, narratology and modern Chinese literature.

Email: sctgh@163.com

度量噪音：皮尔斯符号类型与噪音关系的探讨*

何一杰

摘　要： 度量噪音的最常用方式是确定信噪比，依赖非常明确的数值指标以及技术环境。对于意义的噪音来说，符号意义难以进行技术的量化，并以此确定一个数值比例。本文从皮尔斯符号类型的角度，对噪音与意义的关系进行了梳理，确定了噪音影响可能性的大小，从符号本体的角度对意义的噪音进行了某种程度的"度量"：皮尔斯的十种符号类型有不同的第三性主导程度，噪音作为一种第三性的存在，与符号第三性不同程度的侵占与冲突，对意义产生了不同程度的影响。

关键词： 噪音，符号类型，皮尔斯，信噪比

Measuring Noise: The Peircean Typology and Classification of Noise

He Yijie

Abstract: The most common way to measure noise is by the signal-to-noise ratio, which depends on precise numerical indicators and technical conditions. Noise in the meaning of signs, however, is difficult to quantify, with no easily determinable numerical proportion. This paper investigates the relation between noise and meaning from the perspective of the Peircean typology. It affirms the likelihood of the effect of noise and measures the

* 本文为国家社会科学基金青年项目"网络新闻'噪音'污染与治理研究"（19CXW001）阶段性成果；西华大学校人才引进项目"符号表意中的'噪音'问题研究"（W202205）研究成果。

noise of meaning to a certain degree based on semiotic ontology. There are different degrees of predominance of "thirdness" in Peirce's ten-part sign typology. Noise, existing as a kind of "thirdness" that invades and conflicts with the "thirdness" of signs to different degrees, influences meaning to a varying level.

Keywords: noise, Peircean typology, Peirce, signal-to-noise ratio

DOI: 10.13760/b.cnki.sam.202001006

引　言

噪音难以避免，这是人类表意文化的一个特征。噪音作为"对特定意义不做贡献的符号观相"（何一杰，2018）使意义的传播成为可能，使意义的传播具有效率并且维护了文化的边界。从宏观上对噪音的判断能够引导我们进行一些文化层面的探讨，但难免显得空泛。意义在符号的使用中不断发展，符号总是具体的，特定的意义不断纠缠，其中丰富的个性难以下是非二分的定论。这时，就需要对噪音进一步划分，以探索在不同的符号中噪音的不同性质。噪音与符号本身密切相关，那么符号性质的不同便有可能使噪音有所区别。对噪音的划分应最终归结于噪音与意义的关系，即噪音对意义影响的大小，这样才能形成统一的论述维度。本文对噪音的划分，其实是对噪音影响力的划分，即噪音的度量。

大部分的噪音研究沿用了信息论"信噪比"（signal-to-noise ratio）的概念，即通信或传播中信号与噪音的比率，以此来判断信号的质量。本文并不打算借用此概念，因为意义问题难以量化，符号总是在使用中产生意义，且不断衍义变化。在无确切数值的情况下，"信噪比"对噪音大小的精细区分没有作用。本文依据皮尔斯符号类型学对噪音进行度量的划分，对噪音进行影响能力的排序：当给定两个受到噪音影响的符号或者符号过程时，我们总能判断哪一个受影响更大。

在《噪音法则：皮尔斯现象学视域下的符号噪音研究》一文中，笔者探讨了噪音与第三性的关系（何一杰，2016），噪音的这种特点使得以符号类型为依据对噪音进行的度量，必然采用皮尔斯的符号类型学。皮尔斯对符号的类型进行了相当详细的分类，他区分的符号三元关系可以看作在符号类型上对他的符号现象学基本范畴的一种应用。再现体、对象、解释项分别对应着第一性、第二性和第三性。但皮尔斯并没有满足于此，他继续将符号的三元关系单独划分，对符号再现体、对象和解释项分别进行了第一性、第二性、第三性的划分。于是便有了以下最为基础的皮尔斯符号类型（表1）：

表1　皮尔斯对符号的三重划分（科布利，2013，p.102）

		第一性	第二性	第三性
第一性	呈现品格	质符（qualisign）	单符（sinsign）	型符（legisign）
第二性	再现品格	像似符（icon）	指示符（index）	规约符（symbol）
第三性	解释能力	呈符（rheme）	申符（dicent）	论符（argument）

由于呈现、再现、解释三元关系的不可拆分，皮尔斯通过三个三分构建出的这九种符号类型会产生27种符号分类，即再现体、对象、解释项每一个层面的三种类型，都与其他两个层面的符号类型相组合。此外，皮尔斯还认为，第一位只决定第一位，而第二位则可以决定第二位和第一位，同样，第三位可以决定第三位、第二位以及第一位（Weiss，1945）。根据这一原则，27种可能的类型缩减为以下十种（粗体表示其主导特征）：

1. 呈符性像似**质符**
2. 呈符性**像似单符**
3. **呈符性指示单符**
4. **申符性**指示**单符**
5. 呈符性像似**型符**
6. 呈符性指示**型符**
7. **申符性指示**型符
8. **呈符性规约**型符
9. **申符性规约**型符
10. **论符性规约**型符（CP 2. 254—263）

噪音是一种第三性的存在，但这并不意味着噪音只与第三位的符号类型发生作用。本文认为，越是受到第三性主导的符号，其受噪音影响的可能性就越小；符号越不受第三性主导，其噪音的影响力就越大。

一个具有型符特征的符号，因为具有了某种法则，在面对噪音时，便有了更多使其自身意义符合体裁期望的根据，所以型符受到噪音的影响要弱于单符和质符；一个规约符在处理与噪音的关系上，可以有更多的理据性，而不是由符号自身的品质或与对象的直接关系来决定其意义；同样，一个论符将解释项引向了法则，而非品质特性与存在特征，其受噪音的影响也更少。

由此，我们可以大致为以上的符号类型做一个排序，展示噪音在这些符号类型中的分布情况（表 2）：

表 2　符号类型与噪音的强弱

<table>
<tr><td rowspan="4">噪音影响 强→弱</td><td colspan="3">呈符性像似质符</td></tr>
<tr><td>呈符性像似单符</td><td>呈符性指示单符</td><td>申符性指示单符</td></tr>
<tr><td>呈符性像似型符</td><td>呈符性指示型符</td><td>申符性指示型符</td></tr>
<tr><td>呈符性规约型符</td><td>申符性规约型符</td><td>论符性规约型符</td></tr>
</table>

该图表基于这样一种推论：型符、规约符与论符所占的比重越大，符号受到噪音影响的可能越小。而呈符性像似质符作为唯一具有质符性质的符号，在对其单独进行审视之后，发现其与噪音的关系非常独特，既可谓全，又可谓无。下面就对每一类符号类型与噪音的影响关系进行讨论。

一、呈符性像似质符

按照上文提出的噪音与第三性的关系来看，最易受呈现噪音影响的是呈符性像似质符，这也是唯一一类作为质符存在的符号。呈符性像似质符是最低等的符号类型，它不包涵其他的符号类型，但却时常包含于其他的符号类型之中（皮尔斯，2014，p. 188）。例如我们意识到自己闻到了一种难以辨别的气味，这个气味没有任何动力性、最终性的解释，即我们不会从气味中察觉出危险，或者觉得这种气味似曾相识。这种气味符号时常包含在我们对其他气味符号的符号过程中，我们闻到一阵食物的香味，首先感知到的就是这种符号，然后可能始终停留在这个符号中，或者将符号解释为"附近有人在做饭"，"这家餐馆可能还不错"或者"到了吃饭的时间了"。后者产生的这些解释使得符号不再是一个呈符性像似质符，而变成了其他的符号类型。

在这种符号中，特定的意义就是获取到的符号品质，而这种品质不被抽象化、概念化，因此，呈现噪音的影响直接被作为品质的一部分，甚至噪音本身就是品质。

对这种符号的感知中，噪音只需要被感知，就能够成为其解释项，没有任何其他因素的制约。同样以气味符号为例，如果一个符号作为呈符性像似质符被感知，气味所能呈现出的任何一个观相都可以成为其意义的观相。例如某种不能辨识出意义（闻不出是辛辣还是甜腻）的气味，我们在感知的过程中可能有的一切：气味的类型、强弱、持续的时长、出现的地点等，都是“感受到这种气味”的影响因素，如果改变其中的某个部分，就改变了对这种气味感知的某个品质。又如，视觉刺激突然停止后会出现后像，而一个不指向原本视觉刺激（不思考某个红色的圆形后像是来自灯泡还是电视屏幕）的后像，其涉及的一切在某次获意行为中被感知到的观相，都是其中的关于感受到这个第一性的品质的意义。

这样一来，若只停留在这个符号类型中，噪音的影响可以达到极限，甚至取消自身。对于呈符性像似质符而言，噪音与符号没有区别，我们无法通过对某一特定意义符号过程的判断来确定某个观相是否对其有贡献，它的意义与噪音都是不明确的。我们可以说这种符号完全没有噪音，感知到的所有观相都为意义做出贡献；也可以说它全部都是噪音，意义的分区已难进行。本文倾向第二种看法，将其作为受噪音影响最为强烈的一种符号，以区别于以第三性为主导的论符性规约型符与噪音的关系。

二、呈符性像似单符

呈符性像似单符是任何一个单一的像似符，所以其与噪音的关系，就是单一像似符与噪音的关系。呈符性意味着符号只关注其对象“是什么”或者“怎么样”（而非申符或者论符的“有什么关系”或“导致什么结果”）。这样呈现出的品质，与其对象具有了像似之处。而单符总是单独存在的，如果它不是型符的实例化的话，那么这种单一性就更加绝对。

噪音在这类符号中有如下影响的可能：首先，单符若不是型符的实例化，则其本身就不受某个法则的制约，例如一个圆圈，若不是属于语言系统，就不一定只是字母“o”，或者数字“0”，或者中文的句号，而有可能是更多的东西；在这一层面上来说，更多的可能性给了噪音更大的空间。解释者需要在更大的空间中探求符号的意义，也就更易受噪音的影响。这样，圆圈可以被解释为天体、车轮、禅宗、正确等意义，噪音对其的影响便远比对将圆圈认为是字母“o”这种规约型符的影响强烈。

一张图表所呈现的形状与数据的关系是一个呈符性像似单符——一个呈符性像似型符的实例化。图表这种符号是型符，我们的解释习惯是通过一种可视化的方式将数据呈现出来。但是在具体的符号过程中，这个解释是根据形状的大小、高低、起伏变换的关系而产生的，意义是依据一种单一（并非规约）的观相特征展现的。被污损的图表显然出现了噪音，这种噪音有可能完全遮挡了图表，有可能仅仅处于一个无关紧要的位置，不妨碍人们继续辨认其中数据的关系。这两种可能的噪音都对“图表与数据的关系”这个特定的意义没有贡献，前者完全干扰了意义，后者则被读图者感知，并且忽略。

又例如，纪实照片可以是很多种符号，但如果这张照片的内容没有指涉明显的历史大事件，其中也没有记录什么线索（至少解释者不寻找什么线索），那么这张照片就是一个呈符性像似单符（如图 1）。

图 1　黑白照片

如果解释者同笔者一样，只是无意间看到了这张照片，并不知晓它是否是著名的作品，那么对解释者而言，这是一个呈符性像似单符。我没有去过图中的地方，也完全不知道这是在哪儿，只能感受到这是一处水景，画面中漂浮着水汽，水中还有些杂物，等等。虽然一个摄影品鉴家会告诉我应该怎样理解这幅作品，但实际上我觉得水中的杂物让画面看起来有些乱，甚至让这个照片显得无趣；或者又因为周围的那些植物，让我没有十分注意水面上美丽的水汽；又或者我希望体会到山水画的那种感觉，但却被植物精致的细节打扰了。这些特定的意义总是能在画面中找到一些没有帮助的部分，甚至破坏意义的部分，而这些部分在符号的呈现层面出现。

当然，完全可以为每一个细节都找到完美的解释，比如水中的杂物是突出的“刺点”。巴尔特在《明室》中提出“刺点”这个术语，用来描述照片中的某个细节，某个局部。“不管如何突如其来，刺点总或多或少地潜藏着一种扩展的力量。”（巴特，2011，p. 59）于是，对于水中的杂物，可以说它破坏了非常多的获意尝试：让画面显得不那么纯净，有些让人讨厌；或许这些杂物仅仅是水中的植物刚冒出头，又或许是人类遗弃的废物。这些杂物让那种以纯粹展示自然之美的意义落空，同时又不能明显地支持揭露环境破坏的主题。我们当然可以认为这个画面很糟糕，没有表现什么东西，但同时也可以认为它因为恰好破坏了这些可以明确表现的意义而是一幅不错的作品。这样的判断很可能改变了符号的品质：对于一个能够如此解释的接受者而言，这是一个像似型符；将那些吸引眼球的部分作为刺点，是受到了审视摄影作品的法则的约束。

三、呈符性指示单符

呈符性指示单符仅仅将对象指示出来，而不对符号与对象的联系进行暗示，即“为何由此注意到对象”的解释。它与所有的非型符一样，都缺乏元层次的指引，而其呈符性由于只引起一种指示作用，所以在解释者将注意力转移到对象上后，符号就完成了任务。

呈符性指示单符大部分情况下是呈符性指示型符的实例化符号，拍打肩膀引人注意是型符的实例化，使用这种符号是一种习惯性的表达。当然，呈符性指示单符也可以单独存在，例如李斯卡举出的例子：“一次自发的喊叫，则可能是一个呈符性指示单符。这种喊叫必须是自发的，而且它并不像由于举起重物而发出的哼声或者由于疼痛或恐惧而发出的尖叫声那样具有那种规约式的或者法则式的关系。”（皮尔斯，2014，p. 189）很难想象一个正常人会发出这样的喊叫，它指示了声音的发出者，但却没有让我们觉得他在打招呼，或者他在承受痛苦，就如同一个手机突然响起了铃声却没有任何来电或者提醒。自发喊叫没有使用呼喊的型符性质，脱离了正常的使用方式，作为对象的发声者便很可能被归入非正常的类别中。

呈符性指示单符受到噪音的强烈影响，因为其中依然缺少具有第三性的符号来进行规范。搬运物体或者因为疼痛而发出的喊叫具有一定的社会规约性，它只能具有某些观相，比如声音只能是“哼”“啊”这类的音型，且响度有规则——疼痛的喊叫不应是轻柔的。所以“哇”“哈哈”之类表示惊喜或者开心的声音不会成为此种具有规约性的符号解释。但是，如果声音仅仅指示出了发声者，并且不具有这些规约性的意义，那么嘴巴能够发出的任何声音都指示出了发声者的呈符性指示单符，甚至不仅仅是声音，这个人的动作也变成了此种符号。我们面对一个手舞足蹈、满口胡言的精神病患者，不会认为他乱喊乱叫发出的声音是在打招呼，或者表述某种型符、规约符的意义——至少这种意义没有得到社会的认可；这样一来，病人口中的那些原本在语言中区别语义的音素差异、语气变化，对于解释这个呈符性指示单符来说，全数成为单纯的指示意义的噪音。

声音或者行为上纯粹的呈符性指示单符似乎总有些反常态，但是对于触觉而言，这种符号就常见多了。穿着衣物时感受到的触觉，如果没有被我们忽略，那么它是一种呈符性指示单符，指示出了衣物被穿在我们身上这个状态，而没有其他的意义深度。衣物材质、湿度产生的不同触感，对这个呈符性指示单符来说是噪音，它们没有对指示衣物的状态产生作用。只有当我们意识到某个触觉明显不舒服，比如衣领处的商标没有除去而造成瘙痒感，或者跑完步衣服湿答答地黏在背上时，这些原本的噪音才成为意义的观相。但如果触觉感受到的符号呈现出了这种形态，那么它就不再是一个呈符性指示单符了，它指示了某个明确的对象（商标、湿度），并且实在地受到了对象的影响，由此成为申符性指示单符。

四、申符性指示单符

申符性指示单符除了指示对象，还能够传达符号与对象之间的关系：符号受到对象的影响。"皮尔斯在最终类型学中把这类符号称为'指明符'(designative)。这里所强调的是此类符号的解释方面，即此类符号增强了我们对该符号及其对象进行事实性以及信息性揭露的那种意识。正是由于这个原因，它的对象是更加明确的，并且其解释也是更具有事实性的。"（皮尔斯，2014，p.189）顺水漂去的树叶指示了水流的方向，就此成为一个申符性指示单符，它总是包含着一个呈符性像似单符，在像似性的基础上延伸符号与对象的关系。

符号与对象之间的自然联系被解释者发觉，从而形成了某种意义，噪音在这种符号中便是与这一层次的意义无关的观相，甚至可以产生意义的干扰。在流水与树叶这个例子中，我们感知到的树叶观相不仅仅包括了它运动的方向，还有其形状、颜色、状态（新鲜或枯萎）等，但这些都对作为申符性指示单符的树叶而言无意义贡献，成为此符号过程中的噪音。树叶运动也包含的呈符性像似单符中的噪音，流动的快慢，水中湍流造成的方向的改变，在树叶与水流的像似性层面与意义发生关联，这些观相对判断水流方向无贡献，是意义的噪音。

申符性指示单符在人与自然的关系中地位十分突出，这种关系不仅限于对自然科学的认识，更存在于宗教、仪式等对物质世界的崇拜与模仿中。例如认为绘画不仅仅是像似地再现出了人物肖像，而且通过这种像似性，保留了对象事实性的某些东西（如同绿色保留了香蕉尚未成熟的品质）；对这些指示单符的崇拜或者损毁，可以相应地在对象上产生影响。这样的观念可以追溯到拉斯科洞窟壁画中的牛，原始人认为绘画可以将牛保存下来，可以指示牛的存在，而不仅仅只是其形象的像似（贡布里希，2008，pp. 39－40）。弗雷泽在《金枝》中区分了模拟巫术和交感巫术（1987，pp. 19－21）。交感巫术针对的物体就是一个申符性指示单符，认为头发、指甲可以指示一个人，并且在巫术活动中，认为这是事实上的联系。于是一束头发就具有了申符性，将符号与对象——头发的主人联系了起来。在这样的巫术中，头发、指甲数量的多少，形态的变换，都不及它归属于谁重要，除“取自于谁”之外的观相都被可视为噪音。至于这种噪音如何影响意义，则需要通过人类学的途径进行进一步了解。

五、呈符性像似型符

皮尔斯符号的十种类别中，从第五种呈符性像似型符开始，都变成了第三性主导的型符。相比起质符和单符，型符受噪音的影响更小，因为其本身具有的第三性一定程度上纠正了噪音对意义的干扰。例如我们在讨论一个圆形的概念时可能需要画出一个圆，这个图示的圆就是受到“圆”的概念规范的型符，准确而言是一个呈符性像似型符。这个画出的图示不需要非常精准，我们也不会因为其不精准而否定它是一个圆，因而那些与“圆”这个意义无关的观相便难以对意义产生影响。

同样是呈符性的像似符，呈符性像似型符受噪音的影响就比呈符性像似单符小。呈符性像似型符用符号本身的像似性将对象的特征呈现出来，且由于其型符性，符号和对象的关系是较为确定的。对比上文黑白照片的例子，如果照片是“胜利之吻”，那么其噪音对意义的影响就很小，照片是否清晰，画面背景中各个人物的动作和神情（这些呈现噪音）都对这张照片的意义影响不大。

通过对某些呈符性像似型符的生成过程的分析，同样能够发现其中呈现噪音的隐现。将航拍图绘制成地图就是一个消除噪音的过程。航拍图是一个呈符性像似单符，其中包含着各种信息：天气、植被、建筑、马路上的汽车、行人、各种道路标识，等等。如果以呈符性像似单符的方式解释航拍图，那么寻找其中的道路就会受到各种噪音的干扰。将航拍图制成地图，则是将在其中需找路线信息、位置信息的解释方式固定下来，将其作为呈符性像似型符。这样，与之无关的大部分观相都被清理了出去，地图上只会留下建筑的轮廓、道路的分布、距离与空间位置等。更为极端的做法是地铁图，它在航拍图制成的地图基础上继续消除对特定意义没有贡献的观相，以一种便于阅读的方式标注出了站点之间的位置关系，实际上站点之间的距离，空间上的弯曲变化都被消除了。这种拓扑变换使得特定的意义更为明确，不关心实际的地形、站点的确切间距，只需解释出站点的相对位置、前后关系。也就是说，如果在一张航拍图上以呈符性像似型符——地图、地铁图的方式解释符号，那么需要排除的噪音就比航拍摄影更多，换言之，呈符性像似型符噪音更少。

六、呈符性指示型符

任何一个用作指示符的规约符都是呈符性指示型符，如医院的红十字标志，用一个规约符来指示这个建筑物是医院。红十字与医院的规约关系由《日内瓦公约》决定，是一个成文的解释规则，它与医院这个对象没有明确的像似关系，是约定俗成的符号。这便使得呈符性指示型符在建立符号与对象的联系时有了一定的自由性，如红十字标志，因为一些宗教的原因，部分地区使用红新月、红水晶和红狮子标志代替它表示医院。这种呈符性指示型符所实例化的呈符性指示单符，包含着呈符性像似单符——红色与血液像似，但符号的最终目的不是表明这种像似，而是将解释引向医院、救护组织这个对象。

红十字标志引起的宗教解释是符号受到噪音影响的一个典型例子：其由于与基督教十字架的像似而在宗教的解释体裁中产生了意义，于是红十字标志受到信奉伊斯兰教的国家和地区的抵制，他们认为那是来自异教的物品。这个符号过程中的噪音是红十字与十字架的像似观相，这个噪音在救援组织的协议建立过程中与基督教十字架的意义无关，但是转换到宗教体裁之中，被熟悉宗教的接收者解释过后，原本的噪音就成为意义的观相，对意义产生了影响。

指示代词也是一种典型的呈符性指示型符，它指示了对象，同时表明了自身与对象之间的一种简单关系。比如"这是一个烟斗"，指示代词"这"指代了"烟斗"，但同时也因为我们的约定俗成而指代了一个时间、空间距离

（与“那”相区别）。用像似符表述指示代词的内容就会变得非常困难，而且充满噪音。比如我们如果要用图像表示“这是一个烟斗”，那么可行的方法就是表示出一个烟斗的形状，如图 2 所示：

图 2　马格利特（René Magritte）《图像的反叛》（*The Treachery of Images*）

马格利特的这幅作品是一个烟斗的像似符号，看到这个图像，我们可以将其解释为“这是一个烟斗”。但作者却破除了我们的这一解释，在画作下方写上了一句：“这不是一个烟斗。”马格利特指出，烟斗是可以填满烟草的，但是他创作的这个符号不能填满烟草，因此它不是一个烟斗。对于马格利特阐述的意义而言，所有我们将此图像解释为烟斗的符号观相都是其意义的噪音，他将其作为了一个呈符性像似单符，取消了图像与所表现内容的约定俗成，因此该图取名为《图像的反叛》。

“这是一个烟斗”与《图像的反叛》体现了呈符性指示型符与呈符性像似单符在噪音影响上的强弱关系，后者噪音更多，甚至能完全从意义的噪音出发构建另外的意义，且让人信服。马格利特用这种风格的画作来对绘画的观念发起挑战，本质上就是将一个受噪音影响较小的符号转换为受噪音影响较大的符号，在皮尔斯的符号类别上通过第三性的递减来扩展意义观相的合理化空间。

七、申符性指示型符

申符性指示型符不仅将解释者的注意力引向了对象，还通过符号与对象的联系来传达信息。目录便是一个典型的例子，它是一种规约符，其约定的内容是目录列举的条目与正文内容的指示关系，也正是在这个意义上，它作为一种指示符而存在。目录不仅指示了一个章节，而且表明了章节之间的先后关系。于是，它首先包含了一个呈符性指示型符，如指示代词一样，表明这个条目的对象是一个章节；其次，它还包含了一个呈符性像似型符，通过一种规约的先后顺序来像似正文章节之间的先后顺序和逻辑关系。顺序与内容的位置出现了空间上的像似，在目录中靠前的内容会在后文中较先出现；用缩进格式与另外的规约符（小节）还可以表示次级的逻辑关系。

街上的叫卖声也是一种申符性指示型符。卖牛奶的农户大声喊叫的“牛奶”并不只是让接收者解释出“牛奶”这个对象，还要让接收者意识到这里可以购买牛奶。呈符性指示型符指明了商品的内容，而其中呈符性像似型符则通过呼喊声与叫卖声的那种一致性来传达贩售的意义（牛奶贩子总是拖着长长的声音，就像旧时其他招揽客户的商人一样）。这种符号的噪音受到两个法则的限制，因此比单独的呈符性指示型符、呈符性像似型符更不易受到影响。

对叫卖声所指示的内容而言，声音可能由于习惯而难以让人听出具体的内容。我们在街上听到那些叫卖声，有时因为方言、语调而完全不知道他们叫喊的内容是什么，这时，符号中包含的呈符性指示型符就受到了影响，对应的噪音惯性就是方言、语调等，这些观相对商贩的售卖品这个意义来说是无贡献的，在接收者听来，可能就变成了难以理解的语音。但是，即使是这样一个难以理解的语音，依然保持了它作为呈符性像似型符的特点：通过悠长独特的语调，让人明白这依然是叫卖声，只是需要进一步发现其售卖的内容，而非认为街上来了一个大喊大叫的怪人。申符性指示型符所包含的两种符号是相关联的，能够抵消部分因噪音而出现的干扰，使得符号依然保持其类型。

八、呈符性规约型符

呈符性规约型符的符号与对象之间的联系是约定俗成的，即一种习俗的、法则的联系。同时它又没有纯粹的形式，总是在具体的符号过程中实例化为一个呈符性指示单符。这即是说，规约符总是包含了一类指示符，同时如前文所说，规约符可以作为一种指示符来使用。

符号无法脱离其与对象、解释项的三元关系，任何符号都与对象相连，指示出对象。指示符的目的在于将解释引向对象，而呈符性规约型符则表达了对象的一般意义，是所有实例化的呈符性指示型符的通项。它因为符号使用的重复累积，而形成了习惯性的、法则式的解释方式，是对呈符性指示型符的一种固定的符号衍义。

语言中的名词是这种符号的典型形式。我们使用名词的时候总是将其指向一个对象（此时名词实例化为呈符性指示单符），在此之上，我们还明白名词所表达的那种一般化的意义。例如，“书”可以是一个名词，它的对象是“成本的著作”。需要注意的是，这个对象只能表示为解释项的衍义形式，所以对象本身并不是名词的解释，而我们只能将其表述为解释，否则只有重复使用名词进行循环论证。对于一个包含“书”这个名词的符号过程（如“这本书好厚”），其中的“书”所指代的内容不是一摞装订好的印满字的纸张，而是具有抽象的一般意义。哪怕说话的人手中拿着一本厚书向旁人说出这句话，旁人对名词对象的认识也是规约的，而不是针对手中书的像似符。“这本书好厚”和“这沓报纸好厚”“这沓草稿纸好厚”具有不同的意义，它们的实际呈现出来的观相可以非常相像，但是具有不同的解释项。

这样一来，呈符性规约型符受到的噪音影响就比单纯指示对象的呈符性指示单符小，因为后者可以指示不同的对象，而前者只表达其中的一般通项。试比较“这本书好厚”和纯粹用呈符性指示单符表示的这个意义：眼神指向某一本书，然后说：“好厚。”前者是更为准确的表达，后者则可能产生其他观相的影响，比如书旁边出现的其他物品、放书的桌子，甚至拿着书的人一直霸占着公有的资源（脸皮好厚）。用名词进行的表达比单纯的指示符更为准确，因为蕴含在规约符中的第三性法则已经消除了产生噪音的第三性。

一旦呈符性规约型符脱离这种符号类型的解释方式，噪音的影响就骤然增大。规约符不同于指示符，虽然符号与对象的选择是任意的（其中也可能包含了一定的像似性），但规约符建立的是第三性的法则，通过强制力将符号和对象联系起来。符号与对象之间的联系是人为建立的，可以不依赖于像似性。这种联系十分紧密，以至于一旦忽视其中的联系，符号就退化至了最为原始的呈符性像似质符，或者呈符性像似单符。面对一种完全陌生的语言或者文字时，我们遇到的就是这样的情况，未知的语言符号与对象之间的联系是被动割裂的，于是接受者只能像欣赏图画一般看到的文字，或者如聆听歌曲一般听见某段朗诵。噪音在这样的解释环境中回到了质符和单符，那些文字的线条、语言的音素在最原始的层面影响着意义，这再一次说明了噪音与第三性法则的关系。

九、申符性规约型符

申符性、呈符性规约型符之间的联系与申符性、呈符性指示型符一样，呈符性仅仅表达了对象本身，而申符性则与对象建立一种联系，以此来传递与对象相关的信息。两种申符性符号的不同在于，申符性指示符以指示出实际的对象为目的，而申符性规约符则体现了自身与这个对象的关联。

定义就是一种申符性规约型符，比如我们对书的定义：书是成本的著作。这个表述的这种定义式的逻辑形式表明了书与其一般意义的联系，是一个逻辑中的命题，将“书”与“成本的著作”联系了起来，并且传达出了两者的关系：书“就是”成本的著作。不仅仅是定义这种特定的判断形式，其他的命题也可能是申符性规约型符。例如“这是一本书”，指示代词主项与谓项“书”联系了起来，符号指示的是指示代词指代的内容，而命题这种申符性规约型符将指示代词指代的内容与“书”联系了起来，成为一个解释项。这个解释项既具有申符性单符的解释项特点，即它指示了书的存在；又将指示代词的空间性与书的存在联系起来，传达了另一种深度的意义。

申符性规约型符总是被实例化为一个申符性单符，在每一次实际的符号使用过程中，申符性规约型符再现着与所指称对象的关系，并且受到对象的实在影响。被定义的事物和定义内容的描述是相关的，并且因为事物的不同，定义的内容也有所不同，这本是再直观不过的常识，但却深刻地体现着符号类型的特点。在“这是一本书”这个例子中，指示代词所指示的内容与符号的解释密切相关，“这”可能是一本书，也可能是其他的物体，命题的主项和谓项就如同前文在申符性指示单符中提到的树叶与流水的关系一样，相互影响。

噪音对这种符号的影响，只能以干扰命题表述的形式出现，其他可能的噪音都是将符号放入了别的符号类别中进行解释。例如让“这是一本书”被理解为“这是一支笔”，我们可以由此看出申符性规约型符对噪音的抵抗力，因为这样的意义影响似乎很难实现。不过，如果不以文字形式进行表述，那么在纯粹的图像或者声音中，仍然存在这样的噪音。

十、论符性规约型符

具有论符性的符号最不易受噪音干扰，但在皮尔斯的十种类别中，只有论符性规约型符具有这种特性。皮尔斯对论符性规约型符的著述比较少，其手稿中也仅有一段详细的描述：“论符是这样一种符号，它的解释项通过法则而把其对象再现为一个‘进一步的符号’（ulterior sign）。这种法则是这样的：从所有这样的前提得出这样的结论，就将导向真相的法则。显然，它的对象必须是一般的，也即论符必须是一个规约符。因此，与规约符一样，它进而也必然是一个型符。该符号的副本是一个申符性单符。”（CP 2.254－2.264）三段论就蕴含了一个论符性规约型符，它将前提与结论联系起来。从“哺乳动物都是恒温动物；人是哺乳动物”这个大小前提，推出“人是恒温动物”的结论，论证的前提是论符的对象，而解释项则是前提的进一步符号，即论证的结论。

论符性规约型符将申符性规约型符所表述的命题联系了起来，于是它必然经由申符性规约型符而实例化为一个申符性指示单符。例如我们分辨出了某段音乐的体裁，是由先后加入的相同旋律而形成的卡农（canon），那么我们认为这段音乐具有卡农的形式——音乐的结构指示了这个体裁，并且与体裁具有事实上的联系。卡农与对话具有意义的相关性，特别是在由非复调音乐向复调变化的时候，明显地出现了一种错落的应答感。于是，卡农也是从音乐结构指向对话意义的一个申符性指示单符。面对音乐中的卡农结构，我们可以从论符性规约型符推断出的解释是：音乐含有对话的意义。

逻辑推断是最为抽象的论符性规约型符。维特根斯坦将推断解释为：“如果一定数目的命题所共有的真值基础，同时也是某个命题的真值基础，那么，这个命题的真是从另外那些命题的真得来的。”（1996，p. 63）推断的论符性将解释从一个命题引向另一个命题，并且这个过程是第三性的、规约性的，其再现体、对象、解释项同时蕴含的第三性特征使得其难以被噪音干扰，否则将导致一个逻辑出错的不可能世界。

论符性规约型符受到噪音干扰的例子很少，不过可以在假言三段论的那些反例中发现。例如：“如果这本书在图书馆的书架上，那么没有人借阅这本书；如果没有人借阅这本书，那么这本书可能遗失了；所以，如果这本书在图书馆的书架上，那么这本书可能遗失了。”三段论推理受到了论符噪音的干扰，被语境和多值影响，因而导致在两个前提都为真的情况下，结论为假。“如果这本书在图书馆的书架上，那么没有人借阅这本书”固定了一个语境，在这个语境中，“如果没有人借阅这本书，那么这本书可能遗失了”就不可能实现。这个三段论之所以推导出了错误，是因为将假言三段论能够成立的语境条件排除在外，将原本对意义做出贡献的观相视为噪音，推论由此受到了干扰。

结　语

皮尔斯对符号的分类中蕴含着第三性的递进关系，正是这个关系，让我们能够确定这些符号所受噪音的影响，并在此基础上对噪音进行大致的度量。

这种度量方式是以符号为本体的，是在讨论涉及意义问题的噪音产生与传播的一种有效、可行的噪音模型。该模型可以进一步根据66种符号的分类进行细化，确定更详细的度量类别，为符号意义的研究提供进一步的参考。当然，皮尔斯的符号类型也存在不全面之处，即仅仅从解释者的角度对符号进行现象学式的讨论。而对于一个完整的符号过程来说，符号不仅与解释者相关，还与发送者（作为解释者的发送者）、媒介等问题相关。如何将皮尔斯符号类型学基础上的噪音度量模型拓展至符号的整个传播过程，乃至与信息论的信噪比模式结合起来，有待进一步的研究。

引用文献：

巴特，罗兰（2011）．明室：摄影纵横谈（赵克非，译）．北京：中国人民大学出版社．

何一杰（2016）．噪音法则：皮尔斯现象学视域下的符号噪音研究．载于曹顺庆，赵毅衡（主编），符号与传媒，13．成都：四川大学出版社．

何一杰（2018）．无意义的意义：符号学视野下的“噪音”问题．载于曹顺庆，赵毅衡（主编），符号与传媒，17．成都：四川大学出版社．

科布利，保罗（2013）．劳特利奇符号学指南（周劲松，赵毅衡，译）．南京：南京大学出版社．

皮尔斯（2014）．皮尔斯：论符号；李斯卡：皮尔斯符号学导论（赵星植，译）．成都：四川大学出版社．

维特根斯坦，路德维希（1996）．逻辑哲学论（贺绍甲，译）．北京：商务印书馆．

贡布里希（2008）．艺术的故事（范景中，译）．南宁：广西美术出版社．

弗雷泽（1987）．金枝：巫术与宗教之研究（徐育新等，译）．北京：中国民间文艺出版社．

Peirce, C. S. (2009). *Writings of Charles S. Peirce: A chronological edition*. Bloomington, IN: Indiana University Press.

Weis, P. & Burks, A. (1945). Peirce's sixty-six signs. *The journal of philosophy*, 42(14), 383-388.

作者简介：

何一杰，博士，西华大学人文学院讲师，四川大学符号学-传媒学研究所成员，主要研究方向为符号学、叙述学。

Author:

He Yijie, Ph. D., lecturer of School of Humanities, Xihua University, member of the ISMS Research Team. His research fields are semiotics and narratology.

Email: heyijie235@163.com

中国俗文化的符号学研究*

古今歌词的平仄与音乐性

陆正兰

摘　要：音乐性一直是古今歌词（入乐的诗词）研究的一个核心问题。古今歌词的音乐性至少包括两层：一是歌词声律内在的音乐性，即语言节奏，尤其是平仄的节奏；二是歌词外在的音乐性，主要是指与音乐的配合关系。很多关于歌词音乐性的讨论将二者混杂在一起，部分原因在于中国古代记谱法不发达，歌谱资料缺失。但是仔细审视中国现代歌词的声调与音乐的匹配问题，我们可以发现，自古至今，歌词的平仄并不入乐，而是诗人以不入乐诗的格律为模式生成的“自限”。

关键词：音乐性，平仄，节奏，歌词，声调，曲调

Musicality and the Character-Tones in Chinese Lyrics Ancient and Modern

Lu Zhenglan

Abstract: Musicality has always been one of the central issues in the study of lyrics ancient or modern. It is comprised at least of two different layers: the

* 本专栏由四川大学符号学—传媒学研究所与教育部重点基地四川大学中国俗文化研究所联合主办。

textual musicality created by the prosody (in Chinese, the regulated tones of sounds), and the matching of words with the melody of the tunes. The two are often confused in the study of lyrics. The lack of convenient and accurate notation system in Chinese history has been the main reason for this confusion. But if we concentrate on the musical practice in modern times, we can see that the tones of Chinese characters are not heard once set to music. It is only the limitation that the posts-lyricists imposed upon themselves.

Keywords: musicality, tone, rhythm, lyric, melody

DOI: 10.13760/b.cnki.sam.202001011

一、关于诗词音乐性的讨论

音乐性一直是古今歌词（入乐的诗词）讨论的一个核心问题。古今歌词的音乐性至少包括两层：一是诗词声律内在的音乐性，即所说的歌词语言的节奏，尤其是平仄节奏；二是歌词的外在音乐性，即合乐性，指歌词与音乐的配合关系。但至今很多关于歌词音乐性的讨论，把二者混杂在一起。最早的诗歌，即为歌诗，或称歌词。对早期诗歌音乐性的探讨，也就容易混淆内在音乐性与外在合乐性。实际上，音乐史家讨论的更多是合乐性，王守雪称之为“自然格律”：

> 中国诗从汉到南朝齐梁时期经历了从古诗到近体的衍变，经历了从自然格律到人工格律的衍变，而其核心，则是诗歌音乐美不同内容的衍变。早期古诗中存在的自然格律，是诗乐一体音乐格调的留存，此时人们所认定的诗歌音乐美，是诗乐共同体音乐歌调的美。(2001，p.87)

刘尧民对诗歌和音乐的关系的看法也基本一致，他的总结是：上古至汉代，依乐从诗；汉至六朝，采诗入乐；隋唐以来，倚声填词。他将依乐从诗时期，即上古至汉代称为“诗歌至上的时代”，将汉之后称为“音乐至上的时代”。这个区分很有意思，因为汉代之前，诗即歌词，汉代之后，诗不一定是歌词。而诗即歌词时“诗歌至上”，音乐单出后“音乐至上”，原因主要是中国器乐的滞后发展：“器乐在后产生，而古代之器乐也不十分精良，作曲的规律方法都非常简单粗略，所以古代推重诗歌，而以器乐为附属。”他这个分析有一定道理。

在诗即歌词时，按照杨荫浏对《诗经》《楚辞》及汉乐府的分析，歌曲必然对应于一种曲式，歌词与音乐的关系非常密切。（1981，p. 57）但是最耐不起深究的是唐末诞生的词，唐圭璋在讨论词的起源时，已经指出新曲调是词产生的动力。他的看法是隋唐燕乐本不是中原汉人之音乐，五七言歌词难以相配，迫使长短句产生。由于隋唐燕乐乐谱失落，这个推论无法确证，只能想象“胡部乐”的歌词没有汉语音节那么整齐。其他文学史家也赞同这种看法，但谈到词与乐结合，施议对承认，“唐宋时代所传歌词，有词而无谱，又无法入唱，词与音乐的艺术效果，究竟如何体验，确是一大难题”。看来对这个问题的探讨，似乎从一开始就出现了尴尬。施议对书中举证《定风波》一词，是从歌词文字本身的音乐性拟猜曲调可能的状态。

问题就出在这里：所有的词学研究者，都承认词的文字有平仄规定，然而它究竟是音乐的要求，还是词人自己打制的镣铐，却难以断言。唐圭璋说得很清楚：

> 由于词乐失传，词的音律、音谱也都随之而亡失。虽经后人研究，但唐、宋人具体唱奏情况如何，仍难得其真相。清初人万树所编得《词律》，虽名为词律，实际并非词的音律。王奕清等所编的《钦定词谱》，也非词的音谱，他们考究的都只是词的文字格式。不过词的文字格式，原为配合音乐而形成的，所以直到今天，文字格式也可能作为吟咏及习作的依据。（2004，p. 211）

的确，近日“仍难得其真相”，但是，不少中国诗词音律的讨论者至今声称，他们在讨论词语言的音律时，讨论的实际上是音乐的要求，即曲调要求平仄。这个说法根据何在？这似乎混杂了诗词的内外两种音乐性。

二、“择调”与“依乐用律”

宋人在作词时的确有“择调”的说法，所谓“择调”，夏承焘认为，有三种意义，一为择宫调；二为择腔调；三为“依乐用律”。所谓宫调，就是律调，用来限定乐器声调的高下。宫调由七音十二律构成，在此基础上形成八十四宫调，它们属于音乐的调性系统。而夏承焘所说的腔调，即为词调，最早为歌谱。夏承焘、吴熊和两位先生解释为，“写作一首词必须先创制或选用一个词调，然后按照它对字句声韵的要求以词填之。这样写出的歌词方能协音，可以歌唱。所以作词叫填词，又叫做倚声”（2001，p. 20）。但问题是

“倚声”中“声”是音乐的“声”，还是文字格律要求的“声”？这两者之间的关联，是至今也未明确的难题。两位作者认为，“宋人填词，实不尽依宫调声情。如宋人做小石调的词，大都并不都是‘旖旎妩媚’的，而且每个词调即属于一定的宫调，所以作词时择宫调实际上是与择腔调联系在一起的”(2001，p. 21)。

但这一结论又遭到他们自己的否认：大部分宋词的内部平仄音律要求，实际上与曲调无关。“宋代一般词人填词主要不是为了应歌，所以填词大都并不顾腔调声情。”他们的理由来自沈括《梦溪笔谈》：

> 今声词相从，唯里巷间歌谣及《阳关》、《捣练》之类，稍类旧俗。然唐人填词，多咏其曲名，所以哀乐语声，尚相协会；今人则不复知有其矣，哀声而歌乐词，乐声而歌怨词，故语虽切而不能感动人情，由声与意不相谐故也。(沈括，2015，p. 45)

沈括是在感叹“今人”所作之曲情和词意的不协调，并没有指明词的声音和音乐腔调必须配合。实际上，沈括是认为，所谓填词的平仄声律，其实与歌谱的“倚声”相去甚远。夏承焘等所说的词的音乐性之“依乐用律”，虽然在王灼的《碧鸡漫志》、杨瓒的《作词五要》，以及张炎的《词源》中都有记载，但这些都是理论家们的一种设想和愿望，实际上对填词实践几乎没有影响。夏承焘、吴熊和直截了当地指出了宋人之谬：

> 宋人据以立说，不过附会古乐，并无实际意义。就是大晟乐府诸人及张炎等作词，也并不以此择调。因为词在宋代，虽有不少是按谱协律作为歌词而写的，但一般的词人只把它当作一种抒情的诗的形式，择调时就只考虑词式的长短句格，不再顾及宫调声情与腔调声情，“依乐用律”的更是百无一二。杨瓒、张炎等人论词提倡“依乐用律”。他们只是借古乐来妆点，以此自炫而已。(2001，p. 23)

他们的“依乐用律”目的只是“自炫”，这可能是现代文学史家对南宋词人的最严厉的指责了。夏承焘的指责非常有道理，在所有对于中国古代诗歌的音律的考证中，“倚声”之说都并没有真正依靠乐谱，很少涉及音乐研究，相反都是从诗词自身的音乐性入手的。众多专家关于词的音乐性的讨论已经表明：许多有关文字音律的考究，其实不是音乐曲调的要求。

三、古歌词平仄不入乐

问题出现在何处呢？对这些混乱说法，本文的看法，简单地说，就是平仄等只是词的内部音乐性，因为平仄不入乐。平仄节奏的起源，就是从诗不再入乐开始的。魏晋六朝“徒诗”产生，徒诗即不入乐的诗。它们既然不是歌词，写作时就不必考虑曲调。但偏偏是徒诗开始了中国诗歌关于平仄的近两千年的讲究。内部“协律”，是在诗的内部的音乐性。这种内部音乐性，已经不再是入乐的要求（因为徒诗已经不是为配歌而作），而只能向内追求语言本身的节律。此时出现的沈约“四声八病”论，是为了在拖长音节咏诗时追求“内在音乐美”，它出现在不入乐的五言诗，即所谓“永明体”律诗立足之后，而不是为歌词开的药方。

魏晋以降，随着佛经梵语的传入，音韵学兴起，为文作诗讲究音律，也是文人时尚的一种追求。沈约自炫为“妙达此旨，始可言文”。当时钟嵘对这种格律追求就有所指责：“使文多拘忌，伤其真美。”主张“但令清浊通流，口吻调利，斯为足矣。至平上去入，则余病未能，峰腰鹤膝，闾里已具”（钟嵘，1958，p. 6557）。文字讲究落实在平仄，“于是天下相风，人自藻饰，雕虫之艺，盛于时矣”（裴子野，1958，p. 6524）。沈约指责的“八病”，在钟嵘看来，本是正常。一定要算“有病”，只能说是诗人过分的自我设限而已。

到现代，朱光潜的观点就更为明确：

> 乐府衰亡以后，诗转入有词无调的时期，在词调并立以前，诗的音乐在调上见出；词既离调以后，诗的音乐性在词的文字本身见出。音律的目的就是要在词的文字本身见出诗的音乐……诗既离开乐调，不复可歌唱，如果没有新方法来使诗的文字本身上见出若干音乐，那就不免失其为诗了。音乐是诗的生命，从前外在的乐调的音乐既然丢失，诗人不得不在文字本身上做音乐的功夫，这是声律运行的主因之一。齐梁是……诗离开外在的音乐，而着重文字本身音乐时期。（1998，pp. 219－251）

朱光潜的见解非常确切，恰恰是因为不再入乐，才不得不用“新方法来使诗的文字本身上见出若干音乐”，因为平仄不是音乐对歌词的要求。章培恒、骆玉明也直截了当地判定：“声律论的提出，直接的原因，是诗歌大多已脱离歌唱，因而需要从语言本身追求音乐性的美。”（1996a，p. 386）诗歌摆脱音乐，文字走向独立，诗向书面的语言艺术转化，变成一种视觉语言、内向的语言、更个性化的语言。从历史上看，在歌词时期，诗歌反而无平仄要求。

甚至晚唐、北宋，词再度入乐，此时又不太看到写词要求合平仄的议论。直到南宋（12—13 世纪），词再次出现平仄讲究，这一问题在后来的诗歌文体学史讨论中，是最令人迷惑不解的。

北宋陈师道《后山诗话》批评苏轼“以诗为词，如教坊雷大使之舞，虽极天下之工，要非本色”。有人认为《后山诗话》是后人托名陈师道的伪作，那么“要非本色”的指责看来晚于北宋。不管怎么说，“本色”究竟是指什么，是文字风格，还是声律入乐与否？至少北宋时期，无人深论。

南北宋之交的李清照，晚于苏轼很久，才对此提出较明确的指责。李清照的《词论》说苏轼词只是“句读不箕之诗尔，又往往不协音律”。她是说苏词既不符合律诗，也不符合词的形式要求，但是李清照并没有留下文字说明词的音律应当遵循何种要求。

直到周邦彦担任大晟府提举时，“以他的音律知识并吸收民间乐工曲师的经验，搜集和审定了前代与当时流行的八十多种词调，确定了各词调中每个字的四声，甚至同为仄声的上去入都不容相混”（章培恒，骆玉明，1996a，p. 388）。对入乐之词的平仄，突然严格要求。周邦彦当这个朝廷音乐总监倒是挺尽职，反过来证明，在他之前四百年的词创作无此规定。周邦彦与沈约根本的不同是：沈约的平仄，是为早就不入乐的绝句律诗追加一番平仄讲究，周邦彦是为一开始就入乐的词追加一番平仄讲究。沈约的规定，适合徒诗的朗读，与歌无关，所以几乎一直延续至今；周邦彦以入乐为理由要求平仄，却没有解释曲调有此要求的原因。周邦彦自称是根据音乐制定平仄四声，因为词牌过多，只对应了很少一部分词牌。后世几乎每个词牌有平仄规定，是逐代累积，各种人都来制律，他们作为音乐家的资格很可疑，其平仄制律却都被后人仰视为词必须尊重的格律。

可以明确说：词的平仄规定，是词作为艺术充分发展以后出现的额外规定，曲调能否和歌词的这种平仄的音乐性应和，至今没有见到确实的研究和实践。

章培恒、骆玉明《中国文学史》中列举周邦彦《饶佛图》一词的“双拽头”部分，指出其中五个字的平仄要求合理，因为“读来抑扬变化而和谐婉转，绝无吐音不类而显得拗口的地方。这种词体本身就富于音乐美，同乐曲能完美配合”（1996a，p. 407）。他们明显是从“读”来分析歌词的平仄要求，所谓“词体本身富于音乐美”，是把词当诗读。王力质疑，宋时入声在许多方言中已经消失，周邦彦要求按各词牌填的词符合他定下的四声格律，不知所据是当时“官话”还是何种方言。

南宋的姜夔，同样讲究音律，他却要从周邦彦的平仄规定中脱身。据徐献忠《吴兴掌故》，姜夔“尝著《大乐议》，欲正庙乐”（转引自章培恒，骆玉明，1996b，p. 473），有资格挑战周邦彦。这位学有专长的音律专家，也讲究音律，但却“用各种方式创制新曲来填词，这样就比一般词人更多了一层自由，可以在保持音节谐婉的条件下，相对自由地选择句式长短及字的平仄”（1996b，p. 473）。既能作词又能作曲，姜夔就可以用曲就词，他的乐谱至今留存七首，从其词配曲的方式中，我们能总结出平仄安排的通则。宋代郑樵的总结很尖锐，他反对专讲究诗词格律而与音乐无关的诗歌：

> 古之诗曰歌行，后之诗曰古近二体。歌行主声，二体主文。诗为声也，不为文也……凡律其辞则谓之诗，声其诗则谓之歌。作诗未有不歌者也……二体之作，失其诗矣——纵者谓之古，拘者谓之律。一言一句，穷极物情，工则工矣，将如乐何？（1995，p. 888）

其意大致是说，古代的诗，被称为歌行，后代的诗分为古体诗和近体诗。诗是为了音乐，不是为了文学，讲究格律的就叫诗，诗配上音乐就叫歌。作诗正因为不是为了歌唱，才开始音律工整。

词的艺术高度发达之后，文人的自限意识开始加剧。此时，北方元曲开始兴盛，摆脱了所有这些额外的对平仄的要求，甚至韵部都用当时北方实际口语发音，韵字可以平仄通押。（章培恒，骆玉明，1996c，p. 71）正因为是用来唱的，元曲中有大量口语和衬字，关汉卿《南吕一枝花·不伏老》，一句23字，主体只有7字，加了16个衬字。在谈到元曲音韵时，现代学者任二北说：

> 且所谓曲韵者，既不如诗韵之拘牵，又不如词之泛滥，悉摈古音，较谐俗口，而又无乖废之也。惟北曲中向有入声派作平上去三声用之一法，殊不能遍合于南北人之口，则视其制度惟过去之历史，今日置而不用，仍仿词法，凡入声韵，一首之中，皆单叶之可也。（2004，p. 390）

与此同时，南戏成熟于温州一带，“村坊小曲而为之”，集合民间歌曲而成就中国式歌剧，成为中国地方戏剧的基本模式。北方杂剧有大批文人加入，南戏却被耽于作词的南方文人排斥，一直保持民间作风，直到元末高明《琵琶记》，才引来明清文人加入，传奇才主流化成为昆曲，最后有汤显祖《牡丹亭》那样文辞精致的歌剧出现。即使汤显祖这样精工细作的曲词，吴江派的沈憬也认为不合他推崇的昆曲要求。此后出现的汤沈二人的争论，现在读来变得并不重要，因为昆曲究竟有什么语音要求，现在已经说不清楚。昆曲的念白似乎混杂了多种方言，唱词大抵是半官话。到此时，平仄已经不清，曲调如何配合平仄更无从说起，汤沈之争自然没有结果。

明代民歌大兴盛，至今留下许多文人采集的民歌集。例如冯梦龙的《挂枝儿》《山歌》。这些民歌，哪怕已经经过文人采集、书写、整理，其中也找不出平仄讲究。

王力先生《汉语诗律学》以大篇幅列举词律，但是他开宗明义地指出，八百多首词的格律，大半来自清人追溯，方法是找出第一个写此词牌者的原作，依此为平仄范本，同时参照同代较后出作品，看是否有不同，如有不同，即列为“可变通”。这样的平仄是否真为音乐所要求的规律，就很难说了。大部分词牌曲调已经不传，传下来的也无法看出平仄与曲调相配的规律。因此，大部分平仄格律的延续只是出于对古人的尊重而已。

反讽的是，词的音律中最讲究的、音律家花工夫最大的平仄安排，在词歌唱时几乎完全消失。古曲保存至今，可以做仔细对比研究的典型例子是《阳关三叠》，其最早的词是王维的七言绝句《渭城曲》（又名《送元二使安西》），作为律诗，它严格遵循了平仄规律。可惜唐代《阳关三叠》的原始曲谱没能流传下来，后人对如何“叠”，不得而知。今存有 30 多种《阳关三叠》，段式各异，遑论平仄。目前所见到的《阳关三叠》曲，是以琴歌的形式保存下来的。据靳学东考证：

> 现存最早载有《阳关三叠》琴歌的，是明代弘治四年（1491 年）刊印的《浙音释字琴谱》，而目前最为人们熟悉且流行的曲谱，原载于明代《新刊发明琴谱》（1530 年），后被清代的张鹤编入《琴学入门》之中，这时的《阳关三叠》已经在王维原始的基础上，发展成包括长短句的多段体了。（2001，p. 72）

吴丈蜀《词学概说》中引用的可能是宋代的《阳关三叠》（2002，p. 9），明显是作歌词用的长短句。王维的《渭城曲》原诗只有 28 字，像一首七言绝句，而此歌词字数增加到 113 字。很多赘词明显是根据曲调的需要，在演唱时添加的。这种常被称为“散声”“泛声”和“和声”的各种赘词，才真正是音乐需要的，在汉魏乐府中就开始应用，后代越用越多，不知是否为唐代

《阳关三叠》的歌唱形式。如此多叠字之中，王维诗的内部音律就不可能显明。方成培《香研居词麈》说："唐人所歌，多五七言绝句，必杂以散声，然后可被之管弦，如《阳关》诗必至三叠而后成音，此自然之理。后来遂谱其散声，以字句实之，而长短句兴焉。故词者，所以济近体之穷，而上承乐府之变也。"周颐《蕙风词话》中也说："唐人朝成一诗，夕付管弦，往往声希节促，则加入和声。凡和声皆以实字填之，遂成为词。"

回到本文的基本论证：无论是入乐，还是作为徒诗而创作，诗词的平仄要求，更多的是诗词自身文字音乐性的需要。曲调并不需要歌词的平仄，实际上也唱不出平仄。平仄要求既然对古典歌词已经不是必需，对现代歌词就更是如此。可以这样总结：歌词讲究平仄，或许能帮助歌曲增强音乐性，但不是配曲之必需。

四、现代歌词声调不入乐

现代歌词和音乐发生最密切联系的是语言的音调。这些音调可分成声调（汉语特有的音节发音区别）、声间调（音节之间的声调对比）、句调（整个诗句的结构情绪造成的音调变化，以及诗句之间的声调对比展开）。它们常常笼统地归为歌词的"声调"，其实三者不同，应当仔细区分。

苏珊·朗格认为："歌词进入音乐时，作为一种独立的艺术品便瓦解了。它的词句、声音、意义、短语、形象统统变成音乐的元素，进入一种全新结构，消失于歌曲之中，完全被音乐吞没了。"（1983，p. 80）苏珊·朗格至少说对了一点：歌词一旦进入音乐曲调，各种声调就被乐音"重建"了。我们需要逐一探讨的是，这些不同的"调"如何被乐曲重建。

旋律与歌词的句调的关系相对简单。音乐旋律有平行旋律、上行旋律、下行旋律、弯曲旋律四大类。歌词的句调有平直、昂上、下降、弯曲四大类；很多音乐家认为，曲调每一个乐句总的进行方向和句调的前进方向往往相似。这似乎成了不言自明之理，比如孙逐明先生引用了以下三位作曲家的"体会"，来说明声调、句调和音乐的关系。

作曲家秦西弦认为，乐句与歌词的语句的语调肯定是相配的："在创作歌曲的音乐主题时，要注意音调的进行尽可能与歌词朗诵的语调的起伏达到一致，以便歌词内含有的感情能够自然地表达出来，歌词也让人听得清楚。"（1977，p. 12）作曲家余诠也持相同的看法："曲调和语调在表达感情的方式上基本是一致的。实际上，曲调的本身就包含着语调的色彩。"（1980，p. 37）

李焕之进一步认为歌词语调与曲调必须结合才能成为艺术："诗词和曲调之所以能互相结合而成为一种艺术——歌曲艺术，是因为它们之间有着互相结合的因素，这就是声调上的抑、扬、顿、挫。"（1978，p. 5）几位作曲家用的术语各异，但仔细阅读可以发现，他们说的"语调""声调"，其实都是指歌词的句调，而不是字的平仄。

句调与曲调的关系很明显，因为所谓的句调，主要是由语言、情绪决定的。歌曲首先要表达情感的诸种样式，变化、转折、起伏，至于曲调能否如秦西弦所说的"让歌词听得清晰"，没有举证说明。相反，从本文下面的讨论中可以看到，歌词的很多语音要素，入曲之后变得模糊了，甚至消失了。无论中西歌曲，要听明白歌词，都需要语境的帮助。

这里讨论的是现代汉语诗歌词中普通话的声调，不是古典汉语诗词的平仄。南宋时，平仄已经与实际发音不符，与此后的北方话更不符。现代人讨论平仄，只是一个历史语音学课题，与歌词无关。

声调是指的是音节中具有区别意义作用的音高变化，现代汉语的声调可以从调值和调类两个方面去分析。调值主要由音高构成，决定调值的并不是绝对音高，而是相对音高。一般来说，男人比女人声音低，老人比孩子声音低，即使同一个人在不同的情绪状态下，声音的高低也有差别，绝对音高的对于区别意义没有作用。同一个音"去"，一个成年人和一个儿童发的音，都是从各自的最高音到最低音，虽然儿童的最低音可能比起成年人的最高音还高，但两者变化形式和升降幅度大体相同。在一个音节之内，两个人发音时绝对音高虽然不同，但相对音高类似，所以不会产生交流障碍。

调类是声调的种类，就是把调值相同的字归纳在一起分的类。现代汉语的声调有四种，阴平、阳平、上声和去声，即为四声。阴平高而平，即由5度到5度，没有升降变化，又称高平调或55调。阳平由中音声到高音，即由3度到5度，是个高升的调子，又称高升调或35调。上声由半低音先降到低音再升到半高音，即2度降到1度再升到4度，是先降后升的调子，又称降升调或214调。去声由高音降到低音，即由5度降到1度，是个全降的调子，又称全降调或51调。在实际语流中，相邻的音节会互相影响，产生语流音变。例如，一个上声可能从214变为211，因为后面的字调值比较低。这样，声调就部分取决于声间调，但这变化并不是强制性要求，所以普通话声调可简单归纳为"一平、二升、三曲、四降"。

在音乐旋律中，也存在绝对音高和相对音高。前者指不同的音乐调性，即音乐中的24种大小调；后者指某一种调性中的乐音之间的相对升降幅度，即音程。这种相对音高和普通话的调值并不一致，可以为大三度、小三度、五度、二度、八度，等等。

从以上的分析可以清楚地看到，现代汉语普通话的声调一方面是区分语义的重要标志，另一方面给歌词语言带来了特殊的内部音乐性。于是出现可与上面的乐律学相比的问题：声调这种语言的内部音乐性是否能进入歌曲？

在歌词和旋律的配合中，一个乐音可以对应一个音节，也可以对应两个或多个音节，反之亦然，一个汉语音节可以对应几个乐音，但这两种运动形式并没有特定的配合规律。最重要的是，在汉语歌曲中，汉字的声调被曲调中的乐音“取消”，文字原有的声调无法呈现来。除非有特殊的安排，即使有重要意义区别作用的声调，在歌曲中也常常都消失了。例如《红灯记》中“提篮小卖”，就很难听出是“买”还是“卖”，听众要靠上下文的语境才能区别。又如“你知道我在等你吗?”“飞吧，飞吧，我的马”，很可能被误听为“你知道我在等你妈?”“飞吧，飞吧，我的妈”。这是字词在歌曲中声调消失弄出的笑话。

对这种情况，歌曲翻译家薛范先生谈得非常具体，他称其为“倒字”现象（2002，pp. 137－138），即旋律线条（音高和进行）与歌词的声调不匹配。他列举的歌词是“你是灯塔，你是舵手”。“灯塔”和“舵手”的字调都是由高向低，而曲调在五度上行大跳，恰恰与字调颠倒，使这两句听起来就成了“你是等他，你是躲寿”。

事实上，这种“倒字”现象不可避免，匹配才是例外。在歌词中声调消失是普遍的、正常的情况。听者理解歌词，要脱离声调从语境上猜想。奇怪的是：尽管绝大多数歌曲并不跟着声调走，但很多论者还一直强调声调与音乐的匹配。中国现代音乐史上，赵元任最系统地做过声调与音乐相配实践。赵元任曾批评学堂乐歌时期的作曲家沈心工“因为没有把汉语声调这一音素考虑在内，所以声调的升降和旋律的高低往往不合拍，既难唱又难懂”（榎本泰子，2003，p. 18）。这是否重复了李清照批苏轼的旧例？赵元任自己的《新诗歌集》24 首歌曲中，据称有 22 首注意到音乐与声调相配。（榎本泰子，2003，p. 13）但实际上，正如赵元任自己所说，24 首歌中，“只有第 4 首是略为模仿普通话的四声，还有第 6 首中最后的阴上声，听起来似乎像普通话的上声”（见赵元任，1994，p. 13，注释 8）。赵元任所说的声调，其实包含两个意思，正如他自己的分析：

一层由于中国古老的音乐的传统，二层由于方言的声调的关系，作曲家们有一个公认的处理歌词声调的规则就是按照传统的分类法，

> 把声调归纳为平仄两类，这样凡是遇到平声字旋律就用比较长一点的音或是略微下降的几个音。凡是遇到仄声字的时候，旋律上就用比较短也比较高的音，或是变动很快、跳跃很大的音。（1994，p. 1）

仔细分析，赵元任处理的，并不完全是单纯的声调问题，他注重的实际上是声间调，即相邻音节之间声调的相对变化。旋律的高低对声调配合的要求，指的是声间调的要求。可以取其代表作《叫我如何不想她》分析一下：

3|	5—	3	5 |	5—	6 |	5— |	（旋律）
天	上	飘	（着）	些	微	云	（歌词）
55	51	55	（51）	55	55	35	（调值）

看得出来，赵元任的有意处理并没有做到字字合乐。比如，51 调的“上”和旋律中的“5”，只是发音的开始一致，乐音要求保持“5”的高度，而 51 调的“上”在音乐中并没有从 5 降到 1，所以实际发音为 55 调的“伤”。“云”也是如此。赵元任自己也未完全做到声调的升降与旋律高低的匹配。

赵元任在谱曲时真正考虑的，是声调之间的对比，即声间调。因此，“微”“云”二字调值为 55—35，谱曲为 6—5，“云”相对低一些。但即使声调间的对比，这个乐句中也只有这两个音节被照顾到了，其他的声间调与音乐无关，例如开头的“天上”二字，调值为 55—51，音乐为 3—5，旋律既没有配合声调，也没有配合声间调。

总之，即使自觉如赵元任，在有意以法则为例所作的歌中，声调、声间调与音乐配合的例子，数量也太少，构不成统计学上的意义。自己的例子都不够多，如何成规律？绝大部分现代歌曲的音乐，与声调或声间调无关。正如赵元任总结的那样：“中国现代的作曲家，多半是不受任何歌词声调的限制的，只是很少成份是受到一点作曲家自己的乡音或是文学上的影响。”（1994，p. 12）

我们可以看到，歌词声调可以进入歌曲的音乐，但是在实践中，基本上不与音乐相配。所以说，在歌中，声调与声间调基本消失；字的声调与歌曲无关。从声乐艺术发展来看，比较注意声调的演唱，大部分出现在弹词、评书，以及当代的说唱中，也有歌剧中几近说话的宣叙调，以及像刘大白《卖布谣》、民歌《小白菜》这样极少数接近说话语调的歌唱，这些都是半念半唱，念唱并不入曲，所以声调往往念得很准。循推古例，入乐的汉乐府不讲究声调平仄，而后来的诗歌一旦不入乐，就开始寻找自身的平仄格律。这个现象背后的原因就是歌词一旦入乐，字本身的声调就消失了，不必也无从讲究。

现代作曲者，是否依字的声调高低谱曲？现代词作者，有没有特别注意字的声调？声调为汉语所特有，将来是否会有一种真正意义上“声调歌曲”出现，这超出了我们的想象。笔者至今没有找到足够证据推导出结论，为了避免一概否定一些词曲家的理想追求，这里只能说：当代歌诗，一般不追求特殊的声调安排。

引用文献：

榎本泰子（2003）. 乐人之都——上海，西洋音乐在近代中国的发轫（彭谨，译）. 上海：上海音乐出版社.

靳学东（2001）. 中国音乐导览. 北京：人民音乐出版社.

朗格，苏珊（1983）. 艺术问题（滕守尧等，译）. 北京：中国社会科学出版社.

李焕之（1978）. 歌曲创作讲座. 北京：人民音乐出版社.

裴子野（1958）. 雕虫论. 载于严可均（编），全上古三代秦汉三国六朝文·全梁文（卷五十三）. 上海：中华书局.

秦西炫（1977）. 作曲浅谈. 北京：人民音乐出版社.

任二北（2004）. 散曲之研究. 载于王小盾，杨练（编），词曲研究. 武汉：湖北教育出版社.

沈括（2015）. 梦溪笔谈·乐律一（金良年，点校）. 上海：中华书局.

唐圭璋（2004）. 历代词学研究述略. 载于王小盾，杨栋（编），词曲研究. 武汉：湖北教育出版社.

王守雪（2001）. 从音乐格调到语言声律——中国诗格律化的逻辑. 载于徐中玉，郭豫适（编），古代文学理论研究，19. 武汉：华中师范大学出版社.

吴丈蜀（2002）. 词学概说. 北京：中华书局.

夏承焘，吴熊和（2001）. 读词常识. 北京：中华书局.

薛范（2002）. 歌曲翻译探索与实践. 武汉：湖北教育出版社.

杨荫浏（1981）. 中国古代音乐史稿（上）. 北京：人民音乐出版社.

余铨（1980）. 歌词创作简论. 上海：上海文艺出版社.

章培恒，骆玉明（1996a）. 中国文学史（上卷）. 上海：复旦大学出版社.

章培恒，骆玉明（1996b）. 中国文学史（中卷）. 上海：复旦大学出版社.

章培恒，骆玉明（1996c）. 中国文学史（下卷）. 上海：复旦大学出版社.

赵元任（1994）. 中国语言的声调、语调、唱读、吟诗、韵白、依声填词和不依声填词. 载于赵元任音乐论文集. 北京：中国文联出版公司.

郑樵（1995），通志二十略·乐略第一·正声序论（王树民，点校）. 上海：中华书局.

钟嵘（1958），诗品. 载于严可均（编），全上古三代秦汉三国六朝文·全梁文（卷五十五）. 上海：中华书局.
朱光潜（1998）. 诗论. 北京：生活·读书·新知三联书店.

作者简介：

陆正兰，四川大学文学与新闻学院教授，博士生导师，研究方向为中国诗词、艺术符号学。

Author:

Lu Zhenglan, professor of College of Literature and Journalism, Sichuan University. Her research fields include song lyrics and semiotics of art.

Email: luzhenglan69@163.com

黔中屯堡社会中礼乐文化的符号表征及其传播特质*

谢清果　陈　瑞

摘　要：黔中屯堡的形成源于朱元璋的南征北调之举，屯堡人随屯军由江南迁徙而至，生产生活耕战并举。黔中屯堡社会形态在政治、历史变迁中能够较好地保存，除了经济因素，更得益于其礼乐文化符号系统的传承及其独特的传播结构。从元符号到仪式符号再到符号的传播媒介，散布于其中的符号具有系统性，且深受礼乐文化的浸润。其礼乐文化符号传播的偏心圆结构、时空诉求、风吹草偃的进程等特点，以及深植于礼乐文化中族群认同、社会教化、政治自保等传播效果，共同促成了黔中屯堡数百年不衰的景象。

关键词：黔中屯堡，礼乐符号，符号媒介，传播特点，传播效果

Symbols of Rites and Music Culture and its Communication Characteristics among the Tunpu in Central Guizhou

Xie Qingguo　Chen Rui

Abstract: The presence of the Tunpu in central Guizhou originated from Zhu Yuanzhang's move to the south of the Yangtze river. The Tunpu people then moved from the south of the Yangtze river with the Tun army. Their way of life and production is both military and agricultural. In addition to economic factors, the social form of the Tunpu in central

* 本文为国家社科基金一般项目“华夏文明传播的观念基础、理论体系与当代实践研究”（19BXW056）成果之一。

Guizhou has been well preserved through political and historical changes, benefiting from the inheritance and unique transmission structure of a symbolic system of rites and a musical culture. These symbols, from meta-symbols to ritual symbols to media symbols, are systematic and deeply rooted in the traditional culture of rites and music infiltration. The eccentric circle structure, spatio-temporal demand, the process of wind and grass in the communication of rites and musical cultural symbols, and the communication effects of ethnic identity, social education and political self-preservation, all of which are deeply rooted in the ritual and music culture, have contributed to the enduring image of the Tunpu in central Guizhou for hundreds of years.

Keywords: Tunpu in central Guizhou, symbols of ritual and music, symbolic medium, communication characteristics, communication effects

DOI: 10.13760/b.cnki.sam.202001008

一、屯堡与屯堡文化研究的符号学转向

明代军事屯田的生产组织以屯为基本单位，在边地为防御敌人的侵略，合几个屯或屯所，建立一个屯堡（王毓铨，2009，p.186）。黔中屯堡的形成源于明太祖朱元璋的南征北调之举。为了统一并稳固西南地区，朱元璋广设军屯，黔中腹地作为入滇之咽喉，其军屯的设置在军事战略上显得尤为重要。据《安顺府志·风俗志》载："屯军堡子，皆奉洪武敕调北征南……散处屯堡各乡，家人随之至黔""屯堡人即明代屯军之裔嗣也"。由此形成了贵州颇具特色的屯堡社会，世代生活于其中的屯堡人不是当地百姓，而是随屯军迁移而来的。范增如的《明代普定卫戍屯官兵原籍考》考证黔中军屯人家的原籍多在江苏、安徽、江西三省区。（2009，p.93）他们闲时耕种，战时出兵，生产生活耕战并举，是贵州颇具特色的族群之一。屯堡文化至今经过六百余年的积淀，在世代传承中得到了极好的保存。

在全球化的背景下，民族、地域的文化研究越来越受到重视，彰显地区特色成为应对全球化的有力举措。"黔中屯堡文化是目前国内最具特色的一种地域文化"（朱伟华，2008，p.1），吸引了大批学者，尤其是贵州学者群展开研究，并得到当地政府的支持与重视，相关研究近二十年来取得了尤其丰硕的成果。从社会学角度展开的研究如孙兆霞等著《屯堡乡民社会》基于大量

的田野调查，侧重于对屯堡社会的考察和描写，并对屯堡乡民社会的现代发展提出思考；《屯堡社会如何可能——基于宗教视角的考察》对屯堡社会宗教与社会生活的关系问题进行阐释。从文化及文学的角度，朱伟华《建构与生成——屯堡文化及地戏形态研究》在对屯堡文化、经济进行探讨的基础上着重研究地戏；《黔中屯堡民间文学与传统文化研究》的研究对象扩展至屯堡的山歌、花灯、民族文化交融及传统文化教育等方面。相关论文集有李建军主编，贵州省屯堡研究会、贵州省屯堡文化研究中心编《学术视野下的屯堡文化研究》、《屯堡文化研究》（多卷本）等，对大量学术论文进行汇编。相关学位论文有中央民族大学博士留学生卢百可的《屯堡人：起源、记忆、生存在中国的边疆》，从历史与叙事的角度，系统地梳理了明代、清代、民国、当下的屯堡人及屯堡社会的发展与变迁。研究资料汇编有安顺市政协编《安顺文史资料（第二辑）·屯堡文化专辑》，包含屯堡文化的形成和发展、屯堡家谱、家族村寨名人简介等大量基础资料，为屯堡研究者提供了极大的便利。此外，《六百年屯堡——明王朝遗民纪事》《河里的石头滚上坡——贵州安顺屯堡民居》等以生动的形式对屯堡的风土人情进行图文并茂的呈现。综上研究成果可见，鲜有学者从传播学的角度对黔中屯堡进行研究，研究内容鲜有涉及屯堡古诗文。

在政治的风云变化中，为何黔中屯堡社会形态能够得到较好的保存？首先经济因素必不可缺。王毓铨《明代的军屯》对于内地少数民族地区的屯田，以贵州为例，指出“贵州设都司，建卫所，开置屯田，早在洪武十一年，在正统六年以前，贵州等二十卫的屯地池塘共达九十五万七千六百余亩，所收子粒，据说足给军食”（2009，p.26）。由此可见，中央政府对于贵州军屯势力在物质上给予了充分保障。同时，“贵州的屯田赋税并不重，赋税不重就不会出现军士民户逃亡，其聚落的文化强势就不但不会被分化瓦解，反而会更强”（朱光文，2011，p.90）。来自江南的屯堡人，带来了较为先进的生产力，能够获得物质上的自足。政府在经济上的优待、物质生活上的充分保障，促使远徙而来的屯堡人形成落地生根、安居乐业的观念。此外，屯堡的长久存续更得益于屯堡社会的文化形态、时空格局、传播结构等。本文拟从黔中屯堡社会中礼乐文化的符号表征传统及其传播的角度，探讨黔中屯堡社会形态及其文化得以百年长存的根源。

从符号学角度而言，屯堡文化本质上是一整套中华礼乐文化在黔中地区的在地化符号表征。具体说来，无论是屯堡地戏、祭祀，还是生活仪式、古诗文等一系列符号化呈现，均建构起黔中地区中华礼乐文化中独特的屯堡文化的传播形态。我们力图透过对它的礼乐符号表征系统的深入剖析，展现其背后的意义网络。

二、黔中屯堡文化的礼乐符号表征

黔中屯堡社会数百年不衰，得益于其自身的文化构成。黔中屯堡社会形成于江南地区的军民迁移，在六百余年的历史中始终恪守儒家文化的传统，形成一整套独特的文化、礼仪、习俗、信仰、娱乐方式等，其中体现出大量的礼乐文化因素，并在屯堡社会内部得到广泛认同、遵守和传播，对屯堡社会的稳定存续产生决定性的影响。黄星民《礼乐传播初探》中认为“礼乐传播中的‘礼’，主要指的是在各种场合下举行的各种礼仪；礼乐传播中的‘乐’，不仅只是音乐，还包括诗歌、舞蹈等艺术形式”（2000a，p. 27）。丁鼎认为“礼的本质是‘序’，即等级、秩序；乐的本质是‘和’，即和合、和谐”（2014，p. 67）。结合这样的界定，本文将立足屯堡地戏、祭祀、生活仪式、古诗文等礼乐文化传播的多元符号载体，探讨屯堡社会的礼乐文化的符号表征与传播过程。

（一）人与神同乐：屯堡地戏中的礼乐符号

地戏即跳神，是屯堡村寨特有文化艺术形态，是公认的屯堡的文化标签。郑正强《屯堡民俗奇观——地戏》认为黔中地戏是由“明初戍屯的将士从江淮故地引入并发展起来的”（2002，p. 128）。“地戏起源于军傩”的观点恰恰体现了地戏礼乐精神的渊源。“傩”是一种有一定组织、一定仪式、一定规模的驱逐疫鬼的活动。《周礼》对“傩”有明确记载，《周礼·夏官司马第四·方相氏》曰：“方相氏掌蒙熊皮，黄金四目，玄衣朱裳，执戈扬盾，帅百隶而时难，以索室驱疫。”“大丧，先柩。及墓，入圹，以戈击四隅，驱方良。”（杨天宇，2004，p. 451）这段文字介绍了蒙着熊皮、戴着面具、着玄衣朱裳、拿着武器戈与盾舞动的方相氏，带领百隶行傩法驱逐疫鬼以保一方安宁的场面。此驱疫傩仪发生于宫廷，细分当为宫廷傩，属宫廷仪式。军傩与宫廷傩的最大区分在于傩仪所举行的场所不同，但两者在精神内核上同根植于礼乐文化。《论语·乡党》曰：“乡人傩，朝服而立于阼阶。”朱熹注“傩虽古礼而近于戏”（1983，p. 121），肯定了傩的古礼性质，“朝服而立”体现其严肃庄重。屯堡人在军傩元素的基础上，结合江南母源地的文化记忆，在特殊的历史时期及特定的生存处境中，根据族群生存及情感的需要，在屯堡社区内创造了形式独特的屯堡文化形式——地戏，是对傩之礼乐内涵的传承。

地戏的演出不设舞台，一般就地进行，以说唱为主，或有舞蹈为伴，伴奏的乐器采用的是铜锣、皮鼓等打击乐器，不染丝弦，不惹柔靡，一般一锣一鼓。打击乐器以其便于携带、发音铿锵激昂等特点，曾被广泛用于军旅，以鼓舞士气、激发斗志。地戏的伴奏乐器锣鼓等体现了屯堡人与军事活动的关联及耕战并举的生存境况，同时作为礼乐元素嵌入屯堡文化之中。项阳《以乐观礼》视鼓吹乐（打击乐器与吹奏乐器）为“礼乐重器”，“进入国家礼制之中”，“汉魏以降，鼓吹成为国家礼仪所必备”。（2015，p. 139）鼓吹乐作为国家礼制中的礼乐重器，能够突破阶级的局限，突破宫廷的范围，下移至地方与民间，使之成为普天之下不论贵贱都能使用的礼乐。于是“地方百姓在接衍传统文化中的五礼观念之时，其所能够接触到的更多是国家礼乐中上下相通的鼓吹乐形态”（项阳，2015，p. 20）。沟通朝野的鼓吹乐器为屯堡地戏以打击乐器锣鼓伴奏提供了可能性。作为非语言传播符号的锣鼓，以乐的形式成为地戏文化系统中的重要部分，是礼乐传播的重要载体，也体现出与礼乐文化的内在协同性。

地戏的表演者在演出过程中，不论性别与角色，一律面蒙青纱。由于地戏的演出不设舞台，观众常于高处观看，因此面具置于额上而非覆于面部，而为裸露的面部遮以青纱，以为观者呈现更好的视觉效果。地戏表演者所戴的面具又被称为“脸子”，是地戏的关键要素、精髓之所在。脸子的制作极为考究。根据《地戏面具雕制艺术概观》的记述：“（脸子）在制作时有一套宗教仪式。匠人开凿之前要用禽血祭奠工具，口念一些祝祷的词语。当面具制作完毕后，要举行庄严的‘开光’仪式，将面具供于神龛上，用鸡血点在上边，赋予其神性。”（李端丕，2002，p. 190）朱伟华认为“地戏中的正将往往被视为神，认为他们有驱逐恶魔之威，有赐福纳吉之力”（2008，p. 230），由此，地戏脸子寄寓了人们的美好愿景。脸子制作过程中这一整套的宗教仪式赋予其以神秘色彩和象征意义，屯堡人认为面具代表神灵，体现了“宗教性礼乐”（褚春元，2017，p. 49）的特征。而戴上脸子、青纱遮面进行表演的人，已经超越个体而成为富有寓意的被神化了的英雄化身，是被敬仰、被崇拜的对象。地戏在娱人的同时也达到娱神的重要目的，借此实现人际关系、神人关系的和谐与沟通，是原始礼乐文化的折射。

不同人物角色的脸子造型，整体上体现出一种写实、夸张与节制并存之美，避免对人物面相的过度扭曲与变形，使之夸张而不失真实。此外，头盔和耳翅也是脸子的重要组成部分。头盔包括龙凤装饰、吉语装饰、星宿装饰等，耳翅犹如垂肩之双耳，其造型、图案与头盔相互映衬，能够达到浑然一体而不突兀的效果。脸子整体呈现的浑然之美正是符合礼乐传统的美。李泽厚认为礼乐传统视角下的美是一种儒家所谓“发乎情止乎礼义”的包容、和谐的美，“乐从和”，“乐”追求适度地相互调节、协同、沟通和均衡。（2007，p.49）地戏作为一种艺术形式，其关键要素脸子呈现的和谐之美恰恰体现礼乐之美。“脸”即“面”，普通脸子又可理解为面子、脸面，现代汉语中二者意义相近，而在中国传统文化语境中，脸子、面子的含义又远远超越脸、面的实指范围而具有更多的社会意义及文化意义。谢清果教授认为面子是华夏人际传播的独特媒介，行为符合礼的规范便会有一定的颜面，便会有面子（2017，pp.104—105），即面子的获得来源于对礼的遵守。戴上脸子开始地戏表演的屯堡人代表神的形象，实现了人与神的角色转换，在表演中同时发挥了娱人与娱神的作用，满足了受众驱魔与祈福的心理期待，在与族群的互动中得到认可，获得个人的尊严与荣誉，在尊礼的基础上获得面子、脸面。地戏之脸子与传统文化之面子相呼应，体现出作为面具的脸子就其本身意义而言与尊礼的一致性。

（二）敬神与尊祖：屯堡祭祀中的礼乐符号规范

祭祀之风由来已久，成为滋养中国古代传统文化的沃土。李泽厚认为礼“起源和核心则是尊敬和祭祀祖先”（2017，p.206，p.215）。《周礼・春官宗伯第三・大宗伯》曰：“大宗伯之职，掌建邦之天神、人鬼、地示之礼以佐王建保邦国。”“以吉礼事邦国之鬼神示。”（杨天宇，2004，pp.274—275）大宗伯是掌管对天、地之神即人鬼的祭祀之礼的官职，古礼分为吉、凶、宾、兵、嘉五大类；将吉礼用于祭祀，并将吉礼即祭祀之礼置于五礼之首，可见统治阶级对祭祀的重视与推崇。《礼记・祭统》曰：“凡治人之道，莫急于礼。礼有五经，莫重于祭。”（王文锦，2018，p.631）“祭”为“礼”之重要内涵，为治国、治人之头等大事。纵观春秋时期的社会活动，“祭祀当为两周礼乐文化的核心”（褚春元，2017，p.96）。黔中屯堡社会中祭祀之风极为盛行，是屯堡人生活中必不可少的组成部分，其中规模最大、最为隆重的祭祀活动集中在春节和清明节，分别是祭神活动“抬汪公”及祭祖活动“上坟”。江南地区迁徙而来的黔中屯堡人，把对江南礼乐文化的记忆融入屯堡生活，其祭祀活动带有明显的文化移植的痕迹。

“抬汪公”举行于春节后正月间，不同村寨时间不一。汪公，史有其人：朝廷中人，忠君爱民，义正英勇，深受百姓敬仰。在政府奖掖和民间附会流传的基础上，人们对汪公的态度由爱戴转为信仰，汪公的形象完成了由人到神的转变。后人为其修祠建庙，将其作为神明崇拜祭祀。江南地区迁徙而来的屯堡人把母源地的汪公信仰移植入了屯堡社会，为汪公建庙塑像，定期祭祀，表达对母源地文化的认同，以此作为寄托故土之思的形式，也向朝廷彰显了身为屯军的政治姿态。汪公庙作为“抬汪公”祭祀活动的核心公共空间，要举行完整的仪式，公祭是整个仪式的重头戏，有仪式主持、唱念赞词、鸣锣击鼓、奏乐鸣炮、三跪九叩等环节，“整个程式跟中国传统的祭祀礼仪包括宫廷的祭祀礼仪相类似”（郑正强，2002，p. 199）。接下来有宗族祭祀，最后是村民献祭。在汪公庙中的祭祀完成后，次日抬汪公巡游。巡游路线始于汪公庙，沿中心大街至神台，最后返回庙堂，回归本位，整个祭祀活动结束。巡游之前还有一场祭祀，巡游仪仗盛大，众多表演队各有千秋。对信仰神祭祀本身即是一种礼乐文化，巡游过程突破庙堂这一祭祀场域，更是以一种无声的语言向屯堡人的信仰宣誓，是对汪公精神及其所代表的礼乐文化要素的认同与接受，也是基于自身政治身份的一种自我激励、族群建设。

族制是中国古代文化的重要内容，族制之下有孝悌等人伦之规，以承奉养、祭祀之责。《礼记·祭统》曰：“孝子之事亲也，有三道焉：生则养，没则丧，丧毕则祭。养则观其顺也，丧则观其哀也，祭则观其敬而时也。”（王文锦，2018，p. 632）强调古者“孝”的原则，恭敬并定期的祭祀是其中之一。屯堡人重祭祀，祭祀活动多样、频繁、持续时间长，除了家庭祭祀、宗族祭祀之外，规模最大、影响范围最广也最为隆重的当为清明节的上坟。最具地域特色的清明节“上大众坟”的祭祀对象为入黔始祖或同姓始祖，在天南地北开枝散叶的屯堡人都要回乡祭祖，祭祀队伍极为庞大。组织者会做好各项准备工作的分工安排，在祭祀前筹集资金，各家出份子钱，购买物资，在大众坟茔附近生火做饭，供祭祀参与者就地聚餐。大众坟的存在源自屯堡特殊的社会结构。“屯堡社区的社会结构不是单纯以血缘或地缘为基础，而是发生学意义上的地缘关系与后来族群内通婚形成的准血缘关系二者结合的产物。”（孙兆霞，等，2005，p. 47）屯堡社会形成于移民，共同的母源地及移民地构成了屯堡社会的地缘因素；在地缘的基础上，圈内婚姻产生新的血缘关系。费孝通在《血缘和地缘》中认为“血缘和地缘的合一是社区的原始状态”（2016，p. 80），“血缘是身份社会的基础，而地缘却是契约社会的基础”（p. 85）。屯堡社会的地缘关系是从政治或军事里发展来的，其约定的是屯堡人对源自母源地文化的屯堡文化的认同、接受与遵守，清明节上大众坟是对血缘和地缘共同建构的屯堡祭祀文化的写照，是礼乐传统中祭祀文化的体现。

（三）边缘中的主流：屯堡生活礼俗中的礼乐符号传承

古时屯堡在黔中，周边多是少数民族，即便有汉族，也鲜有来往，且与周边民族处于对立状态，社区处于相对封闭、孤立的状态，同时在政治上与朝廷关系微妙，有着日渐边缘化的趋势，整体而言是在少数民族聚居地处于边缘状态。而作为江南汉族移民群，屯堡人自身的文化与汉文化的传统、官方正统文化是一致的，代表着官方主流文化，因此表现出处境的边缘化及文化的主流化。屯堡人对其母源地的礼俗文化进行迁移，坚持传统，恪守礼仪，在生活的重要场合注重礼仪与仪式，此处具体指生活礼俗，如贯穿人一生的诞生礼、成人礼、婚礼、丧葬礼等。

诞生礼是宣告和庆祝新生命诞生的礼仪，尤其是一个家庭的第一个孩子的诞生礼，庆典隆重。生子庆贺的习俗由来已久，《礼记·内则》载："子生，男子设弧于门左，女子设帨于门右。三日始负子，男射女否。"（王文锦，2018，p. 350）《礼记·射义》："男子生，桑弧蓬矢六，以射天地四方。天地四方者，男子之所有事也。"（王文锦，2018，p. 841）《诗经·小雅·斯干》"乃生男子，载寝之床。载衣之裳，载弄之璋。其泣喤喤，朱芾斯皇，室家君王。乃生女子，载寝之地。载衣之裼，载弄之瓦。无非无仪，唯酒食是议，无父母诒罹。"（程俊英，2019，p. 198）古人根据新生儿的性别悬挂有象征意义的"弧"（木弓）、"帨"（配巾）等物件，以庆祝新生命的诞生，并表示日后需给予不同的物质条件，结合社会文化及时代风尚，赋予不同的角色期待。屯堡社会以"做大客"作为诞生礼的主要内容和形式载体。做大客由夫家和娘家联合操办，邀请亲友参加，表达人们对新生儿及其家庭的美好祝福和期盼，答谢对新生儿的美意，参与者多为女性成员，包括血缘关系下的亲属及地缘关系下的邻里。做大客包括送礼、宴请等庆贺内容，完成新生儿诞生的信息传播及生存意义空间的建构。关于族制，吕思勉《中国文化史》认为，"一姓的人口渐繁，又行外婚之制，则同姓的人，血缘不必亲，异性的人血缘或转向接近"（2014，p. 27）。新生儿使婚姻结合的两姓家族之间有了血缘关系，是连接两姓家族血缘的纽带，强化了家族联结。做大客恰是对这种关系的确认，女性的主导地位也体现出姻亲结合下的家族互动关系。

屯堡成年礼以"剃头"仪式为载体。剃头的日子要结合父亲与儿子的生辰八字来选定。需先做好充分的准备，经过念经、剃头、换新衣、拜忏、摆八仙桌、分发食物等环节（孙兆霞，等，2016，p. 225），完成剃头仪式，并结合仪式进行宴请。头发自古具有象征意义，无论是"身体发肤受之父母，不能有所损毁”的孝道意义，还是“留头不留发”的政治、民族认同的意义。屯堡人的剃头仪式也象征着从幼年到成年的过渡，随之而来的是家庭、社会责任的担当。《礼记·曲礼上》有“男子二十，冠而字”（王文锦，2018，p.16），意思是举行冠礼，并赐以字。冠礼，就是把头发盘成发髻，谓之“结发”，然后再戴上帽子，《说文》认为“冠，弁冕之总名也，谓之成人”。男子行冠礼说明他到了成人年龄，可以婚娶。行冠礼需“筮日筮宾”，对于吉日选择与参与嘉宾极为讲究。《礼记·内则》曰：“女子……十有五年而笄。”（王文锦，2018，p.358）女子年满十五为及笄，表示已经成人，可以嫁人。屯堡的剃头与《礼记》中的冠礼、及笄具有相对一致的意义，都是成年的象征符号。以“头发”作为象征符号而开展的成人礼可谓是古今一致、异曲同工！不同的是《礼记》中的“成年”是可以婚配的年龄，而屯堡社会的“成年”是人生阶段——从幼年到青年的转变，意味着更大的活动空间与更多的责任，与婚姻尚没有直接的关联。如果说诞生礼是对个体存在的一种宣告与接纳，成年礼则是对个体独立的一种认可。

婚姻是不同种族、地域、文化背景的人们生活亘古不变的主题，自古“合两姓之好”“结秦晋之好”，以传宗接代最为宗族所重视。就嫁娶而言，传统文化中向来有严格的程序、仪式、禁忌等规范，也是礼乐文化的重要内容。《仪礼·士昏礼》中记述了士娶妻成婚的礼节仪式，即六礼：纳采、问名、纳吉、纳征、请期、亲迎，涵盖了从提亲到迎亲全过程，在礼制的约束下，一度成为约定俗成的规范。屯堡人对传统的婚姻习俗极为讲究，遵守着古老仪式的既定传统。李尚林《五官屯人婚嫁之“六礼”》通过田野调查，将五官屯人的婚配过程之六礼梳理为：一礼媒人介绍、二礼回口信、三礼发八字、四礼订婚、五礼送日子（报佳期）、六礼接亲，与《仪礼》中成婚之六礼相对应，可见其对传统婚姻礼仪的集成，只是因时代、地域及婚配对象的不同，在具体内容上有所不同。屯堡人婚礼的仪式在嫁方与娶方分别举行，均办酒宴请，接受亲朋贺喜。婚礼的礼节和仪式在很大程度上是建立在屯堡人共通的意义空间基础之上的，是一种象征性的社会互动，是一种新的社会单位、家族地位的建构。中国历来是一个尚礼社会，“礼是社会公认合式的行为规范……维持礼这种规范的是传统”（费孝通，2016，pp.55-56）。屯堡社会的婚姻礼仪是对传统之礼的继承与延续，依靠传统力量推行。

丧葬礼是为生命终结之人举办的礼仪，“是一种完全他历的礼俗，而且与信仰密切相关”（陈华文，2014，p.190），与灵魂信仰、祖先崇拜的思想密切相关，充满着神秘感与宗教气息。礼仪以死者为核心，聚集着最亲近的人及亲朋邻里，彰显的是活着的人的孝道及聚合力。屯堡人的丧葬礼仪尤为复杂冗长，过程中颇多讲究与忌讳，其与诞生礼、成人礼、婚礼一道贯穿人的一生，共同根植于浓厚的传统礼乐文化土壤，是屯堡人生活礼俗的重要内容。

（四）家与国之情怀：屯堡古诗文中的礼乐符号精神

屯堡古诗文是指明清时期屯堡人所创作的，以及非屯堡人创作但与屯堡相关的古文、古诗等文学作品。目前研究者对屯堡古诗文鲜有涉足，成果罕见。《安顺文史资料汇编》列出《屯堡古诗文选辑》一部分，内容包括散文、古诗、楹联等，笔者将以此为依据对屯堡古诗文中所蕴含的礼乐精神略做探讨。总体而言，屯堡古诗文中的礼乐精神主要体现在于家尚“和”、于国尚“忠”两个方面，具有浓郁的家国情怀。家与国是礼乐社会中“夫妻”“父子”“君臣”宗法等级制度的产物，强调家庭和谐、忠君爱国。蕴含着浓郁家国情怀的古诗文是屯堡人精神、情感的内向表达与外向传播的有效载体。

屯堡古诗文彰显出对家庭和谐的推崇。胡纲作《顾夫人俞氏圹志》出土于九溪村，俞氏乃征南将领顾成长子顾统之妻。文中记载俞氏“自幼有淑质”“在家以孝闻”，与丈夫“相敬如宾”“良多内助”，“奉舅姑至谨，待婢妾以恩，衣服饮食务从简朴”（贵州省安顺政协宣教文卫体委员会，2002，p. 395）。该文对俞氏孝、贤、俭的品质给予嘉奖：主夫人的此等品质使得家族中的长幼尊卑秩序得以维护，是家族和谐的基础。屯堡人赵侃《郭太夫人李氏墓志铭》为右军都督府都督佥事郭贵嫡母所作，记述太夫人之德如“天性慈爱，端谨诚庄，事舅姑尽孝敬，睦姻戚以柔和，相夫加肱股之助，训子和熊胆之丸，奉蒸尝必丰腆，待婢妾务宽容，妇道母仪为缙绅家楷范”（pp. 396－397）。文章对郭太夫人李氏孝敬公婆、相夫教子、柔和宽容的秉性给予美誉，可见其对传统礼乐秩序的遵从与维护。自礼乐文明诞生以来，男尊女卑，男女有别，在一个家庭中也有男主外、女主内的分工，女性的活动一般囿于经营家庭，以父慈子孝、夫妻和睦、兄友弟恭、其乐融融的家庭和谐作为终极目标，因此女性往往以此作为日常行为的准则，以实现家庭中的人际和谐。“人际和谐是儒家和谐理论的重要组成部分，人与人的和谐是社会秩序稳定的基础……儒家的礼乐秩序则是以‘仁’作为其理论出发点的。”（谢清果，2016，p. 165）有了家庭的和谐，才有社会及国家的和谐；家和国昌盛，不无道理。在儒家视野中的传统家庭人际传播中，“中庸是方法，仁义是内容，礼乐是形式”（黄星民，2000a，p. 29）。如前文所提到的顾氏、郭氏家庭中的主母，她们品性端庄，富有慈爱之心，以平和中正为行事原则，对上之尊长及对下之婢妾，皆能投之以仁爱之心，宽严相济，宽容大度，能推己及人，恪守妇道，完成社会、时代所赋予的角色期待，使庞大复杂的家庭人际关系处于和谐的状态，实现家族和谐昌盛。

屯堡古诗文也彰显出对国家对朝廷的忠君爱国之心。程正声《补修宗谱序》追述其祖上“上则报效于朝廷，有义士之果烈；中则出镇于边疆，有君子之遗风；下则施训于士卒，有仁人之徽号……不意水西苗变，正公弟兄遂奔安俊之南五官屯而居之，至今十数代矣”（贵州省安顺政协宣教文卫体委员会，2002，p. 399）。程氏祖上效忠朝廷，镇守边疆，训兵有道，水西苗变，国之忧患，毅然出征，于五官屯安营扎寨，以示震慑之威，进而安居，世代守卫，其忠君爱国之心天地可鉴。秦敬《圆通寺记》通过对话的形式，记述征南将领顾城的功勋业绩：“出镇贵州，累次征战，大建勋业，昭昭在人耳目。前后四十余年蒙列圣眷顾之隆，满门显贵光荣无比。公感恩图报，修寺以为祝延圣寿之宇，此亦天保臣子之意。且公精诚布于上国，仁德著于遐方，何功不立，何夷不化?”（p. 398）肯定顾成之赫赫功勋及承蒙圣恩，也肯定其知恩图报之举，其精诚、仁德，足以在蛮夷之地立下万世功勋。纵观顾成之一生及其后人，镇守于西南一隅，为朝廷除暴乱、保安宁，居于屯堡，世代繁衍，均忠君爱国。文章以义正词严的语言反驳质疑之人，使之羞愧而退，更增强了说服力及可信度。《安顺青龙山汪公庙楹联》曰“受皇恩而封越，血食万年”（p. 402），大有皇恩浩荡，万死不辞之气势。魏承柷《冬日游粮仓洞》曰“丞相天威远，蛮方战垒平，凭栏一眺望，阡陌正纵横”（p. 406），描述了朝廷威严远播及战后南蛮之地阡陌纵横、秩序井然、和平安宁的景象。黔中屯堡的将领及屯堡人进入少数民族聚居地区，在其军事生涯及日常生活中履行了守疆卫国的使命，及时平定对南蛮之地少数民族的叛乱，促使西南地区臣服，配合朝廷完成大一统的战略目标。《论语》有言曰：“虽之夷狄，不可弃也。”朱熹注之曰：“之夷狄不可弃，勉其固守而勿失也。”（1983，p. 146）由此可见，夷狄之地也是朝廷辖区中不容放弃的一部分，而统治者要对夷狄进行管辖治理，务必首先使之臣服，其次“用夏变夷”（朱熹，1983，p. 260），即用华夏礼仪对蛮夷之地的少数民族进行治理，使之归属于同一个中央政府的管辖，以确保封建君主专制政体下皇帝的专制权力及国家太平，从而实现蛮夷与华夏一家、夷夏一体的政治目标及政治秩序。由此可见，屯堡古诗文中蕴含着屯堡礼乐文化的精神内核，洋溢着对忠君爱国思想的宣扬，对忠君爱国者的褒扬，对礼乐思想的发扬。

三、黔中屯堡礼乐文化的符号传播特点及传播效果

黔中屯堡社会礼乐文化的符号传播特点及其所达到的传播效果促使其社会结构和社会形态的稳定，是其数百年长存的关键所在。

（一）黔中屯堡礼乐文化的符号传播特点

1. 传播的偏心圆结构

随着历史的发展，黔中屯堡社会的礼乐文化在传播的过程中不断地变化发展着，其传播结构正是吴予敏在《无形的网络——从传播学的角度看中国传统文化》中提出的“偏心圆”类型的“历史－传播结构”。吴予敏认为“传统中国的文化遗产和经验的传承活动大体是按此结构进行的”，“整个历史性的传播活动犹如按着滚雪球式的方式在进行。只是时代决定了这种传播总是越来越远地脱离开原来的文化核心，但是却又不能彻底脱离这个核心”（1988，p.212）。黔中屯堡的礼乐文化在历史的传播过程，不断融入新的时代内容，以适应变化了的时代的需要，但是其礼乐文化的源头依旧根深蒂固，不容撼动。就其成年礼剃头仪式而言，随着时代的发展，男性的剃头仪式相对独立、正式，受重视，而女性的成年礼则更多受到忽视，甚至被合并入其他礼仪中。历史变迁之下，头发、发型越来越失去了原有的象征意义而更加自由随意，以剃头为载体的成年仪式的意义正在不断弱化，但却并未消失，而是在变化中倔强地延续着。屯堡人自来实行族群内婚姻，不与屯堡外的人通婚；随着时代的发展，其原有通婚圈的局限在一定程度上被打破，但无论族群内部婚姻还是与族群外部建立婚姻关系，其原有的婚姻礼仪仍旧续存，体现出传统礼乐文化的规范力。“历史的运动仍然受到时间的一维性的支配，每一层新的传播活动都意味着对遗产的偏离，但是，无论这偏离在实际走得多么远，又不能彻底摆脱遗产的制约。”（吴予敏，1988，p.221）无论传播情境如何变化，传统文化的约束力都不可能消失，传播的内容不会出现历史的断裂。黔中屯堡社会历经六百余年，几经朝代更迭，却能岿然不动，其礼乐文化的偏心圆传播结构功不可没。陈力丹提出“身—家—国—天下”的社会生活传播结构（1995，p.4），而贯穿这个传播结构始终的文化形式便是礼乐，礼乐是偏心圆结构中的核心约束力之所在。因此，国非一家一姓之国，天下乃天下人之天下，礼乐乃天下人之礼乐，恪守礼乐传统，便获得天下的一席之地。在意识形态一元化的社会，守本固元是文化形态得以存在和延续的根

本。而礼与乐正是这个文化形态的本与元，守住了这个本与元，就是把握了生存的根本。在此基础上，黔中屯堡社区在朝代更迭、政治变动中得以世代延续。

2. 传播的时空诉求

黔中屯堡社区具有空间上的封闭性和时间上的延续性，二者相互影响，达到一种相对平衡。黔中少数民族在阶级压迫之下不断掀起武装动乱，成为朝廷的一大内忧，屯军肩负着平叛的责任。屯军的田地，大多夺自当地居民和土司（王毓铨，2009，p. 91），势必造成屯堡人与当地人之间的矛盾与对立，加之于语言的障碍，肩负着政治使命的屯堡人便安守于屯堡之内，与周边居民鲜有往来，这使他们免于被同化而能更好地保持自身文化的单纯性。肩负政治使命、自带母源地区域优越感的黔中屯堡人，具有“华夷之防”的民族本位思想，不与当地少数民族来往。屯堡人移民而来，处于一种事实上的弱势地位，“华夷之防”有助于增强其文化自信，同时与官方及正统建立联系，以心理和思想上的强势弥补现实处境中的弱势。谢清果教授《华夏文明与传播学本土化研究》认为夷夏之防是一种文化上的自我防卫，是一种维护礼仪秩序的行为。（2016，p. 284）为了彰显自身的优越性，维护内部管理秩序，屯堡社会形成了独特的时空传播诉求。屯堡的建筑由石头建成，每一户堪为一个战斗据点，整个村寨俨然军事阵地，于内纵横交错，于外相对独立。屯堡自身的军事防御性质，使其形成空间上的内向聚敛性及外向排他性。就婚姻而言“黔中屯堡人自来就有严格的通婚圈，实行族群内通婚，不与少数民族和非屯堡人通婚，是其婚姻制度的核心”（孙兆霞，等，2005，p. 148）。其通婚圈的限定使得传统得到普遍认同和保存，礼乐秩序得以践行，并具有固定的生存空间以确保其传承不衰。

英尼斯在《传播的偏向》中认为“中国的文字给行政管理提供了基础，它强调的是按照空间来组织帝国，但无法满足时间上的要求，因此中国总是暴露改朝换代的问题”（2003，p. 40）；“在西方文明中，稳定的社会需要这样一种知识：时间观念和空间观念维持恰当的平衡”（p. 53）。在英尼斯看来，时间的偏向与空间的偏向要达到一种平衡，才能带来文明或政治上的长盛不衰。英尼斯推崇口语，认为口语是时间偏向的媒介。黔中屯堡人是一个重视口头传统的群体，口语被视为群体身份的标志，很好地传承了母源地的语言及表达特征，成为日常信息传播的主要媒介。英尼斯认为，“口头传统的灵活性，使希腊人在城邦体制下求得了空间观念和时间观念的平衡”（p. 56）。希腊城邦与黔中屯堡在结构与功能上有相似之处，同是相对独立的辖区，具有政治、军事功能，部分由移民建立。由此观照黔中屯堡，其在传播的时间偏向上主要依赖口语传播，在传播的空间上，由于其明显的地域特点，以口语为媒介的传播主要集中在屯堡内部，能够与活动空间达成相对一致。“对空间问题的强调与对开疆辟土的关注相伴生。”（p.56）屯堡人以屯田作为生活的物质来源，其部分屯田来自对周边民众的侵占，在对屯田的占有与控制上存在一种空间扩张的欲望与现实。这种在空间上的扩张即表现为英尼斯所谓的传播的空间偏向。以屯堡为核心区域，以其控制的屯田为地域空间，形成了一种以空间利益为主导的空间束缚型文化，坚持江南母源地口语习惯，在传播诉求上达到时间与空间的平衡，由此才有了活化石一样的黔中屯堡。

3.“风吹草偃”的传播进程

“风吹草偃”语出于《论语·颜渊》：“季康子问政于孔子曰：‘如杀无道，以就有道，何如?’孔子对曰：‘子为政，焉用杀？子欲善，而民善矣。君子之德风，小人之德草，草上之风，必偃。’”（朱熹，2007，p.138）在此基础上，黄星民教授提出传播的“风草论”——“以风喻信息传播，以草喻受众”（2000a，p.33），谢清果教授认为：“‘风草论’之‘风’突出传播过程的风化功能”，“‘风化’指的是中国传统政治伦理文化通过学校教育等方式灌输于社会成员的过程，它更多强调的是文化推广的循序渐进过程”；“传播者通过‘礼’来推动‘风化’的大力推广”。（2015，p.61）“风吹草偃”在黔中屯堡社会的传播内容为礼乐文化，传播载体为仪式与信仰，传播进程为潜移默化，传播效果最终体现为情感的认同与政治的归附。屯堡人本是命运共同体，但在中央集权的封建政体之下不可避免地存在等级之分，等级制之下的命运共同体采用什么样的手段实现共存共荣是一个关乎存亡的重要问题。承载着礼乐文化内涵的仪式和信仰是屯堡人自我治理的最终选择，治理过程则循序渐进。“风吹草偃”正是通过潜移默化的传播进程，通过循序渐进的礼乐教化，实现了“风化”“风行”的传播效果——“风行指的是文化普及后在社会成员中引起的认同盛行现象”（谢清果，陈昱成，2015，p.61），群体共识由此达成。“个体改变其信仰并非屈服于理性辩论，而是需要为之提供合适的社会环境。仪式提供了这种环境”（科泽，2018，p.111），“仪式的诱导能力主要依赖于它令人们心悦诚服的能力”（p.115）。因此“风吹草偃”也是一种情感传播的模式。行君子之风，泽被于民，民感佩于君子之德而自发归附，“吸附效应是道德传播的核心目标”（邵培仁，姚锦云，2014，p.62）。黔中屯堡社会掌权者的德治体现为仪式的建构与呈现。各类活动仪式成为生活的重要部分，仪式具有一种潜在的感召力，掌权者通过对仪式的组织、呈现，建构了官方的话语体系与治理网络，通过仪式的感召力，潜移默化地引导民众采取符合仪式规制的行为，并将之视为群体约束力，从而不自觉地投入政治的权力框架中。没有暴政与强权，君子之德风以柔和的方式潜入人心，春风化雨，获得了政治控制的韧性与张力，从而维护地方政治影响力与生命力。屯堡的存续与发展均得益于此。

（二）黔中屯堡礼乐文化符号的传播效果

黔中屯堡在其数百年的传承与发展过程中，始终坚守着礼乐文化传统，并反作用于其屯堡人的生活，形成了其独特的价值空间。屯堡场域中的礼乐文化传播极大地促进了屯堡社区中族群关系的整合、族群身份的认同及文化守望，同时也是身负政治、军事使命的屯堡人在政治旋涡中进行自我保全的一种路径。

1. “无形的文化契约”：人际传播中族群情感连接的纽带

黔中屯堡人尚礼，人与人之间不可避免地发生“礼尚往来”的传播事实，传递出一种“礼节的信息”，陈力丹认为：“这种讯息显示的是一种无形的施与报的要求。为了保持和发展某种既定的关系，一旦一方施予（从好话到实际的好处），不用再说什么，它本身就传达了一种礼节性的讯息：另一方至少要对等地给予回报。”（2005，p. 44）宴请活动是这种施予与回报的集中体现，是人际传播的重要形式。屯堡人的诞生礼、成人礼、婚礼、丧葬礼等具有礼仪形式的活动都伴随着宴请，是屯堡人礼尚往来的心理及行为的直接体现，也是屯堡社区内部人际礼乐文化内容传播的重要形式。江林《〈诗经〉与宗周礼乐文明》认为饮食之礼传递着礼乐文化精神，强调同姓宗族之间的共同利益，以加强宗族内部团结，消解矛盾与冲突。（2010，p. 159）屯堡人的宴请活动也具有同样的意义，一方面体现出其礼乐文化的渊源，另一方面在化解矛盾的同时加强族群内部人际联系，增进感情，通过人际传播加强屯堡人在少数民族地区的生存软实力。

宴请中，宴请人往往根据参与宴请人数的多寡、场面热闹与否来判断宴请的成功与否及个人在社区中的地位。以丧葬为例，屯堡社区中流传着一句“人死饭甑开，不请自家来”的俗语，即某家一旦有人过世，将不计成本敞开饭甑请人吃饭，而街坊邻居应当不请自来，方能显出热情。对于丧事主家而言，打开饭甑招待街坊邻居，街坊邻居来者是客，来者即被视为对主家丧葬事务的参与与支持，受到主家的期待与欢迎。对于参与的街坊邻居而言，积极参与别人家的丧事，也是为自家留条后路，在自己面临丧事时，也就会获得相应的参与与支持。宴请的参与者多，场面热闹，说明主人家有面子、有人缘，群众基础好，是对主人家为人处世水平的极大检验。“众人对丧葬礼仪的参与，是建构文化意义从而反过来使个体获得人生关怀和实现社会关联的公共活动”（孙兆霞，等，2016，p. 245），对人气的重视是重视礼尚往来的一种体现。“人总是生活在具体的文化氛围中的，因而人际传播中会有一种无形的‘文化契约’，决定着人际关系，并影响传播的内容、情感的表露，尽管传播双方或多方并没有实际签订什么契约，规则却是潜在的。”（陈力丹，2005，p. 43）对于丧葬事务的相互参与是一种约定俗成的人际传播形式，一方面通过氛围的营造宣泄主人家的悲伤，通过广泛的支持使主人家得到心理安慰，也使得主人忙于招待来者而得以脱离丧亲之痛；另一方面加强了族群内部的联系，平日里为生计奔波的人在这个特殊的场合，为了礼尚往来，放下手中的活计，聚集在一起，加强情感联结，加深彼此了解，有助于营造互帮互助、团结协作的社区氛围，促进族群的内向聚合力。只有联系紧密的族群才能够获得足够的生存空间，屯堡人正是通过对重要场合的相互参与与支持，通过礼尚往来，加强内部族群关系的整合及族群力量的凝聚，进而获得强大的外向生存空间。在这个意义上，宴请已远远超越了“请吃饭”的初级层面，而是以人际传播的形式，促进族群礼乐文化的建构与维系。

2. 无声的教化力量：传播仪式下的族群身份认同与文化守望

屯堡人的婚丧嫁娶及祭祀等活动都有着约定俗成的仪式，仪式强化共同的身份及文化背景，形成族群身份认同，表达对江南母源地的文化守望。这种仪式也是屯堡礼乐文化传播的载体，在传播的过程中，“经过这一套象征意义的行为及程序结构来规范、调整个人与他人、宗族、群体的关系”（谢清果，林凯，2018，p. 65），以无声的传播仪式承载社会教化的功能。

费克斯等认为礼仪（仪式）是指“组织化的象征活动与典礼活动，用以界定和表现特殊时刻、事件或变化所包含的社会与文化意味”（2004，p. 243）。屯堡社会内部不同的传播仪式恰是屯堡人建立并维护社区秩序的方式。屯堡人肩负着朝廷赋予的政治使命，自遥远的江南迁至少数民族聚居的黔中，他们有着相同的政治境遇、地域标签、生存处境，在生存及繁衍的过程中，族群身份认同借助传播仪式的形式完成。詹姆斯·凯瑞的传播仪式观认为“其（仪式）核心是将人们以团体或共同的身份召集在一起的神圣典礼”（2019，p. 40），“它强调的是创造一个有凝聚力的世界”（p. 77）。仪式这样一种具有神圣色彩的传播形式，可以建构一种共同的群体行为，形成共同的族群文化，从而确立族群的内聚力及秩序，提高族群的生存及延续能力。黄星民认为，“媒介的力量不仅在于它提供真实的内容，更在于它提供真实内容的形式……人们可以从参与这个仪式中获得满足感和安全感”（2000b, p.42）。屯堡人参与各项屯堡活动，借助传播仪式，参与屯堡的文化建构及维护。仪式是一种传播形式，也是一种传播媒介，仪式和媒介本身也是一种文化形式，具有教化的力量。黔中屯堡社会的各项仪式本身即是其地域文化的体现，可被视为一种无声的教化。民众参与仪式，可以从中接收信息，获取并分享共同的场域体验和情感体验，建立个体归属感，从而获得个体的安全感和满足感。不同仪式的定期重复不断吸引新的认同力量，强化群体的文化记忆，使群体信仰与情感趋同，维护仪式下的群体和谐。共同的族群文化的建构及维系需要族群的整体参与，从而赋予族群内部每一个个体主动积极参与的责任意识。就清明祭祀而言，已经奔走四方的屯堡人无论身居何处，身份地位如何，都会及时赶回家乡参与祭祀。空间的缺位意味着族群文化维系及认同责任的缺位，更进一步则是身份认同及身份归属的疏离，这在黔中屯堡社会是每一个屯堡后人极力避免发生的。黔中屯堡各项仪式活动与其母源地文化密切相关，对仪式的重视与坚守，是屯堡人寄寓故土情结的一种方式，仪式活动传播出屯堡人对母源地文化的守望与执着。

3. 不容置辩的政治表白：隔空传播以求在政治旋涡中自保

所谓隔空传播是指信息的传播者与传播对象有一定的空间距离，信源无法于瞬间直接到达信宿并获得解码来完成传播活动，难以实现及时的信息互动。在这个传播过程中，信息甚至要经过较长的时间，才能突破空间距离，到达最终的传播对象。这个传播活动的载体可能是人际口语，其使信息在时空中撒播，信息经过众人长时间的口耳相传，最终到达传播对象。而在这个传播过程中，存在不同人的不同解码行为及对初始信息的误读误传，因而存在较多不可控因素。因此对信源性质的把控尤为关键，即保证信源内涵的单一性，使之能够尽可能避免误读。此外，可以经过文字传播，文字传播虽然也需要跨越时空距离，但误读的可能性明显降低。黔中屯堡人对朝廷的政治表白主要表现为对信仰的隔空传播。

黔中屯堡是中央朝廷出于政治、军事的考虑，安置在黔中腹地的棋子，屯堡在空间上远离朝廷，而在现实中又服务于朝廷战略，受制于朝廷管理监控。黔中屯堡能够在远离中央的西南地区延续百年，能够在诡谲多变的政治漩涡中自我保全，与其执着的政治表白密不可分。黔中屯堡人对朝廷的隔空控制给予隔空表白式的回应，通过建构并世代传承独特的屯堡社会礼乐文化，通过信仰、文学、仪式等形式，表达对朝廷的忠心耿耿，由此获得朝廷的认可和信任。抬汪公即是其重要的表白形式之一。黔中屯堡人普遍尊奉汪公。

汪公原名汪华，隋末唐初人，祖籍徽州绩溪，被封为忠烈王，立庙祭祀。黔中《汪氏宗谱》记载：洪武十四年，傅友德帅师征南至贵州山羊岩，遇敌人顽抗而不能进，赖汪公显灵大获全胜，顺利进军，终克云贵。明太祖以其忠贞为国，追封其为灵显大帝。（孙兆霞，等，2016，p.370）经神化的汪公显灵，助阵朝廷大军征南之战，获得皇帝钦封，被视为国家正统教化的象征。汪公是朝廷南征胜利的象征和寓示，以道德的形象嵌入政治教化的体系。汪公的形象内涵具有明晰性与单一性，不容易在传播的过程中被有意或无意地曲解。黔中屯堡人对汪公的信仰恰是对朝廷的表白：以汪公为楷模，助力朝廷的征南大计，忠于朝廷，镇守一方，至死不渝。忠君爱民的汪公作为正义的化身、道德的楷模，由江南迁移至黔中，根植于屯堡人的思想中，促使朝廷需要的、认可的价值观形成。黔中屯堡人为汪公立庙建祠，使之潜移默化地发挥着正统教化的作用，同时也向朝廷表达自身不忘来处、不忘使命、不忘归属的决心；通过文化信仰明确正统，向朝廷表白心迹，使自己够在与当地少数民族对立的处境中获得安身之所，在远离庙堂的边陲能够保持朝廷的信任，从而获得自我保全。此外，如前文所述，屯堡古诗文中也处处流露出向朝廷的表白。因此，通过文化的形式做政治态度及立场的表白，是屯堡人大智慧的体现。朝廷接纳了屯堡人的表白，独特的黔中屯堡文化因而能够百年延续不衰，传承至今。

引用文献：

陈力丹（1995）．论孔子的传播思想．新闻与传播研究，1，2—9．

陈力丹（2005）．试论人际关系与人际传播．国际新闻界，3，42—48．

陈华文（2014）．民俗文化学．杭州：浙江工商大学出版社．

程俊英（2019）．诗经译注．上海：上海古籍出版社．

褚春元（2017）．礼乐文化与象征——对两周礼乐文化的象征性艺术精神之考察．合肥：安徽大学出版社．

丁鼎（2014）．儒家礼乐文化的价值取向与中华民族精神．山东师范大学学报（人文社会科学版），6，66—72，2．

费克斯，约翰，等（2004）．关键概念：传播与文化研究词典（李彬，译）．北京：新华出版社．

范增如（2009）．明代普定卫戍屯官兵原籍考．载于李建军（主编），学术视野下的屯堡文化研究．贵阳：贵州科技出版社．

费孝通（2016）．乡土中国．北京：群言出版社．

贵州省安顺政协宣教文卫体委员会（编）（2002）．安顺文史资料，第二辑．安顺：贵州省安顺政协宣教文卫体委员会.
黄星民（2000a）. 礼乐传播初探. 新闻传播与研究，1，27－35，95.
黄星民（2000b）. 从礼乐传播看非语言大众传播形式的演化. 新闻与传播研究，3，35－44，94－95.
江林（2010）.《诗经》与宗周礼乐文明. 上海：上海古籍出版社.
科泽，大卫（2018）. 仪式、政治与权力（王海洲，译）. 南京：江苏人民出版社.
凯瑞，詹姆斯（2019）. 作为文化的传播（丁未，译）. 北京：中国人民大学出版社.
李端丕（2002）. 地戏面具雕制艺术概观. 载于贵州省安顺政协宣教文卫体委员会（编），安顺文史资料，第二辑. 安顺：贵州省安顺政协宣教文卫体委员会.
李泽厚（2007）. 美学三书. 天津：天津社会科学院出版社.
李泽厚（2017）. 中国古代思想史论. 北京：生活・读书・新知三联书店.
吕思勉（2014）. 中国文化史. 厦门：鹭江出版社.
邵培仁，姚锦云（2014）. 传播模式论：《论语》的核心传播模式与儒家传播思维. 浙江大学学报（人文社会科学版），4，56－75.
孙兆霞等（2005）. 屯堡乡民社会. 北京：社会科学文献出版社.
孙兆霞等（2016）. 屯堡社会如何可能——基于宗教视角的考察. 北京：社会科学文献出版社.
王文锦（2018）. 礼记译解. 北京：中华书局.
王毓铨（2009）. 明代的军屯. 北京：中华书局.
吴予敏（1988）. 无形的网络——从传播学的角度看中国传统文化. 北京：国际文化出版公司.
项阳（2015）. 以乐观礼. 北京：北京时代华文书局.
谢清果（2016）. 华夏文明与传播学本土化研究. 北京：九州出版社.
谢清果（2017）. 华夏传播学引论. 厦门：厦门大学出版社.
谢清果，陈昱成（2015）. “风草论”：建构中国本土化传播理论的尝试. 现代传播，9，59－64.
谢清果，林凯（2018）. 礼乐协同：华夏文明传播的范式及其功能展演. 新闻与传播评论，6，59－68.
杨天宇（2004）. 周礼译注. 上海：上海古籍出版社.
英尼斯，哈罗德（2003）. 传播的偏向（何道宽，译）. 北京：中国人民大学出版社.
郑正强（2002）. 安顺吉昌屯迎春盛会—— “抬亭子”. 载于贵州省安顺政协宣教文卫体委员会（编），安顺文史资料，第二辑. 安顺：贵州省安顺政协宣教文卫体委员会.
朱光文（2011）. 朱元璋南征之谜与安顺屯堡文化. 载于李建军（主编），屯堡文化研究，2010 卷. 贵阳：贵州人民出版社.
朱伟华（2008）. 建构与生成——屯堡文化及地戏形态研究. 桂林：广西师范大学出版社.
朱熹（2007/1983）. 四书章句集注. 北京：中华书局.

作者简介：

谢清果，厦门大学新闻传播学院教授，博士生导师，厦门大学传播研究所所长，华夏传播研究会会长。

陈瑞，厦门大学新闻传播学院博士研究生，贵州师范大学求是学院讲师。

Author:

Xie Qingguo, professor of School of Journalism and Communication, Xiamen University, director of Institute of Communication, Xiamen University.

Chen Rui, Ph. D. candidate of School of Journalism and Communication, Xiamen University; lecturer of Guizhou Normal University Institute.

Email: weirai2002@126.com

中国身体哲学中“气论”的符号学阐释：《黄帝内经》试解*

陈 东

摘 要：气是中国古代哲学的重要范畴，对中国的传统科学具有深远的影响，至今，中医学仍然以气作为人体生命科学的研究对象。论文从符号学的角度分析了“气”符号的生成过程与无限衍义，以及它在《黄帝内经》中医学意义域的形成机制，厘清了《黄帝内经》中“气”概念的理解困境，同时证明了中医学理论身心一元思维。

关键词：气论，符号，意义域，《黄帝内经》

A Semiotic Study of Qi-Theory of Chinese Body Philosophy in *The Yellow Emperor's Classic of Internal Medicine*

Chen Dong

Abstract: Qi is an important concept in traditional Chinese philosophy, which exerted profound impact in traditional Chinese science. Until now, Qi has been the subject of Chinese medicine study. From the semiotic perspective, the paper explores the formation of Qi as a sign, its unlimited semiosis as well as how the medical meaning sphere came into being in *The Yellow Emperor's Classic of Internal Medicine*. It helps to understand the Qi concept and the unity of body and mind in traditional Chinese medicine.

Keywords: Qi-theory, sign, meaning sphere, *The Yellow Emperor's Classic of Internal Medicine*

---

* 本文为成都理工大学中青年骨干教师发展资助计划（10912－KYGG2019－01281）阶段性成果。

DOI：10.13760/6.cnki.cam.20200121

引　言

“气”是中国哲学思想中极为重要的范畴。从先秦诸子至近代章太炎等，对气的研究几乎贯穿整个中国历史。“气”的思想起初被用于阐释宇宙以及生命的本源，自然与人的形成、变化和两者之间的关系。秦汉时期，气的思想得到了系统性的发展，广泛地应用于医学、气象学、堪舆学等领域，《黄帝内经》是以气的思想解释人体健康与疾病的典范。

“气”是整个中医学理论的基础，《黄帝内经》有近3000个“气”字，约占全文五十分之一，“气”字出现的频率，仅次于虚词之、者，在所有实词中，它出现的频率最高。（赵洪钧，2007，p.25）《黄帝内经》中“气”的概念十分复杂，如果要了解其中的气学理论，就必须追本溯源，厘清医学中气思想的发展脉络。气论研究一直以朴素唯物论范式对“气”进行现代化阐释，但是，面对当代物质理论，“气”仍无法自证其合理性。

《黄帝内经》“气”概念的当代阐释困境是：五行之气、阴阳之气、宗气、邪气等各种气从何而来？质料的气与形式的气如何统一在“气”概念之中？刘胜利提出现象存在论，为气论哲学提供了一种全新的研究范式，该范式将元气作为一种存在的元素，一种“现象的存在”或“存在的现象化”。（2011）刘胜利的观点十分新颖，但没能具体展开论述。陈来先生就当前气论哲学研究指出：“我们需要新的研究范式和哲学视野复兴对气论哲学的宏观与微观研究。”（2008，p.4）气论哲学呼唤新的学科理论，以揭示气的本质与发展历史。符号学被认为是文科中的数学，具有跨学科、跨文化特质，是人文科学所有学科共同的方法论。（赵毅衡，2012，p.9）本文从哲学符号学的元符号、无限衍义等概念分析“气”符号哲学意义的形成与医学意义的建构，厘清“气”在中国哲学理论建构中的关键地位，分析了“气”字成为《黄帝内经》中普遍使用的符号的原因，以及现代西方医学中“气”的差异，以解决《黄帝内经》中“气”概念的认知困境。

一、“气”的符号特征

从“气”的字义可以发现中国哲学十分重视自然，中国古代自然观在科学上产生过重要影响。要了解气论哲学，必须追本溯源，探寻踪迹，才能观其思想发展脉络，找出其存在的合理性以及逻辑特点。

《说文解字》说：“气，云气也。象形。凡气之属皆从气。”（许慎，2016，p. 8）关于气的思想最初产生于人们日常生活实践中观察到的自然现象，气与云、雾、烟有相似特点。《说文解字》释云：“云，山川气也，从雨，云象云回转形。凡云之属皆从云。”云属于气，生于山间河流。《说文解字》释雾：“地气发，天不应。”雾由大地之气生发，也属于气。《说文解字》解释烟：“火气也。”烟即火气，仍然归属于气。

作为语言符号的“气”最初是如何生成与传播的呢？首先，何谓符号？符号是携带意义的感知。意义必须用符号才能表达，符号的用途是表达意义。（赵毅衡，2012，p. 1）根据符号的定义，符号必然承载意义，为了表达人类对气的认知，需要借助相应的符号载体。向前推进一步，这样的符号究竟如何锁合意义的？“气”符号的原初获意过程是什么？要回答这些问题，必须从意识、意向性、事物和对象的意义活动几个要素展开讨论。

任何事物只要被感知，受到人的关照，即进入人的意识，与人形成关联，这是意义生成的第一步。康德认为感性就是感性直观，通过感官和时空，认识被给予对象，对于自在之物，由于没有意识的实践，意义无法形成。中国古人在日常生活中反复经验气，感知到气的物质性存在，在意识的作用下发出意向性，对气的不同观相形成不同的认知，意向性决定了物质之气与意义观相的关联。气的形式直观是意识与事物建立契约关系的基础，没有这种获意意向性，就没有其符号的生成动力。

当气被感知时，进入人的意识的是关于气的不同片段，例如，云气是流动不居的，气能为人体所知觉（热气上升、冷气下降等）。为了取得气的形式直观，意识必须将气的形式感知之外的观相予以搁置，存而不论，于是气的流动观相就成了其符号的主要品质。金文的“气”（气）从视觉上体现了气的流动性特点，与对象具有相似性关系。《说文解字》将“气”（气），解释为象形字。皮尔斯根据符号与对象之间的关系将符号分成三类：像似符号、指示符号和规约符号。（2014，p. 51）由此，可以肯定“气”符号就是像似性符号，像似性符号简单直接，易于被感知，具有再现透明性。象形与象声都是模刻自然，金文和《说文解字》中的“气”符号体现出“气”物质的流动品格。“气”符号具有时间性和空间性，不仅能够从空间中去掌握世界，而且能以时间延续展示外在事物。

索绪尔认为，符号的能指与所指的联系是任意的、无理据性的，这一论断是基于拼音文字的特点提出的，因为记音文字无法表达声音以外的形象。

中文是表意符号，音意交融，能指与所指之间本有联系，是有理据的。

“气”符号的像似性特点体现了直觉性思维，是中国哲学思维的基本形式。“气”符号指称的是气的物质性存在，其生成源于物质被感知，体现出中国古代的朴素唯物论。肖峰指出，人在符号世界和表象世界相交织所构成的“符号-表象”世界中进行着符号操作活动，符号常常在操作活动中消失，而画面则经常浮现出来，这正是初步的抽象还不能有效地摆脱形象的纠缠和限制的表现。(1989，p.177) 符号意义与形式的关联携带像似性，无法将意象从符号中抽离，“气”不是纯粹抽象的符号，与西方哲学中的单一概念符号有着根本的区别。西方哲学认为形式与意义的分开是哲学思维的表现，否则逻辑的明确性和系统性无法实现。这种观点自有合理因素，但不无片面性，值得思考和仔细研究。

西方哲学中，概念是高度抽象的思维符号，思维活动依赖概念运作，其内涵与外延十分明确，保证了符号的逻辑性和明确性。这种思维有助于将经验上升为理论，使科学知识不再局限于经验思维，而“气”符号的像似性却始终卷入人的思维活动，这种思维活动是经验的，而非理论的。经验思维是人们运用在日常生活实践中积累的知识而进行的思维操作，是运用生活的直接感受和体验以及社会习俗进行的思维活动。“气”符号是经验思维的体现，未分主客关系。《说文解字注》释“气，云气也”为“象云起之皃”(段玉裁，2018，p.20)。“象云起之皃”是主体对客体的直接体验，主观自我凭借像似性认知外在世界，由此可见，“气”符号的形成是经验思维的结果。

像似符号“气”带有明显的意象思维，无法用概念明确地规定，全靠直观感悟（想象）来追寻意义。意象之象通常借助类比、隐喻、象征以及具体符号语境等方式引申意义，是一种内隐的辩证逻辑。严密的逻辑规范对近代自然科学的发展的影响深远，而意象思维逻辑性不明确，逻辑论证欠缺。中国古代的科技发明通常基于经验层面而非高度抽象的概念层面，因而“气”符号的局限性是不容置疑的。然而，这种缺陷正是“气”符号的价值所在，它使“气”的能指与所指之间的理据性关系避免了机械和僵化的思维操作，促进了主客体的通融与思维的创造性。中国哲学的阴阳、五行符号与“气”符号具有相同的思维特点，是中国思维符号的代表。

“气”符号最初指向物质，属于中国先秦时期名与实的范畴。名实之辩主要围绕名是否源于感性经验和客观实在，概念是否具有客观必然性这样的问题。“气”之名与实是相符的，“气”最初就是指物质。符号的功能在于将注意力引向认知对象，其意义超出认知对象。符号是意义的载体，人凭借符号认知世界，通过形式向意义过渡。“气”最初指物质，后来应实践的要求，人需要扩大认知对象范围，“气”意义延伸到功能。“气”意义随重复而增加，具有累积性，个人和社群的经验在意义的重复实践中形成。赵毅衡认为，重复是意义的符号存在方式，变异也必须靠重复才能辨认，重复与以它为基础产生的变异使意义能延续与拓展，成为意义的基本构成方式。(2017，p.151)符号的生命在于重复，意义在重复中得以延续，意义的延伸离不开重复。“气”符号的意义在重复中获得了生命力，于是就在其他文本中频繁出现，意义范畴不断扩大，各种相关之气成为认识世界的重要载体。

甲骨文、金文以及《尚书》和《诗经》中均未出现名词性的“气”字，只是将其用作副词和动词。李存山认为：“甲骨文、金文和现存《尚书》、《诗经》没有给我们留下名词‘气’字的直接材料。”(1990，p.22)尽管早期文献《尚书》《诗经》中没有名词性“气”字，但是《左传》《国语》中作为明确的哲学范畴的“气”思想已经产生。

“气”原初指物质。张岱年指出，中国哲学中所谓气，可以说是最细微、最流动的物质，以气解说宇宙，即以最细微、最流动的物质为一切之根本。(2017，p.87)中国哲学以气的物质性阐释宇宙万物的运行规律，这与西方哲学所持的气由微小固体形成的原子论有明显差异。皮尔斯把符号载体命名为再现体，即索绪尔说的能指；关于索绪尔的所指，皮尔斯从逻辑上分解成两部分，一部分是符号代替的对象，另一部分是符号引发的思想，被称为解释项。(2014，p.31)皮尔斯的符号意指三分式（对象、再现体、解释项）可以解释中国哲学中“气”符号意义的复数性：气的物世界是唯一，但是意识的作用使意义世界变得多维。解释项需要另一个符号才能表达，而新的符号表意又会形成新的解释项，由此产生无限衍义。

根据《国语·周语上》记载，“土气震发”“阳气俱蒸”，虢文公谏言周宣王，用阴阳之气阐释农事。另记载伯阳父云：“阳伏而不能出，阴迫而不能蒸，于是有地震。”这朴素地解释了气的运动变化与地震的因果关系。又引用了伯阳父对幽王的话：“夫天地之气，不失其序；若过其序，民乱之也。”认为天地之气的变化是民事失序的原因。《左传·昭公元年》载医和之言：“天有六气，降生五味，发为五色，徵为五声，淫生六疾。六气曰阴、阳、风、雨、晦、明也。分为四时，序为五节，过则为灾”。(郭丹，2018，p.1575)谈及气的物质性、运动性以及多样性，阴阳等六气与四时、五行相匹配，蕴含着时空的统一性特点。

战国时期，关于气的认识逐步深化。《管子》最先提出气宇宙观，认为气是万物之本源，自然界一切事物均生于天地之气。《管子·七法》说："根天地之气。"自然界万物的出现以天地之气为基础。《荀子·王制》说："天地合而万物生，阴阳接而变化起。"天地交感产生万物，阴阳运动出现变化。又说："水火有气而无生，人有气、有生、有知亦且有义"。水火有气但是没有生命，人有气、有生命、有智也有义，强调气的生命特征。以上经典文本均暗含了"气是宇宙的根本"的意义。

符号的无限衍义具有空间性和时间性。语言符号"气"从生成起，在不同时期文本中运用，其意义在历史中获得链接式延展并得以积累。祝东指出，语言是最大的符号系统，自然是最广阔的客体对象。(2018）语言符号"气"源于人类在日常生活中对自然世界的感知，为了表达意义而具有了人类交际功能。符号是意义产生的途径，更是意义传播的方式。符号的出现表明人的客观行为转化为主观思维，能通过编码生成意义并传达意义，实现人的目的。美国哲学人类学家卡西尔指出，人是制造和使用符号的动物。(1985，p. 43)"气"符号的出现必然引向其使用，这是人类思维的巨大进步，是人在知觉意象基础上形成的带有社会性和一般性的意象，具有范畴化的特征。"气"符号是皮尔斯所说的"型符"，其意义指向一个类型。"气"符号虽然可以指称某一系列对象，但表意仍然十分模糊，这时就需要符号的双重分节。叶尔慕斯列夫认为双重分节表达层的单元是纯粹形式，是空洞的，他称之为空符；与之对应的内容层面是具体的意义，是实符；两者对应，却不一定重合。(Hjelmslev，1975，p. 56）"气"符号的能指只是形式，与其匹配的内容是具体的意义，即关于气的物质与功能的一切。气的意义域的构成必须在能指分节中进行，否则无法体现复杂的全貌。可以说，符号切分是思维活动从无序向有序转变的关键。

二、《黄帝内经》中"气"符号的意义域

气是如何与身体建立联系并渗透医学的呢?《孟子·公孙丑上》说："夫志，气之帅也；气，体之充也。"(万丽华，蓝旭，2006，p. 57）人的意志是感情意气的统帅，感情意气是充满体内的力量。孟子用气来描述身体与心志的相互影响，体现了气的身体哲学。《管子·枢言》说："有气则生，无气则死，生者以其气。"(李山，2009，p. 85）气是人的生命之本，气决定人的生死。将气作为生命的本质，突显气对生命活动的重要意义。符号是意义的载体，先民对身体的理解和解释必须依靠符号进行，而气是万物之本，是解释

规范的元语言，这种气宇宙观影响了先民的身体观，气进而与身体产生关联。祝东指出："人类社会活动其实是一个不断制造意义，规范意义，而又受意义规范的过程。"（2014）身体之气的意义生成是一元论衍义的结果，这是先民对气的认知的深化与发展，在此基础上，气的意义不断得到延伸和更新。

关于气的流动性特征，《庄子·知北游》说："人之生，气之聚也；聚则为生，散则为死，故通天下一气耳。"（陈鼓应，2018，p. 565）人的出生，是气的聚积，气聚便成生命，气散便是死亡，气是整个宇宙的主宰。庄子不仅强调气是人体生命的本源，还指出气的变动不居是生命活动的本质。虽然庄子通过"气"符号呈现对身体的理解和阐释，但是"气"符号仍然是一个模糊的概念。意识构造"气"符号的意义世界，是先民意义活动的关键。《黄帝内经》是气论思想在医学领域中的具体实践，用气的双重分节表征身体的病理诊断、治疗和摄生规律变化，建构起了以气为根本的医学符号的意义域，使原本模糊的身体认知通过符号得以再现。气贯穿《黄帝内经》整个理论体系的始终，《黄帝内经》在中国哲学"气"范畴的发展史上具有里程碑的意义。《黄帝内经》的"气"符号分为自然之气、生理之气、病理之气等，多种意义域的形成以"气"符号的分节为前提，在意识的意向性压力下向不同的方向衍义，形成以气为核心的医学符号网络。

（一）自然之气

人生活于自然环境中，人体的发展变化必然受到自然界的影响。正是基于这种人与自然的关系，《黄帝内经》认为气指宇宙，涵括天地、阴阳五行、四时等，分为天气、地气、人气。气的内涵与外延逐渐确定，因而可以用来宏观地阐释天地变化的自然规律以及对人产生的作用。人类通过符号"气"的媒介作用呈现出对自然的认知，并通过符号分类表达人化的自然世界。

《素问·阴阳应象大论》说："故清阳者为天，浊阴者为地。地气上为云，天气下为雨，雨出地气，云出天气。"（2016a，p. 39）清阳之气化作天，浊阴之气化为地。地气上升形成云，天气下降形成雨。雨形成的直接原因是天气的下降，但实质是由地气所化生；云形成的直接原因是地气的上升，但根源是天气的下降。这里通过符号的双重分节，用能指切分所指，用天气与地气阐释宇宙之气的升降变化以及云雨的成因。符号的分节使得原本一团模糊之气变得越来越清晰，这也表明人类的思维逐渐走向逻辑化。

《素问·四时刺逆从论》说："春气在经脉，夏气在孙络，长夏气在肌肉，秋气在皮肤，冬气在骨髓中。春者，天气始开，地气始泄，冻解冰释，水行经通，故人气在脉。”（2016b，p.480）意思是春气、夏气、长夏气、秋气和冬气处于人体的不同部位，气根据季节划分，强调自然之气对人体经络的影响，这是针灸治疗的理论基础。自然之气根据时间和功能划分，意在突显人体健康受外部气候的影响。一年中不同时节的气候对人体的作用不同，这是运用气的时间性模塑人体生命的自然观，体现了顺应自然规律的养生思想。

（二）生理之气

生理之气由先天之精、水谷食物之精化生，辅以及吸入的自然之气，通过脏腑而充塞于人体。为了解释生理之气，古人根据所处部位，将气分为真气、宗气、营气和卫气，进而使对气的来源、分布及功能的表述条理化。

《灵枢·刺节真邪》说：“真气者，所受于天，与谷气并而充身者也。”（2016，p.457）真气，是人体最根本的气，人体生命的全部依赖真气而存在，真气属于先天之气，是人体的气结构的最高层次。

《灵枢·邪客》说：“宗气积于胸中，出于喉咙，以贯心脉，而行呼吸。”（p.414）宗气的主要功能是维持人体心跳、脉搏与呼吸，人的生命依赖宗气的推动。

《灵枢·营卫生会》说：“此所受气者，泌糟粕，蒸津液，化其精微，上注于肺脉，乃化而为血，以奉生身，莫贵于此，故独得行于经隧，命曰营气。”（p.175）营气经由血脉进入人体的各个生理组织，是人体生理活动的前提，对人体有关键作用。

《素问·痹论》说：“卫者，水谷之悍气也。其气慓疾滑利，不能入于脉也。故循皮肤之中，分肉之间，熏于肓膜，散于胸腹。”（2016b，p.332）卫气生于水谷之精微物质，活动于脉外，主要分布于人体的皮肤、肌肉和胸腹中。这阐释的是卫气的形成与分布。

气对生理发挥主导作用。根据气的聚散分布而对“气”符号做的分节建构了气的生理学意义。

（三）病理之气

病理之气分正气、邪气、水气、寒气、暑气等。《黄帝内经》不仅认为气是人体形成之本源，还用气解释病理现象。两千多年前，受科技水平的制约，人们无法利用现代的科学仪器从细菌病毒的角度去分析病因。中国古代医家只是用“邪气”概括性地表征所有致病因素，用“正气”指称人抵御疾病的能力，正气无法抵御邪气则生疾病。

《灵枢·刺节真邪》说："正气者，正风也，从一方来，邪气者，虚风之贼伤人也。"（2016，p.458）气分正和邪，正气使人健康，邪气伤害人体，二者可以解释疾病的发生机理。正邪之气的分类是阴阳二元对立思维推演的结果，阴阳思想贯穿整部《黄帝内经》。

《素问·阴阳应象大论》说："冬伤于寒，春必温病；春伤于风，夏生飧泄；夏伤于暑，秋必痎疟；秋伤于湿，冬生咳嗽。"（2016a，p.44）冬天感受寒气过多；春天容易发生热病，春天感受风气过多，夏天容易引发飧泄；夏天感受暑气过多，秋天容易出现疟疾；秋天感受湿气过多，冬天容易产生咳嗽。这一符号分节对指导人类认识气候变化对身体的影响发挥着重要作用。人体由天地之气而生，人的疾病也源于自然之气的变化。仅用自然之气表达疾病成因，表意仍然模糊，而将其分为正气、邪气、寒气则可模塑人们对病理的认知，这种筹划成为医学诊断的关键。

生命由气凝聚而成。《黄帝内经》对气进行双重分节，原动力何在？"气"符号不能单独表意，任何单独的符号都需要语境的帮助才能表达意义。人栖居于意义的世界，任何社群中的人都无法脱离符号系统。（苏智，2018）单独的气无法表征自然、生理、病理规律，解释者更不可能从中解读出气对人体的医学意义。区隔，是意义活动得以展开的前提。（赵毅衡，2017，p.111）区隔是在意向性的压力下分割出意识予以关照的部分，是意义生成的基本操作方式。《黄帝内经》中气的医学意义是区隔的结果。意识对人体生命的诸多观相进行区隔，建构起人体生命规律的"气"符号意义域，人身之气获得秩序，由此形成《黄帝内经》"气"符号的文本组合。

三、中医的身心哲学

作为物质的气在意向性压力下由人的意识变为"气"符号；单个符号无法表达意义，区隔是意义活动的前提，符号通过能指分节分割所指，形成人体生命活动机制的气的医学意义域。分析《黄帝内经》对气的划分，可以发现中医的诸多特点。

第一，中医的唯物主义观。"气"符号的出现源于人的意识在意向性压力下对气的感知，气本是物质性的存在。为了表意的需要，气的意义被延伸，物质之气逐渐转向功能之气。中医之气既指物质，也指功能，体现了中医的唯物主义观。中医之气不同于西方知识体系中的气，西方的气只指作为物质的气，其范畴远没有中医之气广泛。

第二，中医的直觉性思维。直觉性思维是指以感官对事物形象进行直接感知的思维活动。“气”符号的形成是人对于云、雾的感知的结果。《黄帝内经》运用自然之气阐释人体的生理与病理，是在体验自然之气后形成的具象认知。药食之气的温、热、寒、凉以及酸、苦、甜、辛、咸的四性五味均在人品尝等直接感知活动中得到认识。直觉性思维在中医学的基础理论中并不少见，成为中医学的主要的思维方式。

第三，中医的整体论思想。《黄帝内经》宇宙之气、人体之气、生理之气、病理之气，均通过原初“气”符号的双重分节建构气的医学符号域，阐释自然之气对人体的影响，充分说明了人与自然是一个有机整体，体现了“天人合一”整体论思想。人体的生理之气的分割也表明人体是一个有机联系的整体。

第四，中医的辩证思维。人的意识感知气的存在，像似符号“气”由此生成，《黄帝内经》对气进行区隔和分节，并分析不同的气的形成、分布及功能，不同的气相辅相成，对立统一，经察类、求故、明理，才能诊断，这体现了中医的辩证思维。

气是万物之本，这是先民对自然世界的原初认识。先民运用“气”符号从天人同构和天人同质的视域阐释人的身体、疾病和养生思想，形成一种特殊的认知结构，表现出对身体世界的特定理解。人体健康与自然密切关联，“气”符号既指自然之气，也指人体之气，实现了人与自然的统一。中医认为人源于自然，是自然之中的存在。“在世界之中存在，实质上说的是人源自世界，居寓世界之中，依赖于世界，融入世界之中。”（海德格尔，1987，p.65）西方哲学将自然之气当作一个外在于主体的独立对象，以笛卡尔为代表的身心二元论主张身体与心灵各自是独立的实体，身体是一个广延性的实体，心灵是一个不占据空间的实体，身体与心灵相互平行，这种观点区别于中医哲学的整体思维。

结　语

综上所述，对《黄帝内经》中气的符号学分析，阐释了“气”符号的生成过程与无限衍义，以及它在《黄帝内经》中医学意义域的形成机制，厘清了“气”符号的语义——气由最初的指代物质逐渐地转向指代功能，既指自然之气，也指人体之气，同时强调了人体与自然环境、人体内各器官之间的有机统一，最终指向“天人合一”思想。“气”符号研究为当今社会认知

“气”对于人体健康的重要价值提供了指导，也证明了中医理论的身心一元思维。被称为“文科中的数学”的符号学具有跨学科特征，为《黄帝内经》的研究提供了一种新的视野，有利于揭示中国医学的本质。《黄帝内经》中“五运六气”“形气转化”的说法一直处于争论之中，从符号学角度进行研究也许会有新的突破。

引用文献：

陈鼓应（2018）. 庄子今注今译. 北京：中华书局.

段玉裁（2018）. 说文解字注. 北京：中华书局.

郭丹，程小青，李彬源（译注）（2018）. 左传. 北京：中华书局.

海德格尔（1987）. 存在与时间（王庆节，陈嘉映，译）. 北京：生活·读书·新知三联书店.

黄帝内经·灵枢（2016）. 北京：人民卫生出版社.

黄帝内经·素问（上）（2016a）. 北京：人民卫生出版社.

黄帝内经·素问（下）（2016b）. 北京：人民卫生出版社.

卡西尔，恩斯特（1985）. 人论（甘阳，译）. 上海：上海译文出版社.

李存山（1990）. 中国气论探源与发微. 北京：中国社会科学出版社.

李山（译注）（2009）. 管子. 北京：中华书局.

刘胜利（2011）. 对象科学与现象科学——论两种科学的区分与中国古代科学的统一性. 科学文化评论，3，35—52.

皮尔斯，C. S.（2014）. 皮尔斯：论符号（赵星植，译）. 成都：四川大学出版社.

苏智（2018）. 符码特征与周易取象的意义建构. 载于曹顺庆，赵毅衡（主编），符号与传媒，17. 成都：四川大学出版社.

万丽华，蓝旭（2006）. 孟子. 北京：中华书局.

肖峰（1989）. 从哲学看符号. 北京：中国人民大学出版社.

许慎（2016）. 说文解字. 北京：中华书局.

杨立华（2008）. 气本与神化：张载哲学论述. 北京：北京大学出版社.

张岱年（2017）. 中国哲学大纲. 北京：中华书局.

赵洪钧（2007）. 回眸与反思：中西医结合二十讲. 合肥：安徽科学技术出版社.

赵毅衡（2012）. 符号学. 南京：南京大学出版社.

赵毅衡（2017）. 哲学符号学：意义世界的形成. 成都：四川大学出版社.

祝东（2014）. 仪俗、政治与伦理：儒家伦理符号思想的发展及反思. 载于曹顺庆，赵毅衡（主编），符号与传媒，9. 成都：四川大学出版社.

祝东（2018）. 道家语言观的理性精神：道家与马克思主义文化符号思想的比较. 载于曹顺庆，赵毅衡（主编），符号与传媒，17. 成都：四川大学出版社.

Hjelmslev, L. (1975). *Resume of a theory of language*. Madison, WI: University of

Wisconsin Press.

作者简介：

陈东，四川大学符号学—传媒学研究所成员，成都理工大学外语学院讲师，主要研究方向为传播符号学、中国符号学遗产。

Author:

Chen Dong, Ph. D. candidate of College of Literature and Journalism, Sichuan University, member of the ISMS Research Team, lecturer of School of Foreign Languages, Chengdu University of Technology. His research fields are semiotics of communication and Chinese traditional semiotic heritage.

Email: 76010294@qq. com

传播符号学

中西表情包设计比较：基于小黄脸的符号学分析*

林升栋　程　茜　乔巾哲　庞云洁　李亚伟

摘　要： 网络表情已成为虚拟社交中重要的传播符号。目前西方使用最广泛的是绘文字，中国最流行的是微信表情。本文以两种表情中的小黄脸作为文化间设计比较的素材，探索二者在表情使用与平台语境、表情情绪的社会符号学解读、视觉语法框架三方面的差异。不同文化选择了不同的平台界面设计和应用技术，在使用功能上呈现出差异。基于五官特征的符号学剖析，尤其在眼部和嘴部的丰富度比较，表明整体上绘文字设计着重客观的面部表情传递，而微信表情侧重共享的面部表情体验仪式。从小黄脸扩展至其他表情，进一步具体到再现意义、互动意义和构成意义三个视觉语法层次的比较，也说明传递与仪式可以解释二者在设计上的差异。

关键词： 表情，小黄脸，传递，仪式

* 本文为福建省高校人文社科研究基地“厦门大学中华文化传播研究中心”成果。

Comparison of Eastern and Western Emoticon Design: A Semiotic Analysis of the "Little Yellow Face" Emoji

Lin Shengdong Cheng Qian Qiao Jinzhe Pang Yunjie Li Yawei

Abstract: Emoticons are widely used in social interactions in cyberspace. The little yellow face—emoji, which form the most popular set in the world, and WeChat emoticons, which are the most popular set in China, are used as the main materials for a cultural comparison of emoji. We compare them from three perspectives: the platform that transmits the two emoticon sets, social semiotic analysis, and the visual grammar frame. The two platforms, used in different cultural contexts, have different interface designs and operate at different technical levels, as reflected in the different uses and users of the respective emoticon sets. The semiotic meaning expressed by the features of the five senses, especially the richness of the eyes and mouth, indicates that emoticons in the emoji set generally focus on transmission, whereas those in the WeChat set generally focus on ritual. The comparison of the three visual grammar levels of reappearance, interaction and constitution from the yellow face to other emoticons also reinforces our explanation of the two categories of transmission and ritual.

Keywords: facial expressions, yellow faces, transmission, ritual

DOI: 10.13760/b.cnki.sam.202001009

凭借情感表达的丰富性与趣味性，网络表情已成为一种广受年轻人追捧的互联网亚文化，它不仅仅是一张张图片，更决定着未来人们的表达与交流方式。中国互联网发展相对独立于西方，双方发展出各自的社交媒体平台，开发出情趣迥异的网络表情。脸书（Facebook）和推特（Twitter）是西方最有代表性的社交工具，微信是目前中国最有代表性的社交媒体。脸书和推特使用国际上流行的绘文字（emoji）表情。微信在原先 QQ 表情的基础上，独立发展出一套表情系统。互联网公司的用户导向为我们研究不同文化群体对网络表情设计的不同偏好提供了绝佳的素材。

绘文字源于 20 世纪 90 年代，日本年轻人用寻呼机向好朋友们发送一些简单的表情图案，到2010年万国码（Unicode）介入并制定标准后，绘文字正式成为世界通用语言，搭载于美国苹果公司发布的手机操作系统IOS 5中，很快风靡全球。目前绘文字的万国码已更新至12.0版本，在苹果、多普达（HTC）、三星、微软等不同品牌系统，以及脸书、照片墙（Instagram）、推特、瓦次普（WhatsApp）、色拉布（Snapchat）等不同社交平台上产生了二十余种衍生版本。

微信系统表情由微信表情图片、表情包、自定义表情和自拍表情四种构成。微信表情图片即微信自带表情，随微信版本更新不断调整变化。以2018年6.6.7版本为例，微信表情图片包含64个脸部表情、10个手势动作、6个全身表情、20个其他图案表情。表情包是用户自行选择在微信平台下载的动态或静态表情图片，设计者一般会把社会热点、网络流行语、当红人物等素材组合起来，使表情包成为大家“群聊斗图”中一种“趣我”的表达方式。（饶广祥，魏清露，2018）自定义表情是用户自行添加的动态或静态图片，素材可以来源于任何渠道，有助于更个性化地表达情绪。自拍表情是最新推出的，特指由用户拍摄自己表情而制成的表情图像。

绘文字雏形的发明者栗田穰崇（Kurita）最初仅提出6个粗糙的符号，现在大家熟知的绘文字是苹果公司前职员范兰克（Willem van Lancker）的创作，他以实习生身份画了最初的500个写实风格的绘文字，经过长期演化，目前能反映西方用户和开发者的审美偏好。微信表情继承QQ表情，其版本随着用户使用偏好不断淘汰更新，目前已经能反映中国用户和开发者的审美偏好。本文拟选择2018年3月29日发布的苹果手机操作系统11.3版本中自带的绘文字表情和2018年6.6.7版本的100张微信表情图片作为设计比较的素材，脸部表情（小黄脸）为主，其他表情为辅。表情的意义采用绘文字和微信官方给出的定义和解释。实际使用过程中，随着语境变化及使用群体不同而导致的意义流变，本文暂不考虑。

跨文化表情的比较研究，更多从心理或计算机科学角度，研究接收者如何进行面部表情识别，发现人的面部表情存在着跨文化的一致性和文化差异性。目前的研究停留在对真实人脸的识别，只有少数扩展到网络表情上，比如帕克（Park）等人抓取自然文本大资料，发现并解释了集体主义和个人主义文化中网络表情的差异。（Park，Baek，Cha，2014）该文的研究资料是早期基于标点符号组合而成的颜文字，与现在使用的图像很不同。采用自然文本大数据的方式有其所长，但分析略显粗糙。符号学对文化分析的深度和精度可能高于其他方法。本文采用一个自然文本的“小数据”，从符号学入手，初步探讨表情设计的文化差异，并尝试提出一组抽象包容的概念来予以解释。

绘文字使用的官方合作社交平台主要是脸书和推特，其互动模式以评论式为主。这很像中国的微博，使用者发布内容，粉丝在其下评论，粉丝与用户的互动记录左对齐排列，如同第三方的对话记录。微信的互动模式以对话式为主，一左一右，主客分明。这两种不同的呈现偏好，可能使得绘文字设计更追求客观的、精确的情绪传递，微信表情设计则更追求一种共享的、会意的情绪仪式。尽管国内外社交平台提供给用户的可选功能大同小异，但主流接口仍是不同文化群体自然选择的结果。

詹姆斯·凯瑞将“传播”观念分为两大类：传播的传递观和传播的仪式观。本文拟借用这一组概念来概括绘文字与微信表情自带符号之间的差异。从原义来看，传播的传递观将信息的流动比作货物或人的流动，强调信息的传输过程，从一端传送到另一端，关注信息流的速度与传递过程的完整性，以控制为目的；传播的仪式观则从文化传承角度将传播视为一种仪式，强调参与、分享、联合以及拥有共同的信仰。仪式本身是象征性的、表演性的，关注的重点不是信息在时空中“尽可能不失真”的传递，而是在时间意义上建构社会现实和传承文化。仪式不同于日常行为，总是强化或夸张某些行为或装饰，并弱化常见的部分。简言之，传递偏重分享信息的过程，而仪式偏重共享信仰的现实体验。（Carey，2009，pp. 12－13）绘文字的设计可能更体现传递观，而微信表情的设计可能更体现仪式观。

一、两种面部表情系统的拆解分析

艾克曼和弗里森将情绪分为愤怒、惊奇、恐惧、高兴、悲伤和厌恶六类，并依据人脸肌肉群运动及对应的表情，将人脸划分成 46 个运动单元，进而开发出面部动作编码系统。（Ekman，Friesen，1975，pp. 1－9）麦克劳德将这一编码系统从 46 种简化为 12 种，包括斜眼看、挑眉毛等运动单元。（Feng，O’Halloran，2012）马蒂内克提出一个简化的面部表情系统，将脸部动作向前或闭合归为主动，如愤怒；向后或开放归为被动，如恐惧；同时将向上的动作归为积极，如高兴；向下的动作归为消极，如悲伤。（Martinek，2001）这一简单的分法存在很多争议。根据兰考夫的理想化认知模型和韩礼德的系统功能理论，冯和奥哈洛兰（Feng，O’Halloran，2012）从社会符号学的视角来解读视觉影像如何表达情绪，并总结出一套前额、眉毛、眼睛、鼻子、脸颊、嘴的不同形状代表不同情绪的面部图释系统，可用于解读不同五官组合下的不同情绪（图 1）。两位作者谨慎地重申这个系统作为可能的符号编码来源，是描述性的工具，而不是建立情绪意义表达的规定性语法结构。

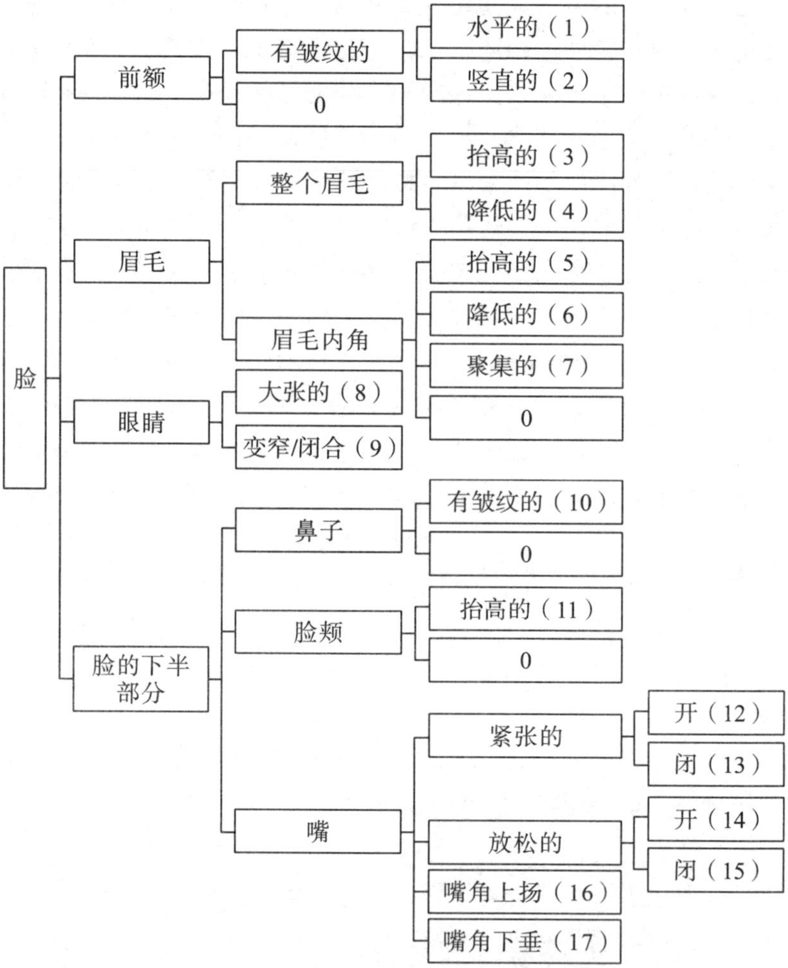

图 1　冯德正和凯·奥哈洛兰的面部图释系统（孙嘉靖，2013）

西方研究对面部动作编码系统精益求精的探索，反映出他们对情绪表达设计标准化的倾向。绘文字由万国码制定标准，万国码为每种语言中的每个字符设定了统一并唯一的二进制编码，以满足跨语言、跨平台文本转换、处理的要求。因此，绘文字在不同语言、不同平台上显示略有差别。微信表情是图片格式，与标准无关。本文预测，相对于微信表情，绘文字的设计通过面部表情的标准化组合来建立情绪意义，系统性更强，即每个运动单元在系统中的重复使用率更高。

已有文献表明，欧美表情设计偏“侧面型”，而日本表情设计偏“正面型”（梁燕碧，2006）。集体主义文化（如日本和中国）偏好垂直设计，例如：^ _ ^，侧重用眼睛表达情绪；个人主义文化偏好水平设计，例如：—），侧重用嘴部表达情绪。（丁尔苏，2012，pp.165—166）在绘文字从标点组合走向图像后，本文预测，微信表情设计侧重眼部，绘文字则侧重嘴部，即绘文字嘴部运动单元的使用频次更高，微信表情眼部运动单元的使用频次更高。

本文将绘文字的87个小黄脸（不区分肤色）与微信自创的55个小黄脸作为比较的素材，把脸部拆分为眉毛、眼睛、嘴、手势四个组成部分，描述其运动形状，并具体说明每个部分的运动形状应用于哪些表情。

（一）绘文字拆解分析

绘文字设计分类更细致，也更具体。例如，绘文字中“笑”可以分为：笑脸、微笑脸、露齿笑、耀眼笑、笑眼、笑得打滚等；“亲”可以分为：亲吻、闭眼亲、鼓脸亲、笑脸亲等；甚至“如释重负”等不常用的表情也分为如释重负、悲伤但如释重负两种。绘文字设计包含以下运动单元：10种眉部、24种眼部、37种嘴部（含4种舌头）和5种手势（见表1—表4）。

表1　绘文字小黄脸眉部的拆分描述

序号	1	2	3	4	5	6	7	8	9	10
眉部										
描述	基本平行	略向下倾斜	八字形	左高右平	左高右低	左低右高波浪形	左低右高	挑眉	向下较大倾斜	向上倾斜
表情	微笑	安静	悲伤、忧伤	思考	眨眼	挑眉	流口水	假笑	笑骂	胜利
	闭眼轻吻	极度痛苦	坚持、冷汗		亲吻	戴单镜片	说谎	阴险	哭泣	噘嘴
	惊讶	担心	累、厌烦					不愉快	大哭	咒骂
	激动	害怕	恶心、呕吐							
	晕	发烧	缠绷带							
	美元嘴	如释重负	悲伤但如释重负							

表 2　绘文字小黄脸眼部拆分描述

序号	1	2	3	4	5	6	7	8
眼部	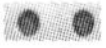				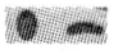	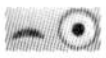		
描述	普通圆眼（微椭）	椭圆眼	月牙笑眼	眯眼	左睁右闭	左闭右睁	星星眼	爱心眼
表情	微笑脸、安静、震惊、恶心	露齿大眼	耀眼笑	坚持	亲吻	眨眼吐舌	眼冒星星	眼冒爱心
	亲吻、拉链嘴、张嘴、无嘴	牛仔	露齿笑	露齿眯眼	眨眼			
	思考、中立、噘嘴、生气		露齿带汗	累				
	冷汗、愤怒、害怕、咒骂		美食	眯眼吐舌				
	吐舌、困惑、担心、哭泣		笑眼	混乱				
	反转脸、书呆子、张嘴皱眉		笑眼亲	笑得打滚				
	困惑、惊讶、皱眉、轻皱眉		天使	呕吐				
	说谎、捂嘴笑、戴单镜片		拥抱	打喷嚏				
	悲伤但如释重负、发烧、缠绷带							
序号	9	10	11	12	13	14	15	16
眼部								
描述	圆眼珠	白眼	眼珠向右	上凸形	八字形	外八字形	下凹形	拱门形
表情	激动	翻白眼	假笑	沮丧	失望	流口水	昏昏欲睡	嘘
			不愉快	笑哭			沉睡中、胜利	
				大哭			如释重负	
							忧伤、担心	

续表2

序号	17	18	19	20	21	22	23	24
眼部	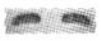							
描述	闭眼	双叉	左眼椭圆 右眼圆	平行 短横	左小右大	流泪	美元	椭圆空白
表情	闭眼亲	晕	挑眉	无表情	露齿 大小眼	哭泣	美元脸	惊恐尖叫
	笑脸							

表 3　绘文字嘴部拆分描述

序号	1	2	3	4	5	6	7	8
嘴								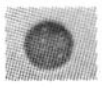
描述	短张嘴	长微张	中长闭嘴	长张嘴	露半齿	露全齿	M 形	小闭嘴
表情	眨眼	笑眼笑脸	微笑脸	爱心脸	露齿脸	耀眼笑	鼓脸亲	安静
	笑脸	拥抱	墨镜脸		露齿大眼		亲吻	沉睡中
	如释重负	天使	反转脸		露齿带汁		笑脸亲	
					露齿笑		闭眼亲	
					露齿眯眼			
					牛仔、 星星眼、 笑到打滚			
序号	9	10	11	12	13	14	15	16
嘴	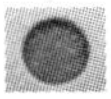			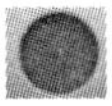				
描述	大张嘴	半张	纵向全张	最大张嘴	纵向 露半齿	短横	长横	右嘴角 微向下
表情	张嘴	生气	惊恐尖叫	晕	惊讶	白眼	无表情	思考
		害怕			大哭	极度痛苦	中立	
		震惊				激动	挑眉	
		皱眉						
序号	17	18	19	20	21	22	23	24
嘴				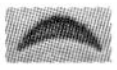		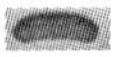		
描述	右嘴角弧 度向下	流口水	W 形	短张嘴 上凸形	露半齿 上凸形	横向椭圆	长闭嘴 上凸形	左嘴角弧 度向下

续表3

表情	缠绷带	流口水	糊涂	害怕、坚持、失望、担心、哭泣	厌烦	睡	皱眉	困惑
				悲伤但如释重负		张嘴冷汗		
				不愉快、冷汗		焦虑		
序号	25	26	27	28	29	30	31	32
嘴			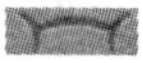		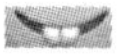		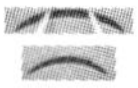	
描述	左嘴角微向下	右嘴角向上翘	H 形	呕吐	兔牙	龇牙	长闭嘴微上凸形	拉链
表情	说谎	假笑	恶心	吐	书呆子	鬼脸	轻皱眉	闭嘴
							发烧	
							胜利	
序号	33	34	35	36	37			
嘴	无							
描述	/	右侧伸舌头	中间伸舌头	左侧伸舌头	中间舌头吐美元			
表情	无嘴	美食	调皮	滑稽	美元脸			

表 4　绘文字手势拆分描述

序号	1	2	3	4	5
手					
描述	双手在嘴边	双手托腮	手枪形	示意别说话	五指捂嘴
表情	拥抱	惊讶尖叫	思考	嘘	捂嘴笑

表 1 至表 4 的分析发现，（1）眉毛在五官中的表现力相对较弱，种类也相应较少。表 1 中，序号 3 眉毛内角抬高的“八字眉”应用最多，均表示悲伤；序号 1、2、9 属于同一种眉形，但眉尾倾斜度逐渐加大，悲伤情绪逐渐强烈；序号 4、5、6、7 属于左右高低不同的眉毛，应用的表情较为分散。（2）表 2 中，眼部形状集中在序号 1 的普通圆眼上，刻画眼部比较单调，变化只体现在眼部形状上，除序号 6、9、10、21 外均“有眼无珠”，缺乏眼睛

内部的刻画。可能是因为眼珠太小，设计者出于传神和简化的考虑做出这一选择。(3) 表 3 中，嘴部形状按照大小、长度、倾斜度、弧度、露齿与否等变化最为丰富，比其他部位的种类数量多出近一倍，说明西方文化偏重嘴部导向的表情设计。嘴部肌肉控制比眼部容易，且面积更大，还可结合舌头，使情绪表达更明确。(4) 表 4 中，手势属肢体语言，出现频率最低，且都固定应用于某一种表情。

(二) 微信表情拆解分析

微信表情设计包含以下不同的运动单元：20 种眉部、37 种眼部、33 种嘴部（含 4 种舌头）和 12 种手势（见表 5—表 8）。

表 5　微信表情眉部拆分描述

序号	1	2	3	4	5	6	7
眉部	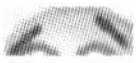						
描述	左低右高八字形	倒八字形角度大	倒八字形角度小	左高右低小弯眉	倒八字弧形	对称拱形	左低右高弧形
表情	撇嘴	发呆	流泪	闭嘴	发怒	龇牙	惊讶
		鄙视				坏笑	
						白眼	
序号	8	9	10	11	12	13	14
眉部							
描述	对称上凸弧形	左高右低不规则曲线	左高右低弧形	对称粗挑眉	挑眉角度大	对称挑眉	对称变八字形
表情	囧	吐	流汗	憨笑	咒骂	嘘	抠鼻
						擦汗	委屈
序号	15	16	17	18	19	20	
眉部							
描述	对称粗短折线	倒 S 形	左低小右高大弯眉	对称下凹弧形	对称平眉	左低右高倒 S	
表情	鼓掌	左哼哼	阴险	皱眉	奸笑	机智	
		右哼哼					

表 6　微信表情眼部拆分描述

序号	1	2	3	4	5	6	7	8
眼部								
描述	竖椭圆眼、眼珠偏下	竖椭圆眼、眼珠右下	爱心眼	水滴眼、眼珠居中	粗平行线	太阳光	竖椭圆眼、小眼珠右下	下凹形
表情	微笑	撇嘴	色	发呆	流泪	害羞	闭嘴	睡
	再见	嘘						
	难过							
序号	9	10	11	12	13	14	15	16
眼部							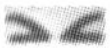	
描述	左右倒V、泪珠	竖椭圆眼、眼珠右上	竖椭圆眼、眼珠左下	倒 V、竖椭圆单眼、眼珠左下	上凸弧形	竖椭圆大小眼、眼珠偏中右	镜像倒 V	横椭圆大小眼
表情	大哭	囧	发怒	调皮	龇牙	惊讶	抓狂	吐
		傲慢			憨笑			
		汗						
序号	17	18	19	20	21	22	23	24
眼部			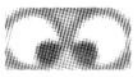					
描述	圆眼、眼珠偏左上	半圆眼	圆眼、眼珠居中偏下	横线	倒八字横椭圆眼	实心圆	左低右高圆眼珠	螺旋
表情	白眼	困	惊恐	流汗	奋斗	咒骂	疑问	晕
						坏笑		
						委屈		
序号	25	26	27	28	29	30	31	32
眼部								
描述	圆眼珠居中	镜像 E	半圆眼、眼珠偏右	横线、偏左眼珠	外八字形	倒外八字形	镜像 E 上长下短	不规则眼球、眼珠偏右下
表情	衰	敲打	擦汗	抠鼻	鼓掌	左哼哼	哈欠	快哭了
				阴险		右哼哼		
				鄙视				

续表6

序号	33	34	35	36	37			
眼部			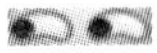					
描述	大圆眼珠闪高光	圆眼球、眼珠偏右	毛毛虫眼、眼珠偏左	半圆眼、眼珠偏右	圆眼珠			
表情	可怜	嘿哈	奸笑	机智	皱眉			
					耶			

表7　微信表情嘴部拆分描述

序号	1	2	3	4	5	6	7
嘴						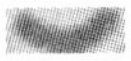	
描述	两端高弧线	波浪线	半圆露齿流口水	圆张	右高凹弧线	两端高粗弧线	十字叉
表情	微笑	撇嘴	色	发呆、睡	得意	害羞	闭嘴
	愉快			抠鼻、白眼	机智		
	再见			疑问、晕			
	皱眉			可怜			
	偷笑						
序号	8	9	10	11	12	13	14
嘴			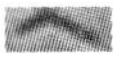				
描述	两端低宽弧线	三角形	中间高折线	舌头	半圆竖齿	不规则圆齿	两端低弧线
表情	大哭	汗	发怒	调皮	龇牙	惊讶	难过
序号	15	16	17	18	19	20	21
嘴			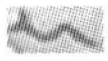				
描述	半圆张	不规则半圆露半齿	不规则曲线	右高凸弧线	椭圆齿	眼镜形齿	半圆露半齿
表情	囧	抓狂	吐	傲慢	困	惊恐	憨笑
					哈欠		
					流汗		
序号	22	23	24	25	26	27	28
嘴						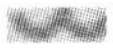	
描述	两端高弧线叼烟	左低右高斜弧线	短横线	不规则半圆露半齿喷飞沫	长椭圆张	倒3	两端高大弧线

续表7

表情	悠闲	奋斗	嘘	咒骂	鼓掌	嘿哈	奸笑
			擦汗		左哼哼		
					右哼哼		
序号	29	30	31	32	33		
嘴							
描述	不规则半圆露齿	两端低折线	扁半圆竖齿	反 3	歪露半齿		
表情	坏笑	快哭了	阴险	亲亲	耶		
					捂脸		

表 8　微信表情手势拆分描述

序号	1	2	3	4	5	6
手						
描述	圆形	横向四指合并	一根手指突出上指	竖向四指合并	一根手指突出左上指	双手侧面轮廓
表情	可怜	哈欠	嘘	再见	抠鼻	鼓掌
	疑问	偷笑				
	抓狂					
序号	7	8	9	10	11	12
手						
描述	双手 V 字形	双臂一上一下	五指分明	手臂横摆右指	两手各一根手指突出下指	两手各一根手指碰尖
表情	耶	嘿哈	捂脸	机智	鄙视	委屈

表 5 至表 8 的分析发现，（1）据表 5，接近一半的小黄脸带有眉毛，但眉毛形状各异，无法按长度、角度等进行归纳，粗细及眉头、眉尾的画法也都有差别。（2）据表 6 眼睛种类最多，微信表情偏重眼部，眼部不仅形状多，且大多带有眼珠，注重瞳孔内部形状的刻画。形状应用较为分散，某个形状通常只为某一个表情设计。（3）据表 7，嘴部相较于眼部种类略少，多是单一线条或简单形状。其他元素上只有叼烟一种。形状应用较为分散。（4）据表 8，手势使用称得上微信表情的一大特色，种类相对较多。

综合上述分析，表 9 系统地比较两种表情每一部位不同形状的种类数量、占各自表情总数的比重、每种形状被组合应用于多个表情的重复情况及其占各部位种类数的比重。

表 9　绘文字与微信表情的系统对比

		总　计		组　合		
		种类	百分比	重复种类	重复率	最多被用次数
眉部	绘文字	10	11%	9	90%	10
	微信表情	20	36%	5	25%	3
眼部	绘文字	24	28%	9	38%	34
	微信表情	37	67%	8	22%	3
嘴部	绘文字	37	43%	13	35%	8
	微信表情	33	60%	7	21%	7
手部	绘文字	5	6%	0	0	0
	微信表情	12	22%	2	17%	3

种类百分比=种类/表情总数（绘文字总数为 87 个，微信表情总数为 55 个）
重复种类：某一形状被应用于多个表情中即为重复
重复率=重复种类/该部位种类数总计
最多被用次数：某一形状被应用在多个表情中的最多次数

微信表情每一部位的种类百分比都远超绘文字，用更为多样化的形状来刻画表情。绘文字除了手部本身形状就很少外，在眉部、眼部、嘴部的重复种类和重复率均高于微信表情，说明绘文字的设计标准化倾向更强，偏向于面部表情系统及组合的逻辑性。微信表情眼部种类占比 67%，而绘文字仅 28%；绘文字嘴部种类占比 60%，而微信表情仅 43%。绘文字在刻画眼部上比较单调，缺乏微信表情那样的对眼睛内部眼珠的刻画；微信表情嘴部大多是单一线条或简单形状，绘文字按嘴部大小、长度、倾斜度、弧度、露齿与否，变化丰富得多。前述预测得到验证。

帕克等人提出，个人主义文化强调自我，集体主义文化强调一个社会共享的价值观。因此，个人主义文化中的个体更有可能从小就被训练明确表达自己的情绪，集体主义文化中的个体则被训练压抑他们的情绪，于是采取间接微妙的表达。当然，所谓压抑，是站在西方人的角度来看的。接着，帕克转到古迪孔斯特在 1997 年提出的“传播中的文化变异模型”，指出文化会影响个体的传播行为，而其中最重要的变异就发生在个人主义与集体主义维度间。帕克认为嘴部肌肉比眼部肌肉更易控制，表达更为明显，符合西方情绪表达明确而东方情绪表达含蓄的文化认知。但在对集体主义偏垂直表情（正面型）与个人主义偏水平表情（侧面型）的解释上，帕克的“垂直”和“水平”的用词暗中迎合了西方世界中的东方垂直型社会（高权力距离）和西方水平型社会（低权力距离）的想象。随着技术进步，原先的绘文字从标点进化到图案，东西方便都使用垂直表情，而不是躺着的水平表情。

绘文字设计不重视眼珠的刻画，可能是因为绘文字本身是面部表情的简化，从写实的角度，眼珠或瞳孔的面积实在太小，据信息传递观，为了尽可能保持面部表情的真实性而做出眼部细节的牺牲。微信表情重视与对象的眼神交流，尤其是对面积更小的眼珠的刻画，从几何比例来说是不写实的，更多是写意。所谓传神，更多是一种现场的、面对面的、共享意义的仪式性体验。尽管在面对面交谈过程中，东西方人都看到了一张真实的脸，但中国人似乎更在意并突出其中的局部，一个眼神，一个秋波，而忽略了那些平淡无奇的部分。微信表情的设计标准化倾向要低得多，由于其比例失实夸大，更多是一种不可分解式的设计。丁尔苏在分析文化的认知代码时，就比较了表10中的几对例子（2012，pp. 165－166）。古埃及用左侧全身画来表现牛、鱼，并借助眼睛来定位鼻子。而古中国则用牛的正面头像表示牛，突出牛角和牛耳；对鱼的表示突出鱼鳞；用正面单独鼻形表示鼻，并突出两个鼻孔。甲骨文只突出了一些局部，而不是描述对象的整体，这一特征在现代汉字“牛”“鱼”和“鼻”上依然有痕迹（需注意，甲骨文也有侧身像的文字）。这几对例子看起来跟早期绘文字的中西偏好（垂直/水平）很吻合，或是巧合，不是本文要探讨的问题。笔者认为，古埃及文字的例子表明其传递信息重在客观陈述和记录，而古中国甲骨文的例子更强化现场的、共享的意义体验。

表10　甲骨文与古埃及文字中水平与垂直呈现的对比

	牛	鱼	鼻
甲骨文			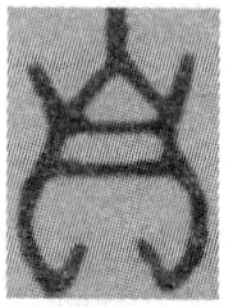
古埃及文字			

在早期标点符号组合的颜文字时代，水平型表情是客观的，这种客观不

仅表现在方向上，而且还体现为眼、嘴、鼻的比例同现实比例接近；垂直型表情眼、嘴比例和间距都失真，但观者会其意，是当场的、实时的仪式性体验。从文字到图像的技术演进后，现在的绘文字无一例外全部转向垂直型表情，尽管从理论上讲西方仍可沿用水平的表情。表情本来就是用于人际互动的，无论是东方人还是西方人，用技术模拟这种面对面的场景，是不可阻挡、符合人性的。现在的绘文字承袭了写实性设计，是一种客观传递的体现；微信表情承袭了写意式表达，眼睛是心灵的窗户，尽管在面部比例中，尤其是在小黄脸中眼珠几乎无法按现实比例写实呈现，设计者明显放大了这一部位。

二、两种面部表情系统的整体与个案比较

本部分采用克雷斯和冯·洛文的视觉语法框架（Kress，Leeuwen，2006，pp. 1—15），从再现意义、互动意义和构成意义三个层次切入分析，既有整体比较，亦有个案比较，分析的素材从小黄脸扩展至其他系统自带的表情。

（一）再现意义

按照视觉语法的分类，再现意义是图像最基本的功能，包括叙事再现和概念再现两种。叙事再现是社会行为的设计，概念再现则是社会构成的设计。叙事再现的图片中，向量由具有明显方向性的事物形成的斜线构成，而概念再现则没有向量。总的来说，绘文字侧重概念再现，其表情设计跟前述面部图释系统的思路如出一辙，是结构化的产物，通过眉、眼、嘴、手各部的逻辑及与现实比例接近的组合来设计表情；微信表情更注重叙事再现，头部前倾后倒、上仰下俯，各种角度，与现实的五官比例与方位都不相符，更加写意（表 11）。

表 11　绘文字与微信表情向量举例

	露齿笑脸	笑得打滚	鬼脸	反转脸	思考脸
绘文字					
	微笑	惊讶	左哼哼	流泪（仰天）	大哭（低头）
微信表情					

表 11 中，绘文字几乎都是采用一个圆圈作为脸廓，尽管这个圆脸可以顺时针、逆时针旋转，甚至完全反转过来（中西方的表情夸张方式也是不同的），但始终是以正面圆脸为构形基础。而微信表情除圆脸外，还会牵涉头部、脖子及全身的活动。前文表 9 中微信表情手势远超绘文字，可见微信表情涉及行为的场景化设计，缺乏绘文字的可分解的组合结构性。绘文字官方释义中形容脸的词语多达 44 个，用语非常丰富，例如露齿笑脸（griming face）、激动而涨红的脸（flushed face），这种“形容词+器官”的形式在微信表情描述中一个都没有。微信表情的官方描述更多采用动词，比如抠鼻、发呆、得意、闭嘴。这些都说明绘文字偏概念再现，微信表情偏叙事再现。

类似的表情设计（表 12），绘文字追求表情信息的写实传递：玫瑰花即是一朵写实的玫瑰花，但现实生活中我们不会只掐下玫瑰花朵去送人；红唇皓齿鲜艳动人，似乎在等待一个亲吻，这种接近写实的画风，可以让读者联想整个面孔以及肌肤娇嫩、美目流盼、桃腮带笑、气若幽兰等形容美女的词汇；拥抱的动作，是表情发送者真实动作的再现，多在庆贺的场景中发出，在中国人看来有点“袭胸”的嫌疑；亲吻的方向则更有趣，绘文字向右方向亲，这或许是跟左对齐评论式中动作发出者在左边有关；“嘘”的动作也非常写实，从对方的角度看到的正是拳头握紧的另一侧；刀把与乒乓球拍手柄都在对多数人来说不顺手的左边。

微信表情追求仪式感，重在会意与实时体验，而不是精确的实像表达：玫瑰花带着长长的花茎，无论对表情发送者还是接收者，都有“握住”的代入感；模糊的红唇，既可看作发送者发出的，也可看作接收者发出的；拥抱更像是卡通形象，一种安慰情境下的可操作表达，既可以是发送者的双臂，也可以是接收者的双臂；亲吻的方向向左，这可能跟左右对话模式中发送者在左边、接收者在右边有关，有趣的是，这种对话中的代入感，即发送者向接收者方向亲去，在接收方手机中却是一个奇怪的呈现——发送者在亲吻自己的头像（图 2）；“嘘”的表情也缺乏立体真实的刻画，掌背掌心不明，可看作掌心，亦可看作掌背，因此收发双方都可代入，不像绘文字那样有清晰的掌心与掌背的区分，明显是发送者的动作；刀把与乒乓球拍手柄都在右边，这是一个顺手的、易代入行为的方向，尽管跟亲吻一样，在接收方手机屏幕上显示会比较奇怪。亲吻、刀和乒乓球的例子也说明，仪式本身重在体验，而不像绘文字那样讲究写实与传递细节。

表 12：绘文字与微信表情再现意义举例

	玫瑰花	嘴唇	拥抱	亲吻	嘘	刀	乒乓球
绘文字							
微信表情							

发送方屏幕显示

接收方屏幕显示

图 2　左右对话模式中发送方与接收方的屏幕显示

（二）互动意义

人际交往中互动意义的接触包括表达和索取两种类型。所谓表达型图像，即图像中的角色或意义精确，写实描述成为核心，观众聚集于对客体表情意义的解读；索取型图像使观看者与图像中的人物角色建立一种实时的、面对面的沟通关系，图像符号是模糊的、写意的，传受双方都有代入感，聚焦于意义的流动性。本文分析的对象主要是人脸，因此更为精细的人脸分解显得极为必要。本文发现，表达型图像绘文字是静态的、写实的刻画，而索取型图像微信表情是动态的、非几何比例的、以眼珠刻画为中心的、会意式的意义流动。

社会距离指的是由取景框架的大小反映出的读者与图像中人物或对象之间的距离。短距一般用于表示亲密，长距则更多展示环境。绘文字表情更大，感觉更近，就像化妆师要给一张脸化妆的距离，是一种细致的情绪表达；微信表情较小，感觉较远，比较接近人际交往的情境。

态度主要由视角体现。从垂直方向上看，绘文字主要是平视，代表双方的关系是平等的；微信表情除平视外，还有仰视和俯视，代表接收方地位有时高于图像，有时低于图像，比如委屈时接收方处于俯视地位，鄙视时接收方处于仰视地位。从水平方向上看，绘文字几乎都是正面，而微信表情则有不同比例的侧面。正面表示收发双方有良好的互动，而侧对或背对则一般表示互动关系差或没有，在中国情境中也用于好友间开玩笑或打情骂俏。

感官情态是指图像的真实度和可信度，可以归纳为高、中、低三类，一般来说色彩越明艳、丰富，感官情态真实度、可信度越高。绘文字拥有更逼真的视觉感受，更趋于写实。

（三）构成意义

构成意义分为信息值、取景框架及显著性。在两套表情中各元素的位置显示了表情的信息值。在平面布局上，左右布局表达已知信息和未知信息；上下方代表理想信息与现实信息；中心至边缘表明信息重要性递减。西方在设计表情时对人们在现实生活中的手势、表情进行写实，而中国更重写意（刘文慧，2013），这两种不同的思路决定绘文字重在传递信息，而微信表情重在仪式。绘文字基本遵循各元素（五官等）在整个表情当中的真实比例与方位，依据情绪种类调整形状。微信表情则没有这么呆板，各元素（五官等）位置也没有明确的范围，有时眉毛甚至可以跳到脸之外。这种写意而非写实的手法，可能跟中国画中讲究散点透视，提倡用活动的视点观察景物，从而使画面内容不受时空的限制有关。西方传统油画采用焦点透视，要求画家让物象处于特定的光照下，通过明暗层次和阴影体现其形象，增强真实感。（安丽，2012）因此，绘文字追求写实、立体，而微信表情为了会意而写意。

取景框架则是指利用线条、阴影、颜色等造成整体上及各元素之间的分割。在线条上，绘文字的轮廓模糊，由光影渐变而成，更接近真实；微信表情中轮廓与区域界线分明。在光源上，绘文字以顶光为主，头顶部分更清晰明亮，脸颊和眼窝处显得较为暗淡，整体呈现更为立体；微信表情的光源以正面光为主且光线较为聚集，脸正中更明亮，没有明显阴影。在微信最近新增的表情中，个别表情也采用顶光源。在颜色上，绘文字的五官轮廓都有阴影和高光，立体感更强，更加真实；微信表情纯色填充，较为扁平化。

显著性指元素吸引注意力的程度，主要体现在饱和度、明度、对比度等方面。虽然两种表情色彩差别不大，但微信表情的颜色不够鲜艳，元素不够突出，而绘文字色彩则饱和度、明度和对比度都更高，更能吸引注意力。（表 13）

表 13　绘文字与微信表情构成意义的对比

	信息值		取景				显著性
	五官位置	透视	线条分割	阴影分割		颜色分割	饱和度、明度、对比度
绘文字			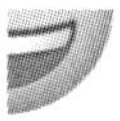				
微信表情							

三、研究小结

绘文字与微信表情的平行比较，首先基于二者的平台。在技术层面上，绘文字由万国码组成，不同平台购买版权后可根据自身需要进行改造；微信表情是由字符串组成并内嵌于微信程序，以唯一的图片形式存在。这一技术基础也直接导致在使用范围上微信表情无法在其他平台上使用，而绘文字则适用于多个平台，尤其是像推特、脸书等完全开放的平台。脸书和推特上绘文字的主接口是评论式，左对齐；微信表情的主接口是对话式，一左一右。使用平台范围以及使用接口的差异，也是不同文化群体自然选择的结果。

微信表情采用更为多样化的形状来刻画表情；绘文字除了手势外，眉、眼、嘴的重复种类和重复率均高于微信表情，其部分之间组合的系统性更强。微信表情眼部种类明显更多，绘文字嘴部种类更多。绘文字各部分比例和位置均符合写实原则，微信表情则更写意，本文借用凯瑞的说法来描述其设计理念上的“传递/仪式”观。在视觉语法和再现意义上，绘文字侧重概念再现，微信表情侧重叙事再现；互动意义上，微信表情发送者对互动性的期待更强烈，更聚焦眼睛的刻画；构成意义上，绘文字追求写实、立体，而微信表情为了会意而写意。就像不久前网络热议的话题：蒙面大侠的形象为什么在东方是蒙嘴，而西方是蒙眼？这也可印证西方人觉得嘴巴比眼睛更能直接传递情绪，而中国人则更希望通过眼神的微小变化来让对方自行体会情绪的差异。这是不同文化群体积累多年后在潜意识下的选择，同时也反映了两种文化的差异。“仪式就像一场令人心旷神怡的游戏”，“在仪式里面，世界是活生生的，同时世界又是想象的……然而，它展演的却是同一个世界。”（彭兆荣，2003）

本文对东西方网络表情设计差异的研究依然是初步的，西方的传递观阐述比较清楚，中国的仪式观仍需进一步的阐释。这个领域仍有许多问题值得研究。很多研究者都是在一个大的英语背景下做研究，将英语和别的语言进行简单的翻译。而且，面部表情的科学知识并不能取代普通大众对它的认识和理解，通常人们是不会使用艾克曼和弗里森的面部表情系统来讨论面部表情的。另外，中国的“愁”在字典里注释为悲伤（sorrow）、烦恼（worry）和忧郁（melancholy），但在英语中是找不到与“愁”对应的词。（韦程耀，赵冬梅，2012）还有学者认为，面部表情系统只是研究者的语言，不一定具有跨语言的可通约性，因而提出了中国民间模型（The Chinese Folk Model）——一个用中国语言来描述面部表情的语言模式。（Ye，2004）该研究也发现，眉毛和眼睛对中国人识别面部表情起到重要作用；美国人一般会对情绪进行离散分类，比如“他怎么看起来那么悲伤?”而中国人对面部表情的描述就不包含情绪术语，比如“他怎么看起来愁眉苦脸的?”中国语言中几乎所有对面部表情的描述都是关于部分的面部运动或者部分的面部结构；中国人在描述一种情绪时，通常会将这个情绪在面部的突出特征与具体某一五官结合起来描述。未来的研究可以朝着这个方向深入。

引用文献：

安丽（2012）. 论中西方绘画的散点透视与焦点透视. 文学界（理论版），8，291－291.

丁尔苏（2012）. 符号与意义. 南京：南京大学出版社.

梁燕碧（2006）. 日本的网络图释“颜文字”及其文化内涵. 广东外语外贸大学学报，2，35－38.

刘文慧（2013）. 发表情，调调情. 21世纪商业评论，6，72－73.

彭兆荣（2003）. 人类学仪式理论的知识谱系. 民俗研究，2，5－20.

饶广祥，魏清露（2018）. “趣我”与浅平化：网络图释的传播与反思. 福建师范大学学报（哲学社会科学版），2，162－172.

孙嘉靖（2013）. 以社会符号视角解读情绪意义. 现代广告（学刊），17，20－23.

韦程耀，赵冬梅（2012）. 面部表情的跨文化表达与识别研究述评. 心理科学进展，10，1614－1622.

Carey, J. W. (2009). *Communication as culture*. New York, NY: Routledge.

Ekman, P. & Friesen, W. V. (1975). *Unmasking the face: A field guild to recognizing emotions from facial clues*. Englewood Cliffs, NJ: Prentice-hall.

Feng, D. & O'Halloran, K. L. (2012). Representing emotive meaning in visual images: A social semiotic approach. *Journal of pragmatics*, 44(14), 2067－2084.

Kress, G. & Leeuwen, T. V. (2006). *Reading images: The grammar of visual design*. New

York, NY: Routledge Press.

Martinek, R. (2001). Interpersonal resources in action. *Semiotica*, 135(1/4), 117－145.

Park, J., Baek, Y. M. & Cha, M. (2014). Cross-cultural comparison of nonverbal cues in emoticons on twitter: Evidence from big data analysis. *Journal of communication*, 64(2), 333－354.

Ye, Z. (2004). The Chinese folk model of facial expressions: A linguistic perspective. *Culture & Psychology*, 10(2), 195－222.

作者简介：

林升栋，中国人民大学新闻学院广告系教授，中美富布莱特学者，研究方向为文化间传播、广告学。

程茜、乔巾哲、庞云洁、李亚伟，厦门大学广告系硕士生。

Authors:

Lin Shengdong, professor of School of Journalism and Communication, Renmin University of China. His research interests are cross-cultural communication and advertising.

Cheng Qian, Qiao Jinzhe, Pang Yunjie, Li Yawei, masters of advertising in Xiamen University.

Email: lincook@163.com

可述性：从符号叙述学界定新闻价值*

冯月季

摘　要：作为新闻学理论中的一个核心概念，传统的新闻价值研究一直徘徊在经验现象归纳和抽象哲学演绎两端。面对各种争议，学界难以就新闻价值概念达成共识。本文从符号叙述学角度出发，认为陈述和叙述是新闻文本构成和表意的两种方式。在此基础上，以可述性作为新闻价值的事件选择标准，以叙述性作为新闻价值的文本评价标准。并且从新闻报道具有无限趋近经验世界的饱满度特征，以及新闻报道的生产、传播和接收的实践维度，认为应当以可述性作为新闻价值的底线标准。

关键词：新闻价值，陈述，叙述，可述性，叙述性

Narratability: Defining News Value from the Perspective of Semiotic Narratology

Feng Yueji

Abstract: Research into news value, a core concept in journalism theory, has extended to both ends of the experiential/phenomenal induction and abstract philosophical deduction spectrum. There are many disputes over the concept and little consensus. This paper argues from the perspective of semiotic narratology that statement and narration are two forms of news text constitution and signification. On this basis, narratability is the standard for selecting news events and narrativity is the standard for evaluating news texts. Given the need for weightiness in a news report, which infinitely approaches the experiential world, and the practical

* 本文为河北省社科基金项目“新闻理论的符号叙述学研究”（HB18XW025）的阶段性成果。

features of the production, communication and reception of news reports, the author claims that "narratability" should serve as the baseline for news value.

Keywords: news value, statement, narrative, narratability, narrativity

DOI: 10.13760/b.cnki.sam.202001010

新闻价值是新闻理论研究中一个核心问题，不过这个核心问题从一开始就存在着许多争端。应当说，包括新闻价值在内的新闻学理论中的许多概念，都或多或少存在着争议性问题，这些问题如果不解决，将会直接损害新闻学作为一门学科的合法性。正如海德格尔所指出的："一门科学在何种程度上能够承受其基本概念的危机，这一点规定着这门科学的水平。"（2010，p.11）笔者通过搜索发现，由于学术界对新闻价值的争论一直达不成共识，所以近年来在新闻理论研究中很少再有人去追究新闻价值的概念界定，而将其作为一个不证自明的概念使用，这种绕过问题本质的现象陈述对新闻学理论研究而言毫无益处。必须把概念说清楚，笔者在此尝试从符号叙述学角度探讨这个问题，希望能够对新闻价值有一个新的认识。

一、新闻价值研究的流变与困境

不得不说的是，新闻价值研究一直难有定论，很大原因在于新闻价值概念的流动性，这也客观造成了新闻价值研究的困境。新闻价值概念的流动性表现在两个方面：其一，新闻现象层面的变化带来概念的变化，例如从硬新闻到软新闻，新闻价值的选择标准发生的变化；其二，新闻价值研究从新闻现象研究向新闻价值概念自身迁移，例如不少学者在文章中讨论"'新闻价值'的价值"。

新闻学自诞生之日起，就建立在实践和应用基础上，因此新闻价值概念的确定必然受制于新闻现象的变化。新闻价值的选择标准从早期的重要性、反常性，演变为日后的趣味性、接近性等，仍然处在不断演变中，继一般意义上新闻价值选择的五要素之外，有学者提出"第三媒介时代"新闻价值的核心要素：全时性、定制性、人性化、必要性、沉浸性、合作性。（李沁，2015）

显然，关于新闻价值的探讨到这里仍没有终结，随着新的新闻现象的涌现，必然还会有新的新闻价值要素的归纳和总结。且不说这是否能够穷尽新闻价值的构成要素（从相对的意义来说，答案必然是否定的），单论这种探讨新闻价值的研究方法，就已然违背了科学研究的逻辑性。卡西尔（Ernst Cassirer）在《人文科学的逻辑》一书中指出：人文科学不能单纯研究历史和社会中个别事件，因此任何一门人文科学的创建必须首先确立自己的概念，并且这些概念具有一种将历史和社会中个别事件“收蓄”的普遍性，否则其理论效力难以持久。（2013，pp. 97－98）柏拉图也曾说过：单纯的现象描述无法构成真正的科学知识。康德在《纯粹理性批判》中也非常明确地指出：理性必须先行于经验，而不能被经验牵着鼻子走。“经验之研究在未能为逻辑反省安立其应占的地位之前是绝对无法觅得‘科学的坦途’的。”（卡西尔，2013，p. 97）

按照上述逻辑来看，新闻价值研究自一开始，就没能在新闻学学科范畴内建立概念的普遍有效性。这是因为新闻价值概念，是西方新闻学界根据新闻业界的经验总结和现象描述，抽象出来的新闻选择标准。毫无疑问，中国新闻学研究中的新闻价值概念延续了西方的学术传统。这种根据经验现象界定新闻价值概念的研究方法，有其重要的实践意义，但是，由于经验现象的丰富性和无限性，我们很难穷尽其全貌，这就显现出经验现象研究方法的弊端，最明显的就是对新闻学学科理论有效性的建构造成的伤害。

经验现象之变化不断动摇概念之有效性，这使得新闻价值研究偏离了人文科学研究的逻辑。不止于此，卡西尔借助艺术作品的三个层次来指明人文科学的根本研究对象，卡西尔认为，艺术作品的存在可分为三个层次：物理存在层次、对象表现层次以及位格表达层次。（2013，p. 62）其中位格表达层次即艺术家的思想和心灵世界，泛指人的世界。人文科学的根本研究对象并非事物的物理存在和对象表现，而必然是卡西尔所说的位格表达层次，即人的世界。以此反观新闻价值的经验现象归纳和总结，便能发现其同样偏离了人文科学研究的根本研究对象。

新闻价值概念的流动性还指新闻价值研究从经验现象的归纳和总结，向新闻价值概念自身迁移，即追问新闻价值这个概念自身的含义。这种转向当然来自新闻学学科自身的压力。自诞生起，新闻学就背负着“新闻无学论”的质疑。于是，一些学者试图从形而上的层面为新闻学寻求理论支持。例如有的学者区分了新闻价值的不同层面：使用价值、认识价值、审美价值、文化价值等。

悖论的是，这实际上与上文所论新闻价值研究的现象和经验总结并无二致。新闻价值层面的划分很大程度上也属于经验现象的范畴。例如，20 世纪

80 年代，我国新闻学界把新闻价值划分为资产阶级新闻价值和无产阶级新闻价值，给新闻价值打上意识形态的烙印。这种状况下，新闻价值的层面突出的是政治价值和认识价值；市场经济条件下，新闻价值突出的层面变成经济价值和使用价值；进入大众文化时代，新闻价值突出的层面就应当是文化价值或审美价值。照此逻辑，新闻价值又成了一个无限衍义的流动性概念。

此外，也有学者从哲学演绎的角度界定新闻价值，试图从价值的哲学概念演绎出新闻价值的概念。不少学者依据马克思关于价值的哲学定义——价值是从人们对待他们满足需要的外界物的关系中产生的，从而推导出“价值是客体在社会实践中所履行的功能，它是客观之于主观的产物”（雷跃捷，1992）。价值就是价值关系，是客体的属性、功能对主体的效应关系，由此“新闻价值关系指的是新闻价值客体之属性、功能对新闻价值主体的效应关系”（杨保军，2002）。这种为新闻价值披上哲学外衣的做法，其学理漏洞早已被挑明，价值理论研究专家李德顺指出：许多人引用的马克思关于价值的定义，恰恰是马克思转述的他所要批评的瓦格纳提出的“商品价值”的概念（2007，p. 20）。此外，这种关于价值的哲学定义“沿袭的仍然是主体哲学的老路，陷入困境自然不可避免”（冯月季，2017，p. 184）。因此新闻学界对新闻价值的哲学演绎，在哲学起点上就犯了大错误，何谈理论有效性。

由是观之，不论是经验总结还是哲学演绎层面的新闻价值研究，最终都走向了困境。客观而言，这两种新闻价值研究的路径并非一无是处，它们分别指向了新闻价值概念的两个层面：新闻事件与新闻文本。当然也有学者意识到了这一点，例如由吉林省广播学院和北京广播学院早年编著的《新闻概论》区分了事实价值和新闻价值；郝雨将新闻价值分为“尺度性新闻价值”和“功能性新闻价值”（2006，p. 71）。不过，上述著作或学者并没有将问题深入下去，而是又返回了传统新闻价值研究的老路。

可以看出，新闻价值研究的经验总结或哲学演绎，都只能涵盖新闻价值的一个层面，前者指向新闻事件，后者指向新闻文本。两者的孤立存在造成了新闻价值概念含义的分裂。经验现象的新闻价值研究，其概念有效性难以持久，而哲学演绎层面的新闻价值的效应或功能到底由谁来界定，主体并不明确。要解决这些问题，必须转换研究思路。笔者尝试从符号叙述学入手，重新界定新闻价值。在重新界定新闻价值之前，笔者不妨先给出一个新闻价值的通俗定义：新闻价值就是媒体或记者选择一个新闻事件当作报道对象之前，考察该新闻事件是否“有必要说”或“可以说”，并且考虑受众是否有需求和兴趣接收。本文余下的论述，就主要围绕这个新闻价值的通俗定义而展开。

二、陈述与叙述：新闻的两种表意方式

新闻之所以有价值，很大程度是因为它满足了受众的某种需求，这种需求与人在现实世界中的思考或认知方式有关，布鲁纳（Jerome Bruner）认为人有“论辩式”（argumentative）和“叙述式”（story）两种思维方式，论辩式思维追求事件真相，叙述式思维追求事件情节生动。（Bruner，1987）狄尔泰（Wilhelm Dilthey）在创立阐释学之初，从更为宏观的意义上指出了这两种认知方式之间的差异。狄尔泰认为人文研究和自然科学具有本质不同：“科学说明自然，人文研究理解生命之表现。”（帕尔默，2014，p. 137）保罗·利科（Paul Ricoeur）认为这也是人在文本阐释行为中所具有的两种认知方式：说明和理解。（2015，p. 153）这两种方式是相互排斥的，“说明”以类似于科学家的运用自然科学的方式解释文本，而“理解”则以历史学家运用的人文学科的方法解释文本。

“说明”是一个结论，而“理解”则是一个过程。“说明”面对的是强编码文本，意义相对恒定，受众不需要做出过多解释，仅仅凭借文本就可以准确解读出文本发送者的意图。“理解”面对的是弱编码文本，意义相对复杂，受众在解读文本的过程中，需要综合把握文本中各意义要素之间的关系。人所具有的这两种认知方式或文本阐释方式，从新闻的角度来说同样适用。新闻，一般意义上分为硬新闻和软新闻，硬新闻要求受众以说明或论辩的方式理解，软新闻要求受众以理解或叙述的方式理解。

基于人的两种认知方式的差异，新闻文本编码的形态相应可分为陈述式与叙述式。陈述是以说明的方式发送和接收新闻文本，是对新闻事件中信息要素客观真实的报道。普林斯（Gerald Prince）在《叙述学词典》中认为“陈述包括历史、理论以及真实的陈述”（2016，p. 17）。对于新闻文本来说，消息类报道就是最典型的陈述，例如天气预报、交通状况等。对于这类新闻报道，受众不需要做出复杂的理解，只要能够明白消息文本所传达的基本信息即可。

与陈述相对应的是叙述，杰拉德·普林斯将叙述定义为“由一个、两个或数个（或多或少显性的）的叙述者，向一个、两个或数个（或多或少显性的）受叙者，传达一个或更多真实或虚构事件（作为产品和过程、对象和行为、结构和结构化）的表述”（2016，p. 136）。与陈述相比，叙述的结构更复杂，主体更加多元。从新闻报道体裁来看，各类深度报道都属于叙述的范畴，

因此有学者建议将新闻定义为“关于新近发生或发现的事实的符号叙述”（李玮，2016，p. 140）。

那么，陈述与叙述之间有什么本质区别呢？通常意义上，我们会说陈述是新闻要素或信息客观真实的说明，而叙述是新闻故事化，叙述就是讲故事，阿瑟·伯格（Arthur Asa Berger）认为：“叙述就是故事，而故事讲述的是人、动物、宇宙空间的异类生命、昆虫等身上曾经发生或正在发生的事情。”（2000，p. 4）詹姆斯·沃特森（James Watson）说：“新闻作为叙述，之所以被受众关注，根本原因是故事性对受众强烈的吸引力。”（Watson，2008，pp. 130－131）赫伯特·甘斯（Herbert J. Gans）也认为“故事的重要性和趣味性”是决定新闻的重要特质（Gans，1979）。

从上述几位学者对叙述的界定来看，陈述与叙述的区别是故事化与非故事化。但是“故事”这个概念在中文当中有虚构的意思，容易造成歧义。例如西摩·查特曼（Seymour Chatman）在其名著《故事与话语》中主要讨论的就是小说和电影的叙述结构。“故事”这个概念的虚构指向与新闻这种纪实型体裁发生冲突，因此以故事性来界定陈述和叙述的区别不够客观。

因此有学者建议，区别陈述和叙述要看是否卷入人物，陈述不卷入人物，只是对自然现象或物质形态变化的客观描述，叙述必须卷入人物（或叙述中物、动物具有伦理取向）。（赵毅衡，2013，p. 8）只有人才有叙述的能力和意向，通过叙述，人获得了存在的意义，如罗兰·巴尔特所说的：叙述是像生命那样存在着。陈述和叙述的这种非人格化与人格化区分，在柏拉图的《理想国》当中有明确表达：苏格拉底划分了“述真”（diegesis）与“模仿”（mimesis）两种话语方式。“述真”是诗人自己说话，而“模仿”则是除了诗人之外的叙述者说话。20 世纪的文学理论将“述真”与“模仿”表述为“展示”与“讲述”。“展示”是客观的、非人格化的，“讲述”则是叙述者隐退到文本之后控制着故事，让故事中的人物出场，通过情节推动故事的展开。

陈述和叙述在新闻报道中是两种常见的手法。例如一般的气象新闻，仅是对天气状况的客观描述，就是陈述式的表达。而如果在气象新闻中使用一些拟人化的修辞或加入人的感觉，例如《新京报》2017 年 4 月 19 日的气象新闻中对天气状况的报道使用拟人化修辞：“北风昨天入夜后变得温柔，尘埃落地。”则该气象新闻就从陈述式向叙述式转化。需要说明的是：因为新闻报道体裁的纪实性特征，一篇新闻报道完全可以使用陈述式的手法，或者使用陈述式和叙述式夹杂的手法。即便是在那些看起来非常接近虚构文本的新新闻主义作品中，陈述式的写作依然不可或缺，例如新闻报道中的时间、地点等新闻要素，必须是客观真实的，这是新闻真实的最低要求。

三、可述性：新闻价值的事件选择标准

根据前文表述，陈述和叙述是新闻文本的两种构成和表意方式，新闻文本是一种被选择的结果，我们需要追问的是：什么样的事件有意义或价值，值得被选择进入新闻文本，即什么样的事件具有可述性？赵毅衡教授将可述性与情节联系起来讨论，笔者认为这实际上首先预设了只有那些具备叙述特征的事件才有可述性。无情节的陈述事件是否具有可述性，例如日全食现象？从新闻的社会功能角度来说，答案是肯定的，类似于像气象报道、天体运行等无情节的陈述事件，受众依然有兴趣接收。因此，在本文对新闻价值的讨论中，可述性指向有情节的叙述事件和无情节的陈述事件。

先来看无情节的陈述事件，这类事件指的是不卷入人物或不具有人格化特征，且无情节展开的事件。在新闻报道中，这类事件依然具有可述性，指的是受众有获取信息的意向性，从新闻作为一种信息的角度而言，信息的客观真实性具有消除不确定性的功能。而有情节的叙述事件有多个人物卷入，且事件被认为具有故事的潜质，因而具有了可述性。从新闻报道的角度来说，可述性是事件的品质，即一个新闻事件是否值得被报道，且受众是否有兴趣接收。

问题在于，可述性是如何判断的？判断的主体是谁？早期的新闻理论研究可能会认为是媒体偏好或记者具有决定新闻价值的权力，随着受众理论的发展，越来越多学者开始倾向于认为受众在新闻价值判断中居于主体性地位。这和可述性的判断主体具有一致性，杰拉德·普林斯说："可述性常常是，甚至总是接收者的一种功能。"（2015，p. 17）但是接收者依然是一个比较模糊的概念，不同的接收者对同一事件的判断并不相同，这样就有可能"众口难调"，可述性的标准就无从界定。

因此，可述性判断的主体就不是社会文化中作为个体的人，而是某个固定的阐释社群（interpretive communities）。新批评主义的斯坦利·费什（Stanley Fish）认为："意义既不是确定的文本的特征，也不是某个独立的读者所具有的属性，而是阐释社群所共有的特征，阐释社群既决定读者阅读形态，也制约了这些活动所制造的文本。"（1998，p. 46）阐释社群是一个集体人格，其中的个体具有大致相似的知识背景、审美品位、信息需求等，阐释社群的意义需求因而成为判断一个事件是否具有可述性的依据。

即便是从阐释社群的角度理解可述性，也依然需要讨论具有可述性事件的特征。因为进入新闻报道的事件与整个经验世界相比，只能是一个子集，正如李普曼（Walter Lippmann）所说的，就算世界上的记者们整天不休息，忙于采访，也不可能把世界上发生的所有事件都写进新闻报道。因此，新闻报道首先是一种事件选择，选择那些值得被报道且阐释社群有兴趣接收的事件。这个问题自世界上第一张报纸诞生之后，就成为媒体和记者一直思考的问题，由此，才涌现出了新闻价值判断的各种标准。

我们可以发现，不论由经验现象归纳的新闻价值标准如何变化，其中有一条不变的就是事件的反常性、新奇性。这种观点从 19 世纪 70 年代出现"狗咬人不是新闻，人咬狗才是新闻"起一直延续至今，成为新闻价值判断的最重要的标准。这种新闻价值的判断标准，实际上是把新闻价值的判断标准统一化了，陷入了一元论的窠臼。从现实来说，这种新闻价值判断标准导致媒体和记者在新闻报道中过度追求猎奇和新鲜，很可能就违背了媒体的职业伦理。

因此，事件是否具有可述性的判断就不能完全以反常性为标准，"接收者并不是都冲着听新鲜而来的，他们期盼某种体裁，完成社会文化规定的表意程式，这也是一种常规性心理满足"（赵毅衡，2013，p. 169）。所以那些具有可述性的事件，除了反常的以外，一些具有常规性、日常化特征的事件也具有可述性。举例来说，当前的新闻报道中，一些非常平凡的人物的经历、命运和生活状态，正在越来越多地成为新闻报道的对象，这类报道就不具有反常性，然而依然具有可述性，因为受众从他人的经验之中获得了有意义的体验。

从人在经验世界的存在来看，反常事件或经验必定属于少数，大多数情况下，人在经验世界中的存在都处在一种程式化的表意机制中。由于人的社会属性，作为个体的人无法完成社会程式化的表意，只有通过不断体验外在世界对象的经验完成自我的社会化。舒茨（Alfred Schutz）认为人对经验世界的体验构成了"经验基模"（Schemata unserer Erfahrung），即"完整的意义脉络，会以'知道某事物'或'已知道某事物'的形式出现，它们是经由范畴秩序化而来的材料构成的，当每一项体验出现时，我们就根据这些基模加以诠释"（2012，p. 110）。通过对外在对象经验的体验和反思，人获得了完成社会程式化所需要的意义素材。

大体上，常规事件和反常规事件构成了新闻报道的主要对象。这里的问题是：反常规和常规间有没有界限？因为新闻报道不可能容纳社会中所有的反常规事件和常规事件，所以新闻价值的判断就必须首先从常规事件和反常规事件中排除那些不适合或没必要报道的事件，如此，新闻价值才有一个基本可以依据的判断标准。杰拉德·普林斯1988年提出了“未叙述事件”的概念，认为“未叙述事件”就是“不能叙述或不值得叙述的事情，其原因可能是它违反了法律（社会的、作者的、类属的、形式的等等），或者是它蔑视了某一特别的叙述者（或任何一位叙述者），或者是它不够所谓可叙述性的门槛（如还不够异常或称为问题）”（沃霍尔，2007，pp. 241—245）。

罗宾·沃霍尔（Robyn R. Warhol）在此基础上从女性主义叙述学以及社会文化规约对叙述行为约束的角度，在“未叙述事件”概念基础上提出“不可叙述事件”概念，分成四种类型：不必叙述（subnarratable）、不可叙述（supranarratable）、不应叙述（antinarratable）、不愿叙述（paranarratable）。（2007，pp. 245—246）“不必叙述”是过于庸常、不值得叙述；“不可叙述”是过于失常或反常规；“不应叙述”是社会文化规范要求不能付诸文本；“不愿叙述”是在经验世界大量存在，但是不符合叙述文类规范。

需要指出的是，沃霍尔讨论的不可叙述事件的四种类型，是以经典现实主义小说作为对象的。之于新闻报道这种纪实型文本来说，并不能简单套用。从时间上看，沃霍尔研究的是19世纪末至20世纪中叶左右，社会文化规范对作家（特别是女性作家）写作内容的约束，例如维多利亚时代的现实主义小说中，性属于禁忌话题，轻易不能碰触；或者是对小说中主人公（特别是女性）命运的操控，例如19世纪的女性主义小说中，女主人公要么嫁人，要么死掉。但是维多利亚时代的社会文化与今天相比显然是“窄幅”的。在讨论20世纪末至21世纪的大众电影时，沃霍尔认为电影中的不可叙述事件的范畴超出了现实主义小说的局限，从而扩大了电影叙述的可能范围。

当今的社会文化与维多利亚时代相比，是“宽幅”的，社会文化规范对不可叙述事件的限定小得多。另外，新闻和小说的体裁不同，讨论小说的底线可述性，应当以事件构成的最简情节为标准，即普林斯所说的“最小故事”（2015，pp. 13—15）。因此无论如何，情节都是讨论小说时无法回避的因素。但是新闻不同，陈述性的事件没有情节，也可以成为新闻报道的对象。新闻报道以经验世界为对象，总是试图再现经验世界的全域，无限趋近于经验世界的饱满度。

在笔者看来，新闻事件的底线可述性，只能以“不必说”和“不可说”为标准，即沃霍尔所说未叙述事件的前两种类型，不包含第三种“不应叙述”和第四种“不愿叙述”。前者指违反社会常规或禁忌，但是社会常规或禁忌是相对的，例如：排泄相关话题过去一般不出现在叙述文本中，但是在今天的社交媒体中，这类话题可以公开来谈，并不是什么社会禁忌。后者涉及文类的限制，例如好莱坞电影固定的大团圆结局，但是这对新闻报道来说并不适用，新闻报道格外热衷于各种“人间悲剧”，例如新闻界流行的“一天给我一桩谋杀案”这一说法。

“不必说”即不值得说。什么样的事件不值得说？沃霍尔认为太微不足道、过于庸常的事没有必要说出来。笔者认为沃霍尔的表述有些模糊，“过于庸常”的界限难以划定。笔者的建议是：从新闻的角度来说，“不必说”或“不值得说”的事件是那些具有常识性且恒定无变化的陈述性事件，例如太阳每天从东方升起，无论如何都不会成为单独的新闻报道对象。也即是说：任何涉及变化的——具有时间向度的陈述性事件，都具备成为新闻报道对象的潜质。

叙述性事件的“不可说”或“不可叙述”，指的是“那些难以用叙事方式再现的事件，凸现出语言或视觉形象充分表征事件的难处”（沃霍尔，2007，p. 245）。从新闻报道来说，叙述性事件的“不可叙述”，既受到社会文化规范的制约，也受到媒体伦理规范的制约，如涉及个人隐私的内容不宜出现在新闻报道中。除此以外，任何叙述性事件都具备成为新闻报道对象的潜质。

四、可述性还是叙述性：新闻价值的底线标准

新闻的叙述性是指基于新闻事件生成的新闻文本卷入了情节，从而被认为具有了故事性。需要说明的是：陈述性事件和叙述性事件都可能具有叙述性。叙述性事件容易理解，无论其情节性强弱，都天然具有叙述性，而陈述性事件若要具有叙述性，则必须经过运用某种特定方式的改造。在新闻报道中，最常见的改造手法就是将陈述性事件情节化，例如对气象报道的人格化处理或拟人化修辞，使得新闻文本呈现出叙述性。

叙述性是新闻价值的文本评价标准，可述性是新闻价值的事件选择标准。那么，新闻价值应当以什么标准来判断，是可述性还是叙述性？笔者的建议是：新闻价值的判断应当以可述性为标准；可述性是新闻事件的品质，叙述性是新闻文本的品质。

从新闻报道的生产和传播过程来看，总是先发生新闻事件，才有新闻采访和报道。这个顺序是一定不能变的，这与小说等文学创作不同，否则就成了“策划新闻”。记者或媒体在对新闻事件进行选择和判断时，当然首先依据

的是阐释社群的兴趣和需要，在此基础上，尽可能地从有必要说或可以说的事件中，选择与报道对象相关的事件进入新闻文本。以报道对象为圆心，散布出若干个与该新闻事件意义相关的文本，从这个层面而言，新闻报道具有穷尽新闻事件本真的文本意向性。

这是由新闻和文学两种文本体裁的差异决定的。瑞安（Marie-Laure Ryan）指出："真正的虚构文本创造自己的世界，并构成该世界的唯一通达模式，而非虚构文本指涉的世界则构成许多文本的潜在目标，因为该世界具有文本外的存在。虚构文本对其指涉世界而言自动为真，但非虚构文本必须同描述同一世界的其他文本竞争才能确立真实性。"（2014，p.49）瑞安的意思是：虚构文本具有文本内在真实性，不指涉经验世界；非虚构文本必须依靠指涉经验世界才能确立真实性。

新闻报道作为非虚构文本，追求再现经验世界的本真，这构成了前文所提及的新闻报道穷尽新闻事件本真的文本意向性。当然，正如瑞安所指出的：新闻文本的这种文本意向性，是在与其他新闻文本的竞争中显现出来的。从现实角度而言，围绕一个新闻事件报道必然有多个新闻文本，众多新闻文本从不同角度挖掘该新闻事件的真相，使得该事件不同程度地扩容和增殖。因此，以再现经验世界本真为追求的新闻报道对新闻事件的选择，锚定的是经验世界的全域，力图在新闻文本中无限趋近经验世界的饱满度。

由此，媒体或记者在判断新闻价值时，必定是以新闻事件的可述性为准则，而叙述性是指受众对新闻事件转化为新闻文本之后的评价。新闻文本是否具有叙述性，媒体或记者不能完全把握，媒体或记者能做的就是对新闻事件的品质进行评估，运用某种叙述方式将新闻事件呈现为新闻文本，从时间顺序上来说，新闻事件的可述性在先，新闻文本的叙述性在后。

新闻事件的可述性既包含陈述性事件，也包含叙述性事件。正如笔者在前文所指出的：新闻报道具有无限趋近经验世界饱满度的特征。因此，以叙述性作为新闻价值的判断标准，无形中就使得新闻报道偏离了经验世界的饱满度。新闻报道可以追求叙述性，但这不具有普遍性，一些陈述性事件依然可以通过不具有叙述性的方式呈现为新闻文本。

用叙述性作为新闻价值的评判标准，实际上窄化了新闻事件的选择范围，又回到传统新闻价值选择的反常规性标准上。并且，叙述性的产生具有滞后性，尽管叙述者精心构造文本，尽量使得文本具有叙述性，但是叙述性的生成最后依然要交由阐释社群来评判。因此，以叙述性作为新闻价值的判断标准，实际上是把新闻文本接收者当成了"理想读者"或"超级读者"，即接收者完全按照叙述者的意图来解释文本，这在现实中是不可能的。一个叙述者自认为叙述性很强的文本，读者可能并不买账，很难说这样的文本具有较强的新闻价值；反之，一些叙述性较弱，甚至陈述性的文本，例如有关地质灾害的消息，读者却有极大兴趣接收，这样的新闻文本当然就具备较高的新闻价值。

因此，笔者从新闻事件出发，而不是从新闻文本出发，主张以可述性作为新闻价值的底线标准，这是综合考虑新闻报道的生产、传播和接收而得出的结论。事实上，一些传统的关于新闻或新闻价值的定义，就是从新闻事件出发的。例如较为常见的陆定一关于新闻的定义："新闻就是新近发生的事实的报道。"再例如艾丰对新闻价值的定义，认为"新闻价值是新近发生的事实的一种社会属性，是指这个事实可能给社会带来的新的信息的分量"。

但是与笔者主张不同的是，这些关于新闻或新闻价值的定义表述比较模糊，"事实"一词涵盖了经验世界的全域，把"不必说"与"不可说"的事件也纳入了新闻报道的对象，这是不合理的。而从可述性出发，将"不必说"与"不可说"的事件排除出新闻报道的对象，那些"有必要说"或"可以说"的事件就构成了新闻报道潜在的对象，这些事件既包含陈述性事件，也包含叙述性事件。这样，我们就得出了一个新闻价值的底线标准，与一般新闻价值的五要素相比，应当说，这个新闻价值的底线标准是宽泛和开放的，既具有学理上的可论证性，也具有实践上的可操作性。

引用文献：

伯格，阿瑟（2000）. 通俗文化、媒介和日常生活中的叙事（姚媛，译）. 南京：南京大学出版社.

冯月季（2017）. 符号与价值：价值研究的符号学考察. 载于曹顺庆，赵毅衡（主编），符号与传媒，1. 成都：四川大学出版社.

费什，斯坦利（1998）. 读者反应批评：理论与实践（文楚安，译）. 北京：中国社会科学出版社.

郝雨（2006）. 回归本义的"新闻价值"研究. 上海大学学报（社会科学版），6，69－74.

海德格尔（2010）. 存在与时间（陈嘉映译）. 北京：生活・读书・新知三联书店.

卡西尔，恩斯特（2013）. 人文科学的逻辑（关子尹，译）. 上海：上海译文出版社.

雷跃捷（1992）. 新闻价值定义再探. 现代传播，3，15－23.

李沁（2015）."第三媒介时代"新闻价值的定位与建构. 当代传播，4，41－44，48.

李德顺（2007）. 价值论（第2版）. 北京：中国人民大学出版社.

李玮（2016）. 语境变迁下的"新闻"定义再思考：以符号叙述学为视角. 载于曹顺庆，

赵毅衡（主编），符号与传媒，1. 成都：四川大学出版社.
利科，保罗（2015）. 从文本到行动（夏小燕，译）. 上海：华东师范大学出版社.
帕尔默，理查德（2014）. 诠释学（潘德荣，译）. 北京：商务印书馆.
普林斯，杰拉德（2015）. 故事的语法（徐强，译）. 北京：中国人民大学出版社.
普林斯，杰拉德（2016）. 叙述学词典（乔国强，李孝弟，译）. 上海：上海译文出版社.
瑞安，玛丽-劳尔（2014）. 故事的变身（张新军，译）. 南京：译林出版社.
舒茨，阿尔弗雷德（2012）. 社会世界的意义构成（游淙祺，译）. 北京：商务印书馆.
沃霍尔（2007）. 新叙述：现实主义小说和当代电影怎样表达不可叙述之事. 载于詹姆斯·费伦等（主编）. 当代叙事理论指南. 北京：北京大学出版社.
杨保军（2002）. 论新闻价值关系的构成. 国际新闻界，2，55-60.
赵毅衡（2013）. 广义叙述学. 成都：四川大学出版社.
Watson, J. (2008). *Media communication: An introduction to theory and process.* Basingstoke, UK: Palgrave MacMillan.
Gans, H. J. (1979). Deciding what's news: Story suitability. *Society,* (4)65.
Bruner, J. (1987). *Actual minds, possible worlds*. Cambridge, MA: Harvard University Press.

作者简介：

冯月季，博士，燕山大学文法学院副教授，四川大学符号学-传媒学研究所成员，主要研究方向为传播符号学、社会符号学。

Author:

Feng Yueji, Ph. D., associate professor of School of Humanities and Law, Yanshan University, member of the ISMS Research Team. His research fields are communication semiotics and social semiotics.

Email: fengyue197997@126.com

回到商品表征：对品牌理论的一个符号学追溯

刘　楠

摘　要：消费社会商品的象征意义对于消费者行为发挥着巨大的影响，为商品赋予象征意义成为营销的重要内容。学术界往往忽视商品和品牌意义构建的关系，将它们割裂开来。本文借助符号学的方法，提出解释商品象征意义形成机制的分析框架，该框架将消费者视为商品象征意义的积极的建构者，而非商品意义消极的接收者，并将商品象征意义的形成概括为几个关键的过程。最后本文讨论了该分析框架对营销观念的意义。

关键词：象征意义，形成机制，商品，品牌

Return to the Representation of Commodity: A Semiotic Review of Brand Theory

Liu Nan

Abstract: The symbolic meaning of commodity has a great influence on consumers' behavior, and giving symbolic meaning to commodity has become an important part of marketing. However, the relationship between commodities and brand meaning has been ignored. With the help of semiotics, this paper puts forward an annalistic framework to explain the formation mechanism of commodity symbolic meaning. Consumers are regarded as the positive constructors of commodity symbolic meaning, rather than the negative receivers of commodity meaning, and the formation of commodity symbolic meaning is summarized as several key processes. Finally, it discusses its significance in marketing theory.

Keywords: symbolic meaning, formation mechanism, commodity, brand

DOI: 10.13760/b.cnki.sam.202001019

符号消费在实践上的盛行受到让·鲍德里亚（Jean Baudrillard）等的批判，他们认为消费社会中符号和商品的物质基础相分离，商品的符号意义完全和它的物质实体无关，商品的能指和所指分离，商品成为漂浮的能指系统，“产品本身并非首要的兴趣所在；必须在该产品上嫁接一套与该产品没有内在联系的意义才能把它卖掉”（鲍德里亚，2001，p.108）。他们批判符号消费的逻辑起点就是消费社会中的商品及品牌与为其赋予的符号意义之间毫无关联。事实上，营销学、品牌学学界对商品和品牌关系的讨论也一直含混不清，以至于对鲍德里亚等人的批判无法做出有力的回应。

一、商品与品牌的纠缠

品牌的塑造问题长久以来都受到学术界和业界的关注，从20世纪50年代开始对品牌管理进行系统性研究至今，管理学、心理学、社会学、人类学等学科的方法和理论都被应用到品牌的研究当中，从不同的角度对品牌进行分析，经历古典品牌理论阶段（20世纪50年代至20世纪80年代）、现代品牌理论阶段（20世纪80年代末至20世纪90年代）和当代品牌理论阶段（20世纪90年代末至今），生产出了大量的非常具有解释力和指导性的理论成果和品牌塑造模型，如品牌形象论、定位理论、品牌蜂窝模型、文化品牌模型等。但是，品牌理论的研究一直以来都存在一个局限——未将品牌与产品很好地结合起来研究，只是停留在品牌问题上。

有关商品的讨论未直接囊括品牌，而有关品牌的研究又未直接把品牌纳入商品的部分，而是用扩展产品、附加产品等词来指代品牌。“扩展”“附加”这些词显得品牌是可有可无的部分，并未充分重视品牌。例如，菲利普·科特勒（Philip Kotler）和凯文·莱恩·凯勒（Kevin Lane Keller）对产品层次的分析指出，产品由核心产品、实体产品和扩展产品构成，实体产品则是由品牌名称、包装、设计、特征、质量水平等构成（科特勒，凯勒，2016）；何建民提出，“品牌作为传播产品价值的工具，是以产品价值为基础的，也是为传播这些价值服务的”（2002，p.47）；王连森认为，“品牌是以企业及其产品为基础、为载体的。品牌总是与企业及其产品结合在一起，没有完全脱离一定企业和产品的品牌。尽管有时候品牌会脱离原来的企业或产品，但是它必须依附于新的企业或产品，才能再次体现它存在的价值”（2004，p. 74）。格拉布（Edward L. Grubb）和格拉斯沃尔（Harrison L. Grathwohl）提出，消费者使用品牌作为象征交流的工具，将品牌作为符号来传播关于他的自我形象的意义，消费者通过内动过程（intra-action process）将品牌具有的符号意义转移到自身，通过互动过程（interaction process）得到他人的回应从而强化、提升自我形象（1967，pp. 22－27）。道格拉斯·霍尔特（Douglas Holt）提出了文化品牌模型，以解释文化偶像品牌的强大力量；偶像品牌的塑造主要是通过合理地利用社会中存在的“严重的文化矛盾”，以及该矛盾所导致的人们的欲望焦虑，通过指出现实和理想的对比形成文化张力，再开发出一个至高无上的概念来应对和解决该文化冲突，从而形成品牌迷思（Holt，2006）。

上述关于品牌意义的讨论，重点或是放在受众和品牌之间的互动关系上，或是放在品牌与文化之间的关系上，均没有提到商品在品牌意义建构中的位置。而唯一提到商品的品牌意义生成模型的，也只是将商品（物）看作品牌未形成阶段的状态，即牌子和品牌都是与商品对立的非物，而商品一旦成为品牌，便与物脱离了关系。

商品和品牌是不可分割的整体，品牌建设的最终目的是促进商品的销售和增加商品的附加值，提高商品的溢价。企业无法向消费者直接出售品牌，而是通过出售商品来实现品牌的价值，没有商品，品牌的价值无法实现，也就是说品牌实质上是基于商品的，商品是品牌价值的载体，并且品牌意义最终是否能够成功地传递、让渡到消费者那里，取决于商品这个意义载体能否承载、匹配品牌的意和形象。脱离商品来讨论品牌将会导致品牌理论脱离实际，无法真正发挥价值。戴维·阿克（David Aaker）认为一位品牌负责人如果想要让旗下的品牌认同具有广度和深度，必须将品牌当作产品、企业、人、符号，以帮助品牌管理人更完备地顾及品牌的不同层面，并且利用这些不同的层面，让品牌认同显得更清晰、更丰富、更与众不同（2013）。也就是说，在戴维·阿克的品牌认同系统中，商品成了品牌的一个层面。蒋诗萍认为品牌是一个三位一体的结构，品牌符号的再现体是名称、标识或者它们的组合，对象是由企业提供的产品或服务，解释项是品牌的社会文化意义与价值。产品或服务是品牌不可或缺的组成部分（2013，pp. 213－221）。

另一方面，品牌对于商品的销售和增值具有重要的意义。因此，品牌和商品相互依赖，相互影响。品牌是增加商品价值的重要工具，商品是品牌价值的载体。商品和品牌的形象、意义一致，能够促进商品的销售和品牌资产的增加，反之则会造成品牌资产的贬值。因此，将商品和品牌结合起来研究不论是对于品牌理论的发展，还是品牌塑造的实践都具有极其重要的意义。

总体看来，目前对于商品/品牌意义的生成的研究具有局限。首先，研究主要集中在较为宏观的层面，主要探讨商品意义主要来源于其他的意义系统，或者说社会、群体的作用，对商品意义生产的微观的、具体的过程关注不够。其次，商品的功能和符号意义被截然二分，商品的物本身所包含的意义被严重忽视，这其中隐含的逻辑就是商品本身并不携带意义，商品要经过转化才能成为符号，商品的符号意义等同于品牌的符号意义。商品意义的生产模型忽略了消费者对商品意义生成的重要作用，虽然有的学者注意到消费者对商品意义的生成有影响，但是他们所提出的消费者的影响，仅是消费者作为意义的接收者从而对于意义的发送者所施加的压力，这类讨论没有认识到消费者同时还作为意义的生产者而存在，尤其是在新媒体时代，消费者的内容生产对于商品意义的影响越发显著。最后，商品意义的生成过度集中在广告和时尚系统中，普遍认为商品/品牌意义的生成在商品生产之后才开始进行，而忽略了商品本身携带的意义。笔者认为，早在商品生产之前，商品意义的生产过程就已开始，因此，对商品意义的讨论应该将商品本身纳入其中。

二、意义滑动：商品与品牌的统一机制

商品的意义主要有三个来源：商品一物承载意义，伴随文本为商品叠加意义（包括品牌），消费者通过购买和消费商品而确证实现商品的意义。这三个意义的来源相互影响，相互制约：商品一物的生产首先来源于对市场信息的洞察，受到消费者需求的压力；商品一物的属性特征又成为伴随文本赋予意义的基础，伴随文本必须依照商品一物的特征对其进行表现，同时在伴随文本的传播中成为商品意义的一个部分，并影响商品意义的解读；消费者对伴随文本的解读影响其消费商品的方式，并且在对商品的消费的同时对商品意义进行了接收和新的创造，它们共同建构了商品的意义。

（一）物的表意：商品一品牌意义的生成

在象征意义的建构研究中，商品一物所表达的意义被极大地忽视了。这主要表现在两个层面：在理论建构层面，学术界在品牌结构的划分中，将商品的物质属性与品牌属性截然对立。研究者使用不同的术语对品牌结构进行

划分，分为产品相关属性和非产品相关属性、内部属性和外部属性、实用价值和享乐价值、硬属性和软属性等。他们使用的术语虽然不同，但是总体上所表达的意思却是大体一致的，即商品被视为没有象征意义的裸物，商品的物理属性纯粹用于满足消费者的物质需要，与消费者对象征性需求的满足无关；满足消费者的自我形象塑造、身份建构、情感体验等精神需要的是品牌等无形属性。在实践操作层面，将商品符号化等同于品牌化，认为商品的符号价值是二次生产的结果，是由广告、营销等大众传播形式赋予的。商品的物质生产阶段对于象征意义的形成没有影响，商品象征意义的形成在于传播阶段和消费阶段。金周汉（Kim Joohan）提出，商品生产的第一个阶段是物理劳动使用材料生产出产品；第二阶段是传播劳动使用产品生产了商品；第三阶段是消费用商品生产出商品的意义或效用。麦克拉肯等创建的商品意义理论模型都将商品意义获取的起点置于商品生产之后，认为商品象征意义通过广告和时尚系统从文化世界转移到商品上（Kim，2000，pp. 75－100）。

实际上，商品符号意义的建构必须要重视商品－物本身的表意，营销者在生产商品的时候必须要能够对商品进行概念化并且清楚商品的各种属性和特征。商品的符号意义并不仅仅靠外在于商品的品牌、广告等纯符号文本赋予，商品是一个复杂的表意联合体，商品的物质方面（如质感、颜色材料等）以及商品的包装等都参与商品的表意。因此，商品－物的象征意义的建构主要包括两个部分，商品概念化和双轴操作。

1. 商品概念化

商品概念化，是指首先对商品进行定位，以商品的目标受众群体以及他们所需要的或者期待的意义为导向，创造商品的概念，并且在市场中已经存在的竞争产品包含的意义中区隔出来，这是商品意义生产的第一步，也是最为关键的一步，它决定了后面的产品设计、包装、广告等一系列意义生产活动的方向。商品意义生产的起点应该是从最远处的环节——产品定位开始，就一步一步把文化、意义消费的预期深度铭刻、植入物质生产的每一个环节之中（吴兴明，2011，pp. 5－15）。例如护肤品的生产，为了给消费者提供新的需求，厂商必须应用市场及其相关信息：用护肤品的消费者群体是谁，他们使用护肤品的时间、场景、原因，哪种类型的护肤品最有可能被选择，等等，总之，厂商需要知道使用护肤品的“模范消费者”。因此，在物质生产之前，护肤品已经被设计成具有某种待消费者解读意义的东西。

2. 商品－物象征意义的双轴操作

过去产品设计主要关注对商品功能的表现，如产品的形状、大小等属性如何表现及优化商品的功能，或商品设计对于消费者物质需要的满足。近年来，产品的表意功能逐渐受到重视，苏珊·维赫马（Susann Vihma）提出，具有不同类型的像似关系的产品设计会引导消费者产生或学习关于产品的不同意义（Vihma，1992，pp. 100－105）。星野（Katsumi Hoshino）将产品的意义划分为内涵意义和外延意义，将内涵意义再划分为表面意义和深层意义（Katsumi，1987，pp. 41－56）。产品设计是将无形的符号意义实体化为有形的商品－物的手段，商品经定位和概念化之后，产品设计将概念通过形状、颜色、材质等通过物的形式呈现出来，将商品的文化意义融入商品的物实体。产品设计不仅仅表现商品的功能和用途，而是服务于商品概念化的表达，产品的形状、材质、颜色等属性都应当从商品的概念意义出发，围绕该意义进行表现，从而使各个表意媒介都表达统一的意义。

商品作为表意的符号文本，其表意活动从组合轴和聚合轴的双轴关系中展开。符号双轴概念首先由索绪尔提出，他将符号中存在的组合关系和聚合关系分别叫作“句段关系”和“联想关系”（1980，pp. 147－170）。雅柯布森（Roman Jakobson）随后将组合轴和聚合轴分别称为“结合轴”和“选择轴”，提出结合轴的功能是邻接黏合，选择轴的功能是比较与选择（Jakobson，1956，pp. 76－82）。赵毅衡提出，“聚合轴是文本组成的方式，聚合轴是符号文本每个成分背后的所有可比较，从而有可能被选择，即有可能代替被选中的成分的各种成分”（2012，p. 157）。商品作为多媒介表意的联合体，其象征意义的生成是从各个表意媒介在聚合轴和组合轴上选择的结果，各个表意媒介相互影响，表达统一的意义。以海蓝之谜（La Mer）精华面霜的意义建构为例，其目标消费者是高端消费人群，产品定位为高端保湿面霜。面霜的成分、膏体的凝固程度、颜色、气味等都是表达意义的媒介，并且这些表意媒介在选择轴上都具有广泛的可选择性。从发送者角度来说，海蓝之谜面霜将“神奇活性精萃”（Miracle Broth™）作为其灵魂成分，采用蛋白石瓷瓶和固体膏体来封存该成分。蛋白石瓷瓶和固体膏体成为其灵魂成分的高活性的确证。聚合轴上的成分，也是符号接收者体会到的本来有可能被选择的成分。消费者在对海蓝之谜面霜的认知过程中，对面霜各个表意媒介的选择进行感知，例如在成分上，在技术高度发展的今天，有许多化学成分都可以用作面霜，而海蓝之谜的灵魂成分“神奇活性精萃”是从大量的可选择成分中筛选出来的；面霜的瓶子也有多种选择，海蓝之谜没有选择主流的塑料、玻璃材质，而是采用蛋白石瓷瓶；面霜大多数都是流质，而海蓝之谜采用固体。各个聚合轴上的可替代性都表达意义，成分的稀有，蛋白石瓷瓶较高的生产成本，以及固体膏体的独特性，都传达出这款面霜的高端感。

（二）伴随文本：意义的叠加

任何符号文本，都携带了大量社会约定和文化联系，这些约定和联系不一定显现于文本之中，而是隐藏于文本之后、文本之外，或文本边缘。它们只是被文本顺带着牵连出来，却积极参与文本意义的构成。在解释中，伴随文本甚至可能比文本有更多的意义。所有的符号文本，都是文本与伴随文本的结合体（赵毅衡，2012，p. 143）。关于商品的品牌、广告、价格等文本都是商品的伴随文本。伴随文本在商品意义的基础上将商品意义丰富化，并且以文本的形式进入各个传播渠道，将商品的意义传递到消费者心智中。

1. 商品意义对伴随文本生成的影响

商品意义与伴随文本相互影响，现有的研究大多只注意到品牌、广告等文本对商品意义的生成和影响，认为商品被动地被赋予意义，而忽略了商品对伴随文本的制约，商品－物本身的意义会影响营销者对商品伴随文本的构想。列维（Levy S. J.）认为，商品的基本属性会限制能够打造出的商品形象的类型，例如，一种商品非常强烈地表现出高质量并且只能在特定场合使用，那么如果尝试将商品的形象塑造为快销和日常使用，可能对商品来说是具有毁灭性的。商品－物的材质、技术、原料等本身携带意义，例如手机、电脑等数码产品的功能与其生产者的技术水平紧密相关，因此它们的广告往往会强调技术研发的新进展对产品性能的提升，而类似可乐、薯片等产品的广告则不会提及其技术的进步等。商品的物质意义与伴随文本赋予的意义要具有一致性，例如沃尔沃汽车的主要物质属性是安全性，因此伴随文本、品牌形象的塑造必然是与安全性相关的家庭责任感。而越野汽车的主要物质属性是在野外的驾驶性能好，因此，它相应的品牌形象是粗犷的硬汉，广告文本也偏向于表现冒险的乐趣。

2. 伴随文本叠加意义

商品的伴随文本为商品赋予意义。伴随文本主要分为前文本、型文本、链文本、副文本、评论文本和先后文本（赵毅衡，2012，pp. 144－148）。文本广告作为商品最直接的评论文本，通过将商品与特定的人群、特定的使用场景等联系起来，将商品建构成为梦想、身份、情感的象征，从而为商品赋予象征意义。链文本是接收者解释某文本时主动或被动地与某些文本“链接起来一同接收的文本”（2012，p. 148），商品的链文本包括商品的代言人、使用该商品的人等，强化广告所塑造的商品象征意义，同时将名人本身的象征意义赋予商品。而商品最为明显的副文本价格则为商品的象征意义提供确证，价格是消费者感知商品档次的最直接的符号，一个品牌属于大众消费品、中档消费品还是奢侈品，消费者难以从其他方面进行判断，价格是判别的主要依据。奢侈品牌保持高价格，可以维护其高端的品牌形象。2018 年，巴宝莉（Buberry）宁愿烧掉价值 2860 英镑的衣物、饰品、香水等，也不愿将其降价卖出，就是因为价格作为其象征价值的符号，对它的象征价值的高低具有重要的影响，降价会使品牌价值受到损坏而不再具有奢侈性。

3. 评论文本设置商品意义解读规则

评论文本为商品意义的解读提供符码，引导消费者对商品意义的解读。商品的评论文本包括广告、消费者以及媒体对商品的反馈评价，为商品各个元素的解读设定规则，促进商品意义的固定。现代企业在对商品进行编码的过程中，有不少对商品符码的元语言的生产。例如，在矿泉水市场中，乐百氏纯净水做了大量的广告和软新闻对消费市场进行培育，宣传纯净水没有有害物质，对人体最好。这就不是对商品本身进行编码，而是对商品的元语言进行编码。而后，华润怡宝矿泉水进入市场，就普及“纯净水缺乏人体需要的矿物质，矿泉水可以补充人体所需的矿物质”的观点，从而将纯净水市场转换成矿泉水市场。农夫山泉、恒大冰泉的进入将矿泉水的判断标准转化成天然、自然。海蓝之谜面霜采用蛋白石瓷瓶作为包装，提出蛋白石瓷瓶能够保护面霜中的珍稀成分，从而保证产品的功效。对任何事物的评估都必然要依据一定的标准进行，对商品价值的评估必然也依照一套评估标准。

（三）消费者互动：商品意义的确证

一方面，消费者作为商品和品牌意义的接收者，对商品和品牌意义的生成起着关键性的作用，商品和品牌意义只有得到消费者的认可才能得到确证，只有在消费者的使用中才能实现。利加斯（Mark Ligas）和科蒂（June Cotte）认为象征意义产生于营销环境、社会环境和个体环境三者之间的“谈判”（Ligas，Cotte，1999，pp. 609－614），象征意义只有在消费者的一致认可下才能存在。消费者并不总是按照营销者的意图解释商品和品牌文本，而是在获取和使用意义的方式上具有主动性，消费者作为意义的接收者和使用者对商品的意义具有的影响——他们不仅仅能选择意义，而且还能够改变商品的意义。消费者可以通过积极主动地对商品进行评论、与营销者进行互动等方式为商品和品牌的解读和传播提供新的、创造性的解释方式和意义；也可能对营销者传播的文本进行对抗式解码，颠覆性地、反向解读营销者传达的意义，从而破坏品牌形象。在新媒体背景下，信息的发散式传播、信息海量化、传播渠道密集化、互动性等特点更是进一步增强了消费者对商品和品牌文本的解读方式的主动性。商品的意义通过电视、网络等不同媒体传递给消费者，而又在受众的评论和转发中不断地被解读和重构。在这个过程中，传受双方的界限十分模糊，受众并不是单纯意义上的受众，而在某些时候成为商品意义的生产者，形成更多传播主体和文本参与的更为广泛的、深层次的互动。例如，联想以“放肆联想，真我主场”为联想粉丝节的主题，倡导年轻人更加自由的表达自我与创造，在抖音发起了“放肆 show 真我”挑战赛，该挑战赛吸引了大量的消费者主动参与创作主题短视频，符合主题的超过1. 3万支，且视频内容非常优质，也进一步提升了联想的年轻化形象。

另一方面，消费者通过交换仪式、拥有仪式、修饰仪式和剥离仪式等仪式获取商品的意义，完成意义从商品到消费者自身的转移，进而拥有商品的意义，同时通过消费仪式、新的商品的使用方式等为商品注入新的意义。例如，消费者在海底捞火锅店吃火锅时，自创鸡蛋灌面筋、“网红蘸料”等吃法，并且将这些吃法做成视频通过抖音短视频等平台分享到网上，引发大量消费者到海底捞消费，模仿这些吃法甚至再自创新的吃法发到抖音短视频等平台上。这让原本以人性化服务攒下好口碑的火锅店再度走红，并且让海底捞在严重同质化的火锅餐饮行业脱颖而出，获得有趣的、年轻的形象。

商品意义的形成是商品-物、商品的伴随文本和消费者之间相互影响、相互作用的结果。商品-物的意义在商品意义的生成过程中发挥着基础的作用，影响和制约了伴随文本的方向；伴随文本一方面受商品-物的影响而偏向特定的文本表现形式和文本内容，另一方面也为商品赋予意义，为消费者制定意义解读的规则；而消费者对商品意义的影响不仅体现在其对商品和伴随文本的解读方式上，其消费行为也同时生产商品的意义。回到商品表征，将商品和品牌结合起来研究，才能更好地解释商品和品牌的意义生成过程中的多方互动，也才能更好指导商品和品牌意义生产实践。

引用文献：

阿克，戴维（2013）. 管理品牌资产（吴进操，常小虹，译）. 北京：机械工业出版社.

鲍德里亚，让（2001）. 消费社会（刘成富，全志钢，译）. 南京：南京大学出版社.

何建民（2002）. 创造名牌产品的理论与方法：品牌经典专著. 上海：华东理工大学出版社.

蒋诗萍（2015）. 论品牌“三位一体”的符号结构与动态位移. 中外文化与文论，29（2），213－221.

科特勒，菲利普；凯勒，凯文·莱恩（2016）. 营销管理（何佳讯，等，译）（第15版）. 上海：格致出版社.

索绪尔，费尔迪南·德（1980）. 普通语言学教程（高名凯，译）. 北京：商务印书馆.

王连森（2004）. 基于符号学的“整体品牌”概念. 北京工商大学学报（社会科学版），19（5），72－76.

吴兴明（2011）. 重建生产的美学——论解分化及文化产业研究的思想维度. 文艺研究，2011（11），5－15.

Grubb, E. L., & Grathwohl, H. L. (1967). Consumer self-concept, symbolism and market behavior: a theoretical approach. *Journal of marketing*, 31(4), 22－27.

Holt, D. B. (2006). *How brands become icons: the principles of cultural branding*. Harvard Business Press.

Jakobson, R. (1956). The metaphoric and metonymic poles. In Roman Jakobson and Morris Halle, *Fundamentals of Language*. Hague: Mouton Press.

Katsumi, H. (1987). Semiotic marketing and product conceptualization. In J. Umiker-Sebeok (ed.), *Marketing and semiotics: New directions in the study of signs for sale.* Amsterdam: Mouton de Gruyter.

Kim, J. (2000). From commodity production to sign production: A triple triangle model for Marx's semiotics and Peirce's economics, *Semiotica*, 132(1－2), 75－100.

Levy, S. J. (1959). Symbols for sale, *Harvard business review*, 37(4), 117－124.

Ligas, M. & Cotte, J. (1999). The process of negotiating brand meaning: a symbolic interactionist perspective. *Advances in consumer research*, 26(1), 609－614.

Vihma, S. (1992). Iconicity and other signs in the form of design products. In S. Vihma (ed.), *Objects and images*. Helsinki: University of Industrial Arts.

作者简介：

刘楠，博士，四川大学文学与新闻学院符号学－传媒学研究所成员，主要研究方向为品牌符号学。

Author:

Liu Nan, Ph. D., member of the ISMS research team. Her research field is semiotics of branding.

Email: 18328582642@163.com

广义叙述学

符号叙述学视野与人类社会演进

唐小林

摘　要： 关于人类社会历史这个大局面叙述文本，不同的视域有不同的社会形态划分，也因此有了不同的社会理解与社会解释。站在我们置身其中的信息社会，以媒介的世界观和符号叙述学的视野，回望人类走过的全部社会历程，我们发现，人类社会经历了口语－身体媒介、文字－书写媒介和数字－网络媒介这三个时期，相应的也经历了演示类、记录类和拟演示类叙述文本的三体演进，呈现为演示类和记录类两种基本社会形态。演示类和记录类这两种基本社会形态，在意义建构方式上表现出不同的特点，演示类社会更偏重于用情节组织经验，记录类社会则更偏重于用范畴组织经验。信息社会属于拟演示类社会形态，虽然也侧重于用情节组织经验，但由于消费欲望的驱动、人工智能的驱使以及多媒介的联动与融合，不仅情节本身被演示化，同时这种演示还更多地呈现出碎片化、拼贴式等特征。

关键词： 符号叙述学，社会形态，演示类，记录类，拟演示类

The Evolution of Human Society from the Perspective of Semio-narratology

Tang Xiaolin

Abstract: In the narrative text of human social history, different perspectives have different social formations, leading to a range of different social understandings and social explanations. Starting from today's information society, and looking back at the whole history of social process from the perspective of a mediatised world-view and a semio-narratology, we find that human society has experienced three periods of mediatisation: oral language/body media, literary/written media and digital/network media. Accordingly, human society has also experienced a three-genre evolution of narrative text: demonstrating, recording and intention-demonstrating. The two basic social formations of the demonstrating and recording types show different characteristics in the construction of meaning. A demonstrating society places greater stress on organising experience by plot, whereas a recording society places greater stress on organising experience by category. The information society belongs to the intention-demonstrating type. Influenced by the two drives for consumption and artificial intelligence, and by the linking and integration of multiple media, it also focuses on organising experience by plot, but the plots are expressed alongside the features of fragmentation and collage.

Keywords: Semio-narratology, social formations, demonstrating, recording, intention-demonstrating

DOI: 10.13760/b.cnki.sam.202001012

一、演示，记录，拟演示：人类社会的三体演进

人类社会的历史可以看作一个大局面文本，而且是充满动人故事、丰沛情节与细节的叙述文本。

从叙述体裁的角度看，人类社会经历了从演示类叙述向记录类叙述再向拟演示类叙述的三体演进。这个“体”是“体裁”的简称。马克思主义将人类社会形态依次划分为原始社会、奴隶社会、封建社会、资本主义社会、社会主义社会、共产主义社会，给人类社会发展以清晰的理论秩序。也有西方社会理论以“现代”作为观察点，用前现代、现代、后现代来描述人类社会的走向。而一般与中国历史相关的教科书，大都潜藏一个古代社会—近代社会—现代社会—当代社会的框架。显然，不同视域下人类社会演进的形态有不同的划分。我们面临的信息社会，只是人类社会这个大局面叙述文本的一

部分，而且还是一个方兴未艾、不断延续、尚未结束的部分。如果从这个叙述文本及其特征出发，回望全部人类历史所经历的社会形态，应该有不同于以往的理解和新的划分。这一新的划分，绝不是为了标新立异，而是为了更好地理解人类历史与我们置身其中的社会。

信息社会，笔者在这里把它当作自明的概念来使用，不再花功夫从头论证，因为不少理论家对此已有相当精彩且令人信服的论述。不过关于信息社会这个符号文本的构成，笔者却有自己的看法。如果按皮尔斯的符号三分，即符号是再现体、对象和解释项的三位体，那么媒介就是信息社会这个大局面符号文本的再现体，智能是它的对象，而消费则是其解释项。这样，信息社会这个符号文本就具有了“媒介”“智能”与“消费”三副面相，它也相应有了三个别称：媒介社会、智能社会与消费社会。也即是说，信息社会是媒介社会、智能社会与消费社会的三位一体。为什么是这样？笔者将专文讨论。

无疑，媒介面相是信息社会最显在的特征，也是我们最直观地感觉到的。网络的出现及网络社会的形成，则把这个特征表现和刻画得淋漓尽致。所以在今天，媒介社会也是可以称为网络社会的。以网络为代表的媒介，越来越凸显为关乎人类生活现状、生存状态和社会发展的关键因素。在这时，用媒介的世界观来观照人类历史，划分社会形态，以深刻理解人类的全部行为，就不得不成为一个紧迫的时代课题。

纵观整个人类社会，出现过两次大的媒介革命：第一次是文字－书写媒介革命，第二次是数字－网络媒介革命。而在这两次革命之前，也就是在文字－书写媒介革命出现之前，还有一个十分漫长的历史时期，这一时期可以称为口语－身体媒介时期。这样，从媒介的角度看，人类社会实际经历了三个时期：口语－身体媒介时期、文字－书写媒介时期、数字－网络媒介时期。当然，这只是一个非常宏观、高度抽象的观察，也是一个挂一漏万的媒介历史划分，它忽略了好些历史细节，比如在数字－网络媒介革命之前，还存在过短暂的电子媒介时期。

有了媒介这个世界观，再从符号叙述学的视野出发，笔者发现，与上述三个媒介历史时期对应的是三种社会形态：与口语－身体媒介时期对应的是演示类叙述社会形态，与文字－书写媒介时期对应的是记录类叙述社会形态，而与数字－网络媒介时期对应的则是拟演示叙述社会形态。今天，我们正处于拟演示叙述社会形态。

从语言、符号的角度解释人类文明、人类历史、社会构成，早有成功的先例。当今最负盛名、最有影响的哲学家之一，约翰·塞尔（John R.

Searle）就曾用“言语行为理论来解释社会本体论”（塞尔，2015，p.1），取得丰富成果，《人类文明的结构：社会世界的构成》是其中的代表。本文只是朝着这个方向努力尝试，希望能走出一步。

二、叙述体裁划分与社会形态关联

以往的叙述学，主要是小说叙述学，因此基本没有体裁划分。赵毅衡的广义叙述学，亦称符号叙述学，把一切符号叙述纳入研究范围，叙述体裁分类就不得不进行，否则全部都以小说对待，各种文体、各种类别的叙述文本“一锅煮”，就必定出现理论乱象。

广义叙述学，严格地说，是叙述学上的革命。赵毅衡在广义叙述学中将叙述体裁划分为三类，即记录类叙述、演示类叙述和意动类叙述，这在叙述学史上是没有过的，完全是创新。记录类叙述诸体裁以小说和历史为代表，其起主导功能的模态是邦维尼斯特说的“陈述”，也就是奥斯汀所说的“以言言事”。这种叙述重在“言”，言说本身就是其重要功能。演示类叙述诸体裁以戏剧、比赛、游戏为代表，其主导功能的模态是邦维尼斯特说的“疑问”，主导语力则是“以言行事”，是为施行某种目的而展开的叙述，“演”是其重点。意动类叙述诸体裁以预言与宣传为代表，主导模态是“祈使”，主导语力是“以言成事”，是为促使听者实施某种目的而进行的叙述，重点在“成”上。（赵毅衡，2013，pp.1－88）在笔者看来，记录类叙述，重在“述行”；演示类叙述，重在“施行”；意动类叙述，重在“实行”。

赵毅衡的叙述体裁分类，适用于所有的叙述文本。文本作为文化的符号，不仅指狭义的文字文本，比如诗歌、小说、通讯；也指中义的文化产品，比如电影、音乐、刘文彩的收租院；还指大局面的社会文本，比如春秋战国时代构筑的文本、环太平洋经济圈形成的文本，等等。这就使这样的叙述体裁分类具有了理论的迁移性，它完全可以用来描述某种社会形态，而不只限于对某些文字文本的分析。这也许也是广义叙述学或者符号叙述学的初衷：能够解释所有以叙述的方式构建意义的符号文本。在这个意义上讲，广义叙述学是走出书斋，走进十字街头，面向万物众生与各种文化文明的叙述学。

叙述体裁的三种分类，与大局面叙述文本——社会的关联点在媒介。赵毅衡叙述体裁的分类标准，是“语气－时向－媒介”的三联式。语气关涉文本的意向、文本的语力。文本的意向，也指文本的意向性。文本是意识的符号，意识具有指向性、关于性，也就是说意识总是关于什么、指向什么的意识。这关于什么、指向什么的意识从文本中表现出来，就构成了文本的意向性。而文本意向性最为显著的表现莫过于语气，所以语气成为叙述体裁划分的一个标准。时间向度，其实也是意义向度，过去、现在、未来三个时态，直接决定了叙述文本的意义如何生成，而“同一的时间向度”也是一个文本得以可能的条件。

把“媒介”作为叙述体裁的划分依据，可谓别出心裁，这恰好因应了当前这个媒介社会，也使叙述理论具有阐释信息社会的适切性和有效性。赵毅衡把媒介分为两类：人造特用媒介、现成非特用媒介。(2013，p. 35) 人造特用媒介，笔者把它称为特有媒介，是人类的创造物，专门用来传达意义，以“语言－文字”为代表。现成非特用媒介，笔者称之为非特有媒介，以“身体－实物”为代表，以身体为中心，这类媒介不是专门用来表意的，而是被“顺手”拿过来当作媒介使用的。这两类媒介分别对应两类叙述体裁的文本：特有媒介对应记录类文本，非特有媒介对应演示类文本。两类媒介的混合，对应意动类文本。(唐小林，2016，p. 71) 这也意味着意动类叙述使用任意一种媒介都是可以的。

“媒介对应叙述体裁”的符号叙述学视野，给予笔者在考察社会形态时以极大的启发。因为人类社会的发展史或者演变史，就是媒介的发展史或演变史。伴随着一次又一次的媒介升级，人类社会形态不断改变而走向今天。重要的媒介升级有两次，一次是文字的发明，让人类有了记录、储存、传达、交流信息的工具，引起了深刻的文化及社会变革。文字代替会说话的鼓，代替马车、轮船，将人类的影响带向天涯海角。第二次就是数字化媒介的出现，使人类进入网络时代，世界变成地球村，人变成实在世界与虚拟世界的两栖动物，并被置于人机共存与对抗的崭新现实中，社会的政治经济、文化科技、人类精神与气质心性等层面都发生了颠覆性变化。说媒介是撬动人类历史发展的杠杆，其实并不为过。

既然是媒介带来社会变动，媒介就必然改变社会状况，用媒介来划分人类历史、考量社会形态，就理所当然。以“媒介对应叙述体裁”视野来观察，人类社会的三个标志性媒介时期，对应的就是三个显著的社会形态：口语－身体媒介时期对应的是演示类叙述社会，文字－书写媒介时期对应的是记录类叙述社会，数字－网络媒介时期对应的是拟演示类叙述社会。

传统叙述学主要是小说叙述学，其对应的媒介是文字－书写，所以它无法用来解释之前的社会，也无法用来解释媒介变迁后的社会，更无法用于考察今天这个以数字－网络为核心的多媒介社会。广义叙述学解决了这个难题。

三、演示与记录：两种基本社会形态及其特点

叙述体裁分为记录、演示、意动三类，但从媒介对应的基本社会形态来看只有两类，即演示类与记录类。也就是说，人类社会由演示与记录这两类基本社会形态构成。

为什么这样说？因为文字－书写媒介出现之前的社会形态是演示的，文字－媒介以后的数字－网络媒介也是演示的。按赵毅衡的命名，应该是“类演示”，笔者用“拟演示”，意在体现出网络社会的演示较之口语－身体媒介时期有了不同的特点，展演的成分更多，虽然具有演示类叙述的基本特点，但又增加了多媒介时代特有的因素：不仅更多表演的成分，而且这种表演已经不是由口语－身体媒介自己直接实行，而是由别的媒介，比如QQ、脸书、推特、微信、表情包等代为实行。演示的方式也大不相同，是拟演示、像演示，而非严格意义上的演示。这样，人类社会演进的三个时期，实际只有两种基本的社会形态，即演示类文本形态与记录类文本形态。从演示到记录再到拟演示，意味着人类社会来了个否定之否定，来了个老黑格尔式的“螺旋式上升”。当然，这是不是上升，人类社会是否遵循自然进化或必然进化规律，还需要仔细辨析。从演示到记录再到拟演示，也意味着历史发展有时有着惊人的相似，这相似后面，似乎隐藏着某种值得我们深入探寻的规律，这些规律也许可以为我们的现实和未来提供某些借鉴。

那么意动类叙述呢，它是否也在人类社会的文本形态中得到表达？回答是肯定的。数字－网络媒介时代，也就是我们置身于其中的信息时代，尽管是以拟演示为突出特征的，但在拟演示叙述中有着明显的意动叙述的因素。这个因素来源于信息社会三面相中的另一副面孔——消费社会。消费社会是一个欲望驱动的社会，因而也是一个意动性社会。所以，在最严格意义上讲，数字－网络社会是拟演示－意动类叙述社会。以意动类叙述的目光观之，这个社会充斥着大量的图像、影像，充斥着广告、未来学家，充斥着各种宣传和预言文本，致使整个社会表现出跃跃欲试的“前倾”姿势：“未来已来”成为时髦的口号。尤其是有关基因工程、人工智能将中断人类进化的预言甚嚣尘上，令人心惶惶，各国快马加鞭，急迫地要在这些领域争夺未来。朝向未来、预支未来，也是消费社会普遍的文化心理。

数字－网络媒介社会之所表现出意动叙述的特征，还在于其所对应的是多媒介。适用于各种媒介，正是意动类叙述的一大特点。语言、文字、声音、

图像、身体、实物、影像等，报刊等传统媒介，微博、微信、知乎等社交平台，手机等终端，以及这些媒介的大融合，都为意动类叙述提供有效支撑。演示与意动类叙述在文本意向上更容易打通，前面说过，演示类叙述重在“施行”，以言行事；意动类叙述重在“实行”，以言成事。施行与实行，行事与成事，都在行为、动作上聚焦，都是驱动性的。

媒介特征决定了人类的生存方式与社会形态，这是以麦克卢汉为代表的不少媒介社会学家的共识。那么记录类社会与演示类社会究竟有着怎样的不同特征呢？笔者认为，特征的不同主要表现在意义的建构方式上。意义是什么？赵毅衡认为，意义是一个符号被另外的符号解释的潜力，这道出了解释学上的事实，也是对符号学意义观的突破。因为符号的意义是一种意指活动，是被感知的符号在接收者心中唤起和引出的一个又一个符号，这个唤起与引出的过程是一个连续、绵延的过程，除非出现意图定点，否则会一直向前，无限衍义。但这个意义观是建立在已经有了符号可供感知的基础上，也就是说，它是以符号和文本的事先给定为前提的。笔者认为，在发生学上，意义是意向的产物，是意向性的结果，即主客体的融合。这种融合实际是一个视界融合，就是说这种融合既不在主体也不在客体，而是在主客体融合的交叉部分，这个交叉部分只能发生在意识上，这种意识由于客体的进入，又只能呈现为一种“视界”：一个即将媒介化的符号。

落到人类活动中，笔者认为，意义是被组织、被解释的人类经验。人类生活在时间之流与感知之流中，并非所有的感知、体验都能成为人类经验，它需要人类的反思，需要意向的抵达。熟视无睹、视而不见，说明只有意识朝向的那部分体验，只有被反思之光照亮的那部分感知，才有可能成为人类的经验。当然，它是否能最终成为经验，还需要人类的组织和解释。

人类组织经验的基本方式有两种：一是用情节组织经验；一是用范畴组织经验。从其主导性说，这两种组织人类经验的方式，分别对应演示类与记录类两种基本社会形态。之所以强调主导性，是想表明这两类组织经验的方式在各种社会形态都可能存在，只是侧重不同。在演示类社会，主要是以情节的方式组织经验，也不排除范畴化经验的可能。在拟演示社会，由于多媒介的融合，范畴化组织经验依然是重要的社会行为，尽管这对大众而言有些遥远。而在记录类社会，也并非全部靠范畴组织经验，以情节组织经验同样存在，只是理性越来越占据重要地位。清楚地说，只要运用符号就会有范畴化，有人甚至反过来说，符号的产生和存在就是根源于人类的范畴化能力的（Harnad，2002，p. 148）。

演示类社会情节组织经验成为主导，是由口语－身体媒介的特点决定的。口语－身体媒介时代，是一个语言行为与行为语言高度结合的时代，身体成为媒介的中心。信息的交流靠声音和身体的动作来完成，声音传播的距离近，信息易于消失，又不能用其他媒介复制，更不能保存。时间上的限制带来空间上的要求，使得人们不得不聚集在一起，在同一个场所内交流。交流的方式，不仅是声音、动作的互动，各部位都必须参加表意，包括眼神、面部表情、肢体语言等，犹如一场实地演出，所以由此形成的社会形态是部落化的、演示类的。空间化、在场性、即兴式、参与性、互动性、亲密性，甚至对话性，构成演示类社会交流的一些重要特征。

意义构筑的在场性与即兴式，给演示类社会的知识生产与传递带来诸多限制。口语－身体媒介缺乏记录功能，信息的保存全靠大脑记忆；大脑记忆屡试不爽的最好方式是叙述，反复的叙述；叙述中最易于记忆的莫过于故事；最好的叙述反复，最有助于记忆的叙述方式，又莫过于有节奏、有韵律、载歌载舞地讲故事。所以，文字－媒介时代之前的民族叙述诗最为发达。口传民族史诗、叙述诗成为人类最早的文化遗产之一。这既是那个时代意义建构的方式，又是那个时代知识生产与传递的方式。

口语－媒介时代，讲故事不仅是维持记忆、生产和传递知识的方式，也是组织社会，协同部落成员完成某项生产活动与生活任务的方式。在这个时代，人类学会了用情节组织经验，却没有完全学会用范畴的方式组织经验。用范畴的方式组织经验，要等文字发明，进入记录类社会以后。

人类用情节组织经验，传递信息，表达意义，是跟演示类叙述同步进行的。语言“发展的基础是不断的日常社交互动和讲述故事”（邓巴，2016，p. 236）。社交互动与讲述故事是同一台大戏。设想只会用口语和身体表达的人们在篝火边聚集、狂欢，“火光跳跃中，人们的想象力被激发出来，于是就有可能开始讲故事”。人类之所以为人类，取决于社群。而社交互动与讲述故事，恐怕是维系前人类社群最为关键的活动：

> 讲故事对于人类来说非常重要，它对维系外围群体的关系起到两个关键的作用，一是它能让我们编造一个社交历史，我们会因此而注重于一段共同的历史，也是因为这段历史才会组成这个社交群体；二是它能让我们以讲故事的形式讲述一个未曾见到的世界，也就是虚构的世界和精神的世界，因此小说和宗教才有可能出现。（邓巴，2016，pp. 235－236）

人类最初的文学出现在口语－身体媒介时代，这时的文学作品大都是讲述故事的，关于口传史诗的研究已经证实了这一点。格雷克（James Gleick）举了一个例子：希腊文学的兴起就源于口语－身体媒介时代，与后来文字的产生无关，直到 20 世纪 30 年代初，结构主义语言学家帕里（Milman Parry）在研究波墨的口传史诗时发现了这个问题，对此学者们才开始有所意识，并不情愿地承认。帕里在当时提出“最初《伊利亚特》和《奥德赛》不仅可能而且肯定是在不借助文字的情况下创作和传唱的。格律、程式化的重复以及史诗本身的诗歌形式，首要的目的无非是为帮助记忆，其朗朗上口的特征使得诗句像时间胶囊一样，可以将一部虚拟的文化百科全书代代相传”（格雷克，2013，p. 33）。藏族的《格萨尔王》、汉族最早的诗歌，都是口传的，比如《吴越春秋》记载的相传黄帝时代的民歌《弹歌》：“断竹、续竹、飞土、逐宍。”《诗经》的叙述性特征以及反复吟唱的特点，也深深地留下了口语－身体媒介时期的文化印迹。有人把“中国古典诗歌的思维方式概括为物态化”（李怡，2008，p. 43），笔者以为这个“模因”其实也是口语－身体媒介文化的残存：只有到了书面文化时代，人类能够用概念、范畴的方式组织经验时，“一个脱离具体事物的抽象世界”（格雷克，2013，p. 34）才逐渐开始建构起来。

文字的发明，使社会出现分割。交流双方的时空距离加大，此时此地发生的事、想说的话，可以通过文字的记录，让彼时彼地的人接收。面对面的交流——曾经传播的主要方式，在文字书写运动中成为过去，社会主导文本从演示类叙述向记录类转向，由此，社会表达总是处于一种过去时态，达成一个叙述的新的社会格局。

文字－书写媒介的出现，是人类的一次最为伟大的飞跃。笔者认为，再没有比这次飞跃更伟大的了。文字－书写媒介使人类没有必要为了信息的交流再聚集在一起，完全可以分散各方。可以沿江而下，到水草丰茂之地定居；可以攀缘而上，到高原牛羊成群的地方生活；也可以漂洋过海，去寻找新大陆，再造人类帝国。没有必要担心失散，因为有文字－书写媒介把分散的各方连接在一起。文字－书写媒介长时间、跨距离的连接功能，使部落化的社会实际上解体，一个非部落化的历史时期已然到来。

口语－身体媒介时期，人类主要生活在“现在时”的文化场景中。也许口传的民族史诗也保留了某些鲜活的民族记忆，也能将部分的历史场景带到眼前；也许通过巫术等形式，也有关于未来生活的某些想象，但更多的是对当下时代的记忆。仪式成为记录方式，也就是依托演示类叙述文本来记录，是口语－身体媒介时期人类文化的一大特点，可惜很少有人从符号叙述学的角度予以说明。有必要强调的是，文字－媒介出现后，生活在由过去、现在和未来共筑的文化场景中的体验，在那以前人类从来没有过。文字－书写媒介不仅能够将自然世界再现目前，还会创造一个从未有过的精神世界、可能世界，将历史复现，让未来以规划的形式先行到来。人类从此生活在文字文本构筑的完整的时间形态当中。

更为关键的是，人类从此学会范畴化的组织经验。文字就是范畴化、理念化的。文字的出现本身就标志着人类范畴化思维得到符号呈现，甚至可以说，文字就是人类范畴化思维的符号。没有哪一个文字不是范畴化的，任何文字都是"白马非马"。一个"树"字，就是一个范畴，意指所有的树。一个词，也是范畴化的，"柏树"，包括所有的柏树，不管是老的小的、高的矮的、死的活的、病的健康的，生长在高原还是生长在平地的，如此等等。文字符号，正因为每一个都是一个范畴，彼此之间才不会交叉，才会基于各自的差异建立系统，覆盖某一文化全域；也正因为建立了系统，才反过来确保其各自的差异，因范畴不同而在一个文化系统中确立自己的地位。每一个文字，都是范畴化组织经验的范例。所以，相对于口语－身体媒介而言，以范畴组织经验，是文字－书写时期人类意识建构的主导。但这并不否认其他的经验组织、意义构筑方式，比如用情节构筑依然发挥作用，只是说这时人类不但多出了这样一个经验，而且这个经验很快后来居上，占去"主座"。

数字－网络媒介时代，已经大不同于口语－身体媒介时代，尽管它们同属演示类叙述的社会形态。数字－网络时代"网遍天下"，无所不有，无时不在，网络文化席卷地球村，人类总体似乎生活在一个巨大的部落当中，仿佛只有与外星人才属于不同的部落。又由于网络上有不同的社交平台，在同一个社交平台，比如微信中，又有不同的"朋友圈"或者"粉丝群"，而且还可以根据某一事件、某一话题、某一会议、某一活动、某一集体建立朋友圈，如此等等。你会发现，我们不仅生活在万维网这个大部落中，还生活在万维网中的无数个小部落中。再部落化，正如麦克卢汉所预言的那样，正成为数字－网络媒介时代这个拟演示社会的特征。

那么，数字－网络媒介时代又用什么来组织和解释人类经验呢？笔者以为，其主导依然情节，也就是说依然是以情节来完成意义的建构。只不过，由于它不再是纯粹的演示类叙述社会，所以已经带有"拟"的性质，用情节组织和解释经验的具体方式发生了变化，再加上消费欲望的驱使、人工智能驱动，人类已经没有心思和足够的耐心去组织一个完整的情节，也没有记忆之需，不必为让这个故事好记而追求必要的形式。这时的情节，已经碎片化为一地鸡毛，或者是文字、图片、视频、表情包等多种媒介的拼贴，并在即兴表演中轻松地完成。这并非说范畴化不存在，只是范畴化存在的方式受到数字–媒介的影响，发生了某种演示化的转折。关于这个问题，拟另文再论。

引用文献：

邓巴，罗宾（2016）. 人类的演化（余彬，译）. 上海：上海文艺出版社.

格雷克，詹姆斯（2013）. 信息简史（高博，译）. 北京：人民邮电出版社.

李怡（2008）. 中国现代新诗与古典诗歌传统（增订版）. 北京：北京大学出版社.

塞尔，约翰（2015）. 人类文明的结构：社会世界的构造（文学平，盈俐，译）. 北京：中国人民大学出版社.

唐小林（2016）. 演述与讲述：符号叙述的两种基本类型. 社会科学辑刊，3，68–74.

赵毅衡（2013）. 广义叙述学. 成都：四川大学出版社.

Harnad, S. (2002). Symbol grounding and the origin of language. In M. Scheutz (ed.), *Computationalism: New directions*. MA: KIT Press.

作者简介：

唐小林，四川大学文学与新闻学院教授，四川大学符号学–传媒学研究所研究员，主要研究领域为符号学理论、符号诗学、信息社会符号学、马克思主义符号学。

Author:

Tang Xiaolin, professor of College of Literature and Journalism, researcher of ISMS, Sichuan University. His research interests include semiotics theory, semiotic poetics, semiotics of information society, semiotics of Marxism.

Email: yz1965@163.com

美杜莎式语象叙事、性别政治与再现的困境*

王 安

摘 要：语象叙事（ekphrasis）是关于词语与形象之间关系的研究。美杜莎这一神秘的、意蕴丰富的形象在语象叙事中具有普遍性。当作为男性的文字试图去观看、言说和控制作为女性的视觉艺术品时，会遭遇后者美杜莎式的反抗。一方面，词语与形象之争体现的不仅是不同符号系统和媒介之间的对比，更是不同体裁间争夺控制权的性别政治博弈，具有广泛的社会和文化意义。另一方面，美杜莎的形象促使人们反思当词语与形象遭遇时所面临的再现困境，它消解了语象二元对立的基础，使语象之间呈现出既对立又统一的动态而辩证的关系，有助于人们更深刻地认识语象叙事的复杂性。

关键词：美杜莎，语象叙事，性别政治，再现的困境

Medusa Ekphrasis, Sexual Politics and the Dilemma of Representation

Wang An

Abstract: Ekphrasis is the study of the relations between word and image. The mythical Medusa with its profound connotations is very common in ekphrastic practices. When the language as a male speaker tries to gaze at, speak for and control the female image of the visual art objects, it encounters the resistance from the latter. On the one hand, the contest

* 本文为教育部人文社科项目“莎士比亚作品中的诗画关系研究”（20YJA752012）的阶段性成果。

between word and image is not only one between different sign systems and different media, but also the struggle for sexual and political power between different genres. In this regard it has profound cultural and social significance. On the other hand, Medusa's image prompts people to rethink the dilemma of representation when the word meets the image. It dissolves the foundation of binary opposition and reveals the dynamic and dialectical nature of ekphrastic antagonism and conflation, which is conducive to a deeper understanding of the complexity of ekphrasis.

Keywords: Medusa, ekphrasis, sexual politics, dilemma of representation

DOI: 10.13760/b.cnki.sam.202001013

语象叙事（ekphrasis）是关于词语（word）与形象（image）之间关系的研究，长期以来是西方文学和艺术理论中的焦点话题，最早可追溯至荷马时代，至今已有逾两千年历史，可谓与西方艺术同龄。不过由于这一概念所涉及的问题域太多，学界对它的理解一直争议不休。目前，关于语象叙事的定义，大家普遍接受的是赫弗南（James A. W. Heffernan）和米切尔（W. J. T. Mitchell）等人提出的“视觉再现的文字再现”一说（王安，程锡麟，2016），即强调文字再现的应是被再现的视觉艺术。自20世纪50年代以来，语象叙事已逐渐发展为西方文学和艺术领域的焦点话题，受到了普遍的关注，涉及的话题极为广泛。不过，有两条线索相对比较清晰和突出，它们都跟语象叙事一词在古希腊罗马的使用有关，大体触及这一概念的广狭二义边界。一是继承卢奇安（Lucian）、阿普列乌斯（Apuleius）与大斐洛斯特拉图斯（Philostratos）等人的传统，将语象叙事研究的范围局限于用文字描写的艺术作品，形成了一种文学体裁，如大斐洛斯特拉图斯的《画纪》（*Imagines*）。（Webb，1999，pp. 7—18）这方面最著名的例子是《伊利亚特》（*Iliad*）中对阿喀琉斯之盾的描述，此外还有济慈（John Keats）的《希腊古瓮颂》（*Ode on a Grecian Urn*）、雪莱（Percy Bysshe Shelley）的《咏佛罗伦萨美术馆达·芬奇的美杜莎》（*On the Medusa of Leonardo da Vinci in the Florentine Gallery*）等。可以将其视作语象叙事的狭义边界。另一条线索延续古希腊时期的修辞学传统，认为语象叙事是一种生动的描绘，即“以言及象”（enargeia），强调运用生动的语言描述人物、战争、暴风雨、瘟疫、地震、节庆、绘画与雕塑作品等，使读者心目中形成如同在场感受到的心像，因此其对象可谓包罗万象。可以将其看作语象叙事的广义边界。公元2世纪前后流行的四种版本的希腊文《修辞初阶》（*Progymnasmata*）以及昆体良（Quntinlianus）的《演说家的培训》（*Institutio Oratorio*）都强调文字描写的生动性及感动观众的心像的重要性。（Webb，2009，pp. 87－130）笔者认为，落在这广狭二义之间的任何“视觉再现的文字再现”都属于语象叙事的范畴，虽然这一定义依然不够清晰，但语与象遭遇时所呈现的复杂情况以及由此形成的对现有语言与图像之间关系认识的挑战，在以文字描绘视觉艺术品的美杜莎式的语象叙事中表现得最为集中，因此有必要进行进一步的深入探讨。

一、西方传统中的美杜莎形象

美杜莎是希腊神话中的蛇发女妖，福耳库斯（Phorcys）与刻托（Keto）所生的三位戈耳工（Gorgon）女妖之一，与共用一只眼睛、一颗牙齿的三位格莱埃（Graeae）女妖，以及福耳库斯与一位缪斯所生的女儿塞壬（Siren）都是姐妹。与她的两位姐姐——斯忒诺（Stheno）和欧律阿勒（Euryale）拥有不死的魔身不同，美杜莎是凡人。关于美杜莎的故事，最流行的版本是，原本美丽的美杜莎受到海神波塞冬引诱，在雅典娜神庙里被化身为骏马的波塞冬强暴，并因此怀上了双胞胎。作为惩罚，雅典娜（Athena）将她的头发变成了一条条毒蛇，将她的面孔变得狰狞可怖，任何看到她面孔的人都会被石化。朱庇特和达娜厄（Danae）的儿子珀耳修斯（Perseus）在赫尔墨斯（Hermes）、雅典娜和冥王哈德斯（Hades）的帮助下，趁美杜莎熟睡之际，砍下了她的头颅。赫尔墨斯给了他一双长翅的飞鞋，雅典娜给了他一面反光的青铜盾牌，哈德斯给了他一顶可以隐形的头盔。珀耳修斯从盾牌的反光中找到了美杜莎，砍下了她的头颅，从她被砍的脖颈处蹦出来巨人克律萨俄耳（Chrysaor）和天马珀伽索斯（Pegasus）。被惊醒的美杜莎的两位姐姐赶紧追赶珀耳修斯，珀耳修斯将美杜莎的头装进一副皮囊逃走了。在珀耳修斯后来的众多英雄行为中，包括他用美杜莎的头将擎天巨神阿特拉斯（Atlas）变成了山脉，将觊觎其妻安德罗墨达（Andromeda）的她的叔叔菲纽斯（Phineus）化为了石头。最后珀耳修斯将美杜莎的头颅献给了雅典娜，后者将其嵌入自己的神盾，神盾成为既可以保护雅典娜，又能置敌人于死地的利器。一方面，正是美杜莎的死导致珀伽索斯和克律萨俄耳的生，她的头颅可以诞生新生命，可谓“某种程度上皮格马利翁的反转”（Schlutz，2015，p. 329）；另一方面，它又能带给敌人死亡，庇佑自己，也同时蕴含着生（自己）与死（敌人）的可能，可以说是典型的避邪意象。这在欧里庇得斯的《伊翁》和阿斯克勒庇俄斯（Asclepius）的神话传说中都有体现（Fasoli，2007，pp. 985－986）。传说医神阿斯克勒庇俄斯从雅典娜那里得到了一瓶美杜莎的血液，如果从左边的血管取，这血液就是致命的毒药，如从右边的血管取，这血液就可以起死回生。作为避邪之物，美杜莎的头颅广泛地出现在西方国家的钱币、珠宝、雕塑、日用器皿装饰和将士的甲胄上，成为西方文化中一个家喻户晓的经典形象。在文学创作中，浪漫主义时期诗人如济慈、雪莱和罗塞蒂（Dante Gabriel Rossetti）等人对美杜莎故事的反复演绎，使她成为当代女性主义作家如普拉斯（Sylvia Plath）、西苏（Hélène Cixous）、斯坦福（Ann Stanford）、博根（Louise Borgan）、萨尔顿（May Sarton）、克兰皮特（Amy Clampitt）等钟爱的形象。（Fasoli，2007，p. 986）

据考证，美杜莎的形象在古希腊就经历过从狰狞可怖的妖怪到具有致命诱惑力的美少女的变化。早在公元前 8 世纪的《荷马史诗》，就提到将美杜莎的头用于装饰盾牌，以起到吓阻敌人的作用。不过《荷马史诗》并未详细交代戈耳工神话的来源。最早较为完整地讲述了美杜莎故事的是公元前 7 世纪赫西俄德（Hesiod）写的《神谱》（*Theogony*），从那时起，关于美杜莎戈耳工的艺术作品已广泛流布希腊各地，通常被描述为面目可憎、吐着舌头、长着猪齿、头缠毒蛇的巨型女妖。这一形象大同小异，在公元前 6 世纪的赫西俄德的《赫拉克勒斯之盾》、斐勒库得斯（Pherekydes）的《神谱》、公元前 498 年品达的《皮托凯歌（10）》（*Pythian Ode* Ⅹ）中均出现过。转折点出现在公元前 490 年前后品达的《皮托凯歌（12）》（*Pythian Ode* Ⅻ），里面提到的美杜莎有着姣好的容颜。此后这一美丽的女妖形象开始出现在希腊各地，包括公元前 460 年埃斯库勒斯（Aeschylus）的《福耳喀得斯》（*Phorkides*）、公元前 2 世纪阿波罗多洛斯（Apollodorus）的《神话全书》（*Bibliotheca*）、公元 1 世纪初奥维德（Ovid）的《变形记》（*Metamorphosis*）。在罗马帝国地理学家帕萨尼亚斯（Pausanias）的笔下，美杜莎是屈顿尼斯湖（Lake Tritonis）一带的守护者，她带领利比亚人狩猎和战斗，在与珀耳修斯的人马的战斗中，她在夜里被偷袭、暗杀。珀耳修斯倾慕于她死后依然如此美丽，便砍下了她的头，展示给希腊人看。在奥维德的《变形记》中，美杜莎原本是一位美丽少女，因海神波塞冬在雅典娜神庙强暴了美杜莎，盛怒下的雅典娜女神将她的头发变成毒蛇，将她的面容变得狰狞可怖，能让看到她的人变成石头。而在阿波罗多洛斯的《神话全书》中，美杜莎被雅典娜惩罚的原因则是她过于美丽，以至于不自量力地要与雅典娜女神比美，雅典娜获胜后，将她变成了女妖。从希腊的传说看，美杜莎这位克里特-爱琴海一带的巴尔干女神，身上融合了两种截然相反的形象：既是狰狞可怖的妖怪，又是美丽的少女；既是生命的守护神，又是死亡的使者。只不过后来她身上美丽的一面逐渐被阿尔忒弥斯（Artemis）和雅典娜所取代，而更容易被人记住的则是她具有可以让敌人石化的“避邪妖女”的作用（Zolotnikova，2016，pp. 353－370）。如果说在《阁楼上的疯女人》中，吉尔伯特和古芭通过对18世纪到19世纪西方文学中由于男权社会的影响而对女性设定的天使与魔鬼形象进行了详细的剖析和批判（Gilbert & Gubar，2004，pp. 812－825），那么美杜莎无疑是男权社会中兼具天使与魔鬼形象的，既是男性欲望的化身又是令他们恐惧的妖怪的完美原型。美杜莎身上兼具的两面性以及她被珀耳修斯砍下头颅的故事，体现的无疑是根深蒂固的男权中心主义对女性的想象与妖魔化。而在美杜莎的凝视中，又蕴含着对男权的蔑视、挑衅，甚至一种能使他们石化、失语乃至精神瘫痪的可怕的革命性和颠覆性力量。美杜莎这一意蕴丰富的形象在以词语（word）描绘形象（image）的语象叙事体裁中具有普遍性，它超越了单纯的语象之间不同符号和媒介的对比，具有明确的性别政治和广泛的文化意义，在斯科特（Grant F. Scott）、赫弗南和米切尔等人的论述中都有体现。

二、美杜莎式的语象叙事

“美杜莎式的语象叙事”是赫弗南、斯科特和米切尔等人所定义的那种作为男性的语言担心作为女性的图像剥夺了其声音与权威的，将图像视为妖女美杜莎的语象叙事，其中又内在地包含由美杜莎的凝视而产生的颠覆性力量。（Heffernan，1993，p. 109）男性的语言一面痴迷于图像，一面又担心被图像褫夺权力而失声，米切尔将这种文字对图像的矛盾情结称为语象叙事的“美杜莎的效果”（Mitchell，1994，78）。

斯科特从语象叙事的性别政治角度，分析了在济慈的《希腊古瓮颂》中，作为男性的文字书写在面对作为女性的图像时产生的“语象叙事的希望”（ekphrastic hope，即“诗如画”，诗画可以结合）和“语象叙事的恐慌”（ekphrastic fear，即男性诗人担心被妖女美杜莎的图像石化、去势、阉割，从而丧失了男性权威），指出希腊古瓮正是美杜莎的形象。这一“美杜莎式的语象叙事”（Medusa ekphrasis）以雪莱所写的《咏佛罗伦萨美术馆达·芬奇的美杜莎》为最典型代表。借用这一术语，斯科特称18世纪的语象叙事诗是美杜莎式的。(Scott, 1994, pp. 120—121) 语象叙事作为一种用词语描绘视觉艺术品的体裁，曾在古罗马风靡一时，不过到了公元4—5世纪时，影响逐渐减弱，主要见于宗教作品中对拜占庭式风格建筑的描绘。到了18世纪，在莱辛（Gotthold Ephraim Lessing）和温克尔曼（Johann Joachim Winckelmann）等人的影响下，酷爱文物的埃尔金伯爵托马斯·布鲁斯（Thomas Bruce）将从希腊帕台农神庙掳掠来的大量珍贵文物卖给英国政府，让欧洲人有机会在大英博物馆里直面古希腊人民创造的璀璨的艺术瑰宝，这再次激发了人们对以文字描写艺术品这一语象叙事体裁的热情。顺应时代的需求，1806年牛津大学和剑桥大学公开向社会悬赏，主办了系列诗歌竞赛，以表彰那些写得最好的描写某件古代艺术品的诗歌，文人竞相掀起了创作语象叙事诗的风潮。在这一时期的语象叙事诗中，为了抵消美杜莎这一具有致命诱惑力的美少女形象（视觉艺术品）可能让男性诗人（语言艺术）石化、失语的危险，诗人们往往想方设法地将其悬置于安全的距离，通过使用框架叙述、作者介入、突出绘画本身的艺术品特性等技巧，来解除她对男性的威胁。斯科特以霍兰德（J. Holland）翻译的普林尼的《咏美狄亚之画》（*On the Picture of Medea*）、雪莱的《咏佛罗伦萨美术馆达·芬奇的美杜莎》和莎士比亚的《鲁克瑞斯受辱记》（*The Rape of Lucrece*）等作品为例，分析了这些作品中的美杜莎式语象叙事。作者指出，在以《咏美狄亚之画》为代表的18世纪语象叙事诗中，女性是静止、沉默、被动的，而积极、主动、凝视并发声的观众与诗人则是男性权威的象征。男性以其话语特权，刻意与沉默而危险的女性图像保持着安全的距离，在窥阴式的想象和远观中，将图像变为文字的他者，以实现词语对意象的权力欲望，并建构了图像女性他者的身份。而雪莱的诗则给予了美杜莎更多的主动，通过直接呈现她的恐怖与美丽，颠覆了此前语象叙事诗在男性观看者与女性被看者之间的主客体对立关系。雪莱通过拥抱而不是物化美杜莎这一他者，拒绝了莱辛的语象艺术二元对立，以饱满的激情书写了她的困境，讴歌了她在压迫中的反抗精神，从而表达了自己反抗权威、实现语象融合的艺术理想。(Scott, 1996)

与米切尔与斯科特的思路类似，赫弗南突出了语象叙事的性别政治，将文字比喻为男性观众，将视觉艺术比喻为女性被看者。他同时指出，语象叙事中的形象并不是完全被动的，它内在地隐藏着一股反抗语言霸权的革命性力量。

> 于是，语象叙事是这样一种文学样式，它取决于那种通常是性属的、在文字再现和视觉再现之间的对抗。因为对抗是在语言本身

> 的领域里展开的，所以总体上是不平等的，不过有一点除外：语象叙事普遍揭示了对视觉艺术的深刻的矛盾心理，一种图像痴迷与图像恐慌、崇拜与焦虑的结合。用文字再现一幅画或一尊雕塑，是为了唤醒它的力量——那种吸引观众，使其激动、惊愕、入迷或感到威胁的力量——尽管语言竭力试图去控制这种力量。（Heffernan，1993，p.7）

文字对形象的再现，一方面展示了男性对美丽女性的窥阴式占有欲望与想象，另一方面又表达了男性因担心美丽女性剥夺了他们的话语权，而试图将她们置于被控制的地位。这就产生了语象叙事的两种常见文本：对美女图（特别是裸女图）与美女受辱图的描写，这两者都是女性语象叙事（feminine ekphrasis），不同于“为了男性和关于男性的”男性语象叙事（Heffernan，1993，p.46）。其中对美女受辱图的文字描绘，通过公开男性语言施加在女性图像上的暴力，“促使读者通过女性的双眼去审视叙事，去倾听那如果不这样便会被压制的声音”（Hefferman，1993，p.70），因而是“形象向词语发起的革命。通过拒绝与引诱的修辞合作、拒绝加入取悦于男性的叙述，美女图变成了美女受辱图，这是一幅被绘制出来用以揭露男性在词语的‘色彩’掩饰下的暴力并使其公之于世的图像”（Heffernan，1993，p.90）。赫弗南进一步阐释道，在美杜莎式的语象叙事中，只有当语与象之间的敌对关系表现为叙述行为与静止图像之间的冲突，即言说的男性试图将作为静止图像的女性植入叙述进程（movement）并赋予其声音（prosopopoeia），使其从画的禁锢中复活时，才体现了语象叙事中的男女性别政治。（Heffernan，1993，pp.108－110）赫弗南从性别之争的角度出发，对美杜莎式语象叙事的特征进行了总结与限定，有助于读者更清晰地把握一个狭义上的、特点鲜明的美杜莎式语象叙事。在他的基础上，卢瓦佐（Elizabeth Bergmann Loizeaux）专门讨论了那些由女性诗人创作的语象叙事作品，称它们是“女性主义的语象叙事”（feminist ekphrasis），它们意识到了充斥着性别权力的男性观看传统，并以此为靶标，挑战其性属机制。女性作为观众的身份，是建立在以男性凝视为文化机制的土壤之上的，这一隐含在男性艺术家与男性观看之中的权力模式和价值体系，可以被女性主义者们揭发、利用、抵制和改写。（Loizeaux，2008，p.81）在这方面，最著名的例子是西苏的《美杜莎的笑声》，在该文中她反复强调了女性写作的重要性。西苏借美杜莎的形象，呼吁女性以自己的方式进行写作。男性作家被深深的阉割焦虑所困扰，他们应该意识到，女性不是被阉割的他者；他们不应聆听诱惑他们的塞壬的声音，而是“只需直视美杜莎的脸，她并非致命的，她美丽而且正在发笑”（Cixous et al.，1976，p. 885）。美杜莎的笑声在西苏笔下成为女性书写的代名词，它挑战了男性的凝视与书写特权。虽然女性的写作并无模式和规律可言，但它确实是存在的，这是不可否认的事实。

综合上述学者的讨论，不难发现，他们对美杜莎式的语象叙事的界定是比较混乱的。笔者认为，这一混乱的产生有多种原因，首先是其出发点并不明确，即“语象叙事”本身的定义到目前为止还是含混的，那么建立在其基础上的、附加了前缀的美杜莎式语象叙事，自然也难以说清。其次，定义的标准也不明确。如果从讨论的对象出发，最狭隘的理解是用文字对某件以美杜莎为原型的艺术品的描绘，再扩展一些，是对以美杜莎式女性人物为原型的艺术品的描绘。如果从讨论的效果出发，那么所有的语象叙事文本都可以纳入这一概念的范畴，即所有的视觉再现的文字再现都隐含着男女性别之间的权力之争，是词语与形象的意识形态博弈，因此均属于美杜莎式的语象叙事。基于这样的定义困局，本文虽主要讨论的是狭义的以美杜莎式女性形象为描述对象的文本，但因主要目的在于揭示词语与形象遭遇时的各种复杂的可能情形，因此范围并不局限于此，而是涵盖了所有的语象叙事。

三、不同体裁间的性别政治

关于语象（或诗画）不同体裁的争论不仅是两种媒介之争，更折射了整个西方文化历史中的性别权力斗争的思想，在埃德蒙·伯克（Edmund Burke）和莱辛等人论诗画有别、弗洛伊德（Sigmund Freud）论美杜莎对男性产生的阉割焦虑和法国学者论巴黎革命等文本中都有阐述。

其实源于古希腊的美杜莎的传说，从一开始就打上了男女性别之争的烙印。文字对形象的描绘，处处体现了两性之间的权力斗争。一方面，在早期的历史中，美杜莎虽然是能让人石化的可怕女妖，但她同时也是一位无辜受害的美少女，既能瞬间置人于死地，也能令人起死回生，因此被广泛用作避邪之物。世界各地出现的大量的美杜莎形象，无疑具有图像崇拜的意味，更多体现的是作为男性的文字对作为女性的图像的窥阴式欲望和想象。另一方面，随着 18 世纪以后“诗如画”理念的逐步式微，尤其是莱辛等人的诗画二分之后，诗以画为理想的根基被动摇了。为了弘扬文字的魅力，绘画被逐步置于他者的位置。在 18 世纪的语象叙事诗中，诗人出于对图像会使自己石化、失语的恐慌，刻意将形象疏远、隔离，让书写代替形象发声。在此语境下，美杜莎自身的悲惨遭遇被淡化了，珀耳修斯斩妖除魔的英雄举止则被广为传颂。美少女美杜莎的凝视具有致命的石化作用，对珀耳修斯构成了巨大的威胁，这如同观赏一幅美丽的绘画，如果被其魅力所俘获而不能自拔，便会失去自我，哑然失声，于是珀耳修斯这位传说中的大英雄，必须受到良好的保护，不受美杜莎凝视的伤害。因此，在雅典娜和赫尔墨斯等神祇的帮助下，他悄无声息地来到如同沉睡的艺术品的美杜莎身边，借助镜子的反光，避开了她的凝视，砍下了她的头颅。珀耳修斯将危险的女性形象置于无害的客体位置，并运用镜子反光的再现方式，巧妙避开了美杜莎目光的凝视，在砍下她头颅的同时，也涤除了自己对美少女不可抵御的魅力的邪念。理智最终战胜了诱惑，男性实现了对女性的完全控制。在此后的英雄行为中，珀耳修斯利用美杜莎的头让阿特拉斯石化成山脉，又解救了被锁在山崖的美丽的安德罗墨达，从自己并不英雄气的杀害美杜莎的行为中，重新找回了自我。在珀耳修斯的系列英雄行为中，美杜莎显然是他克服自身弱点的道具和陪衬，一步步帮助他成长为希腊神话中的著名英雄，而在这一过程中，美杜莎则被无情地牺牲、物化和妖魔化了。故事的背后，隐现着男性言说对女性形象的恐慌，以及他们千方百计压制她言说权力的性别机制。

将语言视作男性，而将图像视作女性，在西方有着悠久的历史传统。柏拉图曾指出，基于诗与画的密切联系，在表达一些抽象而语言难以解释的概念时，不妨借用艺术中的女性形象加以代替。（Hagstrum，1958，p. 5）这一思路已经预示了语象关系中的性别政治：绘画模仿自然，追求的是自然之美，具有直觉的、感官的、身体的、女性化的人格；话语表达理念，倾向知识之真，具有理性的、抽象的、灵魂的、男性化的人格。类似的对比在西方的历史文献中十分常见，其中对现代语象叙事中的性别政治有重要影响的是埃德蒙·伯克（Edmund Burke）和莱辛对诗画关系的讨论。

埃德蒙·伯克和莱辛的目的是为了论证语言优于图像，以为文学进行辩护，因此一反西方从古希腊以来的历史悠久的“诗如画”原则。伯克讨论了诗歌的崇高以与绘画的美之区别，莱辛则提出了著名的时空有别概念：诗歌是时间的艺术，绘画是空间的艺术，最好的艺术形式就是恪守自己的边界。他们的讨论，同时也确立了诗与画的男女性别对立。米切尔指出，伯克“一方面将诗和崇高与男性气质相联系，另一方面将画和美丽与女性气质相联系，这是十分确凿无误的”（Mitchell，1986，p. 111）。莱辛借鉴了伯克的观点，指出诗画之间具有明显的性别差异。简言之，各门艺术若要得体，根本上在于承担恰当的性别角色。绘画是一种空间的自然符号，局限于狭隘的领域，与模仿、身体、外在、沉默、美丽、悦目、女性相关；诗歌是一种时间的任意符号，具有无限的表现力，与表现、灵魂、内在、雄辩、崇高、悦耳、男性相关。“绘画，与对应于男性化的诗歌艺术的崇高和雄辩相比，如同女性，是理想的沉默、美丽、悦人眼目的生物。绘画局限于狭隘的向外部展示其身体的领域和她们起装饰作用的空间，而诗歌则可以自由徜徉于一个行动和表达不受限制的领域，一个时间的、话语的和历史的领域。”（Mitchell，1986，p. 110）莱辛对诗画艺术的性别对比，或许“其体裁法则的最根本意识形态基础是性别法则，不同艺术的得体原则归根结底是扮演适当的性别角色”（Mitchell，1986，p. 109）。米切尔对伯克和莱辛的诗画对立观念的解读，一方面揭示了长期为西方“诗如画”传统所忽略的性别政治，即将形象视作女性他者；另一方面又将其扩展到文化领域里两种敌对意识形态之间的权力斗争：偶像崇拜和偶像破坏。偶像破坏的背后是对女性他者的偶像的恐惧，这便可以解释西方文化中一直存在的对形象的恐惧。米切尔认为，莱辛为我们所揭示的是“诗与画两种体裁之间的关系不是纯粹理论上的，而是类似社会关系的——因此是政治的、心理的，或（综合起来看）意识形态的。各种体裁不是技术上的界定，而是排除或挪用的行为，倾向于将某个‘重要的他者’加以物化”（Mitchell，1986，p. 112）。如果说“诗如画”的悠久传统表明了西方长期以来对图像的痴迷（iconophilia），伯克和莱辛等人的拨乱反正则反映了对图像的恐慌（iconophobia），而“文化的历史，部分是图像与语言符号之间长期争夺控制权的故事”（Mitchell，1986，p. 43）。换言之，语象之争不仅是符号与媒介之争，更折射出西方的整个文化与历史。这是在广阔的社会文化语境中，两种体裁为了争夺男女性别之间的控制权而进行的意识形态博弈，这一观点在米切尔的诸多论著中得到了反复的声明和强调，例如他在评价莱辛的《拉奥孔》时就明确指出，该作是关于诗画两种体裁在时间和空间以及男女性别方面不同的政治体裁。（Mitchell，1984，pp. 98－115）

美杜莎的形象所代表的男性对女性形象的恐慌，被弗洛伊德解释为阉割的焦虑。他在《性与爱情心理》（*Sexuality and the Psychology of Love*）一书中辟有专章讨论美杜莎的头颅。砍头等同于阉割，恐慌产生于看到美杜莎时的阉割焦虑，就像一位不愿意相信阉割情结的男孩不小心看到了一位成年女性，特别是他母亲的裸露身体，发现她缺失男性器官时突然产生的恐慌情绪那样。当他发现她的母亲没有阳具时，无疑也会担心自己的阳具被阉割，出于自恋情结，他必然会激烈地反抗。在这里美杜莎的头颅代替了女性性器官，象征着阳具的缺失，带给人巨大的恐惧，而这一恐惧对敌人同样有效，因此可以用作保护自己的避邪之物。与美杜莎的头颅相比，男性的阳具则有正面的避邪作用。美杜莎头上的毒蛇，显然象征着直立的阳具，这些毒蛇虽然狰狞可怖，但它们却取代了缺失的阳具，缓解了阉割情结带来的焦虑。（Hertz，1983，pp. 30—31）弗洛伊德对原始恋物癖的研究表明，在男性对女性的凝视中存在着男性担心被女性阉割的焦虑，而美杜莎就是这种女性他者的完美原型。

弗洛伊德对阉割焦虑的分析固然有些牵强附会，但他的影响着实不小，使美杜莎成为心理分析中一个经典的原型意象。除了心理学上的讨论外，在19世纪的法国，美杜莎的妖女形象逐渐与暴力革命联系起来，成为其同义词。早在18世纪90年代，伯克就在其《论法国大革命》（*Reflections on the Revolution of France*）中描写暴民将国王和王后从凡尔赛宫押往巴黎时，将他们与妖魔化的神秘女性形象相类比。1792年出现的一幅反对革命的政治卡通画，设计成一枚硬币的两面，将英法两国的自由模式进行了对比。代表英国式自由的是一位坐在橡树下的优雅美丽的贵妇；代表法国式自由的则是狰狞的美杜莎，她左手握剑，右手持叉，叉着一颗被砍掉的男性的头颅，背景是被吊死的贵族。这幅画意味着，英国式自由的同义词是信奉宗教、道义、忠诚、服从法律、独立、个人安全、正义、继承、受保护、财产、勤劳、国家富裕与幸福；法国式自由的同义词则是无神论、伪善、叛逆、背叛、无政府主义和谋杀。法国革命被比喻为“最恶毒的妇人形象”，换言之，一个美杜莎戈耳工的形象。（Hertz，1983，p. 27；Schlutz，2015，pp. 342－343）在雨果（Victor Hugo）对法国巴黎1848年6月大暴动的描写、马克西姆·杜康（Maxime du Camp）对巴黎公社的恶毒攻击以及托克维尔（Alexis-Charles-Henri Clenel de Tocqueville）对1848年底层劳工暴动的回忆中，都出现了以女性形象喻指暴力革命的大段文字。在他们的笔下，财产的分配本质上就是不公平的，它是保证社会秩序的根基，遵循着自然的法则。当无产阶级劳工取得了其他平等权利之后，分配不公便成为他们的最后障碍。他们由于一无所有，属于被阉割的无能男人，因此需要打破旧体制，建立一个新的制度，作为他们新的菲罗斯偶像。在反对他们的人看来，缺失意味着性无能，无法建立一个新制度则导致了混乱与无政府主义。他们没有可以挥舞的男性的武器来进行抗争，只能靠展示没有阳具的女性身体（美杜莎式的避邪物）来吓阻和石化当权者，一方面具有推翻现政府的致命威胁，一方面又带来了暴力和混乱。他们的失败提醒当权者，象征着秩序的现有体制被阉割的后果是极为严重的。因此，他们将革命的暴力和有着致命威胁的美杜莎相类比，意在将其妖魔化，而对革命的镇压则是男性成功地让美杜莎臣服，砍下了她的头颅，完成了自己的英雄之举。(Hertz，1983，pp. 27—40) 政治的威胁被化身为女性的威胁，美杜莎则成为暴力革命的理想替代物，反对革命的男性作家在作品中对其大加挞伐。

从上面的分析来看，文字作品中出现的各种美杜莎式女性形象，早已使语象叙事超越了单纯的不同体裁和媒介之间的对比，具有了广泛的民俗学、心理学、社会学和文化的、历史的意义，这便是美杜莎式语象叙事为我们揭示的复杂的两种体裁之间的性别政治。

四、再现的困境

在 18 世纪的语象叙事作品中，美杜莎作为男性的他者，通常被置于客体化的被控制的权力关系中，文字压制形象的再现暴力表露无遗。词语与形象之间高下有别、截然二分的性别政治，在雪莱的《咏佛罗伦萨美术馆达·芬奇的美杜莎》(Shelley，1924，pp. 139—140) 一诗中受到了质疑、批判和颠覆。美杜莎的头具有美貌、新生和死亡的多重象征。她的凝视，是撬动男女性别政治刻板印象根基的利刃，释放了词语与形象遭遇时的无限可能和无穷潜力，质询了语象之间不同体裁性别政治的有效性，使二元对立的再现模式陷入了困境。这种再现的困境，使以斯科特、米切尔、赫弗南、赫尔茨 (Neil Hertz)、舒尔茨 (Alexander M. Schlutz)、雅各布 (Carol Jacobs) 等为代表的诸多当代学者痴迷，他们在肯定美杜莎对男性凝视的颠覆性力量的同时，也在寻找弥合语象性别之争的可能性。这些努力某些方面与当今女性主义的雌雄同体、非一之性等理念有不谋而合之处。

《咏佛罗伦萨美术馆达·芬奇的美杜莎》写于 1819 年。出于对古希腊雕塑的浓厚兴趣，雪莱访问了佛罗伦萨的乌菲兹美术馆，在那里，他偶然见到了一幅由 16 世纪不知名的画家所作的名为《美杜莎的头颅》的油画，深为画中美杜莎所具有的神秘魅力和她对再现形成的挑战所吸引，于是写下了这首并不被后世评论家看好的语象叙事诗。由于当时人们误传该画为达·芬奇所作，因此雪莱诗歌的标题也便以讹传讹了。雪莱不像此前的诗人那样，以一种居高临下的旁观者身份，去评论和描述一幅等待被发掘的艺术客体，而是一开篇就将美杜莎的头置于主动的地位，“它躺在那里，凝望着午夜的天空，/仰卧着，在云雾缭绕的山巅之上”。诗中的美杜莎的头颅，仿佛一位睡美人，静静地凝望午夜的星空和云雾中沉睡的山巅。它的唇和眼睑依然美丽动人，头上长出的不是头发，而是如同湿漉漉的岩石上的青草一般缠绕在一起的毒蛇，旁边是一只石化的正在窥视的毒蜥蜴和如同飞蛾扑火般拼命扇动翅膀的丑陋的蝙蝠。美杜莎死去的苍白面庞被雕刻得如此活灵活现，既呈现了美杜莎临死一刻的痛苦、愤怒与恐惧，也使观众在惊叹她的美貌的同时，惊惧于会被她的反视变成无生命的石头。诗人指出，是艺术的优雅而非对死亡的恐惧可能让观众迷失自我，使他的精神和思想石化。舒尔茨认为，雪莱创作这首语象叙事诗的目的，不是要保护文字免受美杜莎凝视的伤害，而是要揭露妖魔化美杜莎的男性意识形态和再现的暴力，以颠覆男性的词语强加于女性艺术客体上的权力与再现的欲望和恐慌。雪莱意在告诉我们，正如生活本身是一个谜，美杜莎本来的容颜是不可知晓、不可言说、不可把握和占有的，它存在于词语与形象的再现模式出现之前，因此词语和形象的再现都对它无能为力（Schultz，2015，p. 341），从而从根本上动摇了语象二分的理论根基。雅各布则在讨论该诗时指出，一方面雪莱试图再现美杜莎的头颅这一艺术客体，另一方面，他更深刻的用意还在于通过操演美杜莎的行为，以美杜莎式的凝视颠覆和解构了不同再现媒体之间的区别。（Jacobs，1985，pp. 163－179）

从上述学者的讨论可以发现，除了揭示西方社会和文化中广泛存在的性别政治外，在图像转向的背景下，在对语象关系的讨论成为当前学界焦点话题的当下，美杜莎式语象叙事一个更重要的作用是促使我们反思，当词语与形象遭遇时的再现困境。美杜莎的美貌不可观看，因为那象征的是死亡；也不可言说，因为一旦言说，便表明言说者知道她有多美，或者说已经见过她的美貌，此刻，言说者显然已经被石化了。这解释了为什么在几乎所有的美杜莎式语象叙事诗中，诗人们都尽量避而不谈美杜莎的容颜，“美杜莎的头最了不起的地方在于，它再现了不能被再现或不应被再现之物”（Siebers，1983，p. 8）既然不可观看，也不可言说，那么雪莱在诗歌中所要表达的，就不是作为男性主体的作者或观众要将作为女性审美客体的图像置于言说的语言霸权中，而是利用美杜莎的凝视这一意象来颠覆现有的对美杜莎的男性欲望与想象，同时也颠覆语言对图像的暴力。米切尔指出，男性的凝视与权力话语中所有崇高与美丽、愉悦与痛苦、男性与女性等二元对立的概念都在美杜莎那里被消解了（Mitchell，1994，p. 172），他从心理学的角度，解释了语象遭遇时的三个阶段：语象叙事的冷漠、希望和恐慌（pp. 151－181）。美杜莎的头颅恰好反映了作为男权象征的语言在遭遇作为女性象征的图像时的主体身份的恐慌：他（它）希望与图像保持一定距离（冷漠），以窥阴癖式的远观和抚玩，通过语言的言说将图像变为沉默的他者，从而建构自己在父权制下的主体身份。而在他绘声绘色的图像言说中，女性他者越来越清晰地呈现在他的面前，可能实现图文的融合（希望），从而威胁到他的言说权力，使他变成美杜莎反视中的石头（恐慌），彻底丧失自己的主体地位。伯克曾在论崇高时指出，最能表现崇高主题的是美与恐惧。美杜莎的头颅，表现了死亡前的痛苦、挣扎与恐惧，是男性对女性妖魔化的语言的暴力（冷漠），同时也象征着诗歌作者和男性观众对这幅由语言绘制的美女画作会通过反视让自己变成石头的语象叙事的恐慌。由此可见，美杜莎式语象叙事所折射的是西方社会在图像转向背景下的言说焦虑和图像恐慌。换言之，当语言遭遇图像时，二元对立的话语模式已经彻底无能为力了，言说被颠覆，观看被质疑，图像崇拜与图像破坏并行不悖，图像转向下，再现（representation）陷入了深刻的危机之中。那么语象叙事的可能在哪里呢？米切尔给出的解决之道一是颠覆狭义的语象叙事诗中的二元对立观念（即以文字描述某件艺术品）。他指出，一切媒介都是混合媒介，所有文本都是意象文本（image text），由此抽离男性逻各斯中心主义的根基。换言之，美杜莎的凝视凸显了语象叙事的冷漠、希望和恐慌，使词语（word）与意象（image）之间的克服他者性的再现陷入了危机，因此理解它们之间的关系应当采取辩证的观点：既是对立的，又是统一的；既是独立的，又是融合的。这就像我们观看一幅画，我们本能而直观地知道它是画（冷漠），但如果我们投入这幅画太深，就会觉得自己仿佛与画融为一体（希望），于是又必须惊醒自己，不要陷入太深，否则便会彼此不分（恐慌）。如果把作为观众的我们理解为词语在面对形象时的再现危机，道理也是一样的。因此，美杜莎的头颅，就像德里达（Jacques Derrida）使用的“延异”概念一样颠覆西方逻各斯中心主义，成为米切尔、赫弗南、斯科特、舒尔茨、赫尔茨等人直击语象二分的阿喀琉斯之踵，颠覆了词语与形象二元对立的基础，它们之间呈现出极为复杂的动态、辩证的关系：语既是语又非语，象既是象又非象，象中有语，语中有象。对语象不同再现体裁的区分始于性别政治，又在观看与被看、言说与被说的竞争中被消解、颠覆了，或者说从内部被引爆了。在借助美杜莎的形象消解语象再现的差别之后，米切尔也在尝试着寻找走出再现困境的途径，这一途径或许将指向语象融合的理想。他指出，当语言与意象遭遇时，现存所有的学科均无法有效解释其中的悖论，因此要从所有学科的交叉或影子地带，以超越一切学科的跨学科甚至反学科的高度，以现象学的直观，让语象自由结合、碰撞，从而产生新的认识、新的问题甚至新的学科。由此可见，在美杜莎式的语象叙事中，美杜莎的头颅成为撼动词语与形象再现稳固基石的巨大破坏力量，它在消解和颠覆了语象之分的理论根基之后，为我们留下的是诸多未知的可能。美杜莎已死，从她被砍下头颅的脖颈处，究竟会诞生出什么样的新生命、新事物，或许这才是值得人们期待的。当然在语言学范式依然一统天下，新的图像范式转向正在艰难萌芽的语境下，正如在父权制依然坚不可摧，女性主义仍在不断寻求突破的语境中一样，米切尔将更多的同情给予了形象自我呈现的可能，并孜孜不倦地向着建构一套形象科学的方向努力。

最后，笔者想借用雅各布的一系列追问来结束本文，并将悬置的再现困境留给读者去思考：雪莱在诗中是真如他所写的那样在凝视一位戈耳工，还是在观看一幅伪托达·芬奇的绘画？凝视美杜莎的结果将如何？这对观看一幅画或阅读一首咏画诗有何启示意义？诗歌是否让我们直接暴露在美杜莎的凝视之中，或是如珀耳修斯借助的神盾一样，通过反射和再现让我们免受其害？那些本质上描写艺术作品的文字作品到底是如何运作的？文字描绘本身意味着什么？谁才是观看者——珀耳修斯、他的前辈、画家、诗人，还是读者？（Jacobs，1985，p. 167）本文如果能对读者在反思上述问题时提供些许帮助，也就达到目的了。

引用文献：

王安，程锡麟（2016）. 西方文论关键词：语象叙事. 外国文学，4，77—87.

Cixous, H. , Cohen, K. & Cohen, P. (1976). The laugh of the Medusa. *Signs* (Vol. 1), 4, 875—893. Chicago, IL: The University of Chicago Press.

Fasoli, P. (2007). "Medusa". In F. Malti-Douglas (ed.). *Encyclopedia of sex and gender*, 3 (4), 985—986. Detroit, MI: Macmillan Reference USA.

Gilbert, S. & Gubar, S. (2004). The madwoman in the attic. In J. Rivkin & M. Ryan (eds.). *Literary theory: An anthology*, (2), 812—825. Maiden, MA: Blackwell Publishing.

Hagstrum, J. H. (1958). *The sister arts: The tradition of literary pictorialism and English poetry from Dryden to Gray*. Chicago, IL: University of Chicago Press.

Heffernan, J. A. W. (1993). *Museum of words: The poetics of ekphrasis from Homer to Ashbery*. Chicago, IL & London, UK: University of Chicago Press.

Hertz, N. (1983). Medusa's head: Male hysteria under political pressure. *Representations*, 4, 27—54. Berkeley, IL: University of California Press.

Jacobs, C. (1985). On looking at Shelley's Medusa. In Yale French Studies, *The lesson of Paul de Man*, (69) 163—179. Connecticut, CT: Yale University Press.

Loizeaux, E. B. (2008). *Twentieth-century poetry and the visual arts*. Cambridge, UK: Cambridge University Press.

Mitchell, W. J. T. (1984). The politics of genre: Space and time in Lessing's Laocoon. *Representations*, 6 (Spring issue), 98—115. Berkeley, CA: University of California Press.

Mitchell, W. J. T. (1986). *Iconology: Image, text, ideology*. Chicago, IL: University of Chicago Press.

Mitchell, W. J. T. (1994). *Picture theory: Essays on verbal and visual representation*. Chicago, IL: University of Chicago Press.

Scott, G. F. (1996). Shelley, Medusa, and the perils of ekphrasis. In F. Burwick & J. Klein (eds.). *The Romantic imagination: Literature and art in England and Germany,* 315—322. Amsterdam/Atlanta, GA: Rodopi. https://romantic — circles. org/editions/shelley/medusa/gscott. html.

Schlutz, A. M. (2015). Recovering the beauty of Medusa. *Studies in romanticism,* 54(3), (Fall issue), 329—353. New York, NY: City University of New York.

Scott, G. F. (1994). *The sculpted word: Keats, ekphrasis and the visual arts*. Hannover, GER & London, UK: University Press of New England.

Shelley, M. W. (1924). *Posthumous poems of Percy Bysshe Shelley.* London, UK: John and Henry L. Hunt. https://romantic — circles. org/editions/shelley/medusa/mforum. html. Full editiion in Carol Jacobs (1985). On looking at Shelley's Medusa, *Yale French Studies*, No. 69, The lesson of Paul de Man, 163—179.

Siebers, T. (1983). *The mirror of Medusa,* 8. Berkeley, CA: University of California Press.

Webb, R. (1999). Ekphrasis ancient and modern: The invention of a genre. In *Word and image* 15.1 (January—March), 7—18. Cambridge, UK: Cambridge University Press.

Webb, R. (2009). *Ekphrasis, imagination and persuasion in ancient rhetorical theory and practice*. Farnham, UK; Burlington, VT: Ashgate.

Zolotnikova, O. A. (2016). A hideous monster or a beautiful maiden? Did the Western Greeks alter the concept of Gorgon?. In H. L. Reid & D. Tanasi (eds.). *Philosopher kings and tragic heroes: Essays on images and ideas from Western Greece*. Fonte Aretusa, ITA: Parnassos Press.

作者简介：

王安，文学博士，四川大学外国语学院教授，博士生导师，主要研究方向为英美文学、文学理论与文学翻译。

Author:

Wang An, Ph. D., professor, and doctoral supervisor of College of Foreign Languages and Cultures, Sichuan University. His research interests are English literature, literary theory and literary translation.

Email: wangan@scu. edu. cn

论交流叙述学的研究谱系*

王委艳

摘　要：叙述和交流是人类建构经验世界的基本方式，以叙述的方式交流是存在于人类各种活动领域中的常见现象，但在叙述学的研究历史中，对叙述交流的研究并不充分。经典叙述学强调文本内部研究，对叙述交流性的研究一直处于暗流状态。后经典叙述学将叙述学研究引入文化领域，用理论介入模式，在叙述学研究中渗透各种理论思想，其对叙述交流性的研究基本延续雅柯布森“语言交际图示”和围绕查特曼“叙述—交流情景示意图”展开。叙述转向开启了叙述学研究新视野，探讨叙述一般特性而非某一种叙述类型的特性，成为叙述学研究的一种新的范式。叙述扩容、对叙述的重新界定，都是开启这一研究范式的表现。叙述在各种学科、领域的表现使其交流性凸显，建构交流叙述学成为一般叙述研究范式下的一项紧迫任务。

关键词：叙述转向，一般叙述研究，交流叙述学，研究谱系，研究范式

On the Research Genealogy of Communicative Narratology

Wang Weiyan

Abstract: Narration and communication are the basic ways that human beings construct the world of experience. Communication by narration is common in various fields of human activity, but research into communicative narratology is insufficient. Classical narratology

* 本文为2019年度国家社科基金后期资助项目“交流叙述学”（19FZWB049）阶段性成果；信阳师范学院“南湖学者奖励计划”青年项目。

emphasised the internal study of texts, and the study of narrative communication was never more than an undercurrent. Post-classical narratology introduced the study of narratology into the field of culture, using the model of theoretical intervention to infiltrate various theories with the study of narratology. Currently, the study of narrative communication is basically a continuation of Jacobson's "linguistic communication diagram" and Chatman's "narrative communication scenario diagram". The narrative turn has opened a new field of vision in narratology research. The new paradigm is to explore the general characteristics of narrative rather than the characteristics of a certain narrative type. Narrative expansion and a redefinition of narrative are manifestations of this new paradigm. The performance of narration in various disciplines and fields makes its communication prominent, and the construction of a communicative narratology becomes an urgent task under the general narrative research paradigm.

Keywords: narrative turn, general narrative research, communicative narratology, research genealogy, research paradigm

DOI: 10.13760/b.cnki.sam.202001014

叙述的交流性一直是叙述学研究关注的重要方面，但一直未能充分研究。经典叙述学最具代表性的论文发表于《交流》（*Communication*）杂志 1966 年第 8 期。罗兰·巴尔特在其发表在《交流》杂志的《叙事作品结构分析导论》中不但表明叙述的普遍性，即叙述存在于各种领域，而且同时指出叙述交流性研究的不足。俄国形式主义者雅柯布森提出其著名的语言交际图示，西摩·查特曼以此为基础，提出叙事-交流情景示意图，这些理论架构随后经由诸多学者演绎，并直接影响后经典叙述学下的修辞叙述学研究，如詹姆斯·费伦的“双渠道交流”。当今发生在许多领域的叙述转向，使叙述的交流性凸显，在一般叙述的研究框架下，建构交流叙述学成为叙述学研究的一项紧迫任务。

一、交流性：经典叙述学暗流

叙述的交流性一直是叙述学关注的对象，但经典叙述学对于文本内部研究的强调使这种关注一直作为一种暗流而存在。后经典叙述学打破文本框范，将多种理论、多种视野融入叙述学研究，使叙述学以美国为中心出现复兴局面，尤其是 20 世纪 90 年代以来出现了规模宏大的叙述学转向，叙述学研究向历史、教育、医疗、新闻、法律、影视、广告、网络等多个领域扩展，在历经经典与后经典阶段之后，开始酝酿第三次范式革命，赵毅衡先生的广义叙述学研究适逢其时。交流性成为叙述的核心特性，对于交流叙述的研究因而成为一项非常迫切的任务。要建构“交流叙述学”学科，就有必要对交流叙述的相关论述进行梳理，建构交流叙述理论的研究谱系。

俄国形式主义理论家托马舍夫斯基在《主题》（1925）一文中指出了文学过程的两个重要时刻——选择主题和设计主题，其中心问题则是文学作品的交流性：“主题的选择密切取决于主题在读者中得到的反应。……读者形象即使是抽象的，即使它要求作者尽力使自己成为作品的读者，这种形象也始终出现在作家的意识里”；而“对技巧的关注是作家和他最亲近的读者习以为常的事”。（1989，pp. 234－235）也就是说，对主题的选择与设计均围绕获得最佳交流效果展开。但俄国形式主义并没有发展成为一种交流性的理论，文本形式仍是其研究核心。俄国形式主义的另一位代表理论家雅柯布森在《语言学的元语言问题》一文中第一次提出了著名的语言交际图示，并这样解释：

> 说话者（addresser）把一段话（message）传送给受话者（addressee）。想要使交际运行起来，这段话还需要有一个所指的语境（context），该语境可以为受话者所把握，它或者是语言的，或者是可以语言化的；需要有一套说话者和受话者之间（或者换言之，编码者和解码者之间）完全或者至少是部分共有的代码（code）；最后，还需要有接触（contact），接触是说话者和受话者之间的一条物理通道和心理联系，它使双方能够进入并且保持交际状态。（2001，pp. 52－53）

雅柯布森对于语言交流的影响因素与交流渠道的揭示影响深远。以叙述的方式交流是人类积累和传承经验的重要方式，对纵向的历史层面和横向的共时层面的叙述交流，雅柯布森的语言交际图示均会提供很好的参照。巴赫金则不同，其“对话”“狂欢”理论下的交流基于参与各方的自由、平等，其“复调”理论意为多声部共进，平等观念是其交流对话的核心思想。（2009，p. 4）

经典叙述学受索绪尔语言学、俄国形式主义的影响，以叙述文本的话语和结构为研究对象，对叙述交流性的研究一直是其中的一股暗流。巴尔特在《叙事作品结构分析导论》中指出了叙述作品的多样性，而且同时指出了叙述作品的交流性："叙事作品作为客体也是交际的关键：有一个叙事作品的授者，有一个叙事作品的受者。大家知道，在语言交际中，我和你是绝对互为前提的。同样，没有叙述者和没有听众（或读者）也就不可能有叙事作品。"巴尔特同时指出了叙事作品交流研究方面的问题："这一点也许很简单，但是研究得还很差。""问题不在于探究叙述者的动机，也不在于探究叙述对读者产生的影响，而在于描写叙事作品本身过程中叙述者和读者得以获取意义的代码。"（巴特，1989，p.28）回顾叙述学研究，可以发现，在经典与后经典叙述学之后，在叙述转向的背景下，叙述的交流性已经成为很多叙述类型的普遍特性，但叙述交流性的研究依然停留在对雅柯布森语言交际图示的演绎上，进展缓慢。

普林斯作为从经典叙述学向后经典叙述学过渡的理论家，在其著作《叙事学：叙事的形式与功能》一书中扩展了叙述学的研究视野，尤其在该书第四章《阅读叙事》中探讨了叙事文本与读者之间的交流互动关系。他在对阅读的定义中指出，阅读以"文本与读者的互动为前提"，阅读一部文本就是提出"关于文本的问题并在文本基础上回答它们"（2013，pp.102－103）。在本书中，普林斯提出了许多有价值的概念，对于交流叙述学的研究极具启发价值，比如在第一章《叙述》中的"叙述者"部分提出"'我'信号"；在"受述者"部分提出"'你'信号"；在第四章《阅读叙事》中提出"最大阅读""最小阅读""元叙事信号"；等等。这些概念对于交流叙述中交流因子的辨识与交流语言的建构具有非常重要的价值。

二、后经典叙述学：单向交流叙述图示

后经典叙述学的产生是叙述学研究中的一次范式革命。正如弗卢德尼克指出的："叙事学的青春年华过去之后，是叙事理论的重新定位与分化，结果产生了一系列回应后结构主义的亚学科，学术范式转向文化研究。"（2007，p.23）后经典叙述学并非经典叙述学中时间意义上的继承，因为在叙述学诞生时，一些突破经典叙述学研究范式的理论思想就已经孕育其中，如巴尔特的理论及其对电影、摄影、时装等的研究，就已经突破经典叙述学的研究范围和范式而在符号学意义上具有某种普遍价值。同时，在经典叙述学研究兴盛之时，韦恩·布斯的小说修辞理论无疑具有独特意义，并因此被尊奉为后经典叙述学之修辞叙事学研究的重要理论。值得注意的是，修辞叙述学研究正一步步走向叙述的交流特性，当叙述研究向更广范围的叙述性敞开大门时，

修辞的单向意向性就被交流的双向影响所取代。“在叙述学框架内，叙述被构想为一种交流程序，其中故事层面的信息被一个特定的叙述者传递给一个特定的叙述接受者。”（Herman，2009，pp. 64－65）虽然叙述学（经典和后经典）不排斥叙述的交流性，但这种交流性基本还是在文本的框架内存在，所谓“在叙述学框架内”，即是此意。

在交流叙述方面影响最大的当属查特曼著名的“叙事－交流情景”示意图（图1）。（查特曼，2013，p. 135）

叙事文本

真实作者--->［隐含作者—→（叙述者）—→（受述者）—→（隐含读者）］--->真实读者

图1　查特曼“叙事－交流情景”示意图

查特曼的叙事－交流情景示意图被后来的许多国内外的研究者演绎。这种叙述交流模型在经典、后经典叙述学研究中一直存在，正如赫尔曼指出：“叙述交流模型同时根植于结构主义叙述学（查特曼、热奈特、普林斯）和几乎同时将修辞方法运用于叙述学的先驱——韦恩·布斯。”（Herman，2009，p. 64）由此可见，叙述交流模型从根本上讲存在两方面的缺陷。其一，将叙述交流框范于文本范围之内，这里存在两种交流方式：一者表现为隐含作者与隐含读者之间的交流，一者表现为叙述者与受述者之间的交流。前者的交流基本上是一种虚拟状态的交流，后者包括两种情况：（1）非虚拟交流：戏剧化叙述者与其他人物之间的交流；（2）虚拟交流：非戏剧化叙述者与虚拟受述者之间的交流。其二是修辞性交流，以布斯和费伦的理论为代表。布斯便用隐含作者、作者的“第二自我”等概念，实际上是想对作者进行文本化、虚拟化处理，以解决作者与文本隔断的问题。费伦则强调：“‘作为修辞的叙事’这个说法不仅仅意味着叙事使用修辞，或具有一个修辞维度。相反，它意味着叙事不仅仅是故事，而且也是行动，某人在某个场合出于某种目的对某人讲一个故事。……首先是叙述者向他的读者讲故事，然后是作者向作者的读者讲述叙述者的讲述。”（2002，p. 14）

对于修辞性的强调其实遮蔽了另一种事实，即修辞的反作用，即当人们修辞地进行语言活动的时候，其修辞行为也受到来自修辞的反向支配，即修辞具有反作用，这种反作用来自语境压力、体裁压力、接受压力，等等，也就是说，修辞主体的修辞行为是不自由的。写作的“单行道”给人一种印象，即作者如上帝一样君临一切，这种文学叙述的“单行道”写作模式使交流叙述模型存在难以逾越的发展障碍。在叙述转向背景下，这种基于文学叙述的交流模型必然受到挑战。

值得关注的是，查特曼的图示根本上是修辞性的，单向性明显，读者（包括隐含读者和真实读者）处于交流的末端，作者（真实作者和隐含作者）具有交流的先天优势，其权威决定了交流只能从作者单向流向读者，很难再从读者回到作者。因此，这里的交流只是一种修辞行为。詹姆斯·费伦注意到了查特曼交流图示的单向缺陷，他把人物引入叙事交流，从而获得双渠道交流：（1）作者—叙述者—读者；（2）作者—人物—读者。费伦指出，这两种渠道将会相互作用，这样，交流总量要比查特曼的单渠道大得多。（2012）

修辞叙事学研究从布斯开始，经由查特曼、卡恩斯、费伦发展，从文本内转向文本外，关注文学叙事作品之外的叙述作品，比如电影（查特曼）；关注语境、规约和言语行为（卡恩斯）（Kearns，1999）；关注作者、隐含作者、叙述者、受述者、隐含读者、真实读者之间循环往复的关系（费伦）。修辞叙述学研究对交流叙述研究更具启发意义，而且更加接近交流叙述学。笔者在2013年11月第四届叙事学国际会议暨第六届全国叙事学研讨会（广州，南方医科大学）上提出建构交流叙述学的理论构想，并对查特曼“叙事－交流情景”的单向性提出质疑。谭君强教授提示笔者，费伦曾经在上次叙事学会议（长沙，2011年10月）上指出这种缺陷（会议论文《修辞、伦理即叙述交流：抑或从故事和话语到作者、资源与读者》），并提出叙事交流的双渠道。但费伦的双渠道交流中，每种渠道依然是单向性流动。渠道与方向是两个不同概念，双渠道并非意味着交流可以从读者向作者回溯，其影响基本是一种单向性的，依然难以揭示叙述经验的积累过程以及这些经验对于叙事交流的意义。同时，这种单向性（或者双渠道）很难放置于叙述的历史层面，去揭示叙述作品由简单走向复杂的动态历史过程。

其实，费伦、查特曼的单向交流源于修辞学的理论根基。修辞学提供的是一种经验贯彻模型，即来自创作主体的经验如何通过符号文本在接受者那里获得贯彻，并且，作者希望获得一种无误贯彻，因而忽略了接受者的能动性。费伦的双渠道交流只不过为这种贯彻提供了更多的方式，并没有从根本上改变交流的单向性。中国学者也注意到了这种单向交流的缺陷，谭君强指出：

> 无论是查特曼的模式也好，还是雅恩的模式也好，都存在一个关键的问题，即它们都属于单向传动模式，费伦也注意到查特曼的模式是假设了“一个单一的交流渠道”（a single channel of communication），但他并未对此提出质疑。笔者认为，交流不是一个单一传导的过程，而是一个双向交流的过程。叙事文本内外的交

流过程同样如此。此外，这种交流并不限于两两相对的诸如真实作者/真实读者、叙述者/受述者、人物/人物之间的交流，而是各个不同成分之间可以双向甚或多向交叉的交流。（谭君强，2012，p.176）

谭君强明确指出叙事文本的双向、多向交叉交流特性，可惜谭先生并没有以此为起点，建构叙述参与各方之间的交流机制以及这种交流机制的运行特征，也没有站在叙述转向背景下看到叙述性蔓延使叙述的交流性越发突出并走向叙述建构的核心位置。中国还有其他一些学者对叙述交流图示进行演绎，如亢淑平对叙事交流图的改进（亢淑平，2010），刘江对自传叙述交流图的推演（刘江，2012），等等。但所有这些研究都止步于对叙述交流图的改进，没有更进一步挖掘交流的内在机制，建构交流叙述学的理论模型。

事实上，交流叙述图示一直作为修辞叙述学的核心理论思想被演绎，这种所谓的交流其实是一种修辞，是叙述主体为达到叙述目的而传达其思想的流动链条。但叙述主体的叙述行为并不自由，他受到来自接受者的反向压力，同时还受到文化、语境、体裁等规约性因素的支配。修辞叙述学隔断了来自接受者反向交流的影响，忽略了参与各方之间的中间地带。这其实体现了叙述学研究领域存在的两种观点——修辞观和认知观，“修辞学派认为它是作者劝说读者的一种技巧；认知学派认为它是读者解决文本歧义和矛盾的一种阐释策略，与读者的认知框架有关”（倪爱珍，2018，p.159）。但两种认识均没有解决交流的内在机制问题。交流叙述学的理论建构正是要把这一中间地带的运行机制搞清楚，以便建立一种圆形的叙述交流模型。

因此，建构交流叙述学，必须克服上述修辞性影响，从理论上建构一般叙述学研究背景下的交流叙述学的研究框架。值得关注的是，有些学者已经走到了前面，迪迪埃·科斯特（Didier Coste）在其著作《作为交流的叙述》中指出：“叙述学欲在行动上获取交流，但它仅能够在如下被报道的每一阶段获取交流，即前文本、文本、解释、同文本……上下文、注释、评论、答案和其审问等等。”（Coste，1989，p.6）

也就是说，携带交流性的叙述因子是普遍存在的，而且这些因子会在交流的任何阶段、任何层面，甚至任何时间起作用。叙述学和交流的结合开启了交流叙述学研究的大门。

三、后经典叙述学之后：走向交流叙述学

后经典叙述学之后，有一个少有人注意的理论过渡，也就是说，一种新

的叙述学研究范式正悄然在被认为后经典叙述学的研究中酝酿生成。“80 年代的叙述转向，使得叙述突破了小说的阈限，进入了不同媒介。传统以小说为原型的研究已经无法适应叙述理论的发展”（方小莉，2017，p. 100），这不同于经典叙述学囿于文本内部的形式研究，也不同于后经典叙述学的“叙述学+”模式（叙述学+某种理论范式），而是在更广的背景上，重新认识叙述本身，并在多种叙述类型中寻找“叙述”的共相。同时，对叙述文本的建构方式、存在方式和传承方式进行重新审视，使对叙述的研究在一般意义上获得更新。

罗兰·巴尔特在《叙述作品结构分析导论》中有一段被反复引述的话，其中列举了很多类型的叙述。但经典叙述学研究并没有以这个存在于各种领域的叙述现象为研究对象，而是以文学为中心建构叙述学的理论话语。这给人一种印象：叙述学等同于文学叙述学。但叙述学从来没有囿于文学而限制叙述学的理论拓展力。西摩·查特曼 1975 年出版《故事与话语：小说与电影的叙事结构》，将叙述学研究视野扩展到电影。查特曼指出，“除体裁区别的分析以外，还有对于‘叙事的本质是什么’这一问题的界定。文学批评家们太过倾向于单独地考虑文字媒介，尽管他们每天都通过电影、滑稽连环画、绘画、雕塑、舞剧与音乐来消费故事”（2013，p. 1）。由此可见，查特曼对叙述的理解是很宽泛的。文学之外的叙述一直是叙述学研究的关注对象，从来没有远离叙述学研究视野。

21 世纪以来，尤其是进入后经典叙述学阶段，对文学叙述之外的叙述的关注更成为叙述学研究拓展的重要方向。雅各布·卢特的《小说与电影中的叙事》（*Narrative in Fiction and Film*：*An Introduction*）（2000）探讨了电影的叙述规律。2004 年，由米克·巴尔主编的《叙述学：文学与文化研究中的关键概念》（*Narrative Theory*：*Critical Concepts in Literature and Culture Studies*）（2004）涉及很多领域，如法律、历史、社会等。2005 年，费伦等主编的《当代叙事理论指南》（*A Companion to Narrative Theory*）（2005）代表了 21 世纪以来叙述学研究的新发展。该书第四部分《超越文学叙事》，专门对文学叙述以外的叙述类型，如法律、电影、歌剧、音乐、历史等，进行学理探讨。2006 年，玛丽-劳尔·瑞安出版《故事的变身》（*Avatars of Story*），该书分上下两编，分别探讨了新旧媒介的叙述，尤其是下编，视野对准网络时代的叙述，拓展了传统叙事研究的锋面。尤其可贵的是，瑞安试图拓展对叙述的传统观念，列举了 11 对叙事模式，对于叙述本体的理解更加宽泛和全面。2009 年，桑德拉·埃南（Sandra Heinen）和罗伊·

萨默（Roy Sommer）主编的《跨学科时代的叙述学研究》（*Narratology in the Age of Cross-Disciplinary Narrative Research*）汇集了16位叙述学学者的研究文章，探讨了叙述学研究在跨学科时代的各种表现。

查特曼直接指出，“叙事是一种交流，因此它预设了两个参与者——一个发送者和一个接受者”（2013，p.14）。查特曼前瞻性地提出“叙事-交流情境”示意图，但这种交流链条往往被人解读为一种作者意图诉诸文本并影响真实读者的修辞路线。但查特曼的示意图在真实作者与叙述文本之间、真实读者与叙述文本之间用的是虚线，这意味着，查特曼并没有完全的把握认为真实作者意图会通过叙述文本准确抵达真实读者。而在叙述文本内部，情况会不同，“隐含作者—（叙述者）—（受述者）—隐含读者”这个链条指示的是一种确定的关系，因此用的是实线。查特曼的前瞻性还表现在注意到接受者的能动性，比如对于叙述文本中的人物，他不认为是一个确定的形象，“人物是由受众根据显示或隐含在原始结构中的、由不管什么媒介的话语传达的迹象重构出来的”（2013，p.104）。这与费伦坚持的双渠道之一的“作者—人物—读者”交流渠道具有根本不同，因为后者依然坚持作者修辞的有效性，其传达可以通过叙述者与人物双渠道进行。叙述文本并非一个完备的世界，“叙事唤起一个世界，由于它仅仅是一种召唤，因此我们仍然可以自由地用我们所获得的任何真实或想象的经验去丰富它。不过我们知道何时应该停止推测”（查特曼，2013，p.104）。查特曼的观点意味着叙述文本并非一个稳固的结构，而是一种召唤结构，接受者完全可以根据自己的经验去丰富这个世界。这是一种双向交流思想，这种思想由于其叙事-交流情境而一遍遍被误读或者不完全解读。

费伦在《作为修辞的叙事》一书中指出，“首先，‘作为修辞的叙事’这个说法不仅仅意味着是故事，而且是行动，某人在某个场合出于某种目的对某人讲一个故事”（2002，p.14）。也就是说，某人在向别人讲述故事的同时，也在实施一种行动，这种行动会通过故事的一系列修辞在对方身上达到某种目的。费伦的修辞叙事可表述成如下链条：叙述者意向—故事修辞—接受者反应。这是一种典型的单向交流，没有考虑到接受者的反向叙述能力，或者说接受者文本的建构能力。事实上，这种“叙述者意向”是一种一厢情愿的单向修辞，其目标实现有一个隐含的前提，即接受者能够完全按照叙述者的意向完成对叙述文本的理解，并按照既定的方式做出反应。虽然费伦在其后的研究中对这种单向交流进行了修正，提出双渠道交流，即“作者—叙述者—读者”和“作者—人物—读者”（2013，p.28），但这种双渠道依然是一种单向修辞，只不过多了一条渠道而已，并没有把接受者对叙述的反向交流及其影响考虑进来，本质上依然是修辞性的。

卢特在《小说与电影中的叙事》中用一章的篇幅讨论叙事交流。卢特基本上也是在“叙述者—叙述文本—接受者”的单向思维链条中讨论问题，虽然也看到叙述主体会发生翻转，但难以看到经由二次叙述化之后的“接受者文本”即“二度文本化”后的文本与作者文本的区别，因为组成作者文本与接受者文本的材料并不一样。由叙述者（可靠与不可靠）、叙述文本形式（隐含作者、隐含读者、叙述距离、反讽、叙述角度、叙述层次、声音、人物、引语形式）等组成的作者叙述文本在抵达读者的过程中会产生增殖，诸如伴随文本、读者的个人状况等都会影响叙述交流：“虽则叙事理论仍以文本为中心，它目前却更加强调、也更感兴趣于叙事交流模式的外部环节：即作为作者的信息发送者和作为读者的信息接收者。由于二者都是历史的一部分，也都是一个或更多的文化圈的一部分，晚近文学理论朝向历史和语境转向，并没有降低叙事理论的适切性。”（卢特，2011，p. 16）这里卢特一方面承认作者与读者的不同，另一方面承认叙事理论在二者交流关系中的适切性。卢特对叙述交流的讨论主要围绕文本形式在交流中的作用，或者说这些形式如何影响了接受者的意义判断，“文本意义产生于文本呈示的模范读者与真实读者间的性情和兴趣上的能产性矛盾”。这些讨论运用的是一种修辞学思维，着重解释来自作者并作用于文本的形式如何影响或者引导接受者阅读/观看，忽略了接受者的反塑能力。

因此，从布斯、查特曼、费伦，再到卢特，研究基本沿着修辞学思路进行。尽管查特曼预见到接受者的反向交流能力，但他并没有对此展开研究，而是聚焦于“故事内功能”，“从故事内来说，在一个框架故事中，他为叙述者担当听众，在这个听众身上，各种各样的叙事修辞技巧得以实践”（2013，p. 224）。这仍然属于修辞学思路，用查特曼自己的话说，“尽管理论常求助于逻辑学，但它也严重地依赖于修辞学”（2013，p. 251）。

修辞学虽然也强调修辞链条的完整性，即“作者—文本—接受者”链条的完整，但问题的复杂性在于，单向性遮蔽了来自接受者的能动性，同时对文本持固化观，即过分强调文本的固有形态，而没有考虑到在交流中文本的动态建构过程和二度文本化，所有这些都影响了交流叙述理论的发展。

瑞安在《故事的变身》中用第五章专门讨论新媒介时代“走向互动叙述学”，“倘若说经典叙事学未能通过互动文本性的检验，那么并非意味着互动文本性也未能通过叙事性的检验。相反，这意味着叙述学必须扩展原有的领地”（2014，p. 96）；并指出“互动叙述学的研究对象，不仅包括‘文学’超文本小说，而且还包括基于文本历险游戏、互动戏剧、某些单用户电子游戏、多用户网络角色扮演游戏”（2014，p. 94）。这里，瑞安抓住了在后经典叙述学之后，叙述学发展的一个关键问题，即“叙事性蔓延”，尤其是进入传媒时代，网络成为生活的一部分，“互动”构成了网络的基本特性。

瑞安的可贵之处在于敏锐地抓住了叙事性这个根本问题，同时抓住了网络时代的互动特性，指出建构“互动叙述学”的必要性。虽然瑞安敏锐地发现网络时代叙述学研究必须拓展范围，且指出互动性是网络时代的主要特性。但应当指出，无论互动还是交流，从来都是人类叙述的核心特性，也只有交流性，才使得人类建构了涵盖多学科领域的叙述性经验基础，这些共享的经验靠交流获得合法性，同时也靠交流获得经验的累积、更新与散布。

赵毅衡在《广义叙述学》中提出最简叙述定义，并指出了叙述隐含的两个叙述化过程：其一是叙述者将有人格参与的事件组织进一个符号文本，其二是该文本被接受者理解为具有时间和意义的向度。（2013，p. 7）笔者在这里有必要提醒，这两个叙述化过程是相互支撑和相互建构的，即一个文本只有经过了这两个过程，才能成为叙述文本，缺少任一过程，叙述文本都不能成立。这实际上是说，叙述文本是双向建构的，这种双向性就是“双循环交流”。叙述文本作为一种符号构筑，其意义永远需要在交流中产生并实现。

通过以上的理论梳理，我们可以非常清晰地看到，叙述转向之后，叙述学的发展正在历经又一次研究范式变革，20 世纪 90 年代至 21 世纪头十年，后经典叙述学有两个研究方向：其一是新方法介入叙述学研究，形成“叙述学+”模式；其二是研究对象溢出文学范畴向多领域、多学科扩展。21 世纪第二个十年，后经典叙述学进入所谓第二阶段（以阿尔贝、福鲁德尼克为代表），多种研究方向间有形成壁垒的危机，亟须整合，叙述学研究面临巨大挑战。同时，发生在各种学科、领域的叙述转向已经形成声势，叙述自身特性被赋予新理解，叙述学研究范式发生巨大变革，这一转变为以叙述为核心，而非以叙述的某一类型为核心。在经历经典叙述学意欲建构文学叙述的普遍语法这一宏大目标，和后经典叙述学多元化发展即赫尔曼所谓“复数叙述学”（Narratologies）之后，必须重新思考叙述自身的普遍特性及其对于各领域、各学科的意义，并在多种叙述类型中寻找共相：一般叙述学研究范式已经呼之欲出了。

叙述扩容为叙述学研究提出了新的课题，一种跨学科、跨领域、涵盖所有叙述类型的一般叙述研究正在兴起，这无疑是叙述学研究的又一次范式转换，赵毅衡的广义叙述学研究框架，瑞安的跨媒介叙述学研究，理查森等人的非自然叙述研究等，均试图探讨叙述自身的特性，即让叙述回归一般状态。所有这些研究已经开启了一般叙述研究的大门。交流叙述学正是在一般叙述的研究框架下探讨交流叙述的内在机制，并探索建立交流叙述的理论框架。走向交流叙述学，走向叙述学研究的第三阶段，即一般叙述学研究，是叙述学在新的理论与现实背景下的必然选择。

引用文献：

巴赫金（2009）．陀思妥耶夫斯基诗学问题．载于巴赫金全集（第五卷）（白春仁，顾亚玲，译）．河北：河北教育出版社．

巴特，罗兰（1989）．叙事作品结构分析导论（张寅德，译）．载于张寅德（编选），叙述学研究．北京：中国社会科学出版社．

查特曼，西摩（2013）．故事与话语：小说和电影的叙事结构（徐强，译）．北京：中国人民大学出版社．

方小莉（2017）．“形式”犯框与“伦理”越界．载于曹顺庆，赵毅衡（主编），符号与传媒，14．成都：四川大学出版社．

费伦，詹姆斯（2002）．作为修辞的叙事——技巧、读者、伦理、意识形态（陈永国，译）．北京：北京大学出版社．

费伦，詹姆斯（2012）．修辞、伦理即叙述交流：抑或从故事和话语到作者、资源与读者．外语与外语教学，1，75－80．

弗卢德尼克，莫妮卡（2007）．叙事理论的历史（下）：从结构主义到现在．载于 James Phelan & Peter J. Rabinowitz（主编），当代叙事理论指南（申丹等，译）．北京：北京大学出版社．

亢淑平（2010）．关于叙事交流示意图的商榷．内蒙古农业大学学报，3，367－369．

刘江（2012）．自传叙事交流情景与自传身份隐喻．当代外语研究，1，53－57，& 64．

卢特，雅各布（2011）．小说与电影中的叙事（徐强，译）．北京：北京大学出版社．

倪爱珍（2018）．反讽叙述的形成机制：交流主体的距离．载于曹顺庆，赵毅衡（主编），符号与传媒，16．成都：四川大学出版社．

普林斯，杰拉德（2013）．叙事学：叙事的形式与功能（徐强，译）．北京：中国人民大学出版社．

瑞安，玛丽－劳尔（2014）．故事的变身（张新军，译）．南京：译林出版社．

谭君强（2012）．再论叙事文本的叙事交流模式．河南师范大学学报，6，173－177．

托马舍夫斯基（1989）．主题．载于托多罗夫（编选），俄苏形式主义文论选（蔡鸿宾，译）．北京：中国社会科学出版社．

雅柯布森（2001）．雅柯布森文集（钱军，王力，译）．长沙：湖南教育出版社．

赵毅衡（2013）. 广义叙述学. 成都：四川大学出版社.

Herman, D. (2009). *Basic element of narrative*. New Jersey, NJ: Wiley-Blackwell, A John Wiley & Sons, Ltd. Publication.

Coste, D. (1989). *Narrative as communication*. Minnesota, MN: University of Minnesota Press.

Lothe, J. (2000). *Narrative in fiction and film: An introduction*. New York, NY: Oxford University Press.

Phelan, J. (2000). *Peter J. Rabinowitz, A companion to narrative theory*. London, UK: Blackwell Publishing Ltd.

Ryan, M. R. (2006). *Avatars of story*. Minnesota, MN: University of Minnesota Press.

Kearns, M. (1999). *Rhetorical narratology*. Nebraska, NE: University of Nebraska Press.

Bal, M. (2004). *Narrative theory: Critical concepts in literature and culture studies*. London, UK: Routledge.

Heinen, S. & Sommer, R. (2009). Narratology in the age of cross-disciplinary narrative research, D—10785. Berlin, GER: Walter de Gruyter.

作者简介：

王委艳，文学博士，信阳师范学院文学院副教授，硕士研究生导师，信阳师范学院南湖学者（青年），研究方向为当代文艺理论、叙述学。

Author:

Wang Weiyan, Ph. D. , associate professor of College of Liberal Arts and Nanhu youth talent of Xinyang Normal University. His research interests are contemporary literary theory and narratology.

Email: wangweiy04@163.com

论梦与电影造梦*

方小莉

摘　要： 本文将梦视作叙述文本，尝试从叙述学的角度，结合梦的叙述特性与电影文本的叙述特征来讨论梦与电影的结构性相似。一方面，梦与电影文本在产生与发送方面存在相似性；另一方面，观影体验与做梦也有共通之处。本文主要从文本的叙述主体、发送以及接收三个方面来探讨电影的“梦特性”，分别涉及梦与电影的叙述主体、叙述语言，梦与电影的接收体验以及梦者与观众的认知接收等方面的异同。电影叙述与梦叙述一样，叙述主体主要呈现为框架而非人格，主要的叙述语言均为图像，再加上两种叙述同为演示类，又具有强烈的拟经验性，从而使两种叙述的接收也具有结构性相似。本文将观影作为一种梦境体验，进一步探讨观众对电影的接收以及做梦者对梦的接收两者的认知异同。

关键词： 梦叙述，框架叙述者，拟经验性，观影体验

Dream and the Dream Making of Films

Fang Xiaoli

Abstract: Taking dreams as narrative texts, this essay aims to explore the structural similarities between dreams and films from the semio-narratological perspective, including how film-making mimics the characteristics of dreams, how the experience of watching a movie is similar to experiencing the dream, and how the cognition of the audience and the

---

* 本文为国家社科基金青年项目“奇幻文学的叙述类型研究”（16CWW030）阶段性成果。

dreamers are similar to each other. The narrators of both the dreams and films are usually presented not as a person, but a frame, who tell stories in images. Since the two narratives are similarly produced and disseminated, watching a movie is like experiencing a dream. The dreamer and the audience both, in the darkness, project themselves to the specific characters in the story, thus having their oppressed desires fulfilled in a fantasy as well as getting to know themselves through the characters.

Keywords: dreams, frame-narrator, quasi-experientiality, movie watching experience

DOI: 10.13760/b.cnki.sam.202001015

电影研究从来不缺乏对梦与电影关系的研究，这也许是因为梦与电影的天然联系。我们把好莱坞叫作“梦工厂”，可能这不仅仅是比喻意义上将其视为实现明星梦的地方，同时也意味着好莱坞就是一个造梦工厂。

梦与电影相关联，首先是因为很多导演自述其电影作品受到梦的极大影响，比如英格玛·伯格曼（Ingmar Bergman），克劳德·勒鲁什（Claude LeLouche），罗伯特·奥特曼（Robert Altman），大卫·林奇（David Lynch）等导演都有电影作品灵感来源于自己的梦或他人的梦；某些导演将梦编织进电影作品中，在文本中大量再现各种梦。帕格尔（J. F. Pagel）及其团队对电影制作与梦之间的关系进行了相关调查，他们提出“梦对导演、演员和剧作家等电影创作者均有不同程度的影响，以三种方式呈现：1. 某个电影作品的开创性构思来自梦；2. 剧本写作遭遇思维阻塞时，梦让作者产生顿悟；3. 剧作家在电影中呈现了大量人物的显梦”（1991，pp. 248－249）。无论是电影导演受到梦的影响，电影制作的灵感来自梦，还是电影对梦的使用，都体现了梦对电影的影响。

当然，电影的发生与发展反过也来对人类做梦有影响。寇拉克通过早期的心理学实验证明了电影对实验参与者所做之梦的内容有影响（Koulack，1991）；库克也认为电影对梦的内容和形式都有极大影响（Cook，2011）。在有关梦的色彩研究中，甚至有学者提出 20 世纪四五十年代参与实验的受试之所以报告梦主要呈黑白色，是因为电影是黑白的，而这一现象在 20 世纪 60 年代后发生了大逆转。60 年代后 50％以上的参与者则报告他们的梦为彩色。（Schwitzegebel，2003）虽然学界对电影的流行及其色彩是否对人做梦有直接影响没有确切的结论，但可以确定的是，由于梦与电影的相似性，学者们不仅认为梦对电影有影响，同样也认为电影影响人类做梦的内容和形式。

基于电影与梦之间的密切关系，如上所述，现有的梦与电影关系的研究主要集中在梦与电影的相互影响以及电影对梦的借用和再现。当然也有少量研究关注梦叙述与电影文本的异同以及观影体验与做梦体验之间的异同。本文在前人研究的基础上，尝试从叙述学的角度切入，将梦视作一种叙述文本，结合梦的叙述特性与电影文本的叙述特征来讨论梦与电影的结构性类似。我们虽无法把作为一种叙述的梦完全看作与电影一样的艺术作品，但电影在形式上却与梦有着颇多相似之处。与其说梦与电影类似，不如说电影在形式上具备了“梦的特性”。一方面，梦与电影文本在产生与发送方面存在相似性；另一方面，观影体验也与做梦的经验有相似之处。

一、电影的“梦性质”

有关电影叙述者的研究已经争论了半个多世纪，当代的电影理论主要持两种观点：一种以波德维尔为代表，认为电影的叙述者是“构筑故事的一整套指令（cues）”（Bordwell，1985，p. 62）；另一种则是以列文森或古宁为代表，将电影的叙述者人格化为“呈现者”（presenter）或“显示者”（demonstrator）。第一种观点是将叙述者抽象化为一种指令框架，而第二种则是将叙述者具体化为某种人格。赵毅衡的“叙述者人格—框架二象”论则将这两种对立的观点整合成为一个相反相成的电影叙述者概念——“指令呈现者”。赵毅衡认为，电影叙述者不只是导演、监制、演员、发行公司等一系列人员或制作机构，“电影有一个源头叙述者，他是一个做出各种电影文本安排，代表电影制作‘机构’的人格，电影用各种媒介传送的叙述符号，都出于他的安排”（2013，p. 99）。也就是说，电影叙述的产生是各种指令的集合，即电影通过各种媒介生产出叙述，并通过银幕呈现给观众。与小说叙述者不同，小说的叙述者总是在人格与框架之间切换，特别是在第一人称的小说中，小说叙述者具象为某个人物，主要以人格的形式显现。电影是一种记录演示类叙述，电影叙述者是“指令呈现者”，电影的所谓源头叙述者可以说在电影文本中永远隐身，只是一个抽象的框架。即使是在电影文本中出现了人物的第一人称讲述，这些讲述者也只能是次级叙述者，因为他们的讲述行为是由源头叙述者安排并呈现的。因此电影的源头叙述者始终以框架呈现，就像是呈现影片的大银幕，它不是故事的构成部分，但是所有故事都来自这个框架，都包含在这个框架之中。所谓电影叙述者的人格化，继承了传统小说研究的叙述者概念，认为讲述故事的必然是某个人格，而对各种指令的安排和呈现也归功于某个人格。笔者认为在电影叙述中，叙述者主要呈现为框架。

电影中，叙述者主要呈现为框架，因为源头叙述者永远不显身，这一点与梦叙述十分类似。电影的叙述者不呈现为人格化的叙述者实体，然而既然有叙述文本，则必然有叙述者，因此我们只能构想一个抽象的人格来呈现所有指令。梦叙述也类似，在梦叙述中，梦的受述者如同电影的观众一样观看梦的发生，受述者永远显身，而梦的叙述者却如电影叙述者一样永远隐身，没有实体存在。梦是人类意识的一部分向另一部分讲述故事，入睡的“我”分裂出一个生产梦叙述的人格——叙述者，这一叙述者同在电影中一样，永远隐身。当然电影与梦表面看来有个明显的不同：电影的叙述者呈现为框架，永远隐身，但电影叙述在传播时呈现为一个具象的框架——银幕，从而划分出一个文本的边界，因此观众相信其正在观看的影片有一个文本实体，从而有一个源头叙述者；梦的受述者存在于叙述文本中，他所观看的梦并没有具象的框架，因此梦文本无法划出文本边界。然而这并不意味着我们无法识别叙述者的存在，或划定梦文本的边界。当透明的梦产生时，梦的受述者便如看电影般看到了梦的文本框架，构筑了文本的边界，从而也确定了叙述者的存在。

电影叙述之所以与梦叙述相似，不仅体现为两种叙述的源头叙述者永远隐身，更重要的相似点可能是两种叙述的叙述语言都以图像为主。“电影叙事的基本单元是画面”（戈德罗，2005，p. 106），而同样，梦的“形式或‘语言’主要是图像－隐喻”（Hartmann，2011，p. 5）。正因为梦与电影的主要语言都是图像，所以梦作为一种叙述更接近电影，而电影研究也经常与梦联系起来。很多学者提出电影是一种类梦的媒介：科斯林认为，人们回忆起来的梦是一系列运动的图像（Kosslyn，1994）；奥威尔则提出电影的图像化可以用于模拟梦（Orwell，1970）；这就是为什么博茨－博恩斯町认为梦是个图像问题，而不是语言问题，而电影中图像的主导地位使电影更接近于梦（Botz-Borstein，2007）。因此从形式上来讲，可以说梦与电影都是一种以图像为主导的叙述形式，因此梦无法经语言得到很好的表达，而用电影通过图像则能够更有效地表达。梦与电影都通过使用图像将所要表达的思想或情感具象化。正是因为梦与电影的主导语言形式是图像，库克认为电影能够复制梦经验，而电影图像也更易进入人们的梦（Cook，2011）。

语言是线性的、有序的、抽象的、有距离感的，代表一种逻辑性强的理性文化；图像则空间并置的、无序的、具象的、缺乏距离的，更倾向感性经验。在梦叙述中，梦者之所以能产生强烈的移情作用，认为自己正在经历故事，而不知道自己在做梦，很大程度上正是因为梦者所接受到的是图像，这些图像是具象的、无序的，也是无距离感的，非常接近人类的日常生活经验，从而给人强烈的真实感。同样，电影也符合类似的原理，特别是早期的默片。图像的无序性与具象性使梦与电影具有感性经验特点，因此其叙述逻辑并不像语言文本那般清晰连贯。正如巴克里所认为的那样，梦和电影中充满了不可预测的断裂（Bulkeley，2003）。笔者认为巴克里所提出的不可预测的断裂，正是图像文本无序性的体现。在梦中，梦者所接受到的是一幅幅运动的图像。由于图像本身的具象性，再加上梦的拟经验性，梦者产生了强烈的认同感，因此在整个做梦的过程中，梦者无法识别图像的无序性或者图像之间的断裂，只有醒过来，回想梦的时候，梦者才会发现梦中的逻辑断裂。电影的原理类似，只是后来的有声电影通过人物对话及画外音等语言方式，使图像与图像之间的逻辑联系更为清晰。

梦与电影的叙述主体都始终以框架的形式呈现，其叙述的主要语言形式是图像，这些特点使两种叙述的产生和传播具有相似性，从而也就使两类叙述的接收具有共通之处。接下来，本文将从做梦的体验与电影观众的观影体验来探讨梦叙述与电影叙述在文本接收方面的相似。

二、观影体验与梦境体验

梦具有演示性特点，其媒介是心像，因此只能由梦者在私下当场一次性接收，无法与他者分享。麦茨认为电影是一种似梦的媒介，在最佳状态下，电影像一种集体梦（2006）。若按麦茨所说，电影在最佳状态下模拟了一种集体梦的经历，那么推动电影产生与发展一个很大的动力也许便是对梦的认知。当然，麦茨同时也指出电影与梦不能混淆，因为“做梦者不知道他在做梦；电影观众知道他在电影院”（2006，p.82）。麦茨认为梦者不能等同于观众，因为“观众是一个醒着的人，而梦者却是一个睡着的人”（p.89）。如果仅凭这一点就将电影与梦完全区分开来，那就完全忽略了电影与梦的更多共同点，从而也使梦与电影的研究无法继续。与麦茨相反，卡文将电影视作“观众的梦”（Kawin，1975）：观众可能不认为自己是在看电影，而是在做梦。然而正如博茨-博恩斯町所指出的，如果“简单将观众对等于梦者，那么则否认了电影的本体存在”（Botz-Bornstein，2007，p.38）。也就是说，如果将观众与梦者对等，把电影等同于观众的梦，就相当于否认了电影文本的存在，也就否认了电影叙述者，而只关注观众对电影的接收。

笔者尝试融合这两种观点，倾向于将观众的观影体验视作一种做梦（dreaming）的体验。在这里，笔者既不简单地因观众知道自己在看电影就将他与梦者严格区分开来，也不简单地将观众等同于梦者。笔者所说的“观影体验”包含一系列元素：电影文本、观众以及观影行为发生的场景（比如电影院）。准确来说，本文尝试以梦叙述的特性来分析观影体验。由于梦叙述是一种“受述者主导的心像叙述”（赵毅衡，2013，p. 101），是一种梦者获取的叙述，而叙述者隐身于叙述框架之后——这与电影在很大程度上相似——本文试图以研究梦叙述的方式，通过研究电影的叙述接收者来探讨观影作为一种做梦经验的特性。

梦叙述中的接收者是进入睡眠的梦者，他在梦叙述中永远显身，像观看电影一样接收梦叙述。依据此逻辑，笔者将电影文本和观众划定到同一个观影文本中。那么在这个观影文本中，电影文本类似于梦者接收的梦。梦是人的意识的一部分向另一部分讲故事，虽然梦的叙述者和受述者结合于一个主体中，但梦叙述的研究并不否认梦的叙述者和梦叙述文本的本体存在。梦叙述的叙述者由于始终隐藏在叙述框架背后，因此总是呈现为框架而非人格。这个框架叙述者以图像为主要叙述语言向梦者讲述故事。同理，电影的源头叙述者也始终呈现为叙述框架，这个源头叙述者就像梦的叙述者一样永远不显身，同样以图像为基本语言向观众讲述故事。

笔者将观影文本中的接收者等同于梦叙述的接收者。这里的电影接收者并不简单指在电影放映之前走进电影院的观众。正如梦者是指人入睡后意识分裂出的其中一个人格，本文所说的电影接收者是指电影院灯光熄灭，电影播放启动后进入观影程序的观众。观影程序的启动就像是梦境的开始，此时的观众就像梦者一样开始作为受述者接收电影文本。

电影的接收者可以约等于梦者，首先因为观影环境与入睡环境类似，观众从而陷入一种类似于睡眠的状态或是降低其清醒度。电影学者们常常强调在电影院的黑暗场景中，观众安静地入座，视听信息同步投射到大银幕上，这与梦者所处的情境在形式上基本一致。巴克里认为“我们轻松地静坐在一个安静而黑暗的空间，沉浸在叙述流中，让一波波栩栩如生的声音和视觉图像涌进我们的大脑。在这层意义上，每一个电影作品都模仿做梦经历；每一部电影都能够在形式上重现梦的经验特质”（Bulkeley，1999，p. 104）。电影观众坐在安静而漆黑的环境中，放松心情，开始接收来自银幕的声音和图像，进入类似做梦的环境和状态。电影开始，观影者便进入接收梦的状态。纵然如麦茨所言，观影状态只能算是“一种小型睡眠，一种清醒的睡眠，观众只是相对静止，陷入相对的黑暗之中”（赵毅衡，2013，p.97），但他也不得不承认电影“比其他清醒状态的产物更类似于梦，因为电影是在一种清醒被降低的状态下被接受”（麦茨，2006，p.104）。

除了观影环境为观众设置了适合的“做梦”场景之外，观影者对电影文本的接收本身也模拟了梦者对梦的接收。前文我们已经讨论过，麦茨认为观影与做梦的一个根本的区别是电影观众知道自己在看电影，而梦者不知道自己在做梦。也就是说电影观众有，而梦者却没有自反性。然而笔者认为，电影的叙述形式以及电影观影场景的设置降低了观众的自反性。

当电影院的灯光熄灭，观众安静入座，放松心情，慢慢进入“睡眠”状态，开始接收“梦”。电影院的环境设置本就给观众一种进入梦境的感觉，观众的清醒度在这样的环境中降低，也即自反性降低。同时电影的主要语言是图像，如前文所讲，图像再现是一种非常具象的再现，观众获得具象感知，容易产生一种电影情节仿佛真实发生的感觉，与梦如出一辙。

梦具有强烈的拟经验性，是因为梦者可能产生强烈情感及身体反应。由于这种拟经验性，对于梦者来说梦中情节具有强烈的真实感。这一原理也同样适用于观影体验。库克指出，“电影图像的稳定流动所引起的那种虚构性运动体验与做梦的经验相似”（2011，p.96）。正是因为梦的拟经验性，梦醒以后，梦者回忆起梦中经历的一切，就像真实发生过一样。在电影放映过程中，电影的观众对图像做出具象感知，产生经验错觉，辅以身体的动觉体验，所以看电影跟做梦一样都有强烈的真实感。关于身体的动觉体验，古宁指出，“当我们的身体移动时，我们能够最强烈地经验动觉，但当我们看到物体移动时，我们也能够有此感受，包括电影中的物体移动也能够让观众身体产生动觉感受”（Gunning，2007，p.43）。正是这种动觉感受使观众觉得像是在梦中一样，似乎自己正在经历银幕上的事件。特别是现代电影采用先进的拍摄技术，不仅能够把电影场景拍摄得与生活无异，同时还能让观众产生更细致的动觉感知，从而更有梦一般的感受。库克在讨论《警网铁金刚》（*Bullitt*）中的经典追车场景时提到观众此时会产生强烈的动觉体验，因为摄像机在拍摄时机位在车内，模拟了“在车内”的观众视角（Cook，2011，p.95），观众就像在亲自上演汽车追逐大战一般。类似的电影技巧有很多，比如采用主观视角镜头，让观众与影片人物的视角一致，也会让观众产生真实经历的错觉。古宁认为电影图像的运动使电影产生了一种强烈的真实感，同时也让观众将电影视作一种在场的真实，参与其中（Gunning，2007，pp.40－44）。电影图像的直接具象性以及图像运动引起的在场感容易引起观众对电影的感知回应和情感参与。当然，这与电影作为一种记录演示类叙述也有莫大的关系。电影与梦一样都是演示类叙述，有强烈的在场感，受述者当场完成一次性接收。

由于电影的图像语言以及连续运动的电影图像所产生的动觉效果，电影观众在看电影时有一种强烈的真实感，并产生强烈的动觉体验从而在感知和情感上都容易对电影做出回应，就像是梦者在接收梦时因为对梦有强烈的认同而认为自己正在经历真实的事件。在最佳状态下，电影采用各种方式，也能达到如此效果。

麦茨等学者认为电影的观众是清醒的，他们知道自己在看电影，再加上电影银幕存在一个具象的框架，无时无刻不在提醒观众电影的虚构性，从而打破观众的做梦幻想。接下来笔者从受述者的认知接收角度讨论这个问题。

三、梦者与观众的认知接收

观众走进电影院，室内光线充足，电影尚未启动，银幕框架清晰可见，此时的观众就像没有入睡，保持着清醒，知道自己要来接收一个叙述。如果梦者预先知道自己今晚会做梦，那么他就知道有一个做梦的主体，也就是有一个梦的叙述者——梦者意识的一部分。灯光熄灭，电影开始播放，观众如梦者一样进入睡眠，进入做梦－观影状态。当然，只有在最佳观影状态下，观影体验才可以在结构形式上模拟做梦的状态。电影开始时，观众通常先接收到标题、导演、主演等信息，此时的观影者就如透明梦的梦者一样知道自己在观影，因此也就能够意识到电影的具象框架。由于电影的图像语言使电影有高度的拟经验性，也呈现高度的逼真性，给观众以强烈的真实感，所以观影者随着电影慢慢融入这个虚构世界，认同电影中的人物，产生强烈的移情作用。此时的观众被电影卷入了电影世界，已经完全忘记大银幕的存在，只看到银幕框架内的世界。

事实上，从现实生活的观影经历来讲，当灯光熄灭时，银幕便隐匿于黑暗之中，观众不再关注这个银幕，而是关注虚构世界。此时的观众好似正在做梦的人一样接收以图像为主要语言的叙述，但观众看不到叙述者，也看不到叙述框架，因为观众自身也在这个叙述文本中。在电影播放的全过程，观众都沉浸在电影情节中，直到电影结束，灯光亮起，片尾曲响起，观众才回到知道自己在看电影的状态，重新成为现实生活中清醒的观众。

值得注意的是，观众在观影时能够进入接收梦境的状态，这与观众的认知框架有很大的关系。观众知道自己是在看电影，却自愿与电影的叙述者签下“协议”，暂时放弃清醒的自我而作为虚构叙述的接受者融入虚构世界。也就是说，电影观众在看电影时启动了与虚构世界相符合的认知框架，将自我认识真实世界的元语言转化成为能够解释虚构世界的元语言。准确地说，观众并不是不知道框架的存在，也不是不知道自己作为观众的身份，更不是不知道现实世界的存在，而是出于认知的需要，将电影的叙述框架、自己的观众身份以及现实世界暂时悬搁起来，从而让自己融入虚构世界，更好地认知这个世界，从而在观影时获得强烈的经验感。这样的认知方式不仅用于欣赏电影艺术，我们在阅读小说时也采用这种认知方式，但电影媒介的特殊性以及它与梦的相似性使观影更能模拟做梦的经历。

我们在观影时只集中于电影图像，沉浸于电影的虚构世界而看不到作为框架的银幕，仿佛在做梦，勒温提出，“正在做梦的观众要么是没有注意到梦的银幕，要么是因为梦者被银幕上的图片和行动所吸引而忽略了银幕”(Lewin，1950，p. 104)。勒温的这一观点能清楚地解释观影经验。一方面，由于电影在漆黑的环境中播放，银幕上的内容主要是由光影书写，所以观众只看到电影而没注意到框架；另一方面，观众暂时悬搁了作为框架的银幕，从而卷入电影叙述的虚构世界。这就使电影非常具有梦的特质。博茨-博恩斯町就提出，“我们无法在电影中看到梦，这是因为电影本身就是一个梦”(Botz-Bornstein，2007，p. 23)。勒温在这里似乎是宣称梦与电影一样都有银幕，只是梦者没有看到。我们当然不会认为梦与电影一样有具象的银幕，但梦的接收方式依然与电影类似。

勒温只是在比喻意义上认为梦者从心灵银幕（mindscreen）上接收梦叙述。也许梦者被梦的情节吸引，完全卷入了虚构世界，从而忽略了心灵银幕的存在；或者梦者完全认同梦中的自己，以为梦中的人物就是自己，从而有一种自己正在真实经历的感觉，因此也无法看到心灵银幕。所谓无法看到心灵银幕，其实就是失去了自反性，不知道自己在做梦。那么这个心灵银幕什么时候显现呢？当透明梦发生时，梦者发现了区隔框架，从而知道了自己在做梦，这时，梦者恢复自反性，看到了勒温所说的“心灵银幕”。

梦与电影表面看来还有一个明显的区别：在大多数的梦中，主角都是梦者，而在电影中，观众却无法找到自己。然而无论是做梦经验还是观影体验，都是一个愿望投射和自我客体化的过程。正如麦茨所说，电影像镜子一样，一切都可以得到反映，唯独观众自己的身体得不到反映。电影中出现在银幕上的永远是他者，而观众只是在那里看他。因此观众无法像站在镜子前一样认同作为客体的自己，而只能认同独立于他的客体（麦茨，2006，pp.41－45）。从心理学的角度来讲，可以把观影体验视作观众的心理或欲望投射，观众认同电影中的某个客体，将自己的愿望投射到这个客体身上，因此，观影过程就是一个愿望实现的过程，这与梦类似。同时，我们也发现，观影过程不仅是一种愿望投射，也是一个自我客体化的过程。由于电影与镜子不同，无法反映出观者自己，所以，观者只能将自我客体化，以认同于电影中的某个角色，因此观众在接收电影的时候将自己客体化为认知的对象。这一点与做梦的经历并无二致，梦者接收梦的过程也是一个欲望投射和自我客体化的过程。

约翰·麦克尔斯说："梦者因为直接认同于梦中的人物或景观而有一种经历梦境的感觉；同时梦者又常常有一种作为梦的现场观众的感觉。"（Michaels，1980，p.85）。这正是梦者在梦中的投射与自我客体化的过程。梦叙述的特殊性在于叙述者和接收者是由同一个主体分裂出来的两个部分，而梦的主角正是该主体的投射或是再现，因此甚至可以说叙述者、人物和接收者都是同一个主体。由于梦的接收者与梦者是同一个主体，所以梦者非常容易认同梦中的主角，以为他就是自己，这就是为什么梦者以为自己在经历梦中的事。同时梦者又像是在现场接收梦，特别是在透明的梦中，梦者知道自己在做梦，梦中的自己同时也是被认知的客体。弗洛伊德认为梦是人们认识无意识浮现的途径，也许从某种意义上来说，正是梦让做梦的主体客体化为认知的对象。当然，并非所有梦的主角都是梦者。而主角是他者的情况更能说明梦者在梦中将自己客体化为一个他者。正如弗洛伊德所说，梦里每一个他者背后隐藏的都是梦者自己。哈德菲尔德也指出，"梦中的人物能够被看作剧中人物（dramatis personae），就像在舞台上一样，他们再现特定的观念或不同的心灵，而不是代表本人"（Hadfield，1954，pp.146－147）。

本文主要从电影的叙述主体、电影文本以及电影的接收三个方面来探讨了电影的梦特性。电影叙述与梦叙述类似，叙述主体主要呈现为框架而非人格，主要的叙述语言为图像。正是因为电影与梦的相似特征，再加上两种叙述同为演示类，又具有强烈的拟经验性，所以两种叙述的接收也具有结构性相似。麦茨在讨论观影时说道："当我说'我看'电影时，我指的是两个相反流程的独特混合：影片是我接收到的，同时影片也是我启动的东西，因为在我进入放映厅之前它并不存在，要禁止它，我只要闭上眼睛就可以。启动它时，我是放映机，接受它时，我是银幕。”（2006，p.47）结合梦叙述来研究电影叙述，可以将麦茨这种说法改为：当我看电影时，虽然我无法说电影观众分裂出一个人格成为叙述者，因为这样否认了电影的本体存在，但因为电影的源头叙述者如同梦叙述的叙述者一样始终隐身，所以人格可以不显，那么至少从电影的接收来看，我可以说“入睡”的电影观众接受电影时是梦者，这个梦者在接收银幕呈现的梦时，也自我客体化并认同电影中的他者。最后，笔者想借用苏珊·朗格对电影的认识来结束本文，她把电影定义为以“梦的模式”为主要表达形式的艺术，而正是这种模式使电影最终成为一种独立媒介（Langer，1966，p.200）。

引用文献：

戈德罗，若斯特（2005）. 什么是电影叙事学（刘云舟，译）. 北京：商务印书馆.

麦茨（2006）. 想象的能指：精神分析与电影（王志敏，译）. 北京：中国广播电视出版社.

赵毅衡（2013）. 广义叙述学. 成都：四川大学出版社.

Bordwell, D. (1985). *Narration in the fiction film*. Madison, WI: University of Wisconsin Press.

Botz-Bornstein, T. (2007). *Films and dreams: Tarkovsky, Bergman, Sokurov, Kubrick, and Wong Kar-Wai*. Lanham, MD: Lexington Books.

Bulkeley, K. (2003). Dreaming and the cinema of David Lynch. *Dreaming*, 1(13), 49－60.

Bulkeley, K. (1999). Touring the dream factory: The dream-film connection in *The Wizard of OZ* and *A Nightmare on Elm Street*. *Dreaming*, 1(9), 104.

Cook, R. F. (2011). "Correpondences in visual imaging and spatial orientation in dreaming and film viewing". *Dreaming*, 2(21), 89－104.

Gunning, T. (2007). Moving away from the index: Cinema and the impression of reality. *Differences: A journal of feminist cultural studies*, 18(1), 40－44.

Hadfield, J. A. (1954). *Dreams and nightmares*. Baltimore, MD: Penguin Books.

Hartmann, E. (2011). *The nature and functions of dreaming*. Oxford, UK: Oxford University Press.

Kawin, B. F. (1975). *Mindscreen: Bergman, godard and first-person film*. Princeton, NJ: Princeton University Press.

Kosslyn, S. M. (1994). *Image and brain: The resolution of the imagery debate*. Cambridge, MA: MIT Press.

Koulack, D. (1991). *To catch a dream: Explorations of dreaming*. Albany, NY: State University of New York Press.

Langer, S. (1966). A note on film. In D. Maccann (Ed.). *Film: A montage of theories.* New York, NY: Dutton.

Lewin, B. D. (1950). Interferences from the dream screen. *The yearbook of psychoanalysis*, 6, 104.

Michaels, J. (1980). Film and dream. *Journal of the University Film Association* 32, 1−2, Winter-Spring, 85.

Orwell, G. (1970). New words. *Collected essays, Journalism and letters.* New York, NY: Penguin.

Pagel, J. F., Kwiatkowski, C. & Broyle, K. E. (1999). Dream use in film making. *Dreaming*, 4(9), 248−249.

Schwitzegebel, E. (2003). Do people still report dreaming in black and white? An attempt to replicate a questionnaire from 1942. *Perceptual motor skills*, 96, 25−29.

作者简介：

方小莉，英语语言文学博士，四川大学外国语学院副教授，四川大学符号学-传媒学研究所成员，主要研究方向为叙述学、英美文学。

Author:

Fang Xiaoli, Ph. D. of English language and literature, associate professor of School of Foreign Language and Cultures and member of the ISMS research team, Sichuan University. Her research fields include narratology and British and American literature.

Email: clever-wing@163. com

报告与书评

2019年中国符号学发展研究

段彦会　饶广祥

摘　要：2019年符号学研究在新闻传播学、形象与文化设计、艺术研究、消费等领域全面展开。新闻传播领域集中了最多的符号学研究论文，研究全面打开。艺术符号学的研究迅速发展，从基础研究到深入具体问题，都获得了不少推进。形象与文化设计与应用研究既涉及中国传统文化的开发，也涉及国家形象和城市形象的构建和传播，充分发挥了符号学的分析与建构能力。形成鲜明对比的是，符号学理论研究、符号学和新技术的结合研究相对较少，亟待推进。

关键词：中国符号学，应用，发展，2019

2019 Annual Report of Chinese Semiotic Studies

Duan Yanhui　Rao Guangxiang

Abstract: In 2019, semiotic studies have been conducted extensively in the fields of journalism and communication, and in cultural, image, design, art and consumption studies, among others. The majority of research papers in semiotics can be placed in the field of communication studies, in a broad sense. The rapid advancement of semiotics in art studies has ranged from basic theoretical discussions to specific in-depth case studies. The power of semiotics for analysis and creation has been fully demonstrated in applied studies of image, culture and design that have practical applications, not only for the cultivation of traditional Chinese culture but also in the creation and communication of national and municipal images. However, there has been a relative lack of development in the pursuit of basic semiotic theory and in the cross-disciplinary application of semiotics to new technologies.

Keywords: Chinese semiotic studies, status quo, future trends, 2019

DOI: 10.13760/b.cnki.sam.202001017

2019 年，中国学界共有 1466 篇左右的符号学相关研究论文。[①] 这些论文分布在不同的学科，根据知网的统计，新闻传播学科的论文占比最大，占 16.87%，其次是艺术学科占 15.09%，影视相关符号学研究占 9.89%，位列第三。语言和文学的符号学研究仍然是符号学研究的重要领域，分别占 9.54%和 7.12%。

2019 年出版了 24 部专著，覆盖的领域主要包括了符号学基础理论问题、门类符号学问题、符号学的应用三大方面，其中符号学应用与门类符号学问题相关著作旗鼓相当，二者合计占 2019 年符号学专著中的五分之四。符号学基础理论问题的专著则占比较小。符号学的理论性特别强，很多学者都运用这一理论在各个具体的领域进行研究，其中图像符号学似乎是各位学者比较关注的领域，如皮永生、段于兰翻译的西恩·霍尔所著的《符号崛起：读图时代的意义游戏》用可视化案例而非抽象理论来破译符号的神秘之处，分析符号在当前的文化意义产生和表达。而由严志斌、洪梅所著的《巴蜀符号集成》以及夏勇与朱雪菲所著《图画与符号（良渚原始文字）》则针对具体的区域文字符号进行解读。《叙述与自我》（文一茗，2019）、《戏剧：演出的符号叙述学》（胡一伟，2019）以及谭光辉的情感符号学研究（2019）都尝试建立一个门类符号学体系，这是符号学在中国发展的重要方向和体现。

本文以符号学学术论文为主要的分析对象，对 2019 年符号学研究做一个整体的回溯。从对符号学的学术论文所做的关键共现分析看，2019 年符号学研究可以分为六个聚类，但这些聚类并不是完全区隔的。结合之前的学科分类等数据，大体可以分为四大块研究：传播符号学、形象与文化设计符号学、

① 在中国知网（CNKI），以“符号”为主题，且全文包含了“符号学”的相关研究，检索日期 2019 年 12 月 10 日。

艺术设计符号学、消费符号学。本文将重点对这些领域做分析回顾。

一、传播符号学的研究全面打开

符号学和新闻传播学的结合研究是当代符号学最重要的面向。从关键词的共现分析看，在每个聚类里，都有传播符号学关注的论题：形象传播、话语分析、品牌传播、表情分析、视觉传播等，传播符号学研究全面打开。

有关传播符号学的研究，主要包括了两个层面：传播符号学的基本理论，符号学在传播中的应用。学者们关注到了符号学在中国应用领域的大量应用（赵毅衡，2019），梳理了传播符号学的源头，认为传播符号学研究起源于英法学派。北美一多伦多学派的推进，将皮尔斯的符号学模式应用到传播学研究中，分析传媒中的意义生产问题，而北欧学派则重点研究符号学和新媒介的应用，讨论新媒介社群中的符号活动及其社会影响（赵星植，2019）。

研究者对当下的传播理论问题展开探索。比如，对“后真相”进行符号学分析，提出以“诚”为基础的“意义契约”是“后真相”时代传播追求述真的基本策略，由此探索了格雷马斯符号矩阵的“是”（being）与“似”（seeming）之间“施”（intention）的维度，构筑对象、表象、意向的新的述真模型（胡易容，2019）。对新闻报道中的意动性问题展开研究，提出文本内构筑语力和借助体裁提升参与代入两种方式（林正，蒋晓丽，2019）。而刚出版的译注《媒介的自我指涉》讨论了广告、摄影、电视、游戏等媒介变为自我指涉的各种方式，话题虽小，讨论却极为深入，是传播符号学专门问题讨论的典型（温弗里德·诺特，2019）。

分析具体的传播现象，也是传播符号学发展的重要动力。这些具体的现象覆盖了手机媒介、新闻真实等各领域，是新闻传播符号学研究成果的集中领域。王小英（2019）讨论了移动互联时代手机对人之自我的建构及驯化的机制，认为手机已成为人们必需的常规媒介，主导了人们对世界的解释，在此过程中，人也被手机所驯化。有文章对传统藏戏进行分析，讨论起媒介特性和符号体系，进而提出传承和保护策略。（彭翠，格勒，2019）有学者分析游戏的审美体验格局，提出“符号一场景”合二为一的审美体验格局建构。（白寅，陈俊鹏，2019）也有学者从符号学角度分析传播文化的传播特性，认为传统文化传播具有新的符号规律，呈现出媒介逻辑自洽、话语重组以及日常融入的符号学机制。（晏青，罗小红，2019）还有学者从元媒介的角度，讨论恐怖主义等非传统安全威胁的元传播特征及其带来的安全危害，从符号编码和关系建构两个维度系统梳理了元媒介时代恐怖主义的元传播特性，并从符号编码与人工智能视角提出应对策略。还有学者分析了 VR 新闻中的真实边界，认为“VR 新闻场景中空间和细节的符号意义被放大，语言的符号意义退居其次，同时出现了‘人替（化身）’这样一种全新的符号形式”，由此出现感受真实、情感体验遮蔽新闻真实的风险。（潘晓婷，2019）

传播符号学的研究还涉及动漫、表情符号、话语分析等方面，研究面向广、研究深入是 2019 年符号学研究的一大特色。

二、形象与文化设计研究

2019 年符号学论文大量聚焦于形象研究，涉及的关键词包括国家形象、城市形象、跨文化传播、文化符号学等。有研究者梳理了形象观念在欧洲的演变史。形象这个概念从模仿、譬喻等文艺批评的概念起始，到 19 世纪成为诗学、美学的理想观念，进而马克思主义从辩证唯物主义的立场论述了形象的观念，再到 20 世纪成为精神分析的词语，经历了一个漫长的发展过程。（彭建华，2019）

国家形象与城市形象的构建有赖于中国的象征符号的应用。对国家形象的分析，既有对具体构建的形象分析，也有对建构途径的分析。国家形象总是通过一定的文本表现出来，因此，有关国家形象构建的研究很重要的是确定分析的文本。2019 年度，研究者从国家形象宣传片中的声音（李姝慧，2019）、生态纪录片（杨雪，2019）、历史文化纪录片《如果国宝会说话》（郭萌萌，2019）来研究国家形象，总结出负责任的，“文化历史悠久、地域辽阔；民族文化繁荣、丰满有活力；和平发展、注重相依相生；文化融合与文明冲突的现代化国家”等中国国家形象（沈霄，2019）。

城市形象研究与国家形象研究类似，通过研究符号来探究城市形象构建。城市形象体现在各个具体的场景，如以国际马拉松赛、抖音传播等为个案研究。研究者们结合具体的建构场景，分析城市形象建构的策略。值得强调的是，有学者明确提出了城市文化设计的符号学路径，提出了城市文化设计的步骤：场地结构分析、城市符号分类、意义抽取剥离、运用及新赋义。进而通过符号创作手法，提炼出新的符号媒介、指涉对象、主题，建立新符号作为具体设计元素在城市形象设计中加以应用。（杨琳，许秦，2019）

形象研究往往以文化设计为途径，形象的构建，往往借助中国传统文化的力量。因此，中国传统文化的符号学研究成为形象研究的重要组成部分。

中国传统文化是中国特色的直接体现，学界极为关注如何将传统文化符号应用到具体的文化实践中去。比如，讨论传统文化在国家文化符号建构中的作用（冯月季，李菁，2019）、在写意雕塑中的应用（李凤志，2019）。也有学者反过来，讨论传统文化如何重新进入当代语境。汤强（2019）运用田野调查和“深描”的民族志方法，深入分析了雨崩藏族村寨在旅游发展背景下充分挖掘和利用传统文化及自然环境保护的地方性知识，规范和约束村民旅游开发与资源和自然环境利用的行为，以获得旅游可持续发展。还有不少研究者讨论传统文化节目的传播问题，讨论传统技艺类纪录片的价值与文化自信（陈璃，2019），也有学者提出了中国话语当代构建的路径：道德认同是核心之要，文化认同是必需之举，表述明晰是关键之策。（娄丽景，2019）

三、艺术符号学研究

艺术符号学的讨论既涉及基础艺术，也涉及艺术细节。有学者以郭沫若艺术符号学思想为例，讨论中国艺术符号学的现代性萌芽，提出中国本土化的艺术符号学萌芽于20世纪二三十年代。（安静，2019）不少学者关注艺术符号学的基本问题，例如，扬·穆卡若夫斯基和杜常婧论证了艺术是符号学事实，强调艺术作品具有符号的性质，每一个艺术作品都是自主的符号，是具有意义象征的“作品-物”，也是起着意义作用的“审美客体”；在与指示物之间的关系上，艺术作品并非指向标新立异的存在，而是指向当前环境中社会现象（科学、哲学、宗教、政治、经济等）的整体语境。两位作者还指出，艺术具传达、交流功能。（穆卡若夫斯基，杜常婧，2019）扬·穆卡若夫斯基的论文是布拉格学派的重要文献，也是美学史上第一篇系统讨论艺术符号学的文献。（杨磊，2019）

赵毅衡将符号学推进到更深的层次，讨论艺术与冗余、艺术自身再现系列问题。赵毅衡（2019c）从艺术家的意向性如何进入文本的角度，讨论了艺术家的主体性问题，提出艺术家将自身的名字、形象、思想等部分部件出租给文本，从而让艺术文本携带了一系列主观性意义，这一论述发展了柏拉图的“灵感论”、康德的“先天构架”等理论。

“冗余”与“噪音”在语言学与信息技术领域内涵极为清楚，表示传受双方不需要的内容。艺术因为传播意图不明晰，所以其中某些内容是否冗余就变成了一个难题。赵毅衡从符号学角度进入，理清了冗余、羡余、赘余、噪音等概念，并提出：就对象意义而言，艺术文本的冗余度趋向最大值；就解

释项意义而言，艺术文本的冗余度趋向最小值；艺术性就来自两个趋势之间的张力。（赵毅衡，2019b）

陆正兰的《流行音乐传播符号学》是艺术、传播和符号学的结合研究。该书依次讨论音乐的符号文本结构、音乐符号的意义传播以及音乐符号的社会使用，深入探讨流行音乐符号表意的各个环节，建构起音乐符号传播的理论框架，是深入研究门类艺术符号学的重要著作。

艺术符号学是今年来门类符号学的重要发展方向，也是2019年符号学研究的重要领域。随着泛艺术化的推进，艺术符号学的发展空间极大。

四、消费符号学

消费符号学涉及品牌、广告、消费文化、符号消费、产品设计、平面设计等领域，范围很广。不少研究者关注品牌和广告的符号学研究，重视使用符号学研究品牌与广告的最新现象。饶广祥（2019）从符号学的角度，提出当前语境下广告发生的最大变化是“泛广告化”，并对泛广告化的过程进行了总结，认为泛广告化让广告从传播活动标出项翻转为非标出项，成为信息的主要组成部分。泛广告化让广告文本的意向性融合了新闻等其他体裁的意向性，呈现出多元化的趋势，由此弥合了接收者想要接受的文本和强行置入的广告之间的分歧，推动了当代广告传播的全面演化。张诗婷（2019）关注新出现的广告形态——原生广告的对话性问题，并从文本间性的视角反思了其不足。张诗婷认为，开放的原生广告设计应弱化诉求意图，增加原生广告正文本的展示价值，丰富原生广告可写性伴随文本的形式。

品牌是象征，品牌的研究，既是实践指向的研究，也和符号学有关。（谢佩洪，陈昌东，2019；李雪枫，李雅欣，2019）也有学者直接从符号学进入品牌研究（蒋诗萍，2019；桑森垚，2019；韩冬，2019）。蒋诗萍（2019）从符号矩阵理论出发，提出品牌符号是一个亦正亦负、非正非负的复合项，深层运作机制是欲望与必需的对立，而品牌文化是一种“间性文化自然”。

张殿元（2019）对巴尔特符号学在大众传播分析中的应用进行了反思，他认为符号学对大众文化的分析过分注重符号的解码，而忽视了对意义生产同样重要的符号生产，重视共时性研究而轻视历时性研究，以至于符号学的研究之路越走越窄。他对广告进行了反思：“现代广告产生以来，一直凭借着意义引申和符号转化功能给品牌赋魅而销售产品，近来更是通过积极介入时代观念变革和世风改造的进程，试图给品牌贴上‘世界公民’的标签。这种社会干预的广告手法可以一时带来可观的流量和足够的关注，但现实的转化效果是值得怀疑的。”可疑之处主要在于滥用了广告的真实，侵蚀了人们对广告真实的信任和追求。而网络时代的信息对称性，让原有的操作把戏很容易就被揭穿了。

唐小林和程天悦（2019）也对巴尔特的神话理论进行了反思。两位作者指出巴尔特的神话理论对意识形态分析的有力作用，同时也对该理论在涵指系统与元语言系统的关系以及神话与象征的区别做了进一步辨析。

五、符号学理论研究

符号学理论研究也有不少尝试，主要表现为符号学的理论流派梳理、符号学的理论基础探索、符号学重要理论家思想探讨。赵星植（2019a）对21世纪以来重要的符号学新流派进行了梳理，指出21世纪的符号学运动呈现出多元融合的理论范式，跨学科、跨地域的符号学新流派正在形成。中国符号学成为世界符号学运动中的重要力量。

学者们对知名符号学家思想的研究是符号学理论研究的重要面向。这些符号学家包括皮尔斯、克里斯蒂娃（张颖，2019）、维尔比夫人（孙凤，屠友祥，2019；薛晨，2019）、雅柯布森（罗金，2019）、古斯塔夫·古斯塔维奇·施佩特（赵爱国，2019；贾洪伟，2019；朱有义，2019）等。

赵星植（2019b）通过考察皮尔斯与英国女学者维尔比的学术通信，研究了皮尔斯的意义三分这一重要思想的形成过程。丁尔苏（2019）也对皮尔斯的三分法进行了反思，认为皮尔斯的三分法在扩展索绪尔的二分法时，为分析符号现象提供了更好的基础，但“未能清楚地阐释不同符号之间的相互转换”，导致符号分类时容易出现混乱，为此他倡议建立一符多义的动态符号模式。彭佳（2019）对皮尔斯的指示性的范畴进行了探讨，提出指示性具有多重特征，如直接指出对象，与对象之间具有连续性；在空间上具有方向性；具有动力性，尤其是身体驱动性；逻辑上具有因果性、秩序性、类别化等。彭佳将指示性进一步区分为指示性基础、指示性范畴和指示性趋向。也有学者指出了艺术学界对格雷马斯符号矩阵理论理解和应用出现的偏差与机械化、简单化问题，进而对矩阵进行了重新解读，推动矩阵对意义和价值问题更加客观和精准的分析（陈许鹏，2019）。

2019年，维尔比的符号学思想受到研究者的重视。《维尔比夫人与表意学：符号学的形成》系统地介绍了表意学思想（佩特里利，2019a）。苏珊·

佩特里利（2019b）另撰文介绍维尔比的表意学，将意义区分为表意义的意义、感觉和以为的意义，由此将符义和语言秩序的价值、伦理、审美和符用价值囊括其中。薛晨（2019）也对维尔比表意学的核心概念——感知、意义、意味，展开了进一步的探讨，提出维尔比的表意学充分重视意义的开放性和创造性，推动了符号学由符码符号学向解释符号学的发展。

符号学是一个相对广的论域，难以精确界定。2019 年还有不少对巴尔特、索内松、阿什利·弗劳利、莱昂、安娜·埃诺等国外符号学家思想的译介。从已有的分析数据看，符号学已经成为各个学科重要的方法论，推动着各个领域研究的发展。同时，当代社会文化的演变对符号学的理论建构提出更高的要求，这是当前符号学保持活动的动力，也是中国符号学迅速发展的重要动力。

引用文献：

埃诺，安娜（2019）. 符号学问题（怀宇，译）. 北京：中国人民大学出版社.

安静（2019）. 中国艺术符号学的现代性萌芽——以郭沫若艺术符号学思想为例. 学习与探索，10，171－177，192.

白寅，陈俊鹏（2019）. “场景符号”与“符号场景”：融媒体时代网络游戏的审美体验格局. 新闻界，7，48－55.

陈丹（2019）. 视觉传播如何构建国家形象——基于 2022 年北京冬奥会申奥片的分析. 传媒，19，56－58.

陈静姝（2019）. 基于中国当代艺术经验的中西比较符号学理论建构——“中国当代艺术与比较符号学国际研讨会”会议综述. 当代文坛，3，196－199.

陈璃（2019）. 传播、传承与引领——中国传统技艺类纪录片的价值与文化自信. 当代电视，5，59－62.

陈许鹏（2019）. 艺术理论实践中格雷马斯符号矩阵理论的误读与反思. 湖南包装，34，68－71.

丁尔苏（2019）. 建立一符多义的动态符号模式. 符号与传媒，2，1－12.

冯月季，李菁（2019）. 打造国家文化符号：文化自觉视域下中国传统文化 IP 的价值建构. 中国编辑，9，33－37.

格雷，丁达（2019）. 符号学与翻译问题研究——以皮尔士符号学为纲（贾洪伟，译）. 天津，南开大学出版社.

郭萌萌（2019）. 从空间场景叙事到国家形象传播——以《如果国宝会说话》为例. 出版广角，18，59－61.

郭小安，赵欣茹（2019）. 艺术家群体的身体抗争与符号建构：策略及效果. 新闻与传播评论，72（2），97－107.

韩冬（2019）．奢侈品品牌展示空间多重叙事模式的研究．装饰，3，84－87．
韩晓明，胡晓飞（2019）．城市化进程中传统武术文化传承的困境及对策．体育文化导刊，2，58－62，68．
胡一伟（2019）．戏剧：演出的符号叙述学．成都：四川大学出版社．
胡易容（2019）．“后真相”时代传播符号的“意义契约”重建．湘潭大学学报（哲学社会科学版），43（4），122－129．
胡易容，任洪增（2019）．艺术文本中“空符号”与“符号空无”辨析——电影人物影像符号“不在之在”的表意机制．社会科学，4，177－185．
贾洪伟（2019）．翻译符号学视角下的施佩特符号学思想研究．俄罗斯文艺，1，129－136．
蒋诗萍（2019）．品牌文化现象的深层运作机制及其文化内蕴．社会科学，4，186－191．
莱昂内，马西莫（2019）．论无意味：后物质时代的意义消减（陆正兰等，译）．成都：四川大学出版社．
李凤志（2019）．传统文化视野下吴为山现代写意雕塑的当代性建构．东吴学术，5，131－136．
李静，戴光全（2019）．符号视角下的传统节庆体验研究——以广州迎春花市为例．装饰，4，28－32．
李姝慧（2019）．国家形象宣传片中的声音研究．当代传播，4，66－70．
李雪枫，李雅欣（2019）．祛魅与再塑：奢侈品品牌传播中的“童心”元素分析．山西大学学报（哲学社会科学版），42（4），72－78．
林正，蒋晓丽（2019）．作为信息性社会支持的心理健康干预式报道的意动叙述．符号与传媒，2，111－124．
娄丽景（2019）．中国话语的历史呈现与当代构建．甘肃社会科学，6，123－129．
陆正兰（2019）．流行音乐传播符号学，四川大学出版社。
罗金（2019）．符号学与翻译研究：雅柯布森符号翻译观再探．符号与传媒，2，186－199．
牛旻（2019）．从美、日、韩“漫改剧”看国家形象符号编码．当代电视，1，45－47．
诺特，温弗里德（2019）．媒介的自我指涉（周劲松，译）．北京：社会科学文献出版社．
潘晓婷（2019）．VR 新闻中的真实边界：符号重组与现实建构．当代传播，2，40－43．
佩特里利，苏珊（2019a）．维尔比夫人与表意学：符号学的形成（宋文，薛晨，译）．四川大学出版社．
佩特里利，苏珊（2019b）．维多利亚·维尔比：表意学与语言．符号与传媒，2，36－67．
彭佳（2019）．指示性范畴论：以生物符号学为起点．西北师大学报（社会科学版），56（4），39－47．
彭翠，格勒（2019）．传播符号学视域下的藏戏传承探究．西南民族大学学报（人文社科版），40（2），20－25．

彭建华（2019）. 论“形象”：一个观念史的视角. 华侨大学学报（哲学社会科学版），3，13－25.
饶广祥（2019）. 论“泛广告化”传播的符号学机制. 四川大学学报（哲学社会科学版），3，126－133.
桑森垚（2019）. 符号学视角下的内部地方品牌化探究——以西藏达东村为例. 地域研究与开发，38（2），129－132，146.
沈霄（2019）. “看”中国：作为“他者”的国家形象建构——基于Facebook“中国文化”系列短片的文本分析. 西安交通大学学报（社会科学版），39（5），146－154.
索内松，约伦（2019）. 认知符号学：自然文化与现象学路径（胡易容，梅林，董明来，等，译）. 北京：社会科学文献出版社.
孙凤，屠友祥（2019）. 论维尔比夫人的翻译哲学思想. 符号与传媒，2，83－97.
谭光辉（2019）. 论附加情感编码. 河北师范大学学报（哲学社会科学版），42（6）. 88－94.
汤强（2019）. 传统文化符号的优雅转身——以马赛克设计为例. 美术观察，5，152－153.
唐小林，程天悦（2019）. 大众媒介与意识形态的炼金术——重审符号学家巴尔特的神话理论. 福建论坛，1，110－117.
王婷（2019）. 意义生成与语境建构：“语域”视阈下传统文化类节目研究. 现代传播（中国传媒大学学报），41（1），103－110
王小英（2019）. 论移动互联时代手机对人之自我的建构及驯化. 符号与传媒，2，138－151.
王永祥（2019）. 符号学视阈下的施佩特——纪念施佩特诞辰140周年. 俄罗斯文艺，1，120.
文一茗（2019）. 叙述与自我. 成都：四川大学出版社.
吴坤湖，匡存玖（2019）. 近四十年国外马克思主义符号学的本土化及理论贡献. 江西社会科学，39（6），16－24.
吴来安（2019）. 图像·意旨·场景——基于央视公益广告符号传播变迁的思考. 新闻大学，6，90－107，124－125.
谢佩洪，陈昌东（2019）. 品牌认知的双轨驱动机制与市场细分取向. 管理学报，162，263－272.
薛晨（2019）. “感知”与“母性感知”：符号学之母维尔比表意学的核心概念. 符号与传媒，2，98－110.
穆卡若夫斯基，杨；杜常婧（2019）. 作为符号学事实的艺术. 社会科学战线，11，166－169.
杨磊（2019）. 为何定义艺术：艺术、信息与教化. 社会科学战线，11，183－189.
杨琳，许秦（2019）. 基于场域理论的国际马拉松赛与城市形象传播策略研究. 湖南大学学报（社会科学版），33（4），147－152.

杨雪（2019）．浅论我国生态纪录片对于国家形象的建构——以2008—2018年间作品为例．中国电视，11，79－83．
臧丽娜，刘钰莹（2019）．基于SIVA理论的品牌传播场景构建．当代传播，2，97－100．
张殿元（2019）．罗兰·巴特的结构主义大众文化批判述评——兼论广告的符号学阐释．山西大学学报（哲学社会科学版），42（3），16－21．
张诗婷（2019）．对原生广告对话性不足的符号学反思．编辑之友，10，61－65．
张骁鸣，黄秋芬（2019）．把日常的还给日常：从龙舟赛看传统体育文化遗产的当代适应．旅游学刊，34（5），7－9．
张晓刚（2019）．艺术形态学：历史、现状与当代反思．艺术百家，35（4），12－19，31．
张颖（2019）．论克里斯蒂娃"符义分析"对乔姆斯基转换生成语法的批判性接受．符号与传媒，2，13－24．
赵爱国（2019）．施佩特的"阐释符号学"思想评略．俄罗斯文艺，1，121－128．
赵星植（2019a）．21世纪以来重要符号学新流派的发展趋势．西南民族大学学报（人文社科版），40（8），184－191．
赵星植（2019b）．论意义三分之形成：回顾皮尔斯与维尔比的讨论．符号与传媒，2，68－82．
赵毅衡（2019a）．论艺术的"自身再现"．文艺争鸣，9，77－85．
赵毅衡（2019b）．艺术与冗余．文艺研究，10，11－20．
赵毅衡（2019c）．主体"部件出租"：论作品中艺术家主体性的表现方式．思想战线，45（5），156－163．
郑娟（2019）．艺术信息在艺术表现形式中的编码方式探析．艺术百家，35（3），21－27．
朱有义（2019）．再议"主体性"到"主体间性"的发展之路——施佩特对胡塞尔思想的传承与批判．俄罗斯文艺，1，137－145．

作者简介：

段彦会，四川大学符号学－传媒学研究所成员，主要研究领域为传播符号学。

饶广祥，四川大学文学与新闻学院副教授，符号学－传媒学研究所副研究员，主要研究领域为品牌符号学。

Author:

Duan Yanhui, member of ISMS Research Team. Her main research filed is semiotics of communication.

Rao Guangxiang, associate professor of College of Literature and Journalism, Sichuan University, associate researcher of ISMS Research Team. His main research filed is brand semiotics.

Email: raoguangxiang@163.com

数字社会中的意义问题：评马西莫·莱昂内《论无意味：后物质时代的意义消减》

李俊欣

Meaning in Digital Society: A Review of Massimo Leone's *The Significance of Insignificance*

Li Junxin

书名：论无意味：后物质时代的意义消减
作者：马西莫·莱昂内
译者：陆正兰，李俊欣，黄蓝
出版社：四川大学出版社
出版时间：2019
ISBN：978－7－5690－3001－3
DOI：10.13760/b.cnki.sam.202001018

科学技术的进步总是伴随着人的异化与精神领域的迷失。机器时代到来，人类开始拥有力大无比的帮手，同时也产生了足以摧毁人类文明的敌人。从“文化工业”到“消费社会”，从“单向度的人”到“数字化生存”，冷机器生产出大量的形象与符码，数字设备的进步、再现与控制技术日益完善，使得现实被设想成为一组可以直接计算的参数集合，数字用户从中能够更好地掌握现实，但与此同时，符号与信息的激增导致了符号的泛滥和意义的缺失。按照结构主义“意义在差异关系中产生”的观点，数字时代信息的内爆则会消除这种差异，使来越来越多的符号沦为无意义的噪音，最终形成“能指丰富，所指缺乏”的当代数字文化景观。如果说人是符号的动物，追求意义是人类的生存法则，那么意义的丧失将会使人类沦为机器，变成物。因此，米歇尔·福柯（Michel Foucault）在《词与物》（*Les Mots et les Choses*）中曾留下了这样的警世恒言："人将会被抹去，如同大海边沙地上的一张脸。"（2001，p. 506）

在追求精确和完美的数字冷面孔下，我们的日常生活却也逐渐走向了无意味。那么此刻，我们急需一名符号学家！这是意大利都灵大学的马西莫·莱昂内（Massimo Leone）教授在《论无意味：后物质时代的意义消减》一书中发出的呐喊。"符号学不能也不必教导我们关乎生存的意义，但它可以而且必须警告死亡的意义。"（2019，p. 21）不断前行的数字化，使得我们的生活逐渐被无意义包围。作为一名符号学家，作者试图唤醒沉睡在数字世界中的读者：你是否在追求完美数字图像的同时失去了真我？你是否沉醉在饕餮盛宴中无法自拔，抑或在网络骂战中黯然神伤？《论无意味》一书不同于经典的物质社会学，并非通过系统而抽象的方法解决当今社会的无意味问题，而是聚焦人类的日常活动和生活语境，寻找无意味产生的动因。作者通过在日本乘坐公共汽车的经历开启了发现意味和丢失意味的符号学之旅。

何为无意味（Insignificance）？无意味是否等同于无意义（Meaninglessness）？如果说"意义是一个符号可以被另外的符号解释的潜力"（赵毅衡，2016，p. 2），那么意义则必须通过解释实现，是解释的结果，意味则关乎意义的生成，是解释的前提。因此，莱昂内教授认为"符号可能因为它的符义内容、符用功能或两者兼之却无法被解码而无意义，但一个符号不会是无意味的"（2019，p. 12）。也就是说，对于解释者而言，符号可能因为无法被感知和解码而无意义，但它本身不会停止表意，无意味的符号便不再是符号，而是变成了物。符号的无意义表现在三个层面：不可破译、难以理解以及神秘。当我们无法弄懂符号隐含的所指、代表的实际内容时，符号在不可破译的层面上无意义；当我们理解符号指向的内容却不明白其指向的对象时，符号在难以理解层面的无意义；当我们既不清楚符号指向的内容，也不清楚它指向谁时，这样的符号就好比小说家丹·布朗（Dan Brown）笔下"失落的秘符"，等待着诸如罗伯特·兰登（Robert Langdon）一样的符号学家去破译。无意味则是另外一种情况，既然无意味没有意指，我们又如何发现它的存在与价值？作者提出了两条发现无意味的路径：一是通过无意味到意味的过程，比如通过在日本乘坐公共汽车意识到欧洲公共空间的不稳定因素和暴力行为，只要付出足够的时间与精力，世界上的每件事物都能从其表面的无意味中被唤醒，在意义世界中占有一席之地；二是从意味到无意味的反向过程，比如当人们开始为工具所主宰，或者无休止的数字生产剥夺了我们有意味的时间时，又或当我们沉迷于数字游戏的当下快乐，游戏的娱乐性迫使意义的在场结束时，我们便已身处于无意味的世界里。

《论无意味》一书聚焦看似没有意味却反复进行的无意义人类行为。作者从日常旅行、公共事件以及艺术绘画中获得关于人类生存与意义的价值思考，处处彰显他作为符号学家的敏锐洞察力以及挽救符号意味的责任感。数字技术的突飞猛进改变了我们的日常生活，而它又如何将主客体以及主体间关系转变为空洞的刻板印象？当代社会中的“迷狂”现象与人的存在感缺有着怎样的关系？我们如何抵制数字官僚带来的异化效应？也许我们无法在书中找到完美的答案，但作者关于无意味的符号学思考，同时彰显了符号学方法论的迷人之处，使其成为数字生活中警醒世人的一剂良药。

一、能指数字化：后物质时代的来临

后物质主义（Post-materialism）是罗纳德·英格尔哈特（Ronald Inglehart）在1977年提出的概念，与追求物质的极大丰富与享受的物质主义不同的是，建立在“马斯洛需求层次”和“边际效用递减”理论之上的后物质主义更强调人的精神满足和自我实现。从物质主义到后物质主义的转变，体现的是对经济增长的渴望让位于对生活质量的追求，对物质商品的占有转向对人生意义的问询。而这一转变的动因除了高度发达的工业生产外，还离不开公众对社会信息的追求。信息的激增和数字化节奏的加快在推动社会发展的同时，也使处于临界点的事物出现了质变。

如果说物质主义的典型特征是“物质占有的奢侈浪费”的话，那么后物质时代对意义的空前追求则导致了“符号的浪费”。一方面，精神消费与意义需求导致大量的符号被生产出来，形成现代社会中的符号泛滥和意义危机。作为传媒时代的预言家，马歇尔·麦克卢汉（Marshall McLuhan）曾用“内爆”来形容数字时代的文化裂变。“内爆”是一个消除差异的过程，迅捷的数字媒介突破了时空的限制，抹杀了时空本该具有的意义。而有着“法国的麦克卢汉”之称的让·鲍德里亚（Jean Baudrillard）在此基础上提出了“意义的内爆”，认为当符号信息不断渗透社会，意义也将变得平淡无奇。“我们的生活已经混为一团，过去、未来、遥远或是眼前，这些似乎都没有了区分。个人的、公共的，一切都瞬间‘内爆’于我们面前。”（石义彬，2003，p. 211）另一方面，人的精神世界从物质的束缚中得到了解放，却进入一个数字的迷宫，摆脱了多余的物质性，走向了数字化。“生活不再需要肉体和空间，我们就像世界各地不断流动的数字流量，在这里或在那里，以图标、声音或朋友的面貌出现：这就是我们这个时代的乌托邦，一个并非完全缺乏神秘生命冲动（élan）的乌托邦，一个‘想要远离（cupio dissolvi）’的数字乌托邦。”（莱昂内，2019，p. 91）这便是莱昂内在《论无意味》一书中发出的感叹。作者认为反物质倾向和通信技术的发展导致了“能指的数字化”，即人们开始寻求并发展愈加复杂的能指的非物质化形式，从物质的枷锁中解放，却被稀释在数字的海洋。比如在电话通信中，人们接收到的并非指示符，而是规约符，声音脉冲准确地与声源相对应，这种对应并非由其因果必然性决定，而是由数字代码的任意武断性决定，二进制将所有现象的意义转换成了一系列的“0”和“1”，使我们的身体仿若机器。在后物质时代，符号的大量生产导致人们放弃选择，倾向单轴行为，失去意义；能指的数字化更是突破了表意时空的距离，抹杀了时空本该具有的意义，使我们的生活日益走向无意味。

二、光晕的丧失：对数字生活无意味的批判

从“网络蛮喷”到意见相反者，从图像到购物，从集会再到饮食，处处皆是意味，处处也尽失意味。瓦尔特·本雅明（Walter Benjamin）曾通过“光晕”（Aura）在现代复制技术中的丧失来探讨艺术作品的无意味过程。“光晕”作为一种可感知形式，象征着艺术作品独一无二的神秘韵味，复制技术使得艺术作品时空表意缺失，出现了失真，也使得公众失去了意义的感知力，最终导致“光晕的丧失”，因而“机械复制方法最终是一种贬抑技术，它帮助人们去战胜作品……”（本雅明，2006，p. 23），作为当代符号学家，莱昂内则从意义的角度对数字生活进行了考察和批判。《论无意味》一书的第二至七章揭示了后物质时代人们日常生活的意义消减过程，即数字生活中的各个方面“光晕的丧失”。

作者首先聚焦网络社会这一“数字竞技场”。无论是试图破坏虚拟公共对话的“网络蛮喷”，还是刻意标出自我以寻求意义的意见相反者，都体现出社会生活的数字化引发的人性扭曲和意义交换过程中能指与所指的切割。他认为，“当今数字对话中的大多数观点，都是由持相反意见者创造和捍卫的，这是他们寻求逃避存在无意味的一种方式”（莱昂内，2019，p. 2）。网络社会中，人们的日常沟通愈加演变成“重视形式，忽视内容”的空洞框架，机械地对抗着他人的言论，却不在乎实际争论的内容。如果说机械复制技术消减

了艺术作品原有的光晕，那么在数字图像中，这种光晕或许一开始就不存在，原因在于数字图像的精确与完美不允许“奇点”的出现。在莱昂内看来，数字图像对量化完美的追求，使得任何像素都必须遵循整体的形象工程，而任何想要显示奇特性的像素都只能是故障的像素。数字图像对不完美的剥夺导致了图像的无意味，机械的完美恰如哲学家伊曼纽尔·列维纳斯（Emmanuel Lévinas）所言的“冰冷的华丽”。

在第五至七章中，作者分别对日常生活中的购物、集会以及饮食的无意味进行了批判。从巴黎老佛爷百货公司那近似圣殿的购物空间，到集体仪式和个人惯例的日益消除的边界，再到食品神圣化折射的营销陷阱，种种迷狂无不昭示出一个意义缺失的社会的文化困境。“迷狂”彰显的是认同的“转喻”，即将自己的身份与热衷的事物相连接，以重新获得意义。无论是“网络蛮喷”对虚拟公共对话的破坏，还是通过对抗主流话语来标出自我的意见相反者，都是在反抗数字生活的无意味，以对立和对抗的形式获得某种情感上的认同，逃避存在的无意味。在日常生活中，迫切寻求一种归属感的集体行为则更加彰显了意义的不在场。首先，人们迫切需要通过商品的符号价值建构自己的身份，通过消费行为的差异确立自己的群体归属，通过时尚仪式展示个人的意义崇拜；其次，集体仪式与个人惯例的意义生成则基于主体在时空中保持的重复，尽管这两者的边界日益消除，但独立的个体只有通过集体的仪式才能找到自身的归属感；最后，人们对食物的迷狂引发了诸如“慢食运动”“零公里行动”等备受争议的行为模式，尽管这些活动很大程度上是商家的营销陷阱，但人们依然沉迷其中，渴求通过食物与行动来证明自己的存在。

三、意味的重拾：寻求新的解释与共识

消极的批判是为了积极的构建，《论无意味》一书的写作目的不仅在于批判数字生活无意味，还在于重新发现意味的方向。

莱昂内对意义的关注涵盖了诸多领域，那些看似没有任何意味的事，在他看来都颇具神秘的意味。在《论旅行、厕所与归属：废物世界文化的符号学》（The Semiotics of Waste World Cultures：On Traveling，Toilets，and Belonging）一文中，他将目光集中在旅行中身体消除废物的地方——厕所。厕所既是身体驱逐和拒绝废物的场所，也是意义生产的空间，每一种排泄性的结构选择都与文化息息相关。在他看来，“优雅的厕所和高效污水处理系统

使得我们感知不到我们身体的废物及其代表的意义，一旦我们的生命走到尽头，我们本质上也就成了废物”（Leane，2012，pp. 237－258）。同样，作者漫步在都灵市街道，在与行乞者的相遇中萌发了对城市空间意味的思考，在《城市中的行乞与归属：一个符号学分析》（Begging and Belonging in the City：A Semiotic Approach）一文中，他发现行乞者对路人注意力的“打断”带来了主体性的碰撞，这种“打断”打破了城市居民的日常惯例，使得归属感和边界问题的意味得以显现。这种意味的唤醒也集中体现在《论无意味》一书的论述当中。通过观察日本公共汽车上睡觉的人，莱昂内意识到欧洲公共空间的暴力，对痛苦的习以为常使得痛苦本身变成了无意味的存在；通过对伦勃朗·梵·莱茵（Rembrandt van Rijn）的名作《尼古拉斯·杜尔博士的解剖学课》（*Anatomy Lesson of Dr. Nicolaes Tulp*）的细致解读，呼吁公众关注奇特性的价值，抵抗数字计算带来的僵化思维；通过《百万美元首页》像素拍卖的故事思考像素的符号学研究，像素售卖创造的“价值框架”，将原本无意味的像素变得有意味并且超乎寻常。从厕所的符号学分析到城市空间中的乞讨者，从公共交通中的潜在危险再到伦勃朗的画作，莱昂内无疑是一名杰出的意味发现者，他从画家的视角凝视生活，擅于发现符号习惯背后奇特性的价值。正如作者所言：“符号习惯如同鞋中的沙砾，人们只有摆脱它们时，才能意识到行走的方便。”（莱昂内，2019，p. 16）因此，在追求精确和完美的数字生活中，意味的唤醒需要我们关注奇特性的价值，探索和发现隐藏在符号习惯背后的深层意味。

意味的发现总是源于这样的信念：某物的背后一定还存在别的事物。想要理解这个“别的事物”则需要借助第三要素，如皮尔斯的解释项。皮尔斯认为“传播的最根本问题不再是讨论如何把符号意义从发送者传递给解释者，而是专注于传受双方间如何协商彼此所产生的意义，并通过进一步的互动而达成共同意义的问题”（赵星植，2017，p. 85）。意义在协商之中产生，而意义的实现则依靠解释。莱昂内在《论无意味》一书中认为意味无法单独再生，意味的重拾需要创造新的解释，通过协商达成共识。在数字社会中，精确而复杂的计算方法将社会生活控制在一系列固化的选择之中，而公共话语的非物质化导致了观点的碎片化和机械化，想要突破技术的束缚、数字的牢笼，需要创造新的解释和谈判的空间。在莱昂内看来，符号学在当今数字生活中的重要贡献，一方面在于挑战技术话语的霸权，证明语言领域的问题无法通过先进的技术来解决，而要通过解释、沟通和协商；另一方面，符号学应当而且能够创造用于主体意义交流的共同元话语空间，在虚拟的数字竞技场中重新创造共识。

一场旅行、一幅画作、一家咖啡店、一条满是砾石的小路都能激发作者对日常生活的符号学思考，让我们意识到生活充满了意味，同时也在丧失意味。在以数字化生存为典型特征的后物质时代，对意义的追寻既需要渴望解释的野心，也需要某种“畸形的热情”。莱昂内《论无意味》一书正是从反抗无意味的过程中揭示出当代数字生活的无意味现状，提醒众人“有意义是社会生活的准则，无意味则是一种边缘性的例外”（2019，p. 8）。无意味只是一种错觉。相信在未来的某天，我们会迫切地召唤一名符号学家，带我们探索意味的发现之旅，以更好地满足我们对意义的需求。

引用文献：

福柯，米歇尔（2001）. 词与物：人文科学考古学（莫伟民，译）. 上海：上海三联书店.

莱昂内，马西莫（2019）. 论无意味——后物质时代的意义消减（陆正兰，李俊欣，黄蓝，译）. 成都：四川大学出版社.

赵毅衡（2016）. 符号学：原理与推演. 南京：南京大学出版社.

石义彬（2003）. 单向度、超真实、内爆：批判视野中的当代西方传播思想研究. 武汉：武汉大学出版社.

本雅明，瓦尔特（2006）. 摄影小史/机械复制时代的艺术作品（王才勇，译）. 南京：江苏人民出版社.

赵星植（2017）. 皮尔斯与传播符号学. 成都：四川大学出版社.

Leone, M. (2012). The semiotics of waste world cultures: On traveling, toilets, and belonging. *Culture: International journal of philosophy of culture and axiology*, 2, 237-258.

作者简介：

李俊欣，四川大学文学与新闻学院博士研究生，研究方向为符号学与传播学。

Author:

Li Junxin, Ph. D. candidate of College of Literature and Journalism, Sichuan University. His research fields include semiotics and communication.

Email: lijunxin0411@qq.com

意文的进阶：评《赵毅衡形式理论文选》

贾　佳

Advancing Meaning Studies: A Review of Zhao Yiheng's *Selected Writings in Theories of Form*

Jia Jia

书名：赵毅衡形式理论文选
作者：赵毅衡
出版社：北京大学出版社
出版时间：2019
ISBN:9787－301－29811－4
DOI:10.13760/b.cnki.sam.202001018

符号学从19世纪末20世纪产生之初至今，已经走过了一个多世纪，但直到20世纪80年代，符号学才在中国发展起来。起步较晚，却丝毫没有影响中国符号学的发展速度。经过近40年的历程，中国也逐渐开始继“法国学派”“美国学派”“俄罗斯学派”之后，树立起符号学“中国学派”大旗，成为“第四大符号学王国”（王铭玉，王双燕，2019）。符号学在中国这样迅猛的发展，必然离不开诸多中国符号学者的努力和贡献，赵毅衡先生就是其中的佼佼者。

赵毅衡教授早年师从卞之琳，致力莎士比亚研究，然而他对形式中的逻辑却十分感兴趣，进而投入形式论的研究之中。至今，他已经在形式论的巨流中航行了40余年，成果璀璨。从早年的《文学符号学》（1990）开始，他就尝试为使符号学溢出语言文学范畴做出努力，将文化引入符号学领域，并将符号学定义为“一个社会中所有与社会生活相关的符号活动的总集合”

(1990，p. 89)。直到2011年《符号学：原理与推演》出版，我们才开始更加清晰地了解文化符号学的整个脉络。此外，叙述学也是赵毅衡自始至终坚持的阵地，从《苦恼的叙述者》(1991)、《当说者被说的时候：比较叙述学导论》(1994)，到《广义叙述学》(2013)，他将西方的叙述学理论引介到中国，并结合中国文学传统，进行了一系列具有开创性的理论创新。艺术作为文化意义活动中的重要组成部分，成为赵毅衡近年来所关注的领域，他用符号学意识对艺术领域中的诸多现象予以相关分析和研究，从中我们能够清晰地把握艺术形式与意义之间不可分割的关系。

无论是符号学、叙述学还是艺术符号研究，正如赵毅衡（2019，p. 2）在本书前言中所说，“这条形式论大河，实际上是围绕着意义问题延展的……这本文选是从我40年来的思考中抽取的一些文字，可以看到我的航线是沿着符号学，走向叙述学，走向艺术学。为什么能如此走？因为它们都是围绕着意义流淌。”所以，《赵毅衡形式理论文选》集合了近半个世纪以来在符号学、叙述学、艺术学中具有代表性的论文，意义是统领这三方面的出发点，毕竟“符号学就是意义学”。索绪尔在《普通语言学札记》中提出“各种意指一般区别只根据各种形式的区别而存在……一种意指总是与一种形式有关的”(Saussure，2002，p. 28；转引自怀宇，2019，p. 8)，索绪尔将形式看作意义的集合，而这点也是赵毅衡先生自始至终所追求的形式论。相比索绪尔，赵毅衡拓展了皮尔斯的符号体系，将对意义的思考则延伸到文化意识领域，扩大了意义的研究范围。

《赵毅衡形式理论文选》(以下简称《文选》) 系统地将意义适用的三个领域作为主要论述的方面：符号学、符号现象学，叙述学、叙述哲学，艺术学、艺术风格学。这三个领域看似各自独立，但又都统一于意义理论的框架之中，整体论述都是从“重新定义概念”出发，以实践中的具体现象作结。整个《文选》涉猎三个领域，看似散乱，实则系统，深入浅出，理论功底扎实。

在第一部分“符号学、符号现象学”中，赵毅衡摒弃了传统符号定义的同义反复，重新给符号下了定义，明确提出“符号是被认为携带意义的感知”(2019，p. 5)。而早在1993年他就提出，“符号学”是“关于意义活动的学说”。关于符号学与意义之间的紧密联系之论，并非空穴来风，而是符号学内在研究方式使然。早期符号学研究大多是关于索绪尔所提出的“能指/所指”二分式，近年来对皮尔斯三元符号学的重新发现，则是对索绪尔二元符号体系的纠正，使得意义理论从语言学向更广大的文化和意义领域延展。赵毅衡先生一针见血地指出，“相当重要的一个原因是皮尔斯注重符号的意义解释”

(2019，p. 8)，“解释项”的提出不仅丰富了符号学体系，更为理解人类的意义活动提供了新的范式，所以要研究意义，就离不开对符号学的讨论，《文选》的这一部分即是对意义的生成和表现方式的探索。

为了更加系统地分析意义理论，赵毅衡将符号学与现象学结合，提出了符号现象学理论。他认为，“现象学的关注中心是意识；符号学的关注中心是意义”(赵毅衡，2017，p. 4)。皮尔斯的符号学体系则主要集中于“现象是如何通过感知为意识所理解的”(赵毅衡，2019，p. 20)，这一观点在他关于意义理论的著作《哲学符号学：意义世界的形成》中有较为详细的论述。而在《文选》中，他重点将分析放在了意识的产生上，创造性地沿着皮尔斯符号学方向对意义形式进行思考，并与胡塞尔的意向性和直观形成意识进行联系，提出了“形式直观”(formal intuition)的概念。他认为，形式直观这一意识过程是符号现象学的出发点，它可以回答意识面对的事物如何变成意义对象，即意向性如何将对象变为符号的问题。但与胡塞尔的“本质直观”(essential intuition)不同，赵毅衡并不认为“直观”能够延伸到事物的“本质”，意义的获得需要沿着“形式直观—认识记忆—理解筹划”这三个步骤来落实。其中，在形式直观阶段，事物与符号没有根本区别；在形式还原阶段，事物的诸多观相被悬搁(epoché)了，经过不断的意义积累、认识记忆，才能形成下一步的理解活动。由于意识的片面化感知，先验性的“共现”承担了意识对对象的“最低形式完整要求”。

此外，在第一部分中作者还提出了颠覆皮尔斯将像似性作为符号第一性的大胆假设。赵毅衡先生分别从生物进化序列、儿童成长过程以及指示词语的序列性等方面，证明了“或许‘指示性’才是符号第一性”的结论。这一结论的提出，主要基于在皮尔斯的符号三分中指示符号与意义的邻接方式最为直接，而其他两类则是建立在意义积累和理解筹划的基础之上。

《文选》的第二部分关于叙述学、叙述哲学。由于当代的文化呈现出“严重的叙述转向”倾向，作者重新定义了“叙述”，并提出最简定义，即“有人物参与的事件被组织进一个文本中”(2019，p. 151)。其中，“人物”的参与是区别叙述与陈述的关键。这一定义的确定，为广义叙述学的提出奠定了基础。叙述学不应当仅仅停留于以小说为核心的文学体裁，叙述分析可以与符号学结合起来，打破叙述学的文学界限，为各种叙述研究寻找一个共通的理论基础，这一理论基础即是赵毅衡所提出的“广义叙述学”(general narratology)。

如果说“广义叙述学”只是一个设想，那么《文选》中对诸多叙述体裁的详细分类则印证了叙述学广义化的可能性。第十章提供了叙述体裁的全域分类方案，分别按照叙述体裁“本体地位”的横轴展开，分为纪实型/虚构型；按照“媒介－时间”方向的纵轴展开，可分为过去时记录类诸体裁、进行时演示类诸体裁、过去进行时的记录演示类诸体裁、类演示类的心像诸体裁，以及独立于媒介的未来时（意动型）诸体裁。这一横一纵的两条轴线相互交叉，将文化生活中的各种叙述体裁囊括在内，形成一个统一的完整系统。

第十一章指出，叙述者作为叙述源头，永远处于“框架－人格”两相之间，而这两相之间的关系，则因叙述体裁的不同而有所区别。针对虚构叙述，赵毅衡引入“区隔”理论，分析了虚构叙述与纪实之间的区别。他认为，“一度区隔用媒介化把再现与经验分开，二度区隔把虚构叙述与纪实再现相区隔”（2019，p.179）。虚构之所以被看作真实，是因为区隔被忽略了；而同一区隔内的叙述则永远是纪实。虚构叙述的双区隔原则为讨论文本真相提供了理论依据，在此基础之上，作者进一步说明：叙述交流的可能性，恰恰建立在文本内真实性的基础之上。

《文选》在第一部分中将主体的自我和身份问题延伸到文本身份，并讨论了普遍隐含作者问题，而隐含作者正是叙述学的核心概念。叙述者与隐含作者道德价值上的出入，造成了不可靠叙述。从20世纪50年代布斯在《小说修辞学》中提出隐含作者与不可靠叙述这两个概念开始，隐含作者和不可靠叙述就成为叙述学研究者争相讨论的热点。作为一名符号学家，赵毅衡先生将不可靠叙述和隐含作者延伸到所有符号文本之中，认为这两者是所有符号文本都无法避免的普遍问题，成为广义叙述学的重要论域。

“广义叙述学”这一新的定义方式，是赵毅衡结合符号学理论思考的结果，与此同时他进一步提出了“符号叙述学”（semionarratology）的设想，即“研究一切包含叙述的符号文本的叙述学”，而这也是诸多学者努力的方向。早在1984年，利科在《时间与叙述》中就专门讨论过普洛普、布瑞蒙、格雷马斯等关于“叙述符号学”的论述，恰特曼也明确提出“如果要解决叙述问题，就必须进入符号学”。可见，叙述学与符号学结合，是两个学科内在学理统一性的必然要求。赵毅衡的《广义叙述学》把这一设想通过理论实践的方式呈现出来，将各种广义上的叙述体裁囊括于其中。正如加拿大学者段炼所言，“作为一个具有全局视野的理论，广义叙述学在20世纪晚期和21世纪早期的后经典叙述学中脱颖而出”（Duan，2018）。

“艺术学、艺术风格学”是《文选》论述的第三个重要部分。与前两个部分的行文思路一样，作者首先从符号学角度重新定义了艺术的概念。尽管维特根斯坦等学者一度认为艺术不可定义，但艺术作为社会文化相关符号表意活动的重要部分，在当代社会呈现出越来越重要的地位。赵毅衡认为“定义本身是人类认知的必然过程”（2019，p. 247），是意识给认知归类的过程，而对艺术定义存在与否的讨论，恰恰证明了给艺术定义的必然性。他肯定了程序主义在反本质立场上做出的努力，但否定了程序主义撇开功能主义的莽撞做法，并提出“藉形式达到超脱”（2019，p. 272）的功能说才能够覆盖艺术全域，从而引出了符号学给艺术下的定义：在组成文化的各种表意文本中，艺术是借形式使接收者从庸常达到超脱的符号文本品格。（2019，p. 272）

接下来，针对艺术中的几个重要现象，赵毅衡从符号学角度进行了相关思考。现代先锋艺术以来，尤其是 20 世纪初，艺术中的不协调因素越发成为艺术家和理论家关注的焦点。作者从美术、舞蹈、音乐等诸多艺术门类中总结出艺术与形式之间的微妙关系，认为艺术的不协调是作品有意躲避程式形式的结果。在雅柯布森的符号六主导因素论中“诗性”理论的基础上，作者进一步论述了风格在艺术中的重要性，确定了“风格就是艺术”（2019，p. 305）的关键性结论。在他看来，风格与修辞不同，它是加之于核心文本之上的附加符码。于艺术而言，“风格是附加的，却是本质性存在：无风格不成艺术”（p. 305）。赵毅衡的艺术风格论，从符号学理论上剖析了艺术存在的本质性特征，为艺术本质的研究提供了新的思考方向。对于当今时代呈现出的泛艺术化趋势，作者的思考则更具有理论适切性。他提出，“任何物或事物，都是意义‘三联体’，在物性一实用符号一艺术符号三者之间滑动”（p. 324）。因此，作者认为，社会中的艺术化是潜在的，泛艺术化就是艺术本态。从某种程度上，作者透过符号学视野，为当下受人批判的泛艺术化现状进行了正名。

《赵毅衡形式理论文选》是“中国当代符号学名家学术文库”中首批出版的学者文集之一，该文库体现出总主编王铭玉教授开阔的符号学视野。赵毅衡先生将其近半个世纪对符号的思考精华汇总在《文选》的 21 篇论文之中，其中也不乏他在《广义叙述学》《符号学：原理与推演》和《哲学符号学》中的经典论述。符号学的范畴不仅仅止于文化，更是延及一切有关意义的活动，而人的存在恰好是意义式的存在，所以符号是人存在的本质条件。如果说索绪尔的贡献在于从语言学方法论角度将其对世界的看法进行关系化处理，皮尔斯的贡献在于让符号学溢出语言学，进入更广阔的论域，那么赵毅衡则从意义世界的角度，思考符号意指的诸多方式和形态。感谢赵毅衡先生 40 余年不离“形式论”的初衷，在吸收总结前人符号学理论基础之上，创造了一个具有普遍性的符号学学理模式，为相关学者进行进一步思考和研究指明了方向。

引用文献：

Duan, L. (2018). Framing narrative in the signification process: A review of Yiheng Zhao's *A General Narratology*. *Signs & Media*, 17(2), 248－256.

Saussure, F. de. (2002). *Écrits de Linguistique Générale*. Paris, FRA: Gallimard.

怀宇（2019）. 法国符号学研究论集. 北京：北京大学出版社.

王铭玉，王双燕（2019）.《符号学思想论》之说论. 当代修辞学，211（1），36－42.

赵毅衡（1990）. 文学符号学. 北京：中国文联出版公司.

赵毅衡（2017）. 哲学符号学：意义世界的形成. 成都：四川大学出版社.

赵毅衡（2019）. 赵毅衡形式理论文选. 北京：北京大学出版社.

作者简介：

贾佳，四川大学文学与新闻学院博士研究生，四川大学符号学－传媒学研究所成员，成都体育学院新闻与传播学院助教，研究方向为符号学与叙述学。

Author:

Jia Jia, Ph. D. candidate of College of Literature and Journalism, Sichuan University, member of the ISMS research team, teaching assistant of Chengdu Sport University. Her research fields are semiotics and narratology.

Email: jiajiamail0318@163.com

本书在编辑过程中，得到了四川大学人文社科期刊资助项目、四川大学中国语言文学与中华文化全球传播双一流学科群，以及教育部人文社科重点基地四川大学中国俗文化研究所的支持，特此感谢。